2009

Contexts of Social Capital

Routledge Advances in Sociology

For a full list of titles in this series, please visit www.routledge.com

8. Rave Culture and Religion
Edited by Graham St. John

9. Creation and Returns of Social Capital
A New Research Program
Edited by Henk Flap and Beate Völker

10. Self-Care
Embodiment, Personal Autonomy and the Shaping of Health Consciousness
Christopher Ziguras

11. Mechanisms of Cooperation
Werner Raub and Jeroen Weesie

12. After the Bell
Educational Success, Public Policy and Family Background
Edited by Dalton Conley and Karen Albright

13. Youth Crime and Youth Culture in the Inner City
Bill Sanders

14. Emotions and Social Movements
Edited by Helena Flam and Debra King

15. Globalization, Uncertainty and Youth in Society
Edited by Hans-Peter Blossfeld, Erik Klijzing, Melinda Mills and Karin Kurz

16. Love, Heterosexuality and Society
Paul Johnson

17. Agricultural Governance
Globalization and the New Politics of Regulation
Edited by Vaughan Higgins and Geoffrey Lawrence

18. Challenging Hegemonic Masculinity
Richard Howson

19. Social Isolation in Modern Society
Roelof Hortulanus, Anja Machielse and Ludwien Meeuwesen

20. Weber and the Persistence of Religion
Social Theory, Capitalism and the Sublime
Joseph W. H. Lough

21. Globalization, Uncertainty and Late Careers in Society
Edited by Hans-Peter Blossfeld, Sandra Buchholz and Dirk Hofäcker

22. Bourdieu's Politics
Problems and Possibilities
Jeremy F. Lane

23. Media Bias in Reporting Social Research?
The Case of Reviewing Ethnic Inequalities in Education
Martyn Hammersley

24. A General Theory of Emotions and Social Life
Warren D. TenHouten

25. Sociology, Religion and Grace
Arpad Szakolczai

26. Youth Cultures
Scenes, Subcultures and Tribes
Edited by Paul Hodkinson and Wolfgang Deicke

27. The Obituary as Collective Memory
Bridget Fowler

28. Tocqueville's Virus
Utopia and Dystopia in Western Social and Political Thought
Mark Featherstone

29. Jewish Eating and Identity Through the Ages
David Kraemer

30. The Institutionalization of Social Welfare
A Study of Medicalizing Management
Mikael Holmqvist

31. The Role of Religion in Modern Societies
Edited by Detlef Pollack and Daniel V. A. Olson

32. Sex Research and Sex Therapy
A Sociology Analysis of Masters and Johnson
Ross Morrow

33. A Crisis of Waste?
Understanding the Rubbish Society
Martin O'Brien

34. Globalization and Transformations of Local Socioeconomic Practices
Edited by Ulrike Schuerkens

35. The Culture of Welfare Markets
The International Recasting of Pension and Care Systems
Ingo Bode

36. Cohabitation, Family and Society
Tiziana Nazio

37. Latin America and Contemporary Modernity
A Sociological Interpretation
José Maurício Domingues

38. Exploring the Networked Worlds of Popular Music
Milieu Cultures
Peter Webb

39. The Cultural Significance of the Child Star
Jane O'Connor

40. European Integration as an Elite Process
The Failure of a Dream?
Max Haller

41. Queer Political Performance and Protest
Benjamin Shepard

42. Cosmopolitan Spaces
Europe, Globalization, Theory
Chris Rumford

43. Contexts of Social Capital
Social Networks in Markets, Communities, and Families
Edited by Ray-May Hsung, Nan Lin, and Ronald L. Breiger

Contexts of Social Capital

Social Networks in Markets, Communities, and Families

Edited by Ray-May Hsung, Nan Lin, and Ronald L. Breiger

Routledge
Taylor & Francis Group
New York London

First published 2009
by Routledge
270 Madison Ave, New York, NY 10016

Simultaneously published in the UK
by Routledge
2 Park Square, Milton Park, Abingdon, Oxon OX14 4RN

Routledge is an imprint of the Taylor & Francis Group, an informa business

Typeset in Sabon by IBT Global.
Printed and bound in the United States of America on acid-free paper by IBT Global.

Library of Congress Cataloging in Publication Data

Contexts of social capital : social networks in communities, markets and organizations / edited by Ray-May Hsung, Nan Lin, & Ronald Breiger.
p. cm. — (Routledge advances in sociology)
Includes bibliographical references and index.
1. Social capital (Sociology) 2. Social networks. 3. Social action. I. Hsung, Ray-May. II. Lin, Nan, 1938– III. Breiger, Ronald L.
HM708.C66 2009
302.09—dc22
2008014929

ISBN10: 0-415-41117-3 (hbk)
ISBN10: 0-203-89009-4 (ebk)

ISBN13: 978-0-415-41117-2 (hbk)
ISBN13: 978-0-203-89009-7 (ebk)

Contents

Tables

APPENDIX

Figures

Abbreviations

JES3	Japanese Election Study 3
JGSS	Japanese General Social Survey
LETS	Local Employment and Trading System
NELS88	National Education Longitudinal Study of 1988
ODM	Original Design and Manufacturing
OEM	Original Equipment Manufacturing
SSND	The Survey of the Social Networks of the Dutch
TEPS	Taiwan Education Panel Survey
TSMC	Taiwan Semiconductor Manufacturing Company Limited

Preface

The concept of *social capital* refers to the ways in which people make use of their social networks in "getting ahead." Social capital is not just about the *connections* in networks, however, but fundamentally concerns the distribution of resources on the basis of exchanges. During the past two decades, owing to seminal work in particular by Nan Lin (2001) and James Coleman (1988) in the United States and by Pierre Bourdieu (1986) in France, and joined by leading researchers from around the globe, this has been one of the "hottest" concepts in international academic social science research. In recent years, many researchers around the world have dealt with issues of measurement, data collection, and empirical tests of hypotheses concerning the production of and returns to social capital at the individual level. Significant progress has been made in understanding the dynamics of social capital at both the "top" and the "bottom" of social structure: at the societal (macro) and the individual (micro) levels. At the macro level, much work has explored how social capital, as a collective good, is a force for societal development, national health, and rates of political participation. At the micro level, a body of literature has addressed social capital as a property of individuals, promoting the success of individuals' careers based on the number and quality of their social contacts.

Despite great progress in research at both the macro and the micro levels, however, there remains a prominent gap in our understanding of social capital. The question of *how* the macro–societal and micro–individual dynamics of social capital are linked conceptually and methodologically has largely been left unstudied in the literature. Without an understanding of this linkage, research on social capital is in danger of becoming bifurcated and disjointed, with each level of analysis assuming its own conceptual apparatus and measurement methods and disregarding developments at the other level. The disjunction of research at micro and macro levels has led to concerns as to whether social capital should be seen as multiple concepts, each with its own definition and theories (Portes 1998).

The purpose of this volume is to focus on the mesolevel analysis of social capital—or how social capital interacts with social institutions, beyond individual dynamics yet beneath the surface of entire societies. Social institutions, we argue, constitute the critical social context that operates between society and individuals. This social context provides a necessary link in understanding how individual-level social capital can be "translated" into collective goods at the societal level.

To promote this mesolevel analysis of social capital, an International Social Capital Conference was held at Tunghai University in Taiwan in December 2004, organized by Nan Lin, Ray-May Hsung, and Chieh-hsuan Chen. Authors conducting original research on social capital in markets, communities, and family contexts were invited to present their work. At the conference, each presentation received substantial feedback and suggestions from other participants. Further comments were provided by the editors. This volume is the result of these presentations, interactions, and each author's extensive revision of their original presentation.

The volume is based on the premise that markets, communities, and families are the major contexts within which people meet and build up social networks and the foci to create social capital. The volume makes available a collection of chapters representing some of the most important recent advances in theory, method, and empirical research addressing these issues.

We call the reader's attention to some general features that characterize the chapters collected in this volume. First, they represent recent theoretical and methodological innovations. Theoretically, each chapter reflects, shapes, or expands on the concept of institutional logics. Social capital is captured, for example, as position-generated networks, as the context for recruiting friends, as reciprocity of resource exchanges, as distinguished in both its global and local nature, as childcare networks embedded in family and organizational service providers, and as reflected in the degree of openness or closure of social networks. How these network characteristics determine the gain (or, indeed, the loss) to individuals from investment in instrumental or expressive actions is a common concern in all the included studies.

Paralleling these theoretical advances, innovations in methodology and research design also characterize a number of the chapters. These include an innovative research design that casts diverse contextual settings as "generators" of social relations such as marriage and acquaintanceship, use of diary techniques of data collection on social networks in everyday life, measurement methods for key concepts such as degree and quality of prior social capital, political social capital, restricted network range and limited instrumental resources, and techniques for the uncovering of social logics. Thus, the chapters advance practical methodological work on social capital research. Models ranging from the hierarchical (multilevel) linear model to correspondence analysis are used by several of the chapter authors to understand the interpenetration of individual-actor and more "meso" levels of social capital, such as schools, firms, and economic sectors. These techniques provide promising lines of methodological advance in studying how resources exchanged in networks tie together large-scale institutions and purposive actors, which is the "micro–macro" problem that the concept of social capital uniquely defines.

Another main feature of this book is its recognition that social capital is a worldwide phenomenon that requires international perspective to capture, theorize, and analyze its diverse institutional contexts. We, therefore, feature authors and social capital studies from a wide range of world regions: Eastern and Western Europe, North America, and East Asia. Due to the cascading theoretical interest in new forms of business networks and related issues of civic culture in East Asia, as well as their increasing significance for international markets and the global economy, we place a special emphasis on East Asian business and civic-participation networks, and on the most recent empirical research on social capital based on comparative national surveys in China and Taiwan.

This volume consists of four parts, each featuring chapters that carry forward some of the theoretical and methodological advances mentioned. Part I includes four articles on theoretical and methodological advances in social capital research. In Chapter 1, Ray-May Hsung and Ronald Breiger provide fresh conceptualization of position-generated networks in terms of a duality between types of social ties (the symbolic world) and positions accessed (the material world). In a study of workers in Taiwan high-tech companies, they employ graphical techniques, dual clustering, and generalizations of structural equivalence to understand the typical ways in which people within organizations make use of the structures (both formal and informal) in which they are embedded. They refer to these typical modes as "institutional logics." Finally, the authors note that access to certain positions (those of low prestige) may be associated with having lower income, a "negative" form of social capital, in contrast to the positive boost to income associated with having network ties to high-prestige positions.

In Chapter 2, Beate Völker, Henk Flap, and Gerald Mollenhorst examine how the social composition of contexts such as work, neighborhood, and voluntary associations affects opportunities to meet friends, on the basis of a national representative sample from the Netherlands. The authors uncover striking differences in the degree to which different kinds of social contexts promote friendships. They examine the effects on friendship formation of contexts emphasizing ascription (such as the family) versus achievement (for example, the school), and they examine cohort differences in access to contexts. Their chapter shows how the contexts we enter set an important boundary on our social networks.

In Chapter 3, Rochelle Côté, Gabriele Plickert, and Barry Wellman explore how the golden rule, reciprocity in personal networks, actually works. Reciprocity is seen as a key way that people mobilize resources to deal with daily life and seize opportunities. Such exchanges are a key to obtaining network capital that can provide helpful resources that are flexible, efficient, and effective. People exchange emotional and material aid, information, and companionship. This study tests seven hypotheses concerning the exchange rules of reciprocity, as these rules apply in a neighborhood of Toronto, Canada. The authors find that the principal direct cause of reciprocity is giving support. The parent–child bond is the only relationship that provides minor and major services without regard to the rule of reciprocity. The practice of reciprocity is especially important for the exchange of resources that supply minor services and emotional support. The provision of major services shows little evidence of reciprocity, because the necessarily large expenditures of time and money make it difficult for the recipients to return such major aid. Most reciprocity is, so to speak, "tit-for-tit" and not "tit-for-tat:" People get back the kinds of resources they give.

In Chapter 4, Ken'ichi Ikeda and Tetsuro Kobayashi explore how heterogeneous personal networks can contribute to making democracy work, on the basis of their analysis of panel data from a national voting study in Japan. A principal hypothesis supported by the data analysis is that network diversity is a positive function of political participation. Moreover, the authors elaborate a logic of the importance of weak ties according to which network diversity leads to the accumulation of social power. In addition, they find that network diversity has a measurable effect on reducing intolerance, whereas political talk in networks composed of strong ties increases intolerance. Methodologically, the authors use Heckman's procedures to deal with censored cases resulting from a relatively low response rate to their mail survey.

Part II of the volume emphasizes the implications of social networks for economic organizing as a major context for the production and use of social capital. The chapters range across varied types of markets: a special local employment and trading system in Canada, the outsourcing system of Taiwan manufacturers, and the transformation of network governance mechanisms of Taiwan's small- and medium-sized enterprise organizations.

In Chapter 5, Bonnie Erickson considers contexts for social capital that are local versus global. She is particularly interested in the variety of people whom one knows in a particular social setting, versus the diversity of "everyone else" whom one knows outside that setting. The particular setting that the author investigates is a trading group (Toronto LETS, the Local Employment and Trading System), a community organization of over 700 members who can buy and sell goods or services using their own currency ("green dollars") or a mixture of "green" and federal (Canadian) currency. Erickson's study thus allows observation of theoretically parallel but operationally distinct forms of social capital (global and local) and of two of its important profits, money and a form of personal autonomy that the author refers to as mastery. In both global and local contexts, social location shapes social capital, which in turn yields profits in mastery. The most important difference between the two contexts is the overall strength of the parallel connections: Relationships are generally stronger at the local level than at the global. This is in accord with Erickson's theoretical framework in that the global relationships are a complex combination of many different underlying processes in many particular settings.

In Chapter 6, Jar-Der Luo and Yung-Chu Yeh ask how firms make use of trust relationships to reduce uncertainty in transactions. Their specific context is a review of the outsourcing process in Taiwan's high-tech industry. Noting that there are always some institutional mechanisms to control uncertainty, the authors posit that the uncontrolled part is where trust relationships come into play. Examining the role of trust in each step of the outsourcing processes, they find the network governance of these firms to be a mixture of market bargaining, legal contracts, company regulations, community norms, power, and trust relationships. This chapter provides unique evidence of those Chinese business networks that are embedded in *ren-qing* (a resource that an individual can present to another person as a gift in the process of social exchange and a norm of reciprocity shaped by hierarchically structured networks of *guanxi*; Hwang 1987) and "power dependence" relations. Informal and unwritten contracts are still prevalent in Chinese business transactional networks. Although pointing out that trust is not the only, or even the most important, factor in controlling outsourcing processes, Luo and Yeh nonetheless point out that "real trust" from the heart, manifesting itself in the structuring of social favors and exchanges, remains important in the supply chain networks in Taiwan's high-tech firms.

Chieh-Hsuan Chen explores economic and social action in the transformation of Taiwan's small- and medium-sized enterprises in Chapter 7. He observes that many entrepreneurs transformed their organizational activity from managing "spontaneous networks" to developing "constructed networks" through adjusting and changing the network activity of their firms. Spontaneous networks were typical patterns for the traditional transaction networks of these Taiwanese firms in the 1970s and 1980s. Multilevel satellite production networks (consisting of foreign buyers, trading companies, large manufacturing firms, and outsourcing small factories) were embedded in long-term quasi-family trust networks. Since the 1990s and the emergence of high-tech firms, constructed networks were built according to organizational goals and profit strategies, and not driven by end-products activities. Instead, constructed networks were built up through strategic alliances and information resource sharing.

In part III, social capital is examined within the community contexts of China, Taiwan, Hungary, and the United States. These chapters point the way toward specifying general features of social capital as these features are manifested distinctively at the national and subnational levels.

In Chapter 8, Nan Lin, Dan Ao, and Lijun Song analyze two intertwined processes of social capital: its production and the returns that it generates. The authors employ a nationwide survey of urban residents in China to examine the effects of social, political, and economic factors, as well as geopolitical location on two aims of social capital: general access to diverse occupations, and access to cadres at different bureaucratic levels. The results show that gender, education, and work experience affect both general and political social capital. Further, participation in voluntary associations leads to better general social capital, and party membership contributes to better political social capital. Along with gender, education, work experience, and economic sector, the two types of social capital significantly affect attainment (becoming an executive or professional, having supervisory responsibility, or having higher earnings). There is also some tentative evidence that residence in the core state-administered cities is an added advantage because that environment offers more diverse choices in different economic sectors (the state, private, and foreign-invested) that in turn enhance diversity in social capital.

In Chapter 9, Chih-Jou Jay Chen makes use of a national survey of currently employed respondents in Taiwan to examine the distribution of and returns to social capital. The author seeks to clarify the causal relationship between social capital and status attainment by proposing the variable of prior social capital, defined as the social capital produced earlier than the attainment of the current job. In addition, this study uses occupational categories, authority (supervision), and income to indicate the returns of status attainment. Similar to a finding for China resulting from the model of Lin and colleagues in Chapter 8, Chen finds that position-generated social capital plays an important role in the status attainment process in Taiwan as well. Unlike the case of China, where men had significantly better social capital than women on all three dimensions of social capital (i.e., extensity, range, and upper reachability), Taiwan is shown to be a more equal society in terms of gender difference in access to social capital.

In Chapter 10, Róbert Tardos emphasizes the value of comparative approaches to the study of social capital and community integration, using as his main exemplar case studies of four villages in Hungary. The design of the author's study is to sample villages manifesting high or low rates of community integration (based on voter turnout) in the less-economically developed East versus the more highly developed Western regions of Hungary. Hence, the four communities studied reflect differing levels of cultural and social development. The author uses position and name generators (that is, replies to questions as to which social positions and which individuals a given respondent is connected to) to derive measures on social networks at both individual and household levels. The communities high in integration (whether or not they were in the developed region of the country) tend to have greater social resources across multiple social network measures. The social network outcomes studied include instrumental benefits (income and jobs), expressive benefits (reputation), and political participation. The instrumental returns to position-generated network diversity are significant across the four types of communities. The expressive returns of the in-degree of name-generated networks is also significant. The effects of social capital and political participation varies with the degree of community integration.

Jeanne S. Hurlbert, John J. Beggs and Valerie A. Haines ask, in Chapter 11, whether low network capital is really "the problem" among the urban poor in the United States. Highly influential theories from American sociologists William Julius Wilson and Mark Granovetter portray social isolation as a key factor accounting for the disadvantaged position of the urban poor. Hurlbert and colleagues assess the accuracy of Wilson's and Granovetter's portrayals by testing two propositions. The first is that low network capital, in the forms of restricted network range (the structural element of network capital) and limited instrumental resources (the resource element of network capital), distinguishes the urban poor from their more affluent counterparts. The second proposition is that the restricted range of their networks constrains their access to instrumental resources. They find support for both propositions. Their results also suggest that additional aspects of range, other than those that Wilson and Granovetter highlight, may be important for understanding distinctiveness and disadvantage among the urban poor. Further, they provide evidence that the relationship between the two elements of network capital is complex, with different aspects of restricted range constraining access to different instrumental resources.

Part IV of this volume assesses social capital within the family context. In accordance with a principal theme of our volume, many of the chapters focus directly on the meso level of social capital, an area that deserves greater research emphasis. For example, how (if at all) does the degree of an individual's network closure or openness (his or her propensity to reach a limited, tightly interconnected segment vs. a broad swath of the wider social structure) determine instrumental and expressive action? Family is also the context for the development of parental networks organized around school and the elaboration of social club activities that build the social capital of children. The family is the context for creating social networks and social resources that will shape affective attitudes and school achievement. The chapters in this section address the controversies over the function of social capital in relatively closed versus open networks, and will inspire further scholarly work.

To harness the explanatory potential of the concept of social capital, two diametrically opposed network theories have been proposed, those of Coleman (1988) and of Morgan and Sørensen (1999), emphasizing the value of network closure and diversity of exposure (respectively) in accounting for school success. In Chapter 12, Ly-Yun Chang charts a course that avoids this confrontation, arguing that institutional context and individual-level parental closure should be brought to the center of consideration because the reproduction of school-level social capital depends on the behavior and perception of individual parents in response to the institutional settings of the school system. The author examines how parental closure in two different institutional contexts in Taiwan affects students' cognitive ability. These contexts include a school system that is community-based, and one that is highly stratified by track and sector according to students' academic performance. Chang finds a curvilinear relationship between parental closure and learning outcomes. The optimal parental closure effect on cognitive ability is found in weak parental closure. A liability that reduces learning is found among students whose parents are ignorant about their child's friends. In contrast, parental closure at the school level does not yield any effect on learning growth. This pattern holds for both junior high and higher secondary cohorts.

In Chapter 13, Joseph Galaskiewicz, Beth Duckles, and Olga Mayorova take as their starting point Coleman's (1988) theory of intergenerational closure concerning the benefits that network ties can provide for parents. They use diary data on children's activities on Saturdays, collected through interviews with 1,036 parents and guardians in a major American metropolitan area from 2003 to 2004. Families that lived for a longer time in the metropolitan area had a more extensive childcare network than did newcomers. Also, those who had more extensive childcare networks were more likely to send their children to households where the adults present were family or friends (as opposed to neighbors, coworkers, or others) or where they knew the parents of all the other children present. More surprisingly, the authors did not find that a more extensive childcare network ensured embedded experiences for children when they used organizational providers, e.g., businesses, government facilities, or nonprofits. Thus childcare networks yielded limited returns to parents, being effective in ensuring embedded experiences for children in the household sector, but not in the formal economy of organizational providers. The authors offer two possible explanations for the latter finding. The legal regulation to which organizations are subjected may make them appear trustworthy so that networks are not necessary for dealing with assessing potential risk to the children. Or alternatively, formal organizations may appeal to parents as a means of overcoming the closure of family-based networks.

In the concluding chapter, Yang-Chih Fu compares overlapping networks (where each ego tends to know each alter's family well) to nonoverlapped networks. He finds that stronger expressive returns to time invested in social ties are more likely to be found in a more open network structure. The author collected reports from special diaries kept by fifty-two individuals to record the time investment and the characteristics of ego and alter for each dyadic tie. He used hierarchical linear modelling to explain variation in the significance of contact relations and the probability of pleasant feelings about the contact relation. The significance and pleasure of the dyadic relations were the dependent variables. The overlapping of two peoples' family networks was measured by how well actors knew each other's families. The network closure of overlapped networks was treated as the structural contextual condition that affected the return of time investment on social relations. The pleasure returns of time investment were significant for the open and partially closed networks, but not for the networks exhibiting full closure.

Collectively, these chapters present newly advanced theoretical arguments, statistical analyses, and recent empirical findings. Several articles pursue the debate on closed/dense versus open/sparse networks regarding their usefulness in providing social capital. We often conceive and debate the utility of closed/dense (homophilous) or open/sparse (heterophilous) networks in accessing social capital as a dichotomous choice. In fact, all social networks are homophilous to an extent, but they vary greatly on the extent of heterophily. In the modern associational society, therefore, diversity of network resources should be seen as providing added values for instrumental actions, rather than as a substitution for homophilous and strong networks. Diversity does not negate homogeneity. Future theoretical reformulation should focus on whether and how diversity and richness of social ties add values beyond that offered by strong or homophilous ties in social networks.

We are honored to acknowledge the financial sponsors for this book's production: National Science Council in Taiwan, Ministry of Education in Taiwan, and Academic Exchange Foundation in Tunghai University. We especially express our great gratitude to Jin-ling Huang, chair of the Department of Sociology at Tunghai University, for his strong administrative support for the conference and continued editorial financial support. Finally, we strongly appreciate the assistance from our copy editor, Cyndy Brown, and our graduate students, Pei-Chun Ko and Yen-Chen Lee.

REFERENCES

Bourdieu, P. 1986. "The Forms of Capital," in *Handbook of Theory and Research for the Sociology of Education*, edited by John G. Richardson 241–258. New York: Greenwood.

Coleman, J. S. 1988. "Social Capital in the Creation of Human Capital." *American Journal of Sociology*, 94: S95–120.

Lin, N. 2001. *Social Capital: A Theory of Social Structure and Action.* Cambridge, UK and New York: Cambridge University Press.

Hwang, K. 1987/ "Face and Favor: The Chinese Power Game." *American Journal of Sociology*, 92(4): 944–74.

Morgan, S. L., and A. B. Sørensen. 1999. "Parental Networks, Social Closure, and Mathematics Learning: A Test of Coleman's Social Capital Explanation of School Effects." *American Sociological Review*, 64: 661–81.

Portes, A. 1998. "Social Capital: Its Origins and Applications in Modern Sociology." *Annual Review of Sociology*, 24: 1–24.

Part I

Advances in Theory and Methods of Social Capital

1 Position Generators, Affiliations, and the Institutional Logics of Social Capital

A Study of Taiwan Firms and Individuals

Ray-May Hsung and Ronald L. Breiger

Two of the important tools that have been developed for measuring social capital are position-generated networks and affiliation networks of voluntary associations. Affiliation networks have long been formulated and analyzed as two-mode networks (conceived as linking, for example, persons and the organizations to which they belong). However, very few network researchers have noticed that the structure of position-generated networks could also be conceived as a form of two-mode network data. In this chapter, we employ a two-mode network formulation to map the classification systems that underlie the processes by which actors categorize their social contacts into different occupational positions. In other words, we exploit the embedding of position-generated networks within a two-mode formulation. We therefore see the two-mode network formulation as, in certain respects, capable of unifying the study of position-generated networks (how actors classify their social contacts) and networks of voluntary associations (how actors choose different associations). The institutional logics of these classification and affiliation systems indicate the collective and structural characteristics of social capital.

On the collective level of analysis, network researchers have used correspondence analysis and related techniques to analyze the overall structuring of two-mode network data (Wasserman, Faust, and Galaskiewicz 1990; Borgatti and Everett 1997; Roberts 2000; Pattison and Breiger 2002; Faust 2005) and organizational logics (Breiger and Mohr 2004). With respect to position-generated networks, the two modes are the positions and the types of social ties used to access those positions. (For example, data on these two modes might come from answers to the question, "Do you know anyone who holds the job of division head, and if so, what is their relationship to you?") With respect to affiliation data, the two modes are a set of voluntary groups and a set of actors. (For example, data on these two modes might come in answer to the question, "What kinds of professional associations do you belong to?") For each type of network, the coconstitution of the two modes creates a structure of institutionalized style. This chapter uses correspondence analysis to uncover the institutional logics from the two-mode structuring of position-generated networks and affiliation networks for 369 knowledge workers in four high-tech firms.

On the individual level of analysis, diversity of position-generated networks and memberships in voluntary associations indicate the characteristics of individual social capital (Lin 2001a; Lin, Fu, and Hsung 2001). We classify the position generators and voluntary associations into two types of social capital, according to two criteria. One criterion is based on associational logic between ranks of employees, and access to position and participation in voluntary associations. The other criterion uses the phrase *good position-generated social capital* to refer to the positive consequences that often accrue or become available on the basis of access to valued positions. We use the phrase *bad position-generated social capital* to refer to the negative consequences that may possibly accrue on the basis of accessing disvalued positions or those of low value. Moreover, we identify the income returns to good and bad social capital in regression analyses that control for many other human and social capital and job characteristics.

This chapter first describes our major indicators of human capital and social capital. The data we analyze are drawn from a study of four firms in Taiwan's semiconductor sector. Taiwan's capability in integrated circuit technology has made it a world leader since 1995, and the excellent quality of engineering in the Zones from which we draw our data (the Science Park and Export Processing Zone) has played an important role. Knowledge workers are classified into the ranks of engineers, technology managers, administrative staff, and administrative managers.

INSTITUTIONAL LOGICS OF SOCIAL CAPITAL

Social capital has been conceived in terms of collective assets and individual assets (Lin 2001a). Bourdieu (1984), Coleman (1988, 1990), and Putnam (1993, 1995) conceived social capital as the norms, cultural values, and trust inherent in organizations, classes, or communities. They are concerned with the question of how groups or communities develop and maintain their social networks and enhance their collective interests and identity. Bourdieu (1984) stressed that people of high economic status tend to build up high-density networks with those people who share similar cultural tastes; such networks are, therefore, one mechanism for the reproduction of the collective class identity of the upper classes. Bourdieu went on to posit the semiautonomy of economic and cultural forms of capital (for example, university professors manifest high cultural capital but relatively lower economic capital). Coleman (1988) conceived social capital with reference to the closure of networks that produce social control and norms of obligation. Putnam (1993, 1995) pointed out that the civic engagement of voluntary associations facilitates general trust and a form of democracy that he viewed as efficacious.

The institutional logics of position-generated networks and affiliation networks indicate the collective or structural characteristics of social capital. As mentioned, position-generated networks include a two-mode structure featuring occupational positions (the resource opportunity structure) and types of social ties that actors make use of in daily life. Memberships in voluntary associations have long been conceived as two-mode affiliation networks manifesting a duality of persons and groups (Breiger 1974). These two-mode networks can demonstrate the institutional logics that unify, on the one hand, the meaning structures or classification systems that actors use to classify their social contacts into a set of occupational positions, and, on the other hand, the classifications of voluntary associations that actors develop to organize their affiliations.

These institutional logics are the clustering of meanings that govern how actors arrange the system of their social actions. The institutional logics provide for the "relational structuring of actors and classification" (Breiger and Mohr 2004, p. 18). The idea of institutional logics for action systems is based on action theory and the concept of meaning structure (see Mohr 1998 for a review). Two-mode networks include the meaning structure composed by "a set of material practices and symbolic constructions" (Friedland and Alford 1991, p. 248).

In our study, access to a set of positions or participating in a set of voluntary associations represents a set of material practices (the set of resource opportunities). A set of socially recognized and shared classifications of social ties in daily life represents a set of symbolic constructions.

Social capital is conceived as "the investment in social relations with expected returns" (Lin 2001a, p. 19). Lin proposed that "institutionalized social relations with embedded resources are expected to benefit both the collective and the individuals within the collective" (2001a, 9). On the collective level, the "returns" earned by social relations come in the form of social identity or social recognition (Lin 2001a, 20). Linking social contacts with occupational positions and with participation in voluntary associations provide two avenues for constructing the meaning system of social identity.

We follow Breiger and Mohr (2004) in focusing on two kinds of institutional logics for two-mode networks: logics of structural equivalence of actors' relations, and the logic of mutual constitution of material practices and symbolic constructions. Structural equivalence (along with its generalizations in automorphic and regular equivalence) is an important structuring logic of the classification system of two-mode networks. The basic idea (Borgatti and Everett 1997; Breiger 2000) is that actors organize their relations and social activities in similar ways if they share an equivalent location within a field of action. DiMaggio and Powell (1983) proposed that actors in similar structural positions conform to similar or isomorphic institutional forces or logics (DiMaggio and Powell 1983; DiMaggio 1986; Fligstein and Brantley 1992; White 1992). Structural equivalence, along with its generalizations, provides a foundation for modeling institutional logics.

Duality or mutual constitution is another form of institutional logic. Breiger (2000) used correspondence analysis to compare and contrast Bourdieu's (1990) concept of field and Coleman's (1990) concept of the linear system of action based on dual structures of actors and actions. Bourdieu (1990) realized that the concept of a field is a convenient instrument with which to represent the joint construction of agency and structure. Bourdieu's construction includes one dimension of the pertinent structural properties and another dimension comprising a set of agents. Coleman's (1990) concept of an action system emphasizes the duality of actors and events (or valued outcomes), as well as the dual relations of power and value. (Thus, for example, one actor has power over another, in Coleman's system, to the extent that she controls outcomes that the first actor desires; dually, one event is more valued than another to the extent that it is desired by actors who control the first event.) Social theorists conceived the mutually constitutive character of the relationship between actors and actions or between relations and resource distributions as an empirical linkage between two orders of social phenomena.

SOCIAL CAPITAL AND CORRESPONDENCE ANALYSIS

Correspondence analysis is among the appropriate tools for representing the structural logics of such dual linkages pertaining to social capital. Bourdieu's (1984) social theory makes direct use of correspondence analysis in portraying the relation between positions (such as occupations) and dispositions (such as musical tastes). As to Coleman, although it is not widely known or appreciated, techniques related to correspondence analysis are at the heart of Coleman's theory of social capital. Specifically, Coleman wrote explicitly that "the power of an actor in the equilibrium linear system of action is a direct measure of the social capital available to the actor within that system" (1990, 313). Moreover, Breiger (2000, Appendix) is among those who have shown that Coleman defined an actor's "power" in the equilibrium action system as an eigenvector of a particular network, and this eigenvector is intimately related to the same technique of correspondence analysis that Bourdieu employed (see also Tam 1989). Thus both Bourdieu's and Coleman's concepts of social capital are related, in theory and in practice, to correspondence analysis.

This study explores the institutional logics of two-mode networks for 369 knowledge workers in the field of semiconductor design and production in Taiwan. Different ranks of knowledge workers are interdependent with one another. Knowledge workers at the same rank tend to share similar patterns of position-generated networks and affiliation networks. This means that employees at the same rank tend to share a common framework of organizing rules that pertain both to their social networks and to their social capital. Fields are composed of actors who take each other's actions into account in the framing of their own actions. We make use of contingency tables formed by (a) positions sharing access through the same types of social ties, and (b) positions sharing affiliation with the same types of voluntary associations. Then we use correspondence analysis to map institutional logics of equivalent structures for both types of dual network. The institutional logics of social capital at the field level are interpreted from the profiles of equivalent structures found in the correspondence analyses.

INDIVIDUAL ASSETS OF SOCIAL CAPITAL

Most previous researchers have conceived of social capital as assets of individuals in the form of a return on the individuals' investment in social networks. Researchers have widely used position-generated networks and affiliation networks of voluntary associations. Position-generated networks (such as ties to varied occupational positions throughout a dispersed network) have been found to be efficient resources for attaining instrumental actions and gaining better returns. Participation in work-related voluntary associations has been found to facilitate the acquisition of sought-after information and resources needed at work, and hence to increase returns.

Position-Generated Networks

Position-generated networks provide an effective design for the measurement of individual social capital. Lin defines social capital as "resources embedded in a social structure which are accessed and/or mobilized in purposive actions" (2001a, 12). Flap and Boxman specify that "social capital is the result of the size of the network, the structure of the network, the investment in network members, and the resources of these network members" (2001a, 161). The extent to which a wide variety of positions are accessed, as measured in position-generated networks, has been widely studied and found to be a strong predictor of income returns and of cultural capital (Lin and Dumin 1986; Lin et al. 2001; Erickson 1996, 2001).

Affiliation Networks

The variety of social resources is greater for those who are active in more voluntary associations that are rich in opportunities to meet others. Participation in more voluntary associations facilitates the individual's extensiveness of social circles. Associational activity is a powerful pathway to diversified contacts (McPherson 1981). People often join voluntary associations because their friends in such groups recruit them. Network diversity and the extent of voluntary association activity may well be reciprocally related. The number of memberships in clubs and associations can be conceived as a kind of social capital (Völker and Flap 1991).

Political scientists and sociologists have recently studied the social capital of civic engagement. Putnam (1995) used general social survey data in the United States to demonstrate the correlation between the decline of participation in civic associations and the decline of general trust; see also the recent findings of McPherson, McPherson, and Brashears (2006) on isolation in America. Putnam argued that the voting rate had rapidly declined since 1960 because of a parallel decline in civic engagement. Participation in voluntary associations facilitated the efficacy of social networks, which then produced norms conducive to trust in communities. Putnam's (1995) study conceived of civic engagement with reference to collective assets. Paxton (1999) criticized Putnam (1995) for emphasizing the decline of traditional associations while entirely ignoring the rise of some women's and new movement associations. However, both Putnam (1995) and Paxton (1999, 2002) still focused on the functions of civic engagement for maintaining healthy democratic institutions. Portes (1998) proposed that civic engagement, by producing higher network density, facilitated greater general trust and provided more social support.

In an analysis of Taiwan social change survey data, Lin (2001b) found that there was significant correlation between the degree of civic engagement and the material returns to the investment in civic engagement. He employed factor analysis to classify the organization of civic engagement into global, as distinct from local, associations. Professional, political, and business associations are global associations that are advantageous for prestige and income return; however, they do not significantly affect general trust. Boxman, De Graaf, and Flap (1991) also found that association memberships provided efficient social capital in determining the income returns for managers in the Netherlands. Hsung and Lin (2008) found that specific types of associations, especially work-related associations, are advantageous for income returns.

The duality of access to positions and voluntary associations includes two levels of theoretical implications: institutional logics of social capital at the collective level, and diversity of social capital at the individual level. How to integrate these two levels of analyses has been a puzzle. Access to different positions and voluntary associations is, in part, a function of structural equivalence in job ranks or across multiple types of relations. Clusters or groups of positions and associations often shape the possibilities for access and for gaining social capital. Lin (2001a) stated the basic question for social capital studies as how actors access resources embedded in structural positions. In our model, the position-generated networks contain structurally equivalent clusters based on types of relations or by job ranks. To date, this duality in the theory has not been fully elaborated in research. Few researchers realize that position-generated networks reflect structural equivalence and duality. Integrating these two types of structures, access to positions and to voluntary associations, as well as correspondences between them will make an important contribution to the understanding of the concept of social capital and its empirical foundations.

RESEARCH METHODS

The survey that we analyze was conducted in July and August 2002 under the supervision of the first-listed author. Two firms in Taiwan's Export Processing Zone and two firms in its Science Park were selected: one large and one small high-tech firm in each zone respectively. Contact with many firms was attempted; these four finally permitted face-to-face survey interviews in their firms. All four firms are in the semiconductor industry. The semiconductor industry has been the most important sector among manufacturing industries in Taiwan. One major purpose of this study is to examine the knowledge exchange networks among different divisions within the firm. Knowledge exchanges only exist among engineers, administrative staff, and managers in our case companies. At the time of the survey these high-tech firms were just beginning to promote knowledge exchanges among engineers and staff. For this reason, and also because lower-level workers tend to share a computer and hence do not have unique e-mail addresses that could be used for sampling, we excluded lower-level workers from this study. Because employee information is confidential and held by the personnel offices of these firms, we asked representatives of the personnel offices to randomly select our respondents' names from the employee name rosters of each firm respectively. Each interview took forty to fifty minutes. In all, 369 respondents were interviewed.

Summary of the Data

We distinguish four types of job rankings in our knowledge worker sample: engineer, technology manager, administrative staff, and administrative manager. The descriptive statistics for the variables on individual characteristics, human capital, social capital, and income for these job ranks are summarized in Table 1.1. Technology and administrative managers are mostly men, older and married, and tend to have a higher level of education, more years of work experience, longer job tenure, a greater number of positions accessed, and more voluntary associations engaged than do administrative staff and engineers.

Table 1.1 presents descriptive statistics for six types of positions accessed and the sixteen types of associations accessed. The question for our position generator was: "Among your relatives, friends, or acquaintances, are there people who have the following jobs? If so, what is his/her relationship to you?" Following these questions were six job positions. These six job positions were selected from fifteen job positions listed in the survey of social networks of the Taiwan Social Change Survey of 1997. To examine the capability of resource expansion for these knowledge workers, we chose the six job positions that were the least accessible positions in the 1997 survey (Lin, Fu, and Hsung 2001). These six jobs were distributed into high (lawyer, owner of large factory/firm, assemblymen/women),

Table 1.1 Summary of Human Capital and Social Capital Variables

Variables	*Engineer*	*Technical Manager*	*Admin- istrative Staff*	*Admin- istrative Manager*	*Total*
	N = 218	N = 59	N = 71	N = 21	N = 369
Individual Characteristics					
Gender (1 = men)	.77	.97	.39	.81	.73***
Age	32.49	37.54	33.51	42.86	34.08***
Married = 1	.48	.92	.59	.95	.60***
Human capital					
Years of education	15.85	17.05	15.37	16.43	15.98***
Public univeristy = 1	.40	.56	.37	.43	.42
Science/engineer-ing = 1	.79	.85	.25	.57	.69***
Work years of previous jobs	3.84	5.03	4.45	10.05	4.51***
Current job tenure	4.97	7.79	6.47	9.26	5.96***
Social capital					
# of positions accessed	1.33	2.34	2.11	2.67	1.72***
# of higher-prestige positions accessed	.91	1.63	1.25	1.95	1.15***
# of lower-prestige positions accessed	.43	.71	.86	.71	.57***
# of associations	1.15	2.61	1.79	2.33	1.57***
# of learning associations engaged	.39	1.22	.66	1.33	.63***
# of recreation and philanthropic associations engaged	.76	1.39	1.13	1.00	.95***
Income (N. T.$)	46,388	75,593	42,535	79,762	52,215***

$^{*}p < .05$. $^{**}p < .01$. $^{***}p < .001$.

Table 1.2 Summary of Accessed Positions and Accessed Associations

	Mean Or Percent				
	Engineer	*Technology Manager*	*Administrative Staff*	*Administrative Manager*	*Total*
Position-generated networks					
Extensity (number of positions accessed)	1.33	2.34	2.11	2.67	1.72***
Accessed position (prestige score)					
Lawyer (73)	20.64%	33.90	32.39	57.14	27.10***
Owner of large factory/firm (70)	35.78%	64.41	54.93	71.43	46.07***
Assemblymen/women (69)	16.06%	35.59	14.08	28.57	19.51**
Division head (55)	18.35%	28.81	23.94	38.10	22.22*
Reporter (55)	18.81%	35.59	35.21	33.33	25.47**
Housemaid, cleaning worker (22)	23.85%	35.59	50.70	38.10	31.71***
Accessed associations					
Number of associations accessed	1.15	2.61	1.79	2.33	1.57***
Recreational clubs within firm	22.48%	42.37	25.35	38.10	27.10**
Philanthropic clubs within firm	5.96%	8.47	11.27	9.52	7.59
Study groups within firm	7.80%	28.81	22.54	38.10	15.72***
Knowledge management study groups within firm	7.34%	30.51	14.08	19.05	13.01***
Professional groups within firm	5.05%	15.25	7.04	19.05	7.86**
Recreational associations within zone	6.88%	20.34	16.90	9.52	11.11**
Philanthropic associations within zone	2.29%	1.69	2.82	0.00	2.17
Study groups within zone	1.83%	10.17	1.41	9.52	3.52**
Knowledge management study groups within zone	1.83%	3.39	2.82	4.76	2.44
Professional groups within zone	2.75%	13.56	2.82	9.52	4.88**
Philanthropic groups outside zone	11.47%	22.03%	25.35	23.81	16.53*
Recreational groups outside zone	16.97%	27.12	18.31	9.52	18.43

(continued)

Table 1.2 Summary of Accessed Positions and Accessed Associations (continued)

	Mean Or Percent				
	Engineer	*Technology Manager*	*Admin-istrative Staff*	*Admin-istrative Manager*	*Total*
Religious groups outside zone	10.09%	16.95	12.68	9.52	11.65
Professional groups outside zone	4.13%	5.08	7.04	19.05	5.69*
Study groups outside zone	5.50%	8.47	4.23	4.76	5.69
Knowledge management study groups outside zone	2.75%	6.78	4.23	9.52	4.07

*$p < .05$. **$p < .01$. ***$p < .001$

middle (division head, reporter), and low (housemaid, cleaning worker) occupational prestige positions.

Table 1.2 indicates that there is a significant difference among the four job ranks in terms of their percentages of access to the six positions. Administrative managers have greater percentages of access to higher prestige positions, such as the owners of large factories/firms and lawyers. A smaller percentage of the technology managers (in comparison to administrative managers) can access higher prestige positions. The engineers have less access to most positions. Members of the administrative staff have the greatest access to housemaid/cleaning workers.

Researchers have recently focused on the social capital that is gained through participation in voluntary associations.[1] We designated five types of associations within the firms: recreational clubs, philanthropy clubs, study groups, knowledge management study groups, and professional groups. The same five types were designated within the Zone. With respect to associations outside the Zone to which a respondent has access, we designated six types of groups: philanthropic, recreational, religious, professional, study groups, and knowledge management study groups. The response for each item was "yes" (if a respondent belonged to a group of that type) or "no." Table 1.2 indicates the pattern of participation in voluntary associations among respondents in our four broad occupational categories.

We found that recreational clubs within the firm are affiliated with all ranks of knowledge workers, especially technology and administrative managers. Recreational clubs within the firm thus provide an effective site for social capital for all categories of workers, allowing communication and coordination within the firm. Knowledge management study clubs within the firm are important for technology managers, and general study clubs are important for administrative managers. Philanthropic associations are also very popular for administrative staff and administrative managers.

INSTITUTIONAL LOGICS FROM CORRESPONDENCE ANALYSES: POSITION-GENERATED NETWORKS AND AFFILIATION NETWORKS

As discussed in previous sections, it is useful for certain purposes to recast the study of position-generated networks as a series of studies of two-mode arrays. In this section we present our analyses along these lines. We uncover institutional logics of access to positions on the basis of location within the firm, the type of social relation that is employed, types of voluntary associations with which one is affiliated, and the type of position to which access is sought. We are concerned with how actors make use of varied social relationships in seeking to establish contact with different types of target positions.

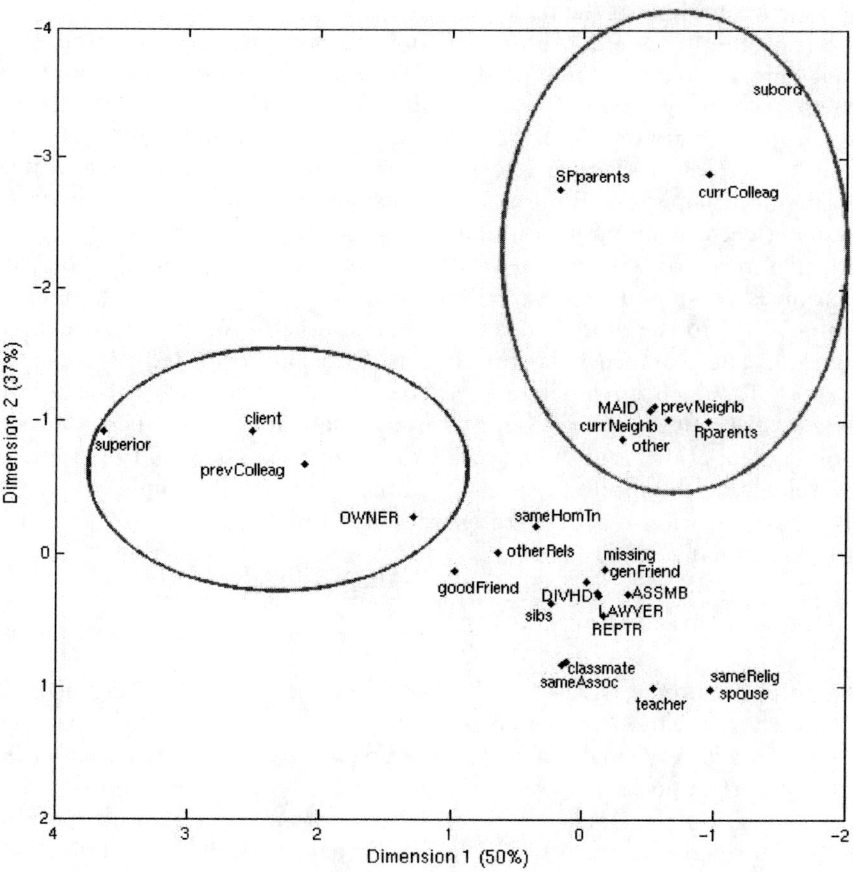

Figure 1.1 An institutional logic: How positions are accessed through intermediary roles.

Notes: preColleag: previous colleague, SPparents: spouse' parent, subord: subordinate, curr Colleag: current colleague, curr Neighb: current neighbor, Prev Nighb: previous neighbor, Rparents: respondent's parent, sameHomeTn: same home town, other Rels: other relatives, genFriend: general friend, DIVHD: division head, sib: sibling, ASSMB: Assembly men/women, REPTR: reporter, same ASSOC: same association, same Relig: same religion

Access to Positions: How to Read a Correspondence Analysis Diagram

How do different types of ties allow access to various network positions? This is the first question we explore with respect to our 369 knowledge workers. For this purpose we use a contingency table with columns naming the six positions in our position-generated network (see the first rows of Table 1.2), and rows naming twenty-four types of relations by which our respondents accessed these positions (for example, through a superior, through the parents of a spouse, via a classmate, and so forth). Each cell in this table reports the number of respondents who used a certain type of relation to access a given position. Figure 1.1 portrays the association between access to positions and types of relations on the basis of a correspondence analysis of the table.

How should we read Figure 1.1 and the other figures in our chapter that report correspondence analyses? Here we take some time to address this question, on the basis of a contribution of Goodman (1996);[2] see also the appendix to our chapter. Looking at the placement of "superior" and "OWNER" in Figure 1.1, we state that owners tend to be accessed through the superiors of our respondents, and that the statistical interaction between owner (a position) and superior (a type of relation) is high. Using a measure (λ_{ij}) proposed by Goodman (1996, 412, 422), the association is computed as +4.924. The distance from the origin (from the point [0,0]) to the point labeled "superior" is 3.7546, which we denote as $\|u_i\|$. The distance from the origin of the point labeled "OWNER" is 1.3121, which we label as $\|v_j\|$. Now imagine standing at the origin (the [0,0] point) of Figure 1.1, and use straight lines to connect the two points ("superior" and "OWNER") to the origin. The resulting angle is extremely small, about 2 degrees, and the cosine of that angle is +.9994. The basic relation we use to interpret correspondence analysis diagrams (see Goodman, 1996, eq. 61) is

$$\lambda_{ij} = \|u_i\| \|v_j\| \cos(u_i, v_j)$$

or, in our example, 4.924 = 3.7546 × 1.3121 × 0.9994. The cosine provides a visualization of the correlation coefficient. If the angle between two points is very small (as in our example), the cosine approaches +1.00 (a near-perfect positive correlation). If the angle between two points is very large (for example, if the two points fall almost on a straight line that also travels through the origin), the cosine approaches–1.00. If the points are nearly at right angles to one another (with respect to the origin), they are approximately uncorrelated and have a cosine near 0.00.

By applying this rule, we can use a correspondence analysis diagram (such as the one in Figure 1.1) to visually assess the magnitudes of many correlations among a set of observations. Moreover, the farther a point is from the origin (e.g., in our example "superior" is farther than "OWNER"), the greater effect or influence that point will have on the association (the λ_{ij}).

We use correspondence analysis diagrams to assess interactions between phenomena of different types (relations such as "superior" and accessed positions such as "OWNER" in the example of Figure 1.1) that are imagined to coconstitute one another and, in this sense, be "dual." Going further, the correspondence analysis diagrams can help us to apply a form of "dual structural equivalence," in the sense that phenomena such as "superior" and "OWNER" have a stronger association with each other to the extent that the angle between them is small, and to the extent that these points are farther from the origin (as specified in the previous equation). On related ways of conceptualizing structural equivalence, see the appendix to our chapter, and see also Breiger and Mohr (2004). Whereas the cosine represents the degree of similarity in the relation of two points to each other, the distance from the origin reflects the "strength" of the relationship.

Institutional Logics of Position-Generated Networks: Relations and Positions Accessed

Applying these principles of interpretation to the correspondence analysis diagram in Figure 1.1, we see three clusters. The one on the left indicates that access to the position of owner is very highly associated with having a tie to a superior, a client, or a former colleague who can access an owner. These are all business and work ties. The cluster at the top right indicates that access to a maid or cleaning person is highly associated with ties to family members or neighbors (spouse's parents, respondent's parents, a current or a previous neighbor) and work contacts (a subordinate, a current colleague). The third cluster indicates that the four other positions (lawyer, division head, reporter, and assemblyman/woman) are relatively equivalent to each other with respect to access. Discovery of this near equivalence prompts us to often refer to these four positions as the "public-service positions." Access to them is particularly dependent on school and association connections in which homophilous relations and social network ties are of some particular importance statistically (same religion, same association, classmate, good friend, siblings, spouse, and others).

Employment Status and Positions Accessed

Next we turn to the question of the ability of knowledge workers in each of our four major categories (engineer, technology manager, administrative staff, and administrative manager) to access the six positions. Figure 1.2 presents the spatial configuration from the CA diagram, as well as the interaction measures (the λ_{ij} defined previously).

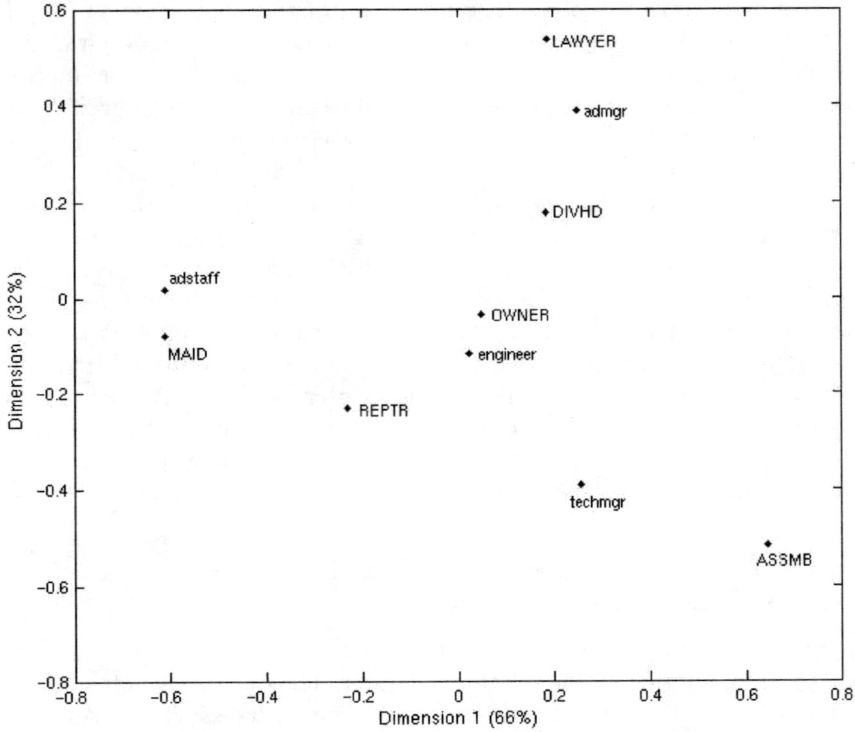

Figure 1.2 An institutional logic: Access of positions through job rank.

Notes: admgr: administrative manager, DIVHD: division head,
adstaff: administrative staff, REPTR: reporter,
techmgr: technology manager, ASSMB: assembly men/women

Engineers have weak associations with each position, as reflected in the extremely small distance from the origin of Figure 1.2. Technology managers have relatively high access to assemblymen/women. Members of the administrative staff (below the level of manager) can access maids and cleaning people relatively easily. Administrative managers have positive association with division heads and relatively extremely high access to lawyers. Technology managers tend to be unlikely to access lawyers. (Notice in Figure 1.2 that they are at opposite ends of the diagram; their interaction score is $\lambda = -.16$, which is the lowest in both its row and column.) Overall, Figure 1.2 indicates that higher ranks of knowledge workers tend to have stronger association with access to higher-prestige positions.

Institutional Logics of Affiliation Networks by Rank

Turning to membership in voluntary associations, the first important point is that managers—both technology managers and administrative managers—

have memberships in the greatest numbers of types of associations among the sixteen association types that we distinguish.[3] The differences in the "total" row of table 1.2a are significant at the .001 level (see also Table 1.2). Engineers have memberships in the smallest number of types of associations. Moreover, these differences (and their patterning) hold for memberships within the firm, within the Zone, and outside the Zone, as well as for the totals (Table 1.2a).[4] We speculate that occupational requisites encourage managers to have a great deal of associational capital, whereas "engineer" is an occupational category that is less embedded as a distinctive identity within voluntary associations.

Table 1.2a Mean Number of Types of Associations

	Mean Number of Types of Associations in Which Respondent Reports Membership			
	Engineer	*Technical Manager*	*Administatrive Staff*	*Administrative Manager*
Within firm	0.49	1.25	0.8	1.24
Within Zone	0.16	0.49	0.27	0.33
Outside Zone	0.51	0.86	0.72	0.76
Total	1.15	2.61	1.79	2.33

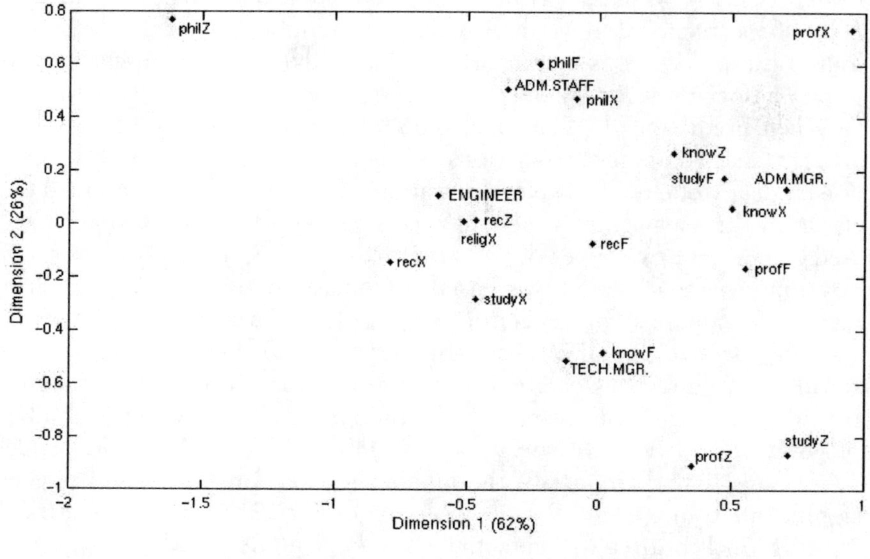

Figure 1.3 An institutional logic: Access to associations through job rank.

Notes: Types of voluntary associations are: professional ("prof"), religious ("relig"), general study group ("study"), managerial knowledge study group ("know"), philanthropic or charitable group ("phil"), and recreational association ("rec"). In addition, voluntary associations are further distinguished as to whether they are within a firm ("F"), within the high-technology zone ("Z"), or outside the zone ("X").

Figure 1.3 reports the spatial configuration, in the form of a correspondence analysis diagram, that relates job category and accessed associations. There is a strong association (λ = .77) between administrative managers and professional associations in the wider world outside the Zone. Technology managers tend to affiliate with professional associations within the Zone (λ = .42). On the other hand, administrative staff members have a strong tendency to affiliate with charitable associations within the firm (λ = .39) and within the Zone (λ = .95). Engineers share a tendency with the administrative staff to join charitable associations within the Zone (λ = 1.07), and engineers tend to go outside the Zone for their recreational memberships (λ = .47).

THE OUTCOMES OF GOOD AND BAD SOCIAL CAPITAL

Model 1 (see Table 1.3) is our baseline model for predicting (the log of) income on the basis of individual characteristics, human capital, and social capital. The individual characteristics include gender and marital status. Age has very high correlation with both marital status and job tenure, so we exclude the age variable from the model. The human capital variables include years of schooling, attendance at a public (vs. private) university, obtaining a degree in a science or engineering field (vs. all other fields), years of experience working at previous jobs, and current job tenure. The variables of social capital in Model 1 include the number of positions accessed (out of the six positions investigated in this study), and the number of voluntary associations accessed.

When predicting (log) income, the effect of the number of positions accessed and voluntary associations engaged is not significant in our baseline model (Model 1). To explore this finding further, we next examined the effect on the dependent variable of accessing two types of position-generated capital and two types of voluntary associations. The classification of position-generated capital was based on the association between employment status and position generator in Figure 1.2. The classification of association-generated capital was based on the association between employment status and voluntary associations in Figure 1.3. Table 1.3 further examines the income returns with respect to the endogenous bias due to the number of good or bad types of social capital (Mouw 2003). Moreover, Model 2 indicates that the effect of the number of positions accessed becomes significant (compare the first variable under "Social Capital" for Model 1 and Model 2) after we input the variable of number of higher-prestige positions accessed. Lawyer, owner of large firm, assemblymen/women, and division head are classified as the higher-prestige positions, and reporter and maid/cleaning position are classified as lower-prestige positions. However, the number of positions accessed becomes insignificant in Model 3 after we input the variable of number of lower-prestige positions accessed. This implies that the aggregated index of "number of positions accessed"

Table 1.3 Unstandardized Regression Coefficients in Models Predicting (Log) Income From Human Capital and Social Capital Variables ($N = 363$)

	Model 1	*Model 2*	*Model 3*	*Model 4*	*Model 5*	*Model 6*	*Model 7*
Gender	.074*** (.013)	.072*** (.013)	.072*** (.013)	.072*** (.013)	.075*** (.013)	.075*** (.013)	.075*** (.013)
Married	.049*** (.012)	.049*** (.012)	.049*** (.012)	.049*** (.012)	.047*** (.012)	.047*** (.012)	.047*** (.012)
Human capital							
Years of education	.021*** (.003)	.021*** (.003)	.021*** (.003)	.021*** (.003)	.020*** (.003)	.020*** (.003)	.020*** (.003)
Public university	.005 (.010)	.005 (.010)	.005 (.010)	.005 (.010)	.004 (.010)	.004 (.010)	.004 (.010)
Science/ engineering	.021 (.013)	.021 (.013)	.021 (.013)	.021 (.013)	.020 (.003)	.020 (.003)	.020 (.003)
Work years of previous jobs	.004*** (.001)	.004*** (.001)	.004*** (.001)	.004*** (.001)	.005*** (.001)	.005*** (.001)	.005*** (.001)
Current job tenure	.005*** (.001)	.005*** (.001)	.005*** (.001)	.005*** (.001)	.005*** (.001)	.005*** (.001)	.005*** (.001)
Rank (contrast-adm. staff)							
Engineer	.010 (.015)	.007 (.015)	.007 (.015)	.007 (.015)	.010 (.015)	.010 (.015)	.010 (.015)
Technical manager	.136*** (.020)	.131*** (.020)	.131*** (.020)	.131*** (.020)	.135*** (.020)	.135*** (.020)	.135*** (.020)
Administrative manager	.153*** (.026)	.146*** (.026)	.146*** (.026)	.146*** (.026)	.148*** (.026)	.148*** (.026)	.148*** (.026)
Social capital							
Number of positions accessed	-.002 (.003)	-.017 (.008)	.007 (.005)	—	-.003 (.003)	-.003 (.003)	-.003 (.003)
# of higher-prestige positions accessed	—	.024* (.012)	—	.007 (.005)	—	—	—
# of lower-prestige positions accessed	—	—	-.024* (.012)	-.017* (.008)	—	—	—
Number of associations engaged	.003 (.003)	.003 (.003)	.003 (.003)	.003 (.003)	-.003 (.005)	.009* (.004)	—
# of learning assoc. engaged	—	—	—	—	.012# (.007)	—	.009* (.004)
# of recreation & philosophic assocications engaged	—	—	—	—	—	-.102# (.007)	-.003 (.005)
Constant	4.150***	4.153***	4.153***	4.153***	4.155***	4.155***	4.155***
Adjusted R^2	.639***	.642***	.642***	.642***	.640***	.640***	.640***
df	12	13	13	13	13	13	13

Note. Standard errors in parenthesis.
$*p < .05$. $**p < .01$. $***p < .001$.

has two opposite components of social capital: good capital accruing from access to positions of higher prestige, and bad capital resulting from access to positions of lower prestige. If we did not decompose these associations, the effect on income of the number of positions accessed would disappear (as it did in Model 1). Model 4 indicates that good and bad social capital creates different directions of effects on income return.

Next, following this line of reasoning, we decomposed the number of associations accessed into two variables: number of learning associations, and number of recreational and philanthropic associations engaged. Model 5 and Model 7 indicate that the number of learning associations engaged has significant positive effect on income returns. However, the effect of the number of recreational and philanthropic associations engaged is negative in Model 6.

Good and Bad Social Capital

In a previous discussion of "negative social capital," Portes (1998, 15–18) distinguished four negative consequences of social capital: exclusion of outsiders, excess claims on group members, restrictions on individual freedom, and unproductive norms. We note that our findings on "bad" capital are related to, but not easily reducible to, any of Portes's types; we have identified a possible distinctive, "fifth" type of negative social capital that leads to negative outcomes (such as reduced income) on the basis of having ties to undesirable positions (such as those of relatively low occupational status). If our findings hold up more generally, we can then say that if an individual wishes to get ahead, it is not sufficient to have as many ties as possible to a variety of social positions. One must pick one's targets carefully, because—just as there is a reward for more ties to desirable target positions—there is also a penalty for developing social ties to positions that are less desirable. In this respect, our research contributes to ongoing efforts—such as those of Gargiulo and Benassi (1999, 298–322) on the "dark side" of social capital, Van der Holst (2006, 5) on gender "downsides" to social capital, and Portes (1998)—that seek to specify the mechanisms and specific contexts (Erickson 2006) by which social capital may have negative as well as beneficial effects.

DISCUSSION AND CONCLUSION

This chapter uncovered the institutional logics of duality of position-generated networks and affiliation networks. The correspondence analyses profiled the structurally equivalent position generators and associations by job ranks of high-tech knowledge workers. We grouped the structurally equivalent position generators into good and bad positions accessed, and also grouped structurally equivalent associations into learning and recreational/philanthropic associations. This chapter found that access to different clusters of positions and associations creates different directions of outcomes. Some clusters of positions and voluntary associations have a positive outcome for instrumental actions; however, some have a negative outcome for instrumental actions.

There are institutional logics of structural equivalence and mutual constitution between social ties and accessed positions. For our total sample, the structures of social ties brought to bear in accessing lawyers, assemblymen/women, reporters, and division heads are relatively equivalent. Largely homophilous ties of school, associations, and friendship tend to be associated with access to these public service positions (institutional sector and structural equivalence of social capital). The structure of social ties used to access owners of large firms or, at a different extreme, to access maids/cleaning workers are quite different (class segregation of social capital).

The logic of mutual constitution in position-generated networks of knowledge workers in high-tech firms implies that there are associational effects between the social ties used to access positions, the type of position accessed, and job rank. It has been suggested by practice theorists that neither the material world (the world of action) nor the cultural world (the world of symbols) can exist or be coherently structured independently (Mohr and Duquenne 1997). In this chapter we have used correspondence analysis to extend this argument. We have related position generators and social ties, exploring precisely how these two aspects of action and representation are interdependent.

If we think of social capital, in part, as one's ability to access positions, will an investment in social capital yield returns? This study found that the aggregated index of "number of positions accessed" has two relevant but opposite components: good capital and bad capital. Good capital boosts income on the basis of social ties that access higher-prestige positions, and bad capital introduces a penalty (lower income) for maintaining ties to lower-prestige positions. If we did not distinguish positive and negative forms of positional capital, the effect on income of the sheer number of positions accessed would disappear. As we have discussed, our distinction leads to an additional, fifth category of negative consequences of social capital, in addition to those identified by Portes (1998).

Correspondence analysis is a powerful tool for identifying the positions and voluntary associations that are structurally equivalent by job rank. The structurally equivalent positions or associations were grouped into common categories and were found to create different directions of outcome for the earnings returns to knowledge workers. This study is based only on 369 high-tech knowledge workers. The job ranks are quite straightforward and the sample represents only white-collar professionals. If we apply the analytical frameworks of this study to a large national representative sample, we may face some complex methodological issues. The classification criteria used here to differentiate structurally equivalent clusters of positions and associations needs to be refined in future studies to be applicable to more complex stratification systems.

APPENDIX: MORE ON READING CORRESPONDENCE ANALYSIS DIAGRAMS

In the text of our chapter, we present some discussion of how to read a correspondence analysis diagram when we introduce Figure 1.1. Here we add just a bit more detail. Our reading methods follow Goodman (1996), to which we refer the interested reader who seeks a comprehensive treatment.

Consider a contingency table that has one column for each of the six positions in our position-generated study (positions such as lawyer, factory owner, maid, and so on) and one row for each type of relation (such as spouse's parents or current neighbor) through which a position might be accessed.

The model of simple statistical independence applied to our table posits no interactions between rows and columns ($\lambda_{ij} = 0$ for all i and j). We can write the simple model of statistical independence as follows:

$$F_{ij} = N\, p_{i+}\, p_{+j}$$

where F_{ij} is the count in the cell in row i and column j that is expected on the basis of the model, N is the table sum, p_{i+} is the proportion of the N counts in row i , and p_{+j} is the proportion of the N counts in column j. Because this model posits the absence of interaction between positions accessed and types of relations used, it is an unrealistic model for our data, serving merely as a baseline.

To model the actual interactions in our table, we seek to focus on residuals from the independence model, and—in particular—we seek to find a dimensional space in which to portray departures from independence. Thus, consider the model

$$F_{ij} = N\, p_{i+}\, p_{+j}\, (1 + \sum_{k=1}^{K} u_{ki} v_{kj})$$

This is the correspondence analysis model (compare Goodman 1996, eq. 26). Here the u and v terms are estimates of the scores of relations (u_i) and accessed positions (v_j) on each of the K dimensions that are postulated. In practice, K is often taken to be equal to 2, providing a "best" simplification of the data structure in just two dimensions ("best" by the criterion of least-squares). Then, a natural descriptive measure of the strength of interaction between a row (u_i) and a column (v_j), which we denote as λ_{ij}, is

$$\lambda_{ij} \equiv \sum_{k=1}^{K} u_{ki} v_{kj}$$

(see the previous equation and Goodman 1996, 412, 422).

Let us illustrate from an example considered in the text: u_i = the relation of "superior," and v_j = the accessed occupation of "owner." The numerical estimates on each dimension (k = 1, 2) that result from the correspondence are as follows:

Relations = "superior"		*Accessed Positions = "owner"*	
u_{1i} = dim. 1	u_{2i} = dim. 2	v_{1j} = dim. 1	v_{2j} = dim. 2
–3.6393	.9234	–1.2821	.2794

Applying these numerical estimates to the equation,

$$\lambda_{ij} = (-3.6393 \times -1.2821) + (.9234 \times .2794) = 4.924$$

is the measure of interaction between "superior" and "owner."

As discussed in our text, there is a convenient alternative way to think about the λ_{ij}, one that yields the same numerical estimate but that allows a visual portrayal of the association. We continue to illustrate with our example of one relation ("superior") and one position ("owner") from our Figure 1.1. We have the alternate formula

$$\lambda_{ij} = \|u_i\| \|v_j\| \cos(u_i, v_j)$$

Here $\|u_i\|$ is the distance of "superior" from the origin (the point [0, 0]) in Figure 1.1. Using the numerical estimates given above and the theorem of Pythagoras, this distance is

$$\sqrt{3.6393^2 + .9234^2} \quad = \quad 3.7546$$

Using a similar calculation, the distance of "owner" from the origin is 1.3121.

The cosine of the angle connecting the two points may be computed as +.9994 (which is the cosine of an angle of about 2 degrees—see Figure 1.1). Thus, using the new equation, we have

$$\lambda_{ij} = 3.7546 \times 1.3121 \times .9994 = 4.924$$

that agrees (as it must; Goodman 1996, eq. 61) with our previous calculation of λ_{ij}.

The advantage of the "geometrical" formula for λ_{ij} is that it encourages a graphical visualization of the interactions in our data. Specifically, it encourages us to interpret correspondence diagrams as follows:

1. Phenomena (such as "superior" and "owner" in this example) have a stronger interaction with each other to the extent that the angle (formed by connecting each point to the origin by a straight line)

between them is small, and to the extent that the points representing them are farther from the origin.

2. Consider the relative interaction of two rows ("superior" and "current neighbor," say, or u_1 and u_2) with respect to the same column ("owner," for example, let us say v_1). We form the projection of each row-point onto the straight line from the origin to v_1. See Figure A1.1 for an example. The interactions (λ_{11} and λ_{21} in our example) are proportional to these projections. Specifically, for the example in Figure A1.1, we have:

$$\frac{\lambda_{11}}{\lambda_{21}} = \frac{a}{a+b}$$

thus indicating that u_2 has a stronger association with v_1 than u_1 does.

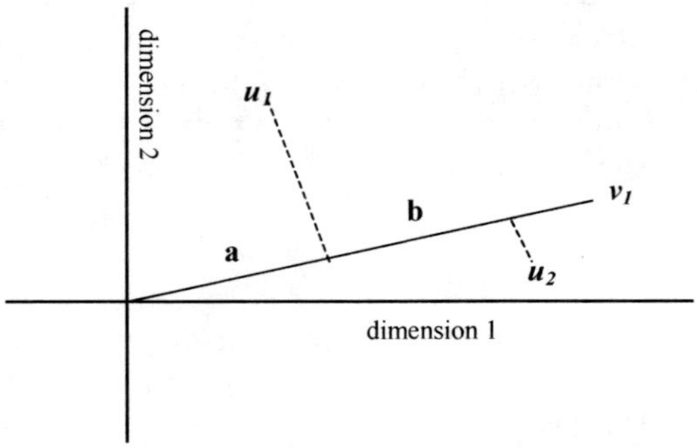

Figure A1.1 The Relative Interaction of Two Rows with the Same Column

The interaction of row u_2 with column v_1 is stronger than the interaction of row u_1 with v_1. In fact, $\lambda_{21} / \lambda_{11} = (a+b) / a$. In this way, we may "use our eye" to infer relative degrees of association from the correspondence analysis diagram.

NOTES

This chapter was presented in International Conference on Social Capital: Communities, Classes, Organizations and Social Networks on 14 December 2004 in Tunghai University, Taichung, Taiwan.

1. Participation in voluntary associations was measured by the following question: "Have you ever participated in the following associations?"
2. We present a simplified treatment of the basic ideas. The reader who wishes a more complete treatment is referred to Goodman (1996).
3. Our sixteen types of voluntary association include five within firms (recreational, philanthropic/charitable, study groups [other than knowledge management], study groups devoted to knowledge management, and professional);

five beyond the firm level but within the zone (the same five as above); and six outside the Zone (the same five as above, plus religious).

4. Differences in memberships by occupational group "outside the Zone" are significant at the .03 level. Differences within all other rows of this table are significant at the .001 level. For each row we have a one-way ANOVA on (3, 365) *df*, with computed *F* ratios (from row 1 to the "totals" row) of 10.74, 6.44, 3.11, and 10.87 respectively.

REFERENCES

Borgatti, S. P. and M. G. Everett. 1997. "Network Analysis of 2-mode Data," *Social Networks* 19: 243–68.

Bourdieu, P. 1984. *Distinction: A Social Critique of the Judgment of Taste*. Cambridge, MA: Harvard University Press.

———. 1990. *The Logic of Practice*. Cambridge, MA: Polity.

Boxman, A. W., P. M. De Graaf, and H. D. Flap. (eds.). (1991) "The Impact of Social and Human Capital on the Income Attainment of Dutch Managers," *Social Networks* 13: 51–73.

Breiger, R. L. 1974. "The Duality of Persons and Groups," *Social Forces* 53 () 181–90.

———. 2000. "A Tool Kit for Practice Theory," *Poetics*, 27: 91–115.

———. and J. Mohr. 2004. "Institutional Logics from the Aggregation of Organizational Networks: Operational Procedures for the Analysis of Counted Data," *Computational and Mathematical Organizational Theory*, 10:11–43.

Coleman, J. S. 1988. "Social Capital in the Creation of Human Capital," *American Journal of Sociology*, 94: S95–S121.

———. 1990. *Foundations of Social Theory*, Cambridge, MA: Harvard University Press.

DiMaggio, P. 1986. "Structural Analysis of Organizational Fields: A Blockmodel Approach," *Research in Organizational Behavior*, 8: 335–70.

DiMaggio, P. J. and W. W. Powell. 1983. "The Iron Cage Revisited: Institutional Isomorphism and Collective Rationality in Organizational Fields," *American Sociological Review*, 48: 147–60.

Erickson, B. H. 1996. "Culture, Class, and Connections," *American Journal of Sociology*, 102(1): 217–51.

———. 2001. "Good Networks and Good Jobs: The Value of Social Capital to Employers and Employees," in *Social Capital: Theory and Research*, edited by N. Lin, K. Cook, and R. S. Burt, 127–58. New York: Aldine De Gruyter.

———. 2006. "Social Capital Across Contexts: Strategies for Theory and Research." Paper presented at the International Sunbelt Conference on Social Network Analysis, Vancouver, April 26–29, 2006.

Faust, K. 2005. "Using Correspondence Analysis for Joint Displays of Affiliation Networks," in *Models and Methods in Social Network Analysis*, edited by P. J. J. S. Carrington and S. Wasserman, 117–47. New York: Cambridge University Press.

Flap, H., and E. Boxman. 2001. "Getting Started: The Influence of Social Capital on the Start of the Occupational Career," in *Social Capital: Theory and Research*, edited by N. Lin, K. Cook, and R. S. Burt 159–84. New York: Aldine De Gruyter.

Fligstein, N., and P. Brantley. 1992. "Bank Control, Owner Control, or Organizational Dynamics: Who Controls the Large Modern Corporation?" *American Journal of Sociology*, 98: 280–307.

Friedland, N., and R. A. Alford. 1991. "Bringing Society Back In: Symbols, Practices, and Institutional Contradictions," in *The New Institutionalism in Organizational Analysis*, edited by W. W. Powell and P. J. DiMaggio 232–63. Chicago: University of Chicago Press.

Gargiulo, M.,and M. Benassi. 1999. "The Dark Side of Social Capital," in *Social Capital and Liability*, edited by R. A. J. Leenders and S. M. Gabbay 298–322. Boston: Kluwer.

Goodman, L. A. 1996. "A Single General Method for the Analysis of Cross-Classified Data: Reconciliation and Synthesis of Some Methods of Pearson, Yule, and Fisher, and Also Some Methods of Correspondence Analysis and Association Analysis," *Journal of American Statistical Association*, 91: 408–28.

Hsung, R. M., and Y. J. Lin. 2008. "Social Capital of Personnel Managers: the Causes and Returns of Position-Generated Networks and the Participation in Voluntary Associations," in *Social Capital: Advances in Research*, edited by N. Lin and B. H. Erickson 234–54. London: Oxford University Press.

Lin, N. 2001a. *Social Capital: A Theory of Structure and Action*, Cambridge and New York: Cambridge University Press.

———. 2001b. "Social Capital: Social Networks, Civic Engagement, or Trust?" Keynote address at the Annual Meeting of the Hong Kong Sociological Association, 25 November 2000 (Revised version).

——— and M. Dumin. 1986. "Access to Occupations Through Social Ties," *Social Networks* 8 365–85.

———, Y. C. Fu, and R. M. Hsung. 2001. "The Position Generator: Measurement Techniques for Investigations of Social Capital," in *Social Capital: Theory and Research*, edited by N. Lin, K. Cook, and R. S. Burt 57–81. New York: Aldine De Gruyter.

McPherson, J. M. 1981. "Voluntary Affiliation: A Structural Approach," in P. M. Blau and R. K. Merton (eds) *Continuities in Structural Inquiry*, London: Sage Publications.

———, L. S. McPherson and M. E. Brashears. 2006. "Social Isolation in America: Changes in Core Discussion Networks over Two Decades," *American Sociological Review*, 71 353–75.

Mohr, J. W. 1998. "Measuring Meaning Structure," *Annual Review of Sociology*, 24: 345–70.

——— and V. Duquenne. 1997. "The Duality of Culture and Practice: Poverty Relief in New York City: 1888–1917," *Theory and Society* 26 (2–3): 305–56.

Mouw, T. 2003. "Social Capital and Finding a Job: Do Contacts Matter?" *American Sociological Review*, 68: 868–98.

Pattison, P. E. and R. L. Breiger. 2002. "Lattices and Dimensional Representations: Matrix Decompositions and Ordering Structures," *Social Networks*, 24: 423–44.

Paxton, P. 1999. "Is Social Capital Declining in the United States? A Multiple Indicator Assessment," *American Journal of Sociology*, 105:88–127.

———. 2002. "Social Capital and Democracy: An Interdependent Relationship," *American Sociological Review*, 67 (April): 254–77.

Portes, A. 1998. "Social Capital: Its Origins and Applications in Modern Sociology," *Annual Review of Sociology* 24 1–24.

Putnam, R. 1993. "The Prosperous Community: Social Capital and Public Life," *The American Prospect*, 13 (Spring): 35–42.

———. 1995. "Bowling Alone: America's Declining Social Capital," *Journal of Democracy*, 6: 65–78.

Roberts, J. M. 2000. "Correspondence Analysis of Two-Mode Network Data," *Social Networks*, 22: 65–72.

Tam, T. 1989. "Demarcating the boundaries between self and the social: The anatomy of centrality in social networks," *Social Networks,* 11: 387–401.
Van der Holst, R. 2006. "The Downside of Social Capital: Examining the Crab Syndrome," paper presented at the International Sunbelt Conference on Social Network Analysis, Vancouver, April.
Völker, B., and H. Flap. 2004. "Social Networks and Performance at Work: A Study of the Returns of Social Capital in Doing One's Job," in *Creation and Returns of Social Capital: A New Research Program*, edited by H. Flap and B. Voelker 172–96. London: Routledge.
Wasserman, S., K. Faust, and J. Galaskiewicz. 1990. "Correspondence and Canonical Analysis of Relational Data," *Journal of Mathematical Sociology,* 15: 11–64.
White, H. 1992. *Identity and Control: A Structural Theory of Social Action.* Princeton, NJ: Princeton University Press.

2 Changing Places

The Influence of Meeting Places on Recruiting Friends

Beate Völker, Henk Flap, and Gerald Mollenhorst

THE IMPORTANCE OF SOCIAL CONTEXTS FOR BUILDING PERSONAL NETWORKS

It is the focus of the sociological program to specify extraindividual conditions that explain behavior and relationships, and result in macro outcomes. Who one socializes with and works with, enjoys leisure time with, or even who one marries depends not only on an individual's sympathy for particular others. Social relationships and networks do not emerge merely as a result of preferences; they also depend on conditions beyond the individual, such as the social contexts he/she lives in. Who one meets at certain places and social contexts is not random; the sociodemographic composition of these contexts constitutes the opportunity structure for meeting particular others and largely affects the resulting personal network. This supply-side perspective follows the lead of many other sociologists (e.g., see Fischer et al. 1977; Feld 1981; Fischer 1982; Blau and Schwartz 1984; Marsden 1990; Podolny and Baron 1997; Kalmijn and Flap 2001; Kalmijn 2002) and stresses the overriding importance of opportunities and constraints over preferences for selecting interaction partners, as there is no "mating" without "meeting"[1] (cf. Verbrugge 1977, p. 577). Demand-side theories, usually applied in social psychology, focus mainly on mating, assuming that differences in personal networks are due to differences in individual preferences. Theories and empirical studies that take both of these mechanisms into account are rare (for exceptions and discussion, see Blau, Blum, and Schwartz 1982; Blum 1985; McPherson and Smith-Lovin 1987; Cook and Whitmeyer 1992). In most theories, the emphasis is on only one side of the explanation, i.e., that of the individual preferences. Hence, in many network studies, explanations of relational patterns are based on person inherent, cognitive, emotional, or normative tendencies toward similarity, transitivity, closure, balance, consistency, and the like.

In this study, we present another case for the importance of the supply-side perspective and analyze the importance of places where one first meets a certain interaction partner who becomes a friend later on. Specifically, we study whether some social contexts or meeting places produce more friendships than others. Furthermore, we inquire into the question whether the importance of specific meeting places as a "birthplace of friendships" has changed through time (see Coleman 1990, p. 579 and passim). In the long run, these changes in contexts are also an alleged cause for changes in personal networks, e.g., a decrease in the density of networks and the strength of relationships (e.g., Putnam 2000, Pescosolido and Rubin 2000).

TRENDS IN SOCIAL CONTEXTS?

In his analysis of modern society, Coleman (1990, 1993) described how social activities that were once enmeshed in the family and the neighborhood, such as domestic care, child rearing, food consumption, preparation for adult tasks, spending leisure time, and work, are nowadays taken over by modern, anonymous, social and economic institutions of the state or the market and their agents. Activities that used to be bundled in what Coleman called the "primordial social structure," such as the family or the neighborhood, became irreversibly unbundled in the "purposive social structure," i.e., organizations and markets (Coleman 1990, p. 585). Bundling of activities can also be understood as overlap in social settings. For example, family and neighborhood used to be bundled formerly but have become unbundled and unraveled nowadays, because family members do not live close to each other in one house or in one neighborhood anymore. Coleman argued that, in consequence, people become less interdependent and less connected to each other. Hence, besides the growing importance of purposive social structures and the fact that corporate actors have taken over activities that were once undertaken by the family, Coleman's argument can also be interpreted as an unraveling of social contexts in which people are involved. This unraveling makes for a change in social ties and the networks that people are embedded in, and probably for a decline in social capital. A popular example is that the the geographical distance between places of work, home, and recreation has increased for many people. Even if one works close to one's home, one meets many people from outside the neighborhood at the workplace, and one's coworkers do not live close to one's home. This is probably typical of modern societies, and especially for urban areas. In more traditional, rural communities, geographical distances are probably smaller and one more frequently meets the same others in different contexts such as work, leisure, neighborhood, and so forth.

The degree to which contexts are bundled affects the structure of personal networks. The stronger contexts are bundled, the more an individual meets the same others and the more the networks of actors will overlap. Personal networks in bundled contexts will be denser and will contain stronger ties than personal networks in separated, unbundled contexts (cf. Feld 1981). If work, recreation, domestic activities, and other activities are undertaken in highly bundled contexts, where people work with others who are members of the same sports club or live in the same neighborhood, many different ties in different contexts cannot exist because there are no opportunities for them to emerge (cf. Mak 1996; Podolny and Baron 1997). Once contexts become unbundled, different network structures will emerge because, in general, the supply of different interaction partners increases. The final result of context unbundling would be a network structure where the focal actor is related to others through ties that are completely unconnected. It is alleged that these ties become more superficial and weaker, but may be more numerous.

In sum, we argue that Coleman's (1993) ideas on changes in contexts over time have two implications: one for the degree to which social contexts become unbundled and one for the degree to which certain contexts (i.e., more purposive social structures like the workplace and education) have become more important at the expense of other contexts (i.e., primordial social structures like family and neighborhood). If activities are taken over more and more by purposive social structures, we can expect these contexts to become more important as a place for the recruitment of friends. This argument can be tested by investigating the contexts where people currently meet new network members, and where they did so formerly. More traditional contexts such as family or neighborhood, which are more or less ascribed or given with birth, can be expected to be less important today than in former times; more modern, achieved contexts such as voluntary organizations and workplaces can be expected to be more important nowadays.

Feld (1981, 1984) was among the first to account more systematically for the impact of social contexts on the emergence of personal relationships. In general, individuals who share a social context have a higher chance to become a member of each other's network than individuals who do not share a context. Yet if one agrees on the importance of social contexts for the emergence of social relationships, it becomes important to understand how contexts differ from each other and whether these different characteristics of contexts account for differences in relationships. Although many dimensions of social contexts can be distinguished, we direct our inquiry to only one characteristic that can be expected to have an impact on the resulting interactions, its degree or level of ascription and achievement. Contexts differ in the degree to which they can be considered as "ascribed" and "achieved." In line with Coleman's (1993) argument, we expect that friends who are recruited more recently will be recruited more often from "achieved" contexts, and friendships established earlier on in life will have been recruited more often from ascribed contexts.

Note that we concentrate on a particular kind of relationship, friendships and their sources (cf. Fischer et al. 1977). Friendship is a kind of relationship that, in general, everyone strives for, but is not as restrictive as marriage; e.g., one can have many friends whereas one only has one marriage partner. Friends constitute an important part of one's network, next to family, neighbors, or colleagues, and friends can form a network by themselves. We focus first on the chance for a certain relationship to be a friendship tie given a particular context of meeting. In a second step, we study the differential impact of contexts on the creation of these friendship relationships; and third, we investigate whether the importance of achieved social contexts for recruitment of friends has indeed increased through time.

DATA AND MEASUREMENTS

We test our expectations using data from a representative survey of the Dutch conducted in 2000, called the Survey of the Social Networks of the Dutch. The data includes information on 1,007 individuals between the ages of 18–65, representing the Dutch population. The sampling procedure was as follows: First, we sampled 40 municipalities that represented the different Dutch provinces and regions, taking into account size differences in municipalities. We subsequently randomly sampled four neighborhoods in each municipality. A neighborhood was defined by a zip code. In the Netherlands, the zip code system consists of four numbers and two letters for every address. We chose to define a neighborhood as the addresses within a zip code area of identical numbers plus one identical letter. On average, such an area includes 230 addresses and corresponds to the route of a postman. Last, we randomly sampled 25 addresses in every neighborhood. We ended up with a data set consisting of 1,007 individual respondents in 168 neighborhoods (because the neighborhoods of one particular municipality were very small, there were 5 neighborhoods sampled, thus the number of 168). The response rate was 40 percent.

All potential respondents in the sample received a letter giving them the background of our research and informing them that we would call to make an appointment. If respondents had no telephone, we announced that one of our interviewers would visit them to make an appointment for the interview. The interviews took about one hour and forty-five minutes on average, and were conducted by thoroughly trained interviewers. In most cases, the interviews took place at the respondent's home and sometimes at his or her workplace. Most questions in the questionnaire had predefined answer categories.

MEASUREMENT

Network Members and Social Contexts

The respondents were interviewed about all kinds of relationships and details of their network. Networks were delineated via so-called name-generating exchange questions, thirteen in total (see Appendix). For example: "With whom did you discuss personal matters during the last months? May I ask for the initials or the first name of these persons?"

In a second step, additional questions were posed about the persons mentioned and the relationship between the respondents and their network members. In the analysis presented in this chapter, we include the following information on the network members: paid work, sex, married/cohabitation (all coded as dichotomous variables), age (continuous variable, scaled in years), highest education (eight categories), and duration of the relationship (continuous variable, scaled in years) between ego and alter. Furthermore, we include information on the kind of role-relation between ego and alter in the analyses, in particular whether a network member was a friend or not (coded as dichotomous variable). Up to three different role relations (friends, family, colleagues, and the like) could be mentioned per network member. We also directly asked about some role relations; i.e., we wanted to know about the respondents' relationship with their boss at work, and two of their direct neighbors. In the analyses presented in this chapter, we included all network members who were labeled as being a "friend," but friends who were delineated after boss or neighbors in reaction to straightforward questions were included only if they were also mentioned in another exchange question.

Information on social contexts or meeting places was collected via the question asking where the respondent met his or her network members for the first time: during education, in a voluntary organization, at work, with family, with friends, at the respondent's home, at the other's home, in the neighborhood, in a place one goes out to, in church, on vacation, at a party, elsewhere (see Appendix). In the analyses, we considered the contexts of school/education, voluntary organization, work, and meeting via friends as achieved contexts, and the contexts of family, neighborhood, and church as ascribed contexts. The remaining contexts such as "respondents' or network members' home," "vacation," "party," and "elsewhere" are considered as "other contexts" and constitute the reference category in the analyses.

Other Measures

In general, we included the same characteristics for respondents (ego) as for their network members (alters) in the analyses. Education was measured in eight categories of highest graduation from an educational training. We also inquired into effects of status and occupational prestige, yet education and occupational status, or prestige, were highly correlated, so we did not include them together in one analysis. We decided to use education throughout the analyses because its coefficients seemed to be somewhat more stable than the others.

Further, a dummy variable indicated whether the respondent was male, married/cohabitating, and held a paid job. In previous analyses we also controlled for being a migrant, but because this parameter has no effect on the likelihood of a certain network member to be a friend we excluded it in later analyses.

As a further characteristic of the respondents we included whether the respondent lived in an urban or a rural area (in the analyses). Urbanization was measured on a five-point scale, based on the density of housing addresses in the neighborhood of the respondent. A value of 1 indicates a highly urbanized neighborhood with more than 2,500 addresses per km^2; a value of 2 indicates a considerably urbanized neighborhood with 1,500–2,500 addresses per km2; 3 indicates that the area is fairly urbanized, i.e., 1,000–1,500 addresses per km^2; 4 indicates a neighborhood that is not really urbanized, i.e., 500–1,000 addresses per km^2; and 5 means the neighborhood is not urbanized, i.e., less than 500 addresses per km^2.

A Note on Period, Cohort, and Age Effects

We interviewed our respondents at only one point in time, yet we aim at investigating an argument on changes through time. In other words, Coleman's (1993) argument is an argument on time periods, yet we have only one moment of measurement. Because we have only one measurement point, we have two problems in our data: cohort and period are confounded, as well as age and cohort. The only thing we could do is divide our sample into different birth cohorts and, in addition, control for the duration of the relationship between respondent (ego) and a particular network member (alter). Controlling for the "age" of relationships solves the problem of confounded cohort and period effects. An indication for a period effect is given if members from older cohorts meet new friends in achieved contexts, yet met their "old" friends in ascribed contexts, which does not hold for the younger cohort. An indication for cohort effects would be if older cohorts always meet their friends at different contexts than the younger cohort.

Moreover, controlling for the duration of relationships also solves the second problem in our data, i.e., confounding birth cohorts with a respondent's age. If we find that older friendships are—independent of a respondent's cohort—always recruited from a certain context, we have an indication for an age effect because these relationships are formed when the respondent was relatively young. If we find that the older cohort recruited older friendships at places other than those of the younger cohort, we have an indication that this finding is due to cohort or period effects.

In sum, although our data are not perfect, we have a proxy to investigate cohort, period, and age effects. Specifically:

- We have an indication for a *period* effect if we find that the oldest cohort recruits newer friends from achieved contexts and has recruited older friends from ascribed contexts, yet the younger cohorts always recruit from achieved contexts.
- We have an indication for a *cohort* effect if the older cohort recruits newer, as well as older, friends from ascribed contexts, but the younger cohort recruits all friends from achieved contexts.
- We have an indication for an *age* effect if the older, as well as the younger, cohort recruit older friends from ascribed (or achieved) contexts and newer friends from achieved (or ascribed) contexts.

We divided respondent's age into three cohorts: the oldest one (cohort 1: those born between 1935 and 1950), the second oldest cohort (cohort 2: those born between 1951 and 1965), and the youngest cohort (cohort 3: those born after 1966).

RESULTS

As we analyze friendship relationships and friendship networks, we first present some descriptive findings on friends of the Dutch. As Table 2.1, Panel A shows, the Dutch have, on average, three friends. The number of friends varies between only one to up to twelve. Furthermore, about 30 percent have no or only one friend; about 25 percent have five or more friends in their personal network. In general, of the 1,007 respondents, 849 do have at least one friend. Table 2.1 also shows the number of contexts

Table 2.1 Descriptive Statistics of Friends, Contexts, and Number of Friends Per Context ($N = 1{,}007$ respondents)

Panel A

Number of friends	*% (n) of respondents*	
No friends	15.7 (158)	
1	14.6 (147)	
2	16.8 (169)	
3	14.0 (141)	
4	13.1 (132)	
5	8.4 (85)	
6	8.6 (87)	
7 and more	8.7 (88)	
Mean number of	Mean (*SD*)	Range
Friends	3.09 (2.47)	1–12
Contexts	2.25 (1.15)	1–7
Friends per Context	1.81 (.90)	1–10

Panel B

Number of contexts	Number of friends	
	1	2 or more (%)
1	100.0%	19.4%
2	—	36.5%
3	—	27.5%
4	—	9.4%
5 and more	—	6.9%

from which friends are recruited. On average, friends are recruited from two contexts.

Panel B of Table 2.1 presents the recruitment of friends from different contexts in more detail. Of those who have two or more friends, the majority, more than 55 percent, have recruited their friends from one or two contexts. The correlation (not shown in Table 2.1) between the number of friends and the number of contexts from which friends were recruited is .74 (Pearson). This indicates that people with many friends found them in many different contexts.

Next, we investigate in more detail whether some contexts produce more friends than others. Table 2.2 focuses on the importance of various contexts for the emergence of friendship relationships, and shows the different odds ratios for becoming friends if one has met in a particular context. As can be seen from Table 2.2, if one meets during education, in a voluntary organization, via friends, or at church, the odds that the relationship will become a friendship are the highest. Neighborhoods are far less productive for the creation of friendship, and a first meeting at work or in the context of the family does not contribute to becoming friends—on the contrary, friends are not met, and hence not made, in these contexts.

Table 2.2 Odds Ratio for Becoming Friends if Met in a Particular Context

	Context	*Odds Ratio*	*Percentage of Friends Within All Relations From That Context (n)*
Achieved	Education	10.10	78.8 (417)
	Voluntary organization	6.61	70.7 (446)
	Work	.33	15.7 (555)
	Friends	7.08	72.6 (365)
Ascribed	Family	.21	9.8 (189)
	Church	5.39	68.8 (66)
	Neighborhood	1.44	36.5 (421)
Other	Vacation, party, going-out opportunity, and "elsewhere"	1.03	29.5 (650)
Total			10,638 relationships with 3,121 or 29.3% friendship relations

Reading example: the odds of becoming friends with someone met in a voluntary organization are about 6, meaning that people who meet in that context have a 6 times higher chance to become friends than to start another type of relation (like acquaintance, colleague, neighbor, etc.) .

To this point, these figures show that the importance of social contexts for meeting friends differs by context. Yet, as argued in section 2, we expect that cohorts differ in their recruitment pattern because "modern," ascribed contexts will become more important. Descriptive analyses not presented here indicate that members of the youngest cohort enter more contexts for recruiting friends, and that their number of friends is higher as well. Furthermore, the network of the younger cohort is less dense and more heterogeneous with respect to social and marital status of the alters, and less heterogeneous with respect to age.

Table 2.3 shows the different figures for the three cohorts concerning the importance of the contexts for recruiting friends in a multivariate multilevel model. It inquires into the dyads of relationships, and the likelihood of a network tie to be a friendship relationship is estimated in a logistic random coefficient model. In all models, it is controlled for characteristics of the respondents (ego), such as the degree of urbanization of their place of residence, whether they hold a paid job, whether they are male or female, the highest level of education completed, as well as whether the respondent lives together with a partner. The same characteristics are taken into account with regard to the characteristics of the network member (alter). We also included the duration of the relationship between ego and alter. Furthermore, we added the different social contexts, i.e., meeting places, as well as one cross-level interaction in the models: that between education of ego and of alter. We did so to have a basic control for the general assumption that people prefer others who are similar to themselves.

Table 2.3 shows that the different social contexts have important effects on the likelihood of a network tie becoming a friendship. The inclusion of meeting places in all models suppresses effects of ego and alters on the likelihood of being friends. We thus found larger effects of characteristics of individuals and their relationships in models that did not include contexts.

The estimated coefficients differ between the three cohorts. For the oldest cohort, born between 1935 and 1950, women and married people generally have more friends than men and those who live without a partner. Although those with a lower level of education mention more friends, those with a higher level of education have more highly educated friends. In addition, a higher education of alter increases the general likelihood that the tie is a friendship tie. Concerning other alter characteristics, those alters that are older are more likely to be friends. With regard to the different meeting places, it is found that —compared to the reference category— all meeting places have an important impact, although some coefficients are negative. The context of church shows the greatest effect, followed by education, other friends, and voluntary organization. The workplace and the family are not places where friends are found, and the impact of the neighborhood is relatively small.

For the second cohort, born between 1951 and 1965, urbanization also plays a role. The higher the degree of urbanization, the lower the likelihood of friendship ties.

Table 2.3 Multilevel Logistic Regression Analyses on the Likelihood of a Tie to be a Friendship Tie, for Three Cohorts (Survey of the Social Networks of the Dutch1, N = 1,007)

	Cohort1 (< 1950) Coefficient (s.e.)	*Cohort2 (1951–1966) Coefficient (s.e.)*	*Cohort3 (> 1966) Coefficient (s.e.)*
Ego-level characteristics			
Urbanization of living area	–.067 (.044)	–.176 (.043)*	–.044 (.064)
Paid job	–.038 (.134)	–.082 (.176)	.036 (.220)
Sex	.260 (.133)*	.139 (.118)	–.017 (.169)
Education	–.119 (.056)*	–.143 (.058)*	–.003 (.103)
Married/cohabitating	–.399 (.144)*	–.461 (.141)**	–.424 (.176)**
Alter-level characteristics			
Paid job	.099 (.117)	.270 (.128)*	.130 (.169)
Sex	.138 (.095)	.092 (.086)	.066 (.125)
Education	.028 (.016)+	.056 (.128)	.224 (.216)
Married/cohabitating	.058 (.108)	–.099 (.010)**	–.341 (.135)*
Age	.036 (.004)**	–.019 (.003)**	–.056 (.006)**
Duration of relationship	–.008 (.003)*	.005 (.004)	–.006 (.008)
Meeting places			
Education	1.988 (.245)**	1.605 (.186)**	1.723 (.253)**
Voluntary organization	1.622 (.180)**	1.505 (.181)**	1.307 (.264)**
Workplace	–.726 (.137)**	–1.219 (.126)**	–1.496 (.181)**
Family	–1.292 (.170)**	–1.517 (.157)**	–1.110 (.224)**
Friends	1.797 (.206)**	1.625 (.194)**	1.430 (.277)**
Neighborhood	.308 (.146)*	.289 (.139)*	–.021 (.220)
Church	1.992 (.359)**	1.025 (.417)*	—
Other (ref.)	—	—	—
Interaction terms			
Education ego*education alter	.049 (.020)**	.030 (.021)	–.014 (.036)
Intercept	–2.508 (.451)	1.055 (.046)	1.772 (.667)
Deviance (–2 loglikelihood)	2885.2	3601.15	1676.33
Difference to empty model	1855.58	1834.39	1209.14

Note. ^{+}p .< .10. $^{*}p < .05$. $^{**}p < .01$.

Furthermore, contrary to the older cohort, it matters whether the network member has a paid job. Alters who do paid work are more likely to be the friend of ego. In addition, age of the network member also matters, yet in a different manner than for the first, older cohort: for the first cohort, elderly network members were more likely to be friends; for the second cohort, the younger network members are more likely to be friends than another type of relation. Considering the different contexts, the effect of church is considerably smaller for this cohort, and family and workplace make the recruitment of friends even less likely.

Last, for the third and youngest cohort of those born after 1966, those who are not married cite more friends, and the likelihood of a tie to be a friend is still greater if the network member is not married. Furthermore, similar to the second cohort, younger network members are more likely to be friends than older ones. Note that the duration of a relationship has no effect in the two younger cohorts, but only in the older one. This means that friends in the older cohort are relatively new relationships if compared to other network members, yet in the other two cohorts the duration of a relationship is not associated with being friends. Concerning the different meeting places, the effect of voluntary organization is here somewhat smaller than in the other two cohorts and the effect of workplace has increased (negatively). Neighborhoods have no effect at all, and the number of friends recruited from church for this cohort was too small to be computed.

In sum, the analyses presented in Table 2.3 show that social contexts differ in the likelihood that a network member is a friend. Although the context of education for all three cohorts is a very important predictor, the coefficient for church and neighborhood has declined. Last, the association between workplace and friendship became even more negative in the youngest cohort than it was for the older one. Overall, it seems that the importance of meeting places for recruiting friends has declined for the younger cohort.

Table 2.4 presents the odds ratios calculated on the basis of the analyses presented in Table 2.3. These ratios can be calculated as the exponential of the estimated coefficient; they provide the odds ratios for the different meeting places while controlling for characteristics of ego (respondents) and alters (the network members). Table 2.4 shows that the odds ratios of education and voluntary organization are largest for the first cohort.

Furthermore, the odds ratio of having met via other friends and neighborhoods declines in cohorts 2 and 3, compared to cohort 1. Most drastic is the decline in the odds ratio for church. From these analyses, we can conclude that (a) the influence of different contexts on becoming friends is noteworthy, and (b) that this influence differs between the three cohorts. The latter conclusion is an indicator for the argument that meeting places have indeed changed through time. For the youngest cohort, the odds for recruiting friends from ascribed contexts are lowest.

Table 2.4 Odds Ratios for Becoming Friends if Met in a Particular Context; Calculated From Figures Provided in Table 2.5 (Survey of the Social Networks of the Dutch1, *N* = 1,007)

	Context	*Cohort 1*	*Cohort 2*	*Cohort 3*
Achieved	Education	7.300	4.970	5.600
	Voluntary organization	5.060	4.500	3.690
	Work	.483	.295	.224
	Friends	6.030	5.078	4.178
Ascribed	Family	.274	.219	.329
	Church	6.830	2.787	—
	Neighborhood	1.460	1.375	.979
Odds ratios for achieved and ascribed contexts compared				
Education and	Family	26.642	22.694	17.021
	Church	1.060	1.785	—
	Neighborhood	5.000	3.614	5.720
Voluntary organization and	Family	18.460	20.547	11.215
	Church	.740	1.614	—
	Neighborhood	3.465	3.272	3.769
Workplace and	Family	1.762	1.347	.680
	Church	.086	.105	—
	Neighborhood	.294	.214	.228
Friends and	Family	22.007	23.187	12.699
	Church	.880	1.822	—
	Neighborhood	4.130	3.693	4.267

Note. The odds ratios are calculated as exponentials of the estimated coefficients in Table 2.3; odds ratio = e^{β}. Comparisons between pairs of odds ratios in the second half of the table are calculated as the fraction between two odds ratios. Reading example: for cohort 1, the odds of recruiting a friend via the context of education are 7.3/.274 = 26.642 times the odds for recruiting a friend via the context of family.

In the lower half of Table 2.4, pairs of odds ratios are compared. This way, we studied the differences in importance of achieved, compared to ascribed, contexts for the three cohorts. Table 2.4 shows that recruiting friends via education and voluntary organizations is clearly more important than recruitment via family, church, or neighborhood. This holds for all of the three cohorts. Furthermore, the workplace—although not a place for making friends—is still more important than the family, but only for the two older cohorts. Compared to church and the neighborhood, the workplace does not lead to friendship. Finally, recruitment via friends is clearly more important than via other family or neighborhood, yet for the older cohort it is less important than the church.

So far, our results suggest that, with the exception of the place of work, achieved contexts are in general more important for the recruitment of friends than ascribed contexts. However, we also want to know whether the degree of bundling of contexts has changed and whether there is a general trend in contexts, i.e., whether the importance of contexts changed through time. As to the first question, whether contexts became unbundled, we do not have clear information on the degree of bundling or overlap of contexts in our data. In other words, we do not know whether people meet their colleagues at work as well as in a voluntary organization, or whether one meets friends in the neighborhood as well as at work. We can reconstruct ties between contexts while creating an affiliation matrix and study the pattern of contexts. We did so only for the oldest and the youngest cohort. The affiliation network between contexts is based on the answers of the respondents to the question of where they met each of their friends. A connection between two contexts occurs if a person has a friend in both of these contexts. The affiliation matrices have been used as input for a multidimensional scaling that resulted in Figure 2.1 and Figure 2.2.[2]

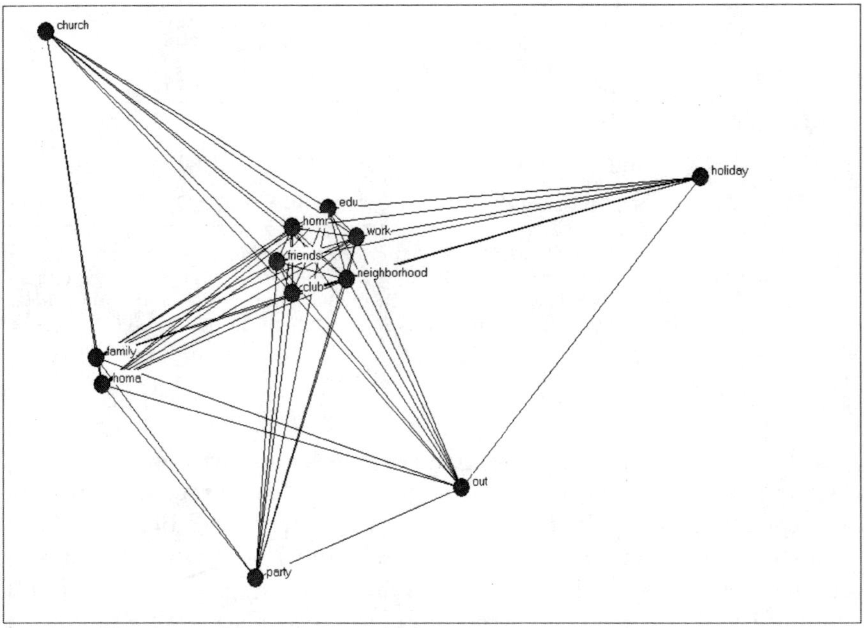

Figure 2.1 Network of social contexts where friends are met for the cohort of individuals born between 1935 and 1950.

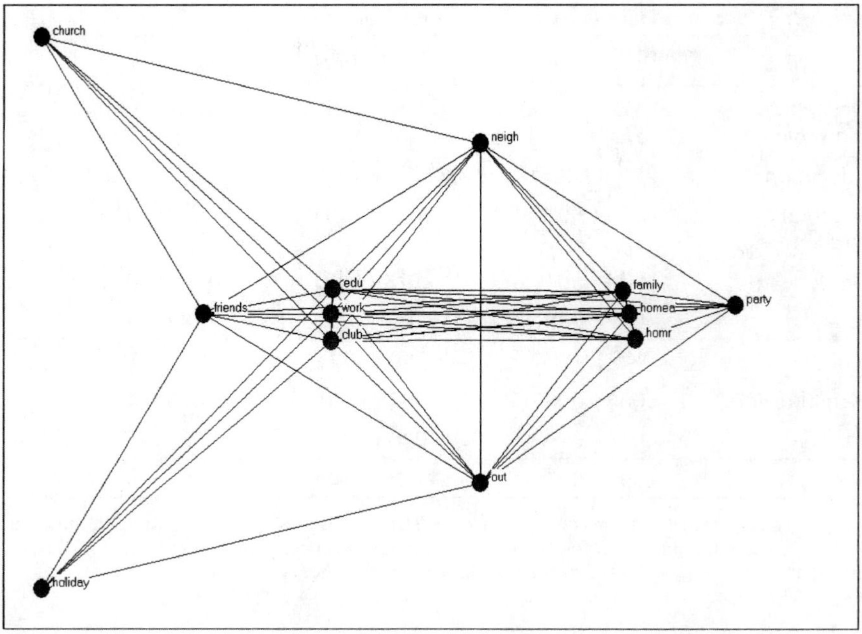

Figure 2.2 Network of social contexts where friends are met for the cohort of individuals born between 1966 and 1982.

These affiliation matrices represent hypernetworks (see McPherson 1982; see also Breiger 1974). As can be seen, Figure 2.1 shows a much more centered network than Figure 2.2. Figure 2.2 shows more segregation. Nodes in Figure 2.1 are much closer together than in Figure 2.2, in particular if we look at the cluster in the middle of the figure consisting of education, work, voluntary organizations (clubs), neighborhood, home, and friends ("friends" indicates that one met a friend via another friend). Education, work, voluntary organizations, and friends are examples of purposive or achieved social structures; neighborhood and family circles are examples of primordial or ascribed social structures. In Figure 2.2, a cleavage between these two types of structures has emerged. The two figures indicate that in the younger cohort, fewer people recruit their friends from family as well as from education, yet in the older cohort both ascribed and achieved contexts were recruitment places.

Finally, we inquired into the question of whether older or newer friendship relationships in the different cohorts have been recruited from different contexts. Specifically, we expect that newer relationships of the older cohort are recruited from achieved contexts, and older relationships of that cohort are recruited from ascribed ones. Table 2.5 presents a logistic multilevel regression analysis with context as the dependent variable. The trend

Table 2.5 Trends in Contexts for Different Cohorts

	Cohort 1	*Cohort 2*	*Cohort 3*
Dependent variable	Trendparameter (*SE*)	Trendparameter (*SE*)	Trendparameter (*SE*)
Education	.096 (.012)**	.087 (.010)**	.056 (.015)**
Voluntary organization	–.026 (.009)**	–.029 (.011)*	–.009 (.019)
Work	–.024 (.004)**	–.078 (.011)**	–.198 (.032)**
Friends	–.007 (.009)	–.015 (.010)	–.080 (.024)**
Family	.045 (.011)**	.090 (.013)**	.137 (.023)**
Neighborhood	–.008 (.008)	.007 (.010)	.033 (.020)+
Church	–.045 (.019)**	.020 (.029)	.005 (.070)
Other	–.055 (.007)	–.008 (.008)	–.010 (.015)

Note. Trendparameter is the coefficient for the effect of duration of relationship (continuous scaled in years) in a multilevel logistic regression model with context as dependent variable. In the analyses it is controlled for characteristics of ego and alter; see Table 2.3.

parameter is the estimated coefficient for the duration of the relationship. In this analysis, it is controlled for the same characteristics of ego and alter as in the analysis presented in Table 2.3. Note that meeting places are the dependent variable in these analyses, while the duration of friendships, the trend parameter, is one of the independent variables.

Table 2.5 shows that for the two older cohorts, the effect of duration of relationship is positive with regard to the regression on education. Older friends are thus more likely to be recruited from education. Furthermore, newer friends are more likely to be recruited from work or from a voluntary organization, but also via other friends. Finding friends via friends is important only for the third cohort and accounts for the newer relationships. Finally, older friends are also found via family; this holds, in particular, for the youngest cohort. The duration of a friendship has no effect on the analyses of the contexts neighborhood and church, indicated by the nonsignificant coefficients.

In sum, these analyses provide a partial confirmation of the expected period effects: as mentioned, an indication for such an effect is provided if the older cohort recruits newer friends from achieved contexts and older friends from ascribed contexts, while the younger cohort recruits from achieved contexts (see Table 2.4). This has been shown to be correct for voluntary organizations. These findings cannot be explained by cohort or age differences. Yet it is not in line with this hypothesis on period effects that the older cohort also has recruited older friends via the context of education and relatively newer friends via the context of church. With regard to education, we have found an age effect. As mentioned, such an effect is indicated if the older, as well as younger, cohorts recruit older friends from other contexts than newer friends. Regardless of which cohort one belongs to, important friends who (at least to a substantial part) stay with each other are formed during adolescence when one pursues one's education. We did not find any indication for particular cohort effects because we did not find systematic differences between the cohorts.

DISCUSSION AND CONCLUSION

Our analyses lead to a number of conclusions. In general, people in the Netherlands have about three people that they call friends in their network, and these friends are met in two contexts, on average. Those who visit more contexts also have more friends (or vice versa). Yet, above all, the analyses show that the place where people have met their network members has an important consequence for the resulting relationships. Friends are found most frequently in contexts of education and voluntary organizations. Although there are not many friends found in church, for the oldest cohort church provides an important meeting place for finding friends, in the sense that persons who are met in this context are highly likely to become friends.

There are striking differences in social contexts concerning the degree to which they promote friendship. In particular, it is intriguing that, although many friends are met at work, the chance that a network member who is recruited from the workplace will become a friend is small, at least in the Netherlands. Also, the family is not a good context for finding friends, which might indicate a specific kind of closure among family ties: via one's family, one meets only other family but no others that become friends later on. Note that it is not negative *per se* if a context does not produce friends, because it still might produce acquaintances or marriage partners.

Second, as to the difference between achieved and ascribed contexts, we found that, for all cohorts, the chance of recruiting friends via the context of education is at least more than 17 times greater than recruiting friends via family. Also, the chance of recruiting friends via voluntary organizations is at least 11 times, and via friends 12 times, greater than recruiting friends via family. When comparing the contexts of "education," "voluntary organization," and "via friends" with recruitment in the neighborhood, we found smaller, yet still clearly greater, odds in favor of these achieved contexts. In general, achieved contexts have been shown to be far more important than ascribed ones, yet not all achieved contexts are equally important. Compared to church and neighborhood, the workplace is a place where the chance to recruit friends is very small. Furthermore, for the oldest cohort (1935–1950), church is an important place for recruiting friends, which changes for the younger cohorts. In the youngest cohort, those born after 1966, the number of respondents who found a friend via the context of church are so small that the program (Mlwin) does not calculate them.

Third, when inquiring into the pattern of contexts, we found that the members of the oldest cohort seem to use almost equally ascribed and achieved contexts for recruitment of friends. Members of the youngest cohort get friends from contexts of education less often, as well as from family or neighborhood (see Figures 2.1 and 2.2).

Fourth, when inquiring whether new friends are found in contexts different from those of older friends, we found the following. In all three cohorts, older relationships are found in the context of education and newer relationships in the context of work although there are not many friends found at the workplace. Furthermore, newer relationships are recruited from voluntary organizations, but this holds only for the two older cohorts; for the youngest cohort, the duration of a relation is not associated with voluntary organizations as a recruitment place for friends. This third cohort does recruit their newer friends via other friends, an association that is not found for the older two cohorts. All three cohorts also find relatively old friends via their family; this holds best for the youngest cohort. Finally, newer friends are also found via the church, but this only holds for the oldest cohort.

Our general conclusion from these findings is that achieved contexts are more important for recruiting friends than ascribed ones. However, this is not true for the workplace, which is an achieved context as well. Furthermore, "church" as an ascribed context does play a role, but only for the oldest cohort. In addition, our expectation that the older birth cohort recruits older friends from ascribed contexts is refuted when we consider education. The context of education has been and still is a very important market for friendships. This is probably due to a respondent's age when an education is pursued, and which did not change between cohorts or periods in time. The expectation regarding the importance of achieved contexts for older cohorts is corroborated when we consider voluntary organizations and the place of work (although, as already mentioned, the latter is not a good place to find friends). New friends are often found in these contexts. This holds for all three cohorts. In a general way, the idea that changes occurred in social contexts is confirmed, although not for all types of contexts or meeting places. In two of the four achieved contexts considered, we found an indication for a period effect (for the contexts of work and voluntary organizations), i.e., a change through time that cannot be explained by cohort or age differences. In the context "meeting via friends" there was no significant finding at all, and in that of education our expectation is refuted.

It seems that more dimensions of social contexts are of importance than the straightforward partition into ascribed and achieved. These other dimensions may be related to the degree to which they constrain an individual's interaction (Fischer et al. 1977; Feld 1981). For example, education, or more precisely a classroom, is a context in which individuals stay together for quite some time and in which few come and go during that time. Furthermore, those who are met in that context are highly similar in terms of age; education, of course; but also according to social class or ethnicity. This may explain why the context of education is so important for finding friends. Voluntary organizations are probably places where people's activities are not constrained as well.

One criticism of our analyses is that we do not know which network members have been lost or which relationships have been broken after some time. Our data provide only information about the "successful" friendships that lasted until we undertook our research. With regard to education, it could be that many friends have been lost who were recruited from the setting of education. Methodologically, our data are left-censored, yet it remains important that so many friends are found in that context and that a substantial part seems to stay friends with the respondent after education is completed. It might also be the case that the friends met in education are most similar to ego and that they, therefore, have very stable relationships. In further studies we have to inquire more deeply into the similarity between ego and his or her network members with regard to relevant social characteristics (see Mollenhorst et al. 2008a, 2008b). Here, we have found, in particular for the oldest cohort, that education of a network member seems to be associated with the likelihood of being a friend, and that higher-educated respondents have also higher-educated friends.

To sum up, our analyses provide another case for the importance of social contexts as sources of social networks, and that there have been important changes in these contexts over time. Moreover, they indicate that one's network is bounded by the social contexts that one enters. These boundaries of social networks deserve more study in future research.

APPENDIX

1. *Getting a Job:* Who helped you get your current job?
2. *Asking for Advice:* If you have a problem at work, whom do you ask for advice?
3. *Providing Advice*: Are there any colleagues who come to you and ask for advice regarding a problem at work?
4. *Sour Social Capital*: People at work do not always get along and sometimes get in each other's way. Are there any persons who cause you trouble at work?
5. *Cooperation:* Who are the two colleagues with whom you cooperate most frequently?
6. *Supervisor:* Who is your boss?
7. *Getting a House:* Who are the people who helped you get your house/apartment, or the people from whom you bought your house/apartment?

8. *Minor Repairs:* If you are doing minor repairs in or around your house and you need help, whom do you ask?
9. *Keys:* Is there somebody outside of your household who has a key to your house/apartment?
10. *Direct neighbors:* Who are your direct neighbors? May I have the names of two of them?
11. *Visiting:* Who are the people you visit from time to time?
12. *Core Discussion Network:* With whom did you discuss important personal matters during the last half year?
13. *Open question:* If you look at the list of names we made during this interview, are there people who are important to you, in whatever area of your life, who should be added?

For every name generator, a maximum of five different persons could be mentioned. Contexts where network members have been met for the first time:

1. school/education
2. voluntary club/organization
3. workplace
4. via family
5. via friends
6. respondent's home
7. network member's home
8. neighborhood
9. public places one goes out to
10. church
11. vacation
12. party
13. elsewhere

NOTES

An earlier version of this chapter was presented at the XXIV International Sunbelt Social Network Conference, 12–16 May 2004, Portoroz, Slovenia. Correspondence should be addressed to Beate Völker, University of Utrecht, Department of Sociology/ICS, Heidelberglaan 2, Nl–3584 CS Utrecht. E-mail: b.volker@uu.nl. We thank Ron Breiger, Ray-May Hsung, and Bonnie Erickson for their useful comments.

1. Hedström and Swedberg (1998, p. 23) call this a situational mechanism, which opposes an action-formation mechanism. Put differently, the auxiliary assumption that describes the social situation in which people exercise their preferences is extremely important in delivering an adequate explanation for social phenomena.
2. The figures have been drawn using NetDraw, a program implemented in UCINET VI.

REFERENCES

Blau, P. and J. E. Schwartz. 1984. *Crosscutting Social Circles. Testing a Macro-structural Theory of Intergroup Relations.* Orlando, FL: Academic Press.

Blau, P. M., T. C. Blum, and J. E. Schwartz. 1982. "Heterogeneity and intermarriage," *American Sociological Review,* 47: 45–62.

Blum, T. C. 1985. "Structural constraints on interpersonal relationships: A test of Blau's macrosociological theory," *American Journal of Sociology,* 91: 511–21.

Breiger, R. L. 1974. "The duality of persons and groups," *Social Forces,* 53: 181–90.

Coleman, J. S. 1990. *Foundations of Social Theory*, Cambridge, MA: Harvard University Press.

———. 1993. "The rational reconstruction of society," *American Sociological Review,* 58: 1–15.

Cook, K. S. and J. M. Whitmeyer. 1992. "Two approaches to social structure: Exchange theory and network analysis," *Annual Review of Sociology,* 18: 109–27.

Feld, S. L. 1981. "The focused organization of social ties," *American Journal of Sociology,* 86: 1015–35.

———. 1984. "The structured use of personal networks," *Social Forces,* 62: 640–52.

Fischer, C. S. 1982. *To Dwell among Friends. Personal Networks in Town and City,* Chicago: University of Chicago Press.

———. R. M. Jackson, C. A. Stueve, K. Gerson, L. M. Jones, and M. Baldassare. 1977. *Networks and Places. Social Relations in the Urban Setting.* New York: Free Press.

Hedström, P. and R. Swedberg. 1998. "Social mechanisms," in *Social Mechanism. An Analytical Approach to Social Theory,* edited by P. Hedström and R. Swedberg, pp. 1–31. Cambridge, UK: Cambridge University Press.

Kalmijn, M. 2002. "Sex segregation of friendship networks: Individual and structural determinants of having cross-sex friends," *European Sociological Review,* 18: 101–18.

———. and H. Flap. 2001. "Assortative meeting and mating: Unintended consequences of organized settings for partner choices," *Social Forces,* 79 : 1289–1312.

Mak, G. 1996. *Hoe God verdween uit Jorwerd.* Amsterdam, The Netherlands: Atlas.

Marsden, P. 1990. "Network diversity, substructures and opportunities for contact," in *Structures of Power and Constraint. Papers in Honor of Peter M. Blau,* edited by C. Craig, M. W. Meyer, and W. R. Scott, pp. 397–410. Cambridge, USA: University Press.

McPherson, J. M. 1982. "Hypernetwork sampling: Duality and differentiation among organizations," *Social Networks,* 3: 225–49.

———. and L. Smith-Lovin. 1987. "Homophily in voluntary organizations: Status distance and the composition of face-to-face groups," *American Sociological Review,* 52: 370–79.

Mollenhorst, G., B. Völker, and H. Flap 2008a. "Social contexts and core discussion networks. Using a choice constraint approach to study similarity in intimate personal relationships." Forthcoming in *Social Forces.*

———. 2008b. "Social contexts and personal relationships: the effect of meeting opportunities on similarity for relationships of different strength." Forthcoming in *Social Networks,* 30: 60–78.

Pescosolido, B. A. and B. A. Rubin. 2000. "The web of group affiliations revisited: Social life, postmodernism and sociology," *American Sociological Review*, 65: 52–76.

Podolny J. and J. Baron. 1997. "Resources and relationships: Social networks and mobility in the workplace," *American Sociological Review*, 62: 673–93.

Putnam, R. D. 2000. *Bowling Alone. The Collapse and Revival of American Community*. New York: Simon & Schuster.

Verbrugge, L. M. 1977. "The structure of adult friendship choice," *Social Forces*, 56: 577–97.

3 Does *The Golden Rule* Rule?

Rochelle R. Côté, Gabriele Plickert, and Barry Wellman

TIT-FOR-TAT AND ALL THAT. . . .

> "What goes around comes around," we learned as children on the streets of Saskatoon, Berlin, and New York.
>
> "Where were you when we needed you?" we thought when others did not repay the help we had given to them.

Reciprocity—doing for others what they have done (or would do)—is a key way that people mobilize resources to deal with daily life and seize opportunities. Such exchanges are a key to obtaining network capital that can provide helpful resources that are flexible, efficient, and effective.[1]

In principle, reciprocity is a universal norm. In practice, it is variable. Reciprocity varies in *content*: people exchange emotional and material aid, information, and companionship. It varies in *specificity:* exchanges can be of the same resource—a hug for a hug—or of different resources—a hug for childcare. It varies in *immediacy:* compare two people giving each other emotional support with adult children giving eldercare to aged parents who had provided childcare decades ago. It varies in *directionality*: support sometimes flows only in one direction rather than reciprocally. It varies in *tie or network* focus: exchanges can reciprocate between two persons or move indirectly through the social network in which their tie is embedded.

The loosely coupled networked nature of contemporary society means that social support does not come reliably from one group. Tie attributes such as proximity, frequency of contact between exchange partners, role relationship, and tie strength mediate the reciprocal provision of social support, as do the personal characteristics of individuals—which include the resources available to them—and of the networks in which these ties are embedded. As such, personal networks rarely operate as solidarities; network capital can come from a variety of ties and through multiple networks (Wellman and Leighton 1979; Wellman 1999, 2001; Kadushin 2004).

The consequences of reciprocity go beyond the specific resources exchanged. With reciprocity, network capital multiplies in positive feedback cycles. What goes around comes around—helpfulness stimulates further helpfulness, encouraging social bonds. Not only does reciprocity have this practical function, but sages worldwide have prescribed it as a guide to moral and ethical behavior. After Cain's immortal question, "Am I my brother's keeper?" [Genesis 4:2],[2] Leviticus (19:18) preached, "Love thy neighbor as thyself," echoed by Jesus' teaching of what has become known as The Golden Rule: "Do unto others as you would have them do unto you" [Matthew 7:12]. Yet such norms are not limited to Judeo-Christian traditions. For example, the Prophet Muhammad had similar sentiments in about 600 CE: "No one of you is a believer until he desires for his brother that which he desires for himself" (Hadith recorded by al-Bukhari). Sociologist Alvin Gouldner (1960) summarizes these ideas as "the norm of reciprocity": "People should help those who have helped them and people should not injure those who have helped them."

But not all reciprocity is altruistic: self-interest is also a factor. Rational choice and exchange theorists assume reciprocity to be a function of satisfying goals in a way that will give the greatest amount of personal satisfaction (Coleman 1973, 1990; Scott 1999). Individuals are not motivated through a sense of higher purpose, but more in the hope that an act will be reciprocated either directly or indirectly through opportunities. For example, gift giving can increase access to social networks by creating new ties that allow people to connect through a series of exchanges (Gouldner 1960; Sahlins 1965, 1972). By helping others, a person can also develop a reputation as a helpful person. When needing help in return, others may be more forthcoming. Reciprocity becomes a practice by which people cooperate to gain advantage in society. It helps to start and maintain interactions, as well as to encourage relationships to remain stably balanced (Gouldner 1960).

"Prisoners' Dilemma" simulations shed some light on reasons why people reciprocate support. Cooperative behavior is more likely when: (a) sufficient repetitions of successful exchanges have occurred, and (b) adequate time has passed to formulate an opinion about the trustworthiness of the exchange partner (Axelrod 1984; Baker and Rachlin 2001; Braun and Gautschi 2006; Buchan, Croson, and Dawes 2002; Komter and Vollebergh 1997; Molm, Quist, and Wiseley 1993; Stephens, McLinn, and Stevens 2002; Takahashi 2000). Such studies suggest that people who give money to other players do so to the extent that they believe others will reciprocate (Molm, Takahashi, and Peterson 2000). Players who show unselfish exchange behavior and trust by giving away half their money usually receive returns in excess of what they gave away (Hoffman, McCabe, and Smith 1998; Kurzban et al. 2001; Parks and Rumble 2001; Yamagishi and Cook 1993).

Although "Prisoners' Dilemma" research is based on laboratory simulations, ethnographic fieldwork has documented reciprocity in villages and urban neighborhoods. For example, one study in rural England has delineated how the exchange of resources combines with paid labor to provide different types of reciprocal help (Pahl 1984), while a study in rural China has documented the interdependence of villagers during Maoist upheavals in China (Chan, Madsen, and Unger 1992). Many urban studies have focused on poor people's heavy use of reciprocal relationships for supplying social support, both in the less-developed world (e.g., Lewis 1961; Peattie 1968; Roberts 1978) and in the industrially developed world (e.g., Young and Willmott 1957; Gans 1962; Liebow 1967; Stack 1974).

Nor are reciprocal exchanges limited to humans. Animal studies have documented reciprocal support (Ridley 1997; Fehr and Rockenbach 2004; Melis, Hare, and Tomasello 2006).[3] Animals are most apt to use cooperative strategies when the possibility of future gain is greatest (Sanabria, Baker, and Rachlin 2003; Wilkinson 1986). One experiment showed that blue jays work together cooperatively to obtain a larger, but delayed, reward of food despite temptations to cheat and get a smaller, immediate reward. The jays vary their cooperation, with the characteristics of their partners affecting their tendency to reciprocate (Noë 2001; Mesterton-Gibbons and Adams 2002).

Our own investigation complements these laboratory, ethnographic, and animal studies by using multivariate survey analysis to tease out how the interplay of relationships, social network characteristics, and personal characteristics (e.g., gender, age) affect the nature of reciprocal relationships. We use evidence from the second East York (Toronto) study of social networks to identify what kinds of support are available from whom, and in which kinds of relationships. Regardless of whether the exchange is pursued for self-interested or altruistic reasons, the language of the Golden Rule still applies. In its strictest interpretation, "Do onto others . . ." necessitates that one act is reciprocated with a similar act. However, in real-life situations one act is sometimes reciprocated with something different. For our study, we analyze one-to-one exchanges, both restricted to one type of thing (e.g., emotional support) or mixed (as when emotional support is exchanged for minor services), to provide evidence about what types of goods are exchanged and which types are more likely to be exchanged for similar and for different types. We analyze whether people follow the Golden Rule in everyday exchanges of social support and how they do so. The questions we address are:

1. What kinds of supportive resources are more likely to be reciprocated? Are different dynamics associated with the reciprocal exchange of different types of resources? For example, reciprocal emotional aid exchanges intangibles, while providing major aid for healthcare can entail large commitments of tangible resources.
2. Does reciprocity restricted to the exchange of similar resources operate differently than the exchange of one type of resource for another

kind? What are the circumstances under which people exchange similar or different things? What characteristics affect the likelihood that these two types of exchanges will occur?

WHERE DOES RECIPROCITY COME FROM?[4]

Testing the Golden Rule

We turn first to the Golden Rule: *Do unto others as you would have them do unto you*. Defined most strictly, if I give you X, I expect that you would give me X back. In our study, X could be emotional aid, minor services, or major services. Stated more formally, this is:

Hypothesis 1: People are likely to exchange the same type of resource.

In addition to such specific exchanges, the research literature is filled with accounts of people giving some other kind of resource in return for help given. Someone may have lent a supportive ear about family problems for years but receives childcare in return.

Hypothesis 2: Giving one type of resource is associated with getting other types of resources in exchange.

Note that Hypotheses 1 and 2 are not mutually exclusive. Reciprocity can entail exchanges of both similar and different resources. Previous research has shown that relational, network, and personal characteristics are related to the one-way provision of supportive resources that, in turn, can affect reciprocity. It is reasonable to expect that the characteristics associated with the one-way provision of resources are also associated with the reciprocal provision of resources.

Our Possible Factors

Is the Golden Rule the only guide for reciprocating social support? Do other aspects of a tie foster reciprocity? To assess this, we add a series of variables that may affect the likelihood of reciprocal exchanges of supportive resources.[5]

Tie strength.

The strength of ties is likely to affect reciprocity exchange: if two people see their relationship as intimate, voluntary, and special, and they have much contact in a variety of ways, there should be more mutual awareness of need that results in supportive exchanges (Homans 1961; Wellman

1992). For example, the second East York study (using the same data as we do here) found that most ties provide small services, emotional support, or both. Socially close friends—but not socially close kin—were the most important sources of sociable companionship (Leighton 1986; Wellman and Wortley 1990; Wellman and Frank 2001; see also Uehara 1990, 1994, 1995).

But are strong ties more apt to reciprocate? We define a strong tie as one that has at least two of the attributes of social closeness, voluntariness, and multiplexity. Given the high performance of tie strength in one-way provision of resources, we expect it to be significantly associated with reciprocal, two-way, resource exchange.

Hypothesis 3: Strong ties increase the likelihood of reciprocal exchange.

Kinship.

There are cultural and structural reasons for kin to be supportive and reciprocating suppliers of network capital. The norm that "blood is thicker than water" idealizes the promotion of family welfare, encourages kin to share resources, urges them to give other kin privileged access to these resources, and celebrates long-term reciprocity (Schneider 1984). Kin are also the most likely of network members to be densely interconnected, fostering communication about needs and norms of providing help. Thus, most North Americans distinguish between kin and friends in their expectations for supplying social support, and they also distinguish among types of kin, expecting more from immediate kin (Farber 1966, 1981; Allan 1979; Argyle and Henderson 1985). Our East York research has found three distinct types of kinship roles—*parent–adult child, sibling,* and *extended kin,* as well as roles of *friendship, neighbor,* and *workmate.* Affines (in-laws) behave like consanguines; because support effectively goes to the household rather than to the person, kin often feel that they are supporting their own blood relatives (Goetting 1990).

Friends.

Friends and neighbors make up about half of most active personal networks (Wellman 1979; Fischer 1982a, 1982b; Willmott 1987; Wellman and Frank 2001) and they usually comprise about half of the ties that provide each kind of support. Friendship ties are less densely knit and normatively bound than kinship ties. For better or worse, getting social support from friends is more problematic than getting it from kin. Whereas people are born into—or marry into—kinship, friendship is more voluntary and often functions as discrete ties outside of bounded groups. The voluntary, one-to-one nature of friendship means that people must maintain it more actively and be more concerned about reciprocating a friend's help

(Blieszner 1988; Crohan and Antonucci 1989; Allan 1989; Adams 1990; Wellman and Wortley 1990; Adams and Torr 1998).

Hypothesis 4: Kin are more likely than friends to be reciprocally supportive. Parents and adult children are especially likely to reciprocally exchange major services.

Proximity, contact and neighboring.

Do contact and proximity help explain reciprocity? Contact and proximity foster shared values, increase mutual awareness of needs and available resources, reduce feelings of loneliness, facilitate resource delivery, and encourage reciprocal rounds of resource exchange (Homans 1961). This should be true especially when the resources exchanged depend on the delivery of tangible goods and services, where sizable travel effort might deter the providing of help.

Hypothesis 5: Physical access—in the form of contact, proximity, and neighboring—will promote the reciprocal exchange of services, especially minor services.

Personal characteristics.

The personal attributes of people, as well as their relationships, can clearly affect the provision of social capital. For example, research supports the popular observation that women provide and receive more emotional support than men. As the saying goes, "Women express, men repress." Women tend to interact "face-to-face" by exchanging emotional support, yet men tend to interact "side by side" by exchanging goods and services (Perlman and Fehr 1987, p. 21). Indeed, gender is the only personal characteristic that our previous one-way research has found to be related to the provision of social support, with women being more supportive than men (Wellman 1985; Wellman and Wortley 1990; Wellman and Frank 2001).[6]

Hypothesis 6: Being female increases the probability of exchanges of emotional support.

Network characteristics.

Exchanges of social support may depend not only on the characteristics of ties but on the nature of the networks in which these ties are embedded. Size probably matters, but in which direction? People with larger networks may be more network savvy, able to garner more ties and a higher proportion of supportive ties. Larger networks are also more diverse and increase the likelihood that someone in the network will supply different kinds of supportive resources (House, Umberson, and Landis 1988; Burton et al. 1995; Oxman and Hull 1997; Hurlbert, Haines, and Beggs 2000; Sammarco 2001; Williams and Dilworth-Anderson 2002).

Hypothesis 7: Ties in larger networks will be more likely to reciprocate.

STUDYING SUPPORTIVE RELATIONSHIPS IN EAST YORK[7]

Interviewing East Yorkers

Our data come from interviews conducted from 1977 to 1978 in the East York section of Toronto. Although the data are not new, they have the benefit of being well studied and validated by research elsewhere (Wellman 1985, 1999; Wellman, Carrington, and Hall 1988; Wellman and Wortley 1989, 1990; Wellman and Wellman 1992). Twenty-nine people were interviewed, with a combined total of 335 active ties in their personal networks. The interview participants were a subset of the random sample of adults surveyed in 1968 for the first East York study (Wellman 1979). Although most had hundreds of people in their social networks, constraints on time meant that we were only able to ask participants in detail about active network members, comprising *strong* network members (socially close, intimate ties extending beyond the household); and *significant* network members, who were active network members but not as socially close.

The interview participants ranged in age from 29 to 66 years old. Most (71 percent) were married. Ninety percent of the men held a full- or part-time job. Somewhat fewer women, 66 percent, were employed, 8 percent were not in the labor force, and 26 percent were homemakers. Like the interview participants, the majority of network members were married (67 percent), employed (75 percent), and had attended at least trade school or some college (90 percent). They ranged between 18 and 90 years in age.

The Resources that East Yorkers Exchange

We asked the East Yorkers which of the twelve different kinds of resources they received from—or gave to—each active network member. We identified four broad types of social support—*emotional support, minor services, major services*, and *financial aid*—and discovered which types of ties were likely to send different kinds of support (see Wellman and Wortley 1989, 1990 for details).

Emotional support is provided in one direction or another in 61 percent of the ties: 41 percent of network members provide East Yorkers with emotional support, and 38 percent of East Yorkers' ties with network members are emotionally supportive. The fact that 61 percent—and not 79 percent—of the ties

Table 3.1 Percentage of Network Members Providing Support to Participants

Network Member	*Emotional Support (%)*	*Minor Services (%)*	*Major Services (%)*	*Financial Aid(%)*
No exchange	39	36	71	84
One-way exchange				
Network member to participant	23	24	12	8
Participant to network member	20	19	13	6
Reciprocal exchange	18	21	4	2
Total	100	100	100	100
% One-way exchange	30	33	14	12

Number of ties = 335.

are emotionally supportive is because some ties are reciprocally supportive; see Table 3.1 for details. The widely given emotional aid is intangible, with little financial cost, and can be given to some extent over the telephone, as well as face-to-face.

Minor services are also provided in one direction or another in 64 percent of ties. Forty-five percent of network members (24 percent one-way + 21 percent reciprocally) and 40 percent of interview participants provide minor services. Minor services include giving or lending household items (38 percent), helping with small household jobs (35 percent), providing other minor services (40 percent), and help in dealing with organizations (10 percent). Thus, tangible aid—goods and services—is widely given.

Major services are provided in one direction or another in a far lower percentage of ties—29 percent. They are provided by 16 percent of the network members and by 17 percent of the interview participants. Major services include help with big household chores (such as repairs or regular help with housework: 16 percent) and other large services (such as day care for children or long-term health care: 7 percent). Providing such major services usually requires a major commitment of time, effort, and sometimes skill. Major services are, thus, less likely to be reciprocated. Not only is the need rarer than for minor services and emotional support in predominantly working/middle-class East York, it is less likely that both the respondent and the network member have the capacity to provide major services.

Financial aid is provided in one direction or another by a lower percentage of ties: 16 percent. It is provided by 10 percent of the network members and by 8 percent of the interview participants. Only a tiny percentage (2 percent) of ties reciprocally exchange financial aid: seven ties in all. We believe that this is because financial resources, generally, are fungible. Those who have substantial amounts of it do not need to exchange with others, except at different times of their lives. For example, parents aid young adult children who may reciprocate many years later to their aged parents. Given that exchanges of financial aid are indiscriminate, the proportional odds assumptions for our cumulative logit models do not hold. Consequently, we do not include financial aid in continuous analyses. However, our data do suggest that reciprocal exchanges of financial aid are most likely to occur between parents and adult children, in particular between fathers and adult daughters. Women neighbors of roughly similar ages also help each other financially.

The Extent to Which East Yorkers Reciprocate

We use one-way exchange as an independent explanatory variable, from participant to network member. This allows us to examine the extent to which the participants' provision of resources is associated with reciprocal exchange.

Previous research using these data has shown how different kinds of relationships, networks, and personal characteristics provide different types of resources. Analyses have shown that although East Yorkers do obtain resources from their networks, different types of resources are received from different network members. The type of relationship—the strength of ties, whether kin or friend, and physical accessibility—are especially related to who provides emotional aid, minor services, and major services.[8]

The evidence shows that East Yorkers are supportive in many ways, and that they reciprocate support most fully in providing emotional support and minor services. The next to the last row in Table 3.1 shows the extent to which network members who give one kind of resource receive the same kind of resource in return. Yet even for the most prevalent types of support—emotional support and minor services—only about one-fifth of the ties reciprocate. However, reciprocity is contingent on one-way exchange, and when emotional support or minor services are given, it is only reciprocated in a minority of the ties. Thirty percent of all emotional aid is reciprocally exchanged, as are 33 percent of minor services.[9]

A smaller percentage of major services are given and reciprocated. Giving major services entails a greater commitment of time and effort, and only a minority of East Yorkers (29 percent) give or get major services. Most major services are not reciprocated: only 4 percent of all ties have relationships in which major services are reciprocated. Even in those ties when major services are given, only 14 percent of the giving relationships are reciprocated. Although the small number of reciprocating ties limits our analysis, the data suggest that either the need for major services has not been present or the receiver does not have the ability to reciprocate by providing major services in return.

Statistical Method

The logistic regressions used for our multivariate research describe the relationship between the reciprocity of each type of resource—emotional support, minor services, and major services—with sets of explanatory variables discussed in the previous section, from tie strength to network size and density. For each of the three reciprocity variables that we study, there are three values:

1. No resource provided by either participant or network member.
2. One-way resource provision by participant to network member, but not in the other direction.
3. Two-way reciprocal resource provision between participant and network member.

The models we use describe the reciprocal exchanges of active network members. The explanatory variables predict the probability of being in a higher category (two-way exchanges), rather than in a lower category. Our cumulative logit models make no assumption about the distances between observed categories. It takes into account the proportional odds score, testing the assumption that the three-value ordinal restrictions are valid, with desired *p*-values. The proportional odds assumption evaluates the null hypothesis that the explanatory coefficients are equal.

EXPLAINING RECIPROCITY: OUR RESULTS

Baseline Models: Measuring the Golden Rule

We use three models to study the reciprocal exchange of each of emotional support, minor services, and major services. We first examine whether the provision of a supportive resource in one direction is associated with reciprocity in the other direction—as the Golden Rule suggests. We do this in two ways, the *specific* (restricted) exchange of a resource and the *mixed* (generalized) exchange of one resource for another. Subsequent models examine if tie and network characteristics and personal characteristics add to the explanations provided by the Golden Rule.[10]

Our operational definition of reciprocity is that the interviewed East Yorker has given a resource (for example, emotional support) to a network member and that the network member has given that (or another) resource to the East Yorker. However, we do not have systematic information about the direction in which the support was given first. In many cases, it is an ongoing dance of reciprocal exchanges.

The first model straightforwardly supports a narrow construction of the Golden Rule: East Yorkers are significantly likely to do unto their network members as their network members have done onto them (the main diagonal of Table 3.2). Put another way, there are significant associations between the giving and receiving of emotional support, the giving and receiving of minor services, and the giving and receiving of major services. This does not mean that all who get a resource give it in return, but they are more likely to do so than those who never got the resource. All three statistical associations are significant and large, with minor services having a somewhat stronger association than emotional support: odds ratios of 7.5 and 5.4. (We repeat our caution that the small number of reciprocated cases of major services makes its statistics problematic, beyond basic percentages.)

There are two other Golden Rule phenomena. The first is between emotional support and major services: participants who have given emotional support to network members are more likely to have received major services from them. The second is between minor services and emotional support where participants who helped with a minor service received emotional support from the network member. However, in neither case do we know which form of support came first.

Although importantly supporting the Golden Rule, the analysis based on Table 3.2 looks at reciprocal exchange only in isolation from other potential explanatory variables. Hence, we performed logistic regressions that include the potential explanatory variables as controls discussed earlier (tie strength, etc.). Table 3.3 presents our final models for emotional support, minor services, and major services respectively. Although they contain many variables, they are the pared-down results of numerous logistic regressions. For example, because kinship and network density are statistically associated, we ignore network density as an explanatory variable and instead, use several types of kinship as variables.

Table 3.2 Reciprocal Pattern of Resource Exchange Between Network Members and Participants

Participants' Support	*Emotional Support*			*Minor Services*			*Major Services*		
Network Members' Support	*b*	*SE*	*Odds Ratio*	*b*	*SE*	*Odds Ratio*	*b*	*SE*	*Odds Ratio*
Emotional support	1.70****	.16	5.4	0.27	.14	1.3	0.87***	.24	2.4
Minor services	0.37*	.15	1.4	2.02****	.18	7.5	0.43	.26	1.5
Major services	0.17	.25	1.2	0.02	.24	1.0	1.91****	.27	6.7
Likelihood ratio	191.26			222.79			111.63		
N	335			335			335		

Note: Data shown as coefficients with standard errors (in parentheses) obtained from cumulative logit regressions.

*$p < .05$. **$p < .01$. ***$p < .001$.

Table 3.3 Final Models of Cumulative Logit Analyses for Reciprocal Exchanges of Network Members (N = 335)

		Emotional Support		*Minor Services*		*Major Services*	
		b *(s.e)*	*Odds Ratio*	*b* *(s.e)*	*Odds Ratio*	*b* *(s.e)*	*Odds Ratio*
Participants' services	Emotional support	1.58*** (0.17)	4.84	0.28 (0.16)	1.33	0.97*** (0.29)	2.65
	Minor Services	0.55** *(0.17)*	1.73	-2.04*** *(0.20)*	7.67	0.22 *(0.29)*	1.24
	Major services	–0.05 *(0.29)*	0.95	–0.05 *(0.27)*	0.94	1.97*** *(0.32)*	7.22
Relational attributes	Tie strength (strong ties=1)	0.43 *(0.31)*	1.54	0.04 *(0.31)*	1.05	0.16 *(0.44)*	1.17
	Frequency of phone contact	0.03 *(0.23)*	1.03	–0.01 *(0.22)*	0.98	–0.01 *(0.31)*	0.99
	Frequency of face-to-face contact	0.07 *(0.26)*	1.07	0.06 *(0.25)*	1.06	–0.42 *(0.40)*	0.66
Network member's role relationship	Parent/adult child	0.65 *(0.60)*	1.91	1.75** *(0.60)*	5.80	2.52* *(1.18)*	12.4
	Siblings	0.74 *(0.41)*	2.10	0.31 *(0.43)*	1.36	1.61 *(1.12)*	5.00
	Friend	0.61 *(0.39)*	1.83	0.93* *(0.41)*	2.53	1.70 *(1.12)*	5.51
	Neighbor	–0.56 *(0.43)*	0.56	1.22** *(0.43)*	3.42	2.83* *(1.12)*	16.9
Network members' personal characteristics	Sex (female = 1)	0.86** *(0.31)*	2.37	-0.51 *(0.30)*	0.59	–0.90 *(0.44)*	0.41
	Marital status (married = 1)	0.36 *(0.29)*	1.44	0.05 *(0.29)*	1.04	0.01 *(0.43)*	1.01
	Age	0.03** *(0.01)*	1.03	–0.03** *(0.30)*	0.97	–0.01 *(0.02)*	0.99

(continued)

Table 3.3 Final Models of Cumulative Logit Analyses for Reciprocal Exchanges of Network Members ($N = 335$) (continued)

		Emotional Support		*Minor Services*		*Major Services*	
		b (s.e)	*Odds Ratio*	*b (s.e)*	*Odds Ratio*	*b (s.e)*	*Odds Ratio*
Participants' personal characteristics	Sex (female = 1)	0.22 *(0.34)*	1.24	0.38 *(0.33)*	1.46	0.29 *(0.48)*	1.34
	Marital status (married = 1)	–0.01 *(0.33)*	0.98	0.39 (0.33)	1.47	0.66 *(0.59)*	1.95
	Age	0.02*** *(0.02)*	0.91	0.02*** *(0.02)*	1.02	0.02 *(0.02)*	1.02
Size of network	Net size	0.02*** *(0.03)*	1.01	0.04† *(0.02)*	1.05	0.03 *(0.04)*	1.03
	–2 Log L	462.0		465.2		231.3	
	N	335		335		335	

Note. Data shown as coefficients with standard errors (in parentheses) obtained from cumulative logit regressions.

†$p < .10$. *$p < .05$. **$p < .01$. ***$p < .001$.

Preliminary analyses led us to retain a variable indicating whether a network member was a neighbor, and to delete a measure of residential distance between network members and participants. Although we examined models for major services, we do not discuss them extensively because the log percentage of ties providing major services makes statistical analyses problematic.

The three baseline models examining the narrow definition of the Golden Rule—specific exchange—shows that giving emotional support, minor services, or major services in one direction strongly increases the odds of receiving it in the other direction. With respect to the generalized Golden Rule, the association between participants giving emotional support and getting major services is joined by a weak association between giving minor services and getting emotional support.

Taken together, the two Golden Rule models in Table 3.3 show that most exchanges are for similar resources, such as the exchange of minor services for minor services. However, all of the other associations for resource exchange are positive, suggesting that there is an additional tendency toward generalized exchange. Hence, Hypothesis 1 is confirmed, and there is some support for Hypothesis 2.

Relationships and Reciprocity

Is it all just support provided in one direction bringing forth reciprocal support, or are there other influences when the Golden Rule is observed? To examine this, we add to the baseline models measures of other aspects of the ties between participants and network members (i.e., tie strength, frequency of contact, and indicators of role relationships: parent–adult child, sibling, friend, and neighbor).

Other aspects of ties add little to the Golden Rule items in explaining the likelihood of receiving reciprocal resources. There are no significant tie characteristics related to the reciprocal exchange of emotional support. However, in addition to the Golden Rule, several role relationships are associated with reciprocally receiving minor or major services: being a neighbor, a parent, or an adult child. Tie strength has no impact, nor does frequency of contact—either face-to-face or by phone, or being a friend or sibling. In short, there is no support for Hypothesis 3 (tie strength), and partial support for Hypothesis 4 (the parent–child kinship relationship) and Hypothesis 5 (access/neighboring). Thus, the traditional community norms of socially close kinship ties and physically close neighboring continued in East York in the 1970s to facilitate reciprocity.

We have been surprised at the low number of associations between tie characteristics and reciprocity, because these same data have shown all of the tie characteristics to be appreciably related to one-way provision of supportive resources (as previously discussed; see also Wellman and Wortley 1990). We found an association then; why not now? We believe that we have discovered a chain of causality that is more complex than we had originally imagined. Tie strength, frequent contact, and role relationships affect the one-way provision of resources, but once these resources have been received, it is the sheer fact of getting them that engenders reciprocity, both specific and generalized.

Personal Characteristics, Network Characteristics, and Reciprocity

Do the personal characteristics of participants and their network members affect reciprocity in addition to—or even instead of—the Golden Rule and tie characteristics? Once again, the Golden Rule measures remain strong and significant in the final models (Table 3.3), but there is an additional effect of two personal characteristics: gender and age. In Table 3.3, the model for emotional support shows that gender is important for reciprocity as well as for one-way support: female participants significantly reciprocate emotional support, confirming Hypothesis 6. There are also negative effects of the age of both participants and network members on reciprocated emotional support and of network members' age on reciprocated minor services.

The relative unimportance of personal characteristics is evident even when we analyze such characteristics relationally: preliminary analyses showed no relationship to reciprocity of the similarity of the personal characteristics of the participants or the members of their networks. The lack of importance of similarity suggests that the reciprocal exchange of resources is not based on "sameness" but on resources previously supplied. The implication is that prior supportiveness fosters the bond of reciprocity rather than class, gender, or marital status.

The final models also include network size as the only significant network characteristic. The larger the network, the more likely it is that each tie in the network will reciprocate with emotional support. Having more people in a network increases the chance of reciprocal exchange. Rather than the quality of ties compensating for a lack of quantity, the quantity of ties is associated with the greater emotional quality of ties in a network. Hence, Hypothesis 7—that ties in larger networks will be more likely to reciprocate—is supported for emotional support and is almost significantly supported for the reciprocation of minor services. However, reciprocity in major services is not linked to the size of networks, because it depends solely on prior supportiveness and parent–child bonds.

SUMMARY AND CONCLUSIONS: SUPPORT LEADS TO RECIPROCAL SUPPORT

Our evidence is clear: the principal direct cause of reciprocity is giving support. Analyses show that getting support from network members is the key to East Yorkers reciprocating—usually in kind, but sometimes with other forms of support (see the odds ratios in Figure 3.1). The parent–child bond is the only relationship that operates without much regard to near-term reciprocity: providing minor and major services.

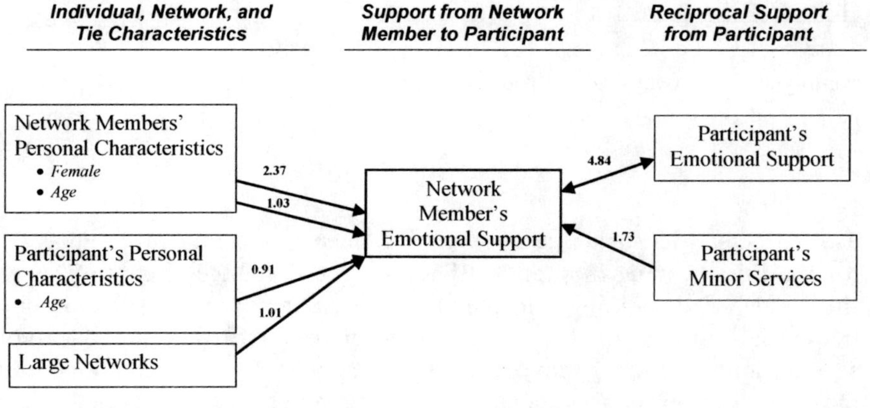

Figure 3.1a Pathways to reciprocated emotional support.
Note: Pathway values depict odds ratios.

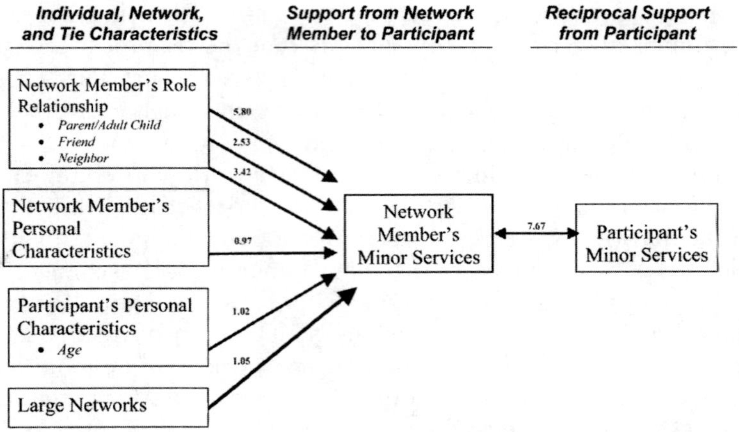

Figure 3.1b Pathways to reciprocated minor services.
Note: Pathway values depict odds ratios.

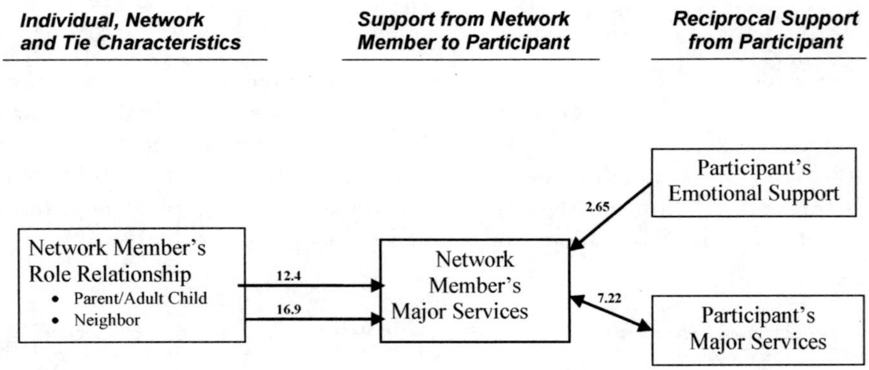

Figure 3.1c Pathways to reciprocated major services.
Note: Pathway values depict odds ratios.

Tie characteristics such as strength and frequency of contact are important for the initial giving of support. They set the exchange in motion, with the Golden Rule coming into play thereafter. The practice of reciprocity is especially important for the exchange of resources that supply minor services and emotional support. Each exchange strengthens the bond and makes further exchanges more likely. Our reading of the interviews suggests that both self-interest and norms are at work, an area we leave for future investigation.

The exception is the provision of major services where there is little evidence of reciprocity, because the necessarily large expenditures of time and money mean that return engagements are difficult for the recipients of such major aid. Perhaps our time frame in the interviews was too short. This is probable when the most common supply of major services is between parents and their adult children. Usually many years pass between parental help to children and filial help to aged parents. Given that other kin are less supportive and that most ties operate independently of each other, we believe that the parent–child norm of mutual support continues even when other kinship norms are weaker.

Even though personal networks stretch well beyond neighborhoods, it is gratifying to know that neighboring still has its payoffs in the exchange of services. Yet neighbors are only a small fraction of the East Yorkers' networks. In 1977, phone contact substituted for much of the neighborly interaction, supplemented by intermittent trips by car or plane to visit with distant network members (Wellman and Tindall 1993). Today, e-mail, list-servs, and the Internet can also reduce the importance of physical proximity (Wellman 2001; Wellman and Haythornthwaite 2002). Yet the importance of proximity will persist for services until it is possible to transport a cup of sugar electronically.

What do our findings mean for reciprocity? First, as the sages have counseled, people should invest in their ties and amass generalized credit that can be called upon for reciprocal exchange in the future (Kadushin 1981). As the action philosopher Don Corleone said via the voice of Marlon Brando: "Some day, and that day may never come; I'll call upon you to do a service for me. But until that day—accept this justice as a gift on my daughter's wedding day" (Puzo and Coppola 1972).

Second, for reciprocity in East York—and probably in most of North America—it is not who one's network members are, but what their relationships are to the individual. Gender, socioeconomic status, and other personal characteristics do not strongly affect reciprocity. The nature of relationships do, through the accessibility of network members and their role relationships as kin and friends.

Third, "do unto others as you would have them similarly do unto you." The evidence shows that most reciprocity is tit-for-tit and not tit-for-tat: people get back the kinds of resources they give. Although the reasons for this are beyond the scope of this chapter, we suspect that it is not so much careful bookkeeping but the specialization of relationships: ties that specialize in emotional aid often do not specialize in material aid. Hence, people respond in kind.

Fourth, it is probably for similar reasons of specialization that the key to supportiveness among our respondents is the nature of their ties and not the nature of their networks. Moreover, the prevalence of networked individualism—rather than solidary groups—suggests that the ties themselves are more important than the network (Wellman 2001; Wellman and Frank 2001). Network density has no effect on reciprocity and network size has only a small effect.

We close by pointing out some scope conditions to what we have described. These data are not from the era of the Internet: the greater ease of communication today may have engendered increased supportiveness, especially in intangible exchanges. However, we also wonder if the decline of people available to discuss important matters over the past twenty years (Smith-Lovin, McPherson, and Brashears 2006) is manifested in a reduced availability of support (reciprocal or not) in contemporary North America. Our third East York study is examining this (Wellman, Hogan, et al. 2006).

Finally, note that the supportive exchanges that we have discovered focused on reproduction, rather than on production. East Yorkers rarely discussed using their relationships to go into business, invest, or even to get a job. They discussed relationships and exchanges that centered on themselves and their households, and secondarily on their networks and the neighborhoods. The East Yorkers' investments in their ties have provided *havens*: a sense of belonging and being helped. When needed, the ties have provided *bandages*: routine emotional aid and small services that have helped people cope with the stresses and strains of their everyday lives. More rarely, a few ties have provided *safety nets* that have lessened the effects of acute crises and chronic difficulties such as serious illness, childcare, and unemployment.

Where does reciprocity come from? Is it an outgrowth of general human goodness? Perhaps the sages got the reciprocity norm right. As Mikhail Bakunin said in 1867: "No person can recognize or realize his or her own humanity except by recognizing it in others and so cooperating for its realization by each and all".

Or, does reciprocity spring from a utilitarian analysis, as suggested by "Matron Mama Morton" in the musical *Chicago* (Kander and Ebb 1975):

> They say that life is tit for tat; and that's the way I live.
> So I deserve a lot of tat, for what I've got to give.
> Don't you know that this hand washed that one too?
> When you're good to Mama, Mama's good to you!

NOTES

Our research has been supported by the Social Science and Humanities Research Council of Canada, Intel Research and by Microsoft Research. We appreciate the prior collaborations on which this work builds, especially with Barry Leighton (Wellman and Leighton 1979), Scot Wortley (Wellman and Wortley 1989, 1990) and Kenneth Frank (Wellman and Frank 2001). We are grateful for the advice of Juan Carrasco, Bonnie Erickson, Ann Sorenson, Beverly Wellman, and David W. Wright and for the assistance of Lauren Bot, Tony Massimo, Alexis Kane Speer, Phuoc Tran, Julie Wang, and Natalie Zinko.

1. We see network capital as social capital embedded in interpersonal relations that can provide custom-tailored helpful resources that are flexible, efficient,

and effective. Consistent with a network view, we view social capital as a resource embedded in a person's social network and accessed through network ties (Lin 2001, 2006).

2. All Biblical quotations have been translated by Logue (2002).
3. For our discussion of laboratory and ethnographic works, please see the extended version of this chapter, Wellman, Côté, and Plickert (2006) online.
4. See Plickert, Côté and Wellman 2007 for an extended version of this chapter
5. See Plickert, Côté, and Wellman 2007; and Wellman, Côté ,and Plickert 2006 for a more detailed review of the research literature with respect to other possible factors that are related to reciprocity.
6. Previous research with these data did not show that marital status and socioeconomic status were important for the provision of social support (Wellman and Wortley 1990); these variables were excluded from further analyses.
7. For a more extended discussion of measurement and method, please see Plickert, Côté, and Wellman 2007.
8. For more information, see Wellman (1985); Wellman, Carrington, and Hall (1988); Wellman and Wortley (1990); Wellman and Gulia (1999); Wellman and Potter 1999; Wellman and Frank (2001).
9. We calculated the reciprocal exchange of emotional support in the following manner: as Table 3.2 shows, 61 percent of the ties have an emotional support component (100—39 = 61). Dividing the percentage of reciprocating ties (18 percent) by this number—18/61—shows that 30 percent of all ties that contain emotional support reciprocate it.
10. We present only the final models here. For detailed model steps see Plickert, Côté, and Wellman 2007.

REFERENCES

Adams, R. 1990. The Structure of Adult Friendships. Presentation to the International Society for Personal Relationships, May, Oxford, U.K.

Adams, R. and R. Torr. 1998. Factors Underlying the Structure of Older Adult Friendship Networks. *Social Networks* 20: 51–61.

Allan, G. 1979. *A Sociology of Friendship and Kinship*. London: Allen & Unwin.

———. 1989. *Friendship*. London: Harvester Wheatsheaf.

Argyle, M. and M. Henderson. 1985. The Rules of Relationships. In *Understanding Personal Relationships*, ed. S. Duck and D. Perlman, 63–84. London: Sage.

Axelrod, R. 1984. *The Evolution of Cooperation*. New York: Basic Books.

Baker, F. and H. Rachlin. 2001. Probability of Reciprocation in Repeated Prisoner's Dilemma Games. *Journal of Behavioral Decision Making*, 14: 51–67.

Bakunin, M. 1867. Solidarity in Liberty: The Worker's Path to Freedom. http://marxists.org/reference/archive/bakunin/works/writings/ch04.html.

Blieszner, R. 1988. Individual Development and Intimate Relationships in Middle and Late Adulthood. In *Families and Social Networks*, ed. R. Milardo, 147–167. Newbury Park, CA: Sage.

Braun, N. and T. Gautschi. 2006. A Nash Bargaining Model for Simple Exchange Networks. *Social Networks*, 28: 1–23.

Buchan, R. N., R. Croson, and R. M. Dawes. 2002. Swift Neighbors and Persistent Strangers: A Cross-Cultural Investigation of Trust and Reciprocity in Social Exchange. *American Journal of Sociology*, 108: 168–206.

Burton, L., J. Casper, A. Shore, K. Cagney, T. LaVeist, C. Cubbin, and P. German. 1995. The Structure of Informal Care: Are There Differences by Race? *The Gerontologist*, 35: 744–52.

Chan, A., R. Madsen, and J. Unger. 1992. *Chen Village Under Mao and Deng*. Berkeley: University of California Press.

Coleman, J. 1973. *The Mathematics of Collective Action*. London: Heinemann.

———. 1990. *Foundations of Social Theory*. Cambridge, MA: Belknap.

Crohan, S. and T. Antonucci. 1989. Friends as a Source of Social Support in Old Age. In *Older Adult Friendship*, ed. R. Adams and R. Blieszner,129–146. Newbury Park, CA: Sage.

Farber, B., ed. 1966. *Kinship and Family Organization*. New York: Wiley.

———. 1981. *Conceptions of Kinship*. New York: Elsevier North Holland.

Fehr, E. and B. Rockenbach. 2004. Human Altruism: Economic, Neutral, and Evolutionary Perspectives. *Current Opinion in Neurobiology*, 14: 784–90.

Fischer, C. 1982a. *To Dwell Among Friends*. Berkeley: University of California Press.

———. 1982b. What Do We Mean by Friend? *Social Networks*, 3: 287–306.

Gans, H. 1962. *The Urban Villagers*. New York: Free Press.

Goetting, A. 1990. Patterns of Support Among In-Laws in the United States: A Review of Research. *Journal of Family Issues*, 11: 67–90.

Gouldner, W. A. 1960. The Norm of Reciprocity: A Preliminary Statement. *American Sociological Review*, 25: 161–78.

Hoffman, E., A. K. McCabe, and V. L. Smith. 1998. Behavioral Foundations of Reciprocity: Experimental Economics and Evolutionary Psychology. *Economic Inquiry*, 36: 335–53.

Homans, G. 1961. *Social Behavior: Its Elementary Forms*. New York: Harcourt Brace Jovanovich.

House, J., D. Umberson, and K. Landis. 1988. "Structures and Processes of Social Support," *Annual Review of Sociology*, 14: 293–318.

Hurlbert, J., V. Haines, and J. Beggs. 2000. Core Networks and Tie Activation: What Kinds of Routine Networks Allocate Resources in Nonroutine Situations? *American Sociological Review*, 65: 598–618.

Kadushin, C. 1981. Notes on the Expectations of Reward in N-Person Networks. In *Continuities in Structural Inquiry*, ed. P. Blau and R. K. Merton, 235–254. London: Sage.

———. 2004. Too Much Investment in Social Capital? *Social Networks*, 26: 75–90.

Kander, J. and F. Ebb. 1975. *Chicago: A Musical Vaudeville*. New York: Samuel French.

Komter, A. and W. Vollebergh. 1997. Gift Giving and the Emotional Significance of Family and Friends. *Journal of Marriage and Family*, 59: 747–57.

Kurzban, R., K. McCabe, V. Smith, and B. J. Wilson. 2001. Incremental Commitment and Reciprocity in a Real-Time Public Goods Game. *Personality and Social Psychology Bulletin*, 27: 1662–73.

Leighton, B. 1986. Experiencing Personal Network Communities. PhD dissertation, Department of Sociology, University of Toronto, Canada.

Lewis, O. 1961. *The Children of Sanchez*. New York: Vintage.

Liebow, E. 1967. *Tally's Corner*. Boston: Little Brown.

Lin, N. 2001 Building a Network Theory of Social Capital. In *Social Capital: Theory and Research*, ed. R. Burt, 233–274. New York: Aldine de Gruyter.

———. 2006. A Network Theory of Social Capital. In *Handbook of Social Capital*, eds. D. Castiglione, J. van Deth, and G. Wollbe, 50–59. New York: Oxford University Press.

Logue, F. 2002. Turn the Golden Rule Inside Out. *King of Peace Tribune* [online]. http://kingofpeace.org/religioncolumn/101102.html.

Melis, A. P., B. Hare, and M. Tomasello. 2006, Chimpanzees Recruit the Best Helpers. *Science*, 311(5765): 1297–1300.

Mesterton-Gibbons, M., and E. S. Adams. 2002. The Economics of Animal Cooperation. *Science* 29813 (December): 2146–47.

Molm, D. L., T. M. Quist, and P. A. Wiseley. (1993) Reciprocal Justice and Strategies of Exchange. *Social Forces*, 72: 19–26.

Molm, L. D., Takahashi, N., and Peterson, J. T. 2000. Risk and Trust in Social Exchange: An Experimental Test of a Classical Proposition. *American Journal of Sociology*, 105: 1396–1427.

Noë, R. 2001. Biological Markets: Partner Choice as the Driving Force Behind the Evolution of Cooperation. In *Economics in Nature: Social Dilemmas, Mate Choice and Biological Markets*, eds. R. Noë, J. A. R. A. M. van Hooff, and P. Hammerstein 93–118. Cambridge, UK: Cambridge University Press.

Oxman, T. E. and J. G. Hull. 1997. Social Support, Depression and Activities of Daily Living in Older Heart Surgery Patients. *Journal of Gerontology: Psychological Sciences*, 52B: P1–P14.

Pahl, R. E. 1984. *The Divisions of Labour.* Oxford, UK: Blackwell

Parks, C. D. and A. C. Rumble. 2001. Elements of Reciprocity and Social Value Orientation. *Personality and Social Psychology Bulletin*, 27: 1301–09.

Peattie, L. 1968. *The View from the Barrio.* Ann Arbor: University of Michigan Press.

Perlman, D. and B. Fehr. 1987. The Development of Intimate Relationships. In *Intimate Relationships*, eds. D. Perlman and S. Duck, 13–42. Newbury Park, CA: Sage.

Plickert, G., R. R. Côté, and B. Wellman. 2007. It's Not Who You Know, It's How You Know Them: Who Exchanges What With Whom? *Social Networks*, 29: 405–29.

Puzo, M. and F. F. Coppola. 1972. *The Godfather.* Los Angeles: Paramount Pictures.

Ridley, M. 1997. *The Origins of Virtue: Human Instincts and the Evolution of Cooperation.* New York: Viking.

Roberts, B. 1978. *Cities of Peasants.* London: Edward Arnold.

Sahlins, M. 1965. On the Sociology of Primitive Exchange. In *The Relevance of Models for Social Anthropology*, ed. M. Blanton, 139–216. New York: Praeger.

———. 1972. *Stone Age Economics.* New York: Aldine.

Sammarco, A. 2001. Perceived Social Support, Uncertainty, and Quality of Life of Younger Breast Cancer Survivors. *Cancer Nursing*, 24: 212–19.

Sanabria, F., F. Baker, and H. Rachlin. 2003. Learning by Pigeons Playing Against Tit-for-Tat in an Operant Prisoner's Dilemma. *Learning & Behavior*, 31: 318–31.

Schneider, D. 1984. *A Critique of the Study of Kinship.* Ann Arbor: University of Michigan Press.

Scott, J. 1999. Rational Choice Theory. In *Theory and Society: Understanding the Present*, eds. G. Browning, A. Halell, N. Hewlett, and F. Webster, 1–11. London: Sage.

Smith-Lovin, L., McPherson, M., and Brashears, M. 2006. Social Isolation in America: Changes in Core Discussion Networks Over Two Decades. *American Sociological Review*, 71(June): 353–75.

Stack, C. 1974. *All Our Kin.* New York: Harper & Row.

Stephens, D. W., C. M. McLinn, and J. R. Stevens. 2002. Discounting and Reciprocity in an Iterated Prisoner's Dilemma. *Science*, 298: 2216–18.

Takahashi, N. 2000. The Emergence of Generalized Exchange. *American Journal of Sociology*, 105: 1105–34.

Uehara, E. 1990. Dual Exchange Theory, Social Networks and Informal Social Support. *American Journal of Sociology*, 96: 521–57.

———. 1994. The Influence of the Social Network's 'Second-Order Zone' on Social Support Mobilization: A Case Example. *Journal of Social and Personal Relationships*, 11: 277–94.
———. 1995. Reciprocity Reconsidered: Gouldner's 'Moral Norm of Reciprocity' and Social Support. *Journal of Social and Personal Relationships*, 12(4): 483–502.
Wellman, B. 1979 Community Question: The Intimate Networks of East Yorkers. *American Journal of Sociology*, 84: 1201–31.
———. 1985. Domestic Work, Paid Work and Net Work. In *Understanding Personal Relationships*, eds S. Duck and D. Perlman, 159–191. London: Sage.
——— 1992. Which Types of Ties and Networks Give What Kinds of Social Support? *Advances in Group Processes*, 9: 207–35.
———. 1999. The Network Community. In *Networks in the Global Village*, eds B. Wellman, 1–48. Boulder, CO: Westview.
———. 2001. The Rise of Networked Individualism. In *Community Networks Online*, ed. L. Keeble, 130–184. London: Taylor & Francis.
———, P. Carrington, and A. Hall. 1988. Networks as Personal Communities. In *Social Structures: A Network Approach*, eds. B. Wellman and S.D. Berkowitz, 130–184. Cambridge, UK: Cambridge University Press.
———, R. R. Côté, and G. Plickert. 2006. Tit-for-Tat and All That: Reciprocity in East York. http://www.chass.utoronto.ca/~wellman/netlab/PUBLICATIONS/_frames.html.
———, and K. A. Frank. 2001. Network Capital in a Multilevel World: Getting Support From Personal Communities. In *Social Capital*, eds. N. Lin, R. S. Burt, and K. Cook, 233–273. Hawthorne, NY: Aldine De Gruyter.
———, and M. Gulia. 1999. A Network is More Than the Sum of its Ties: The Network Basis of Social Support. In *Networks in the Global Village*, ed. B. Wellman, 83–118. Boulder, CO: Westview.
———. and C. Haythornthwaite, eds. 2002. *The Internet in Everyday Life.*, Oxford, UK: Blackwell.
———, B. Hogan, K. Berg, J. Boase, J. A. Carrasco, R. Côté, J. Kayahara, T. L. M. Kennedy, and P. Tran. 2006. Connected Lives: The Project. in *Networked Neighbourhoods: The Online Community in Context*, ed. P. Purcell, 157–211. Guildford, UK: Springer.
——— and B. Leighton. 1979. Networks, Neighborhoods and Communities. *Urban Affairs Quarterly*, 14: 363–90.
——— and S. Potter. 1999. The Elements of Personal Communities. In *Networks in the Global Village*, ed. B. Wellman, 49–81. Boulder, CO: Westview Press.
——— and D. Tindall. 1993. Reach Out and Touch Some Bodies: How Telephone Networks Connect Social Networks. *Progress in Communication Science*, 12: 63–94.
——— and S. Wortley. 1989. Brothers' Keepers: Situating Kinship Relations in Broader Networks of Social Support. *Sociological Perspectives*, 32: 273–306.
——— and S. Wortley. 1990. "Different Strokes From Different Folks: Community Ties and Social Support," *American Journal of Sociology*, 96: 558–88.
——— and B. Wellman. 1992 Domestic Affairs and Network Relations. *Journal of Social and Personal Relationships*, 9: 385–409.
Wilkinson, G. S. 1986. Social Grooming in the Common Vampire Bat, Desmodus Rotundus. *Animal Behaviour*, 34: 1880–89.
Williams, S. W. and P. Dilworth-Anderson, P. 2002. Systems of Social Support in Families Who Care for Dependent African American Elders. *Gerontologist*, 42: 224–36.

Willmott, P. 1987. *Friendship Networks and Social Support*. London: Policy Studies Institute.

Yamagishi, T. and K. Cook. 1993. Generalized Exchange and Social Dilemmas. *Social Psychology Quarterly*, 56: 235–45.

Young, M. and P. Willmott. 1957. *Family and Kinship in East London*, Harmondsworth, UK: Penguin.

4 Making Democracy Work via the Functioning of Heterogeneous Personal Networks

An Empirical Analysis Based on a Japanese Election Study

Ken'ichi Ikeda and Tetsuro Kobayashi

EQUAL OPPORTUNITY TO PARTICIPATE AND TOLERANCE FOR HETEROGENEITY

In a well-known comparative political participation study, Verba, Nie, and Kim (1978) stress that political participation and equality of opportunity to participate is important for a well-functioning democracy. Liberal democracy requires both citizen participation and the acceptance of the participation of others. It is important to note that the latter implies an acceptance of the right of every party to speak out, including disliked minorities. Then intolerance of another's participation sets a double standard for democratic practice (Sullivan, Piereson, and Marcus 1982). Unless both of these basic requirements—political participation and tolerance—are fulfilled, trust in democratic institutions, such as the government and political parties, will lose its liberal democratic value.

Recently developed social capital theory has much relevance to this argument. Based on his empirical study of Italian local politics, Putnam (1993) posits that social networks, deep generalized interpersonal trust, and a high sense of reciprocity among citizens bring positive effects to social, as well as political participation, which in turn contributes to the development of liberal democracy. Putnam (1995, 2000) applies this logic to the United States in the 1990s, and finds that society is losing the basic conditions for well-developed social capital.

Despite its alarming predictions, the Putnamian logic of social capital is more or less optimistic, bringing severe criticism that he did not focus on the dark side of social capital (Portes and Landolt 1996; Schulman and Anderson 2001). Indeed, closed social networks—defined as trustful and reciprocal relationships among cohesive group members—have the possibility of fortifying the borders between in-groups and out-groups, and may brew intolerance against the social/political participation of out-groups.

Therefore, developing social capital itself can possibly lead to political intolerance. It is indeed, a double-edged sword.

Politics is an arena of mutual compromises among the parties with heterogeneous ideas through the processes of discussion, confrontation, and consensus building, all of which are often divided into in-groups and out-groups. This built-in heterogeneity can develop conflicts in the positive construction of social capital, allowing it to degenerate into its dark side. Nevertheless, unless citizens participate in collective deliberations despite these heterogeneous cross-pressures, politics will lose the chance to create new ideas for managing society and will merely result in confrontations between antagonistic partisans. The hidden presumption is that democracy will not function well without trusting relationships that allow open debates, even if different worldviews collide. Huckfeldt, Morehouse, and Osborn (2001) conclude, through an analysis of the 2000 American National Election Study, that citizens do, indeed, encounter heterogeneous political information. Their findings show that this heterogeneity does not interfere with citizens' political participation, implying that citizens share some basic trustful relationships.

Mutz (2002a), however, showed that the evidence is unstable. Her analysis revealed that those who have political dissent in their personal networks are reluctant to participate. Moreover, in the situation where partisan cleavage accelerates "politicized collective identity" (Simon and Klandermans 2001, p. 319) on both sides of the camps, confrontation will be sensitized, conformity pressure among in-group members will be more severe, and differentiation from out-groups will take clearer shape. In such situations—for example, Northern Ireland or Israel/Palestine—mutual trust is difficult to maintain among opposing groups, even though the situation promotes radical styles of participation. Although they are contrary to the findings of Huckfeldt et al. (2001), examples of such circumstances are not hard to find in reality, such as Anpo–Tousou (the Japanese movement against the Japan–U.S. Security Treaty) in the 1960s; unstable political situations in developing countries; and altercations over racial, environmental, or military issues in postmodern societies.

Therefore, although the dark side of social capital has not been studied sufficiently in an empirical and quantitative manner, analyses of the dark side have much relevance to the theory of participation and equal opportunity (Verba et al. 1978). We will use political intolerance to represent the dark side of social capital and assume it leads away from the notion of equal opportunity.

One beneficial strategy is to focus on the effect of heterogeneity/homogeneity of one's social network (Ikeda 2004, 2007). In a "bonding" social network (Putnam 2000) such as homogeneous, tightly knit, and cohesive relationships, we easily lose the chance of exposure to heterogeneous information, different political orientations, or other perspectives that differ from our own. On the other hand, in an open "bridging" social network we have a greater chance of encountering heterogeneous citizens with different viewpoints and knowledge, which, in turn, increases the possibility of more tolerant attitudes toward these citizens. Although exposure to heterogeneous networks (encounters) possibly produces the political tolerance necessary for liberal democracy by overriding the deep borders between in-groups and out-groups, we cannot deny that, contrary to wishful thinking, encounters may fuel the fire between groups such that the poor may be repulsed by meeting the rich, i.e., the encounters may increase out-group hostility. Yet without these encounters there may be no chance of developing tolerance. Thus, although we should admit that optimistic prediction is only possible under certain fortunate conditions, the possibility is worth focusing on, for it is one of the few breaching points for an open society. It makes possible an effective counterattack against a pessimistic viewpoint that citizens do not (or would not) encounter heterogeneous others by emphasizing the closed-mindedness of citizens' daily talk and social identity (Walsh 2004), or against the viewpoint that citizens are reluctant to talk about politics to avoid being seen as principled and confrontational (Eliasoph 1998). Accordingly, by focusing on the bridging function of social networks, this analysis contributes to the study of social capital in democratic societies.

POSITION GENERATOR AS AN INDEX OF HETEROGENEOUS NETWORKS

In the following analysis we use a position-generator battery as an index of heterogeneous networks that estimates the diversity of one's social network. The position-generator battery (Lin, Fu, and Hsung 2001) enables only a few indicators to determine the diversity of the respondent's social networks. One is a scale that assesses the diversity ("extensity" in Lin, Fu, and Hsung's terms) to which citizens have access to other citizens with different social positions (social status in the sense of occupational prestige). This scale, which we call "network diversity," identifies to the respondents the extent to which their weak ties are spread in the social strata beyond their daily bonding social network. Specifically, the position-generator battery asks every respondent whether he or she is personally acquainted with people of different occupations. Previous studies on these occupations have determined their social prestige scores. This enables the researchers to measure the extent of access to the various positions on the social ladder, i.e., the heterogeneity of access in terms of social status. Some people have access to almost pansocial strata; others have a more limited range. In other words, some have more bridging social networks and others have less.

Another approach is to estimate the heterogeneous elements in one's intimate personal network—i.e., an index of heterogeneity in strong ties—whereas the current approach measures heterogeneity in one's weak ties. As weak ties are known to introduce heterogeneous knowledge and ideas in networks (Granovetter 1974), the current approach is more advantageous than using strong ties for determining the effect of network heterogeneity.

In addition to the network diversity index, we also measure whether the respondents know local/national high-ranking civic servants and local/national politicians, as well as executive members of a number of voluntary organizations. We are assuming that these measurements are indices of the social power of respondents as used in social stratification theory (Imada 1989), because having connections to powerful positions indicates latent social influence ability. We expect that analyses on the relationship between network diversity and the social power related index (henceforth *political diversity index*) will reveal that a part of the powerful resource of network diversity comes from its high correlation with these connections.

PARTICIPATION, TOLERANCE, AND INTERACTING FACTORS

The measurement of network diversity here enables us to test hypotheses that network heterogeneity is a positive function of participation and tolerance to equal opportunity. Because, as we have contended, the sunny side of social capital is easily turned into the dark side, we posit that the effect of network heterogeneity potentially has an interaction with other key factors that contribute to the differentiation. Here we analyze two groups of factors: generalized trust/reciprocity and private life orientation. In the following sections, we examine each of the targeted variables.

Social/Political Participation

Some empirical evidence shows that social and political participation are related to heterogeneous networks. In addition to Huckfeldt et al. (2001), another study in Japan (Ikeda 2008) using Japanese General Social Survey data for 2003 revealed that the political heterogeneity of networks measured by a social network battery (network on talking politics) related positively with political participation, as well as a feeling of political efficacy. Other studies are consistent with this view in various measurements of heterogeneity (Gimpel and Lay 2005; Kwak et al. 2005; McLeod et al. 1999). As discussed earlier, however, there is also some counterevidence. Findings by Mutz (2002a) showed the existence of heterogeneity in terms of political dissent being a deterrent to participation. Costa and Kahn (2003) also suggested that heterogeneity in terms of macro-level diversity of race, ethnicity, and income at the community level decelerates civic engagement. We thus need to specify the sources of this contrasting evidence.

However, in this analysis, a problem arises concerning the causal relationship, i.e., whether diverse network exposure accelerates participation or whether participation enables citizens to obtain diverse network exposure.

Both may be possible, and to strictly test the causality we require long-term panel data. Although the data we use here comprise a panel, they extend only to one year at most, which is not sufficient for the effect to emerge. We thus conduct partial correlation analyses on this particular relationship. Moreover, as participation itself does not represent the dark side of social capital, the analysis of participation is supplementary in this chapter.

Intolerance

Although the concept of political intolerance is important in democratic politics, translation of the variables of interest into specific questions is difficult. Most often the concept is measured on whether respondents accept the freedom of expression of their most hated (political) groups or political/social minorities in various public settings (Bobo and Licari 1989; Mutz 2002b; Sullivan et al. 1982). We have doubts, however, about the frequency of encountering such situations, even though the measurements are conceptually relevant. In this chapter we focus on milder and commonly experienced intolerance, i.e., intolerance of dissent with individuals encountered frequently in daily life, rather than with those whose existence is often indirectly experienced via the mass media or hateful hearsay (as is typical for extremist minorities).

Liberal democracies do not often go to the extreme of excluding or rejecting all radical or minority citizens. Nevertheless, even where milder intolerance is prevalent (which is more often observed in daily situations), suppression of open opinion expression may exist. Such conditions are enough to interfere with the frank confrontation of heterogeneous ideas and stifle the positive advances in social capital. We call this the weak version of political intolerance, as compared with the strong version of intolerance for minorities, extremists, or hated groups. This weak version of intolerance occurs when open communication is disturbed by the pressure for conformity, social reality maintenance motivation, and/or by other suppressing forces as tools of social control (Portes 1998).

The absence of the strong version of tolerance is observable in people's attitudes but is rarely manifested in behavior, simply because of infrequent opportunities. On the other hand, the weak version of intolerance is observed more frequently. For instance, informal personal relationships are often the seed of group identity and, at the same time, this type of relationship is a factor that suppresses heterogeneous ideas, which may result in the prevention of spontaneous and frank political communication. In Japan, for instance, revealing one's political orientation in the workplace can be a risky undertaking, for it can invite negative sanctions and/or alienation.

Generalized Trust and Reciprocity as Interaction Factors

Putnam (1993, 2000) strongly posits that generalized trust and reciprocity are essential for civic life, which promotes civic engagements. The implication of this logic is that trusting others reduces the risks of our participation. When we have *reciprocal* relationships, our participation connotes acceptance of the participation of others. This is acceptable, however, only as long as we believe that *trust* in others also implies that others are willing to contribute to improving our social life (i.e., their will is similar to ours). In this context we hypothesize that trust and reciprocity are positively related to participation and tolerance (accepting the right of others to participate).

However, the relationships possible are not so simple. Using the broader term of "social capital," in an aggregate analysis of 47 countries Norris (2000) finds a positive correlation between social capital and tolerance. However, she suggests that this relationship is largely due to social capital through the participation of voluntary organizations rather than trust, and many studies do not find a clear relationship between trust and participation at the individual level (Newton 2001). It is, therefore, possible that trust and reciprocity may not be directly influential factors for participation/intolerance, but may help other factors to facilitate participation/tolerance; i.e., trust or reciprocity has some interaction with other contributing factors, in this case network diversity. The inference is that where the level of trust/reciprocity is high, we will find that network diversity is positively related with tolerance. In other words, where trust/reciprocity functions well, the sunny side of social capital emerges. If citizens are open-minded, the heterogeneity of others stimulates more tolerant attitudes as well as participation. On the other hand, where these factors function poorly, the sunny side is overridden by the dark side and the heterogeneity causes antagonism.

Private-life Orientation as an Interaction Factor

People do not participate in politics automatically, even if they have a full diversity of social networks. In other words, not everyone necessarily thinks of political life or associational/network life as positive or attractive and, therefore worthy of participation. Based on the well-known argument by Inglehart (1977, 1990), the more citizens that support postmaterialist values, the greater is the orientation to social/political participation. The reality, however, appears less simple. For instance, even in advanced industrial societies, voter turnout rates are not very high and the reverse is often true. That is, the greater the industrialization, the lower the turnout rate, as in the case of the United States or Japan. This may be due to the fact that postmaterialist values lead not only to the awareness of social/public life, but also to an emphasis on an affluent private life. Self-actualization may mean that citizens are eager to make efforts to attain a worthwhile social goal, but it also opens the way for enjoying one's private life with its various consumer aspects, such as a fashionable life or entertainment activities. Therefore, the greater the number of people with a private life orientation, the fewer who will emphasize their public life, resulting in lower social/political participation. The data from Japan support this inference (Ikeda 2007), i.e., a private orientation in terms of detachment from political life decelerates social as well as political participation. The analysis also shows that private-life orientation decreases the level of political sophistication (Ikeda 2007). We posit here that the lower the level of political sophistication, the lower the possibility of understanding heterogeneous ideas in the political, as well as the public, arena, which in turn causes an intolerance of differences. Although a diversity of networks promotes tolerance, a decrease in effect will likely be observed where a private orientation is strong.

Hypotheses

In the following analyses, we attempt to determine how social network diversity mitigates the dark side of social capital. Therefore, our hypotheses are:

Main Hypothesis: Network diversity is a positive function of participation and of tolerance to equal opportunity.

- H1a. Network diversity has a positive correlation with social/political participation, even after controlling for demographic factors.
- H1b. Network diversity has a positive correlation with politically-related network diversity.
- H1c. Social/political participation is a positive function of the interaction between social capital variables (trust/reciprocity) and network diversity.
- H1d. Social/political participation is a negative function of the interaction between private-life orientation and network diversity.
- H2a. The more network diversity respondents have, the lower their intolerance.
- H2b. Intolerance is a negative function of the interaction between generalized trust/reciprocity and network diversity.
- H2c. Intolerance is a positive function of the interaction between private life orientation and network diversity.

DATA

We used panel data from the Japanese Election Study 3 (JES3) that provides a position–generator battery and a measure of intolerance. The principal investigator of this project is the first-named author. The project, titled "Nationwide chronological studies on voting behavior in the 21st century" (2001–2006), is supported by the Specially Promoted

Research on Science (Ministry of Education). The primary data are from the 2003 Unified Local Election mail survey, conducted as the third wave of the JES3 panel survey. The composition of the sample consists of the panel sample as well as new entries. The total N is 1,461 (a return rate of 48.7 percent). We also used several variables (trust, reciprocity, and private orientation) from the fourth wave of the same panel survey conducted in the fall of 2003, although the main focus of the data is from the third wave.[1]

Network Diversity Indices

First, we created an index of network diversity from the position-generator items to measure the diversity of weak-tied networks in the different hierarchical positions in society. Respondents indicated if they had acquaintances in any of 23 categories of diverse occupations for each gender.[2] The respondents indicated whether they knew a man, a woman, or both in each of the 23 occupations that vary in occupational prestige and gender composition. For 16 of the 23 occupational categories, we followed the prestige scores constructed by the SSM surveys of Japanese occupations held in 1985 and 1995 (Naoi and Seiyama 1990; Umino 2000). The sampled positions had prestige scores ranging from 38.1 to 90.1, and can be roughly grouped into three classes: an upper class (consisting of high-status professionals such as physicians, lawyers, owners of large companies, and congressmen); a middle class (comprising middle-level professionals such as elementary school teachers, nurses, and policemen); and a lower class (consisting of janitors and restaurant waiters/waitresses). In addition to the 16 categories with prestige scores, we introduced seven new categories of occupations thought to be highly relevant to political behavior ("Official of neighborhood association/Self-governing body," "Official of volunteer group/Civic movement group," "Official of trade association," "Official of labor union," "Executive above director in prefectural office," "Mayor/village chief," "Manager of support group for politicians [*Koenkai*] including secretary of assembly members").

We measured the network diversity for each respondent by counting the number of occupational categories with prestige scores, yielding a score ranging from 0 to 32 (16 categories for each gender), with a higher score indicating greater network diversity. On average, the respondents accessed almost 5.6 sampled positions. Besides network diversity, we measured the political network diversity for each respondent by counting the number of different occupation categories related directly to politics, yielding a score ranging from 0 to 14 (seven categories for each gender), with a higher score indicating greater political network diversity. On average, almost 2.3 sampled positions were accessed by the respondents.

Participation, Intolerance, and Other Intervening Variables

Social participation.

(a) Membership in formal voluntary organizations: Given a list of six organizations, respondents named those to which they were affiliated, and responded to questions on these affiliations ($\alpha = 0.63$). In this analysis, the scale of affiliation was weighted by the level of involvement in the organization in question. The most frequent response was "Jichi-kai/residential association" (50 percent). *(b) Membership in informal groups*: Membership in three types of informal group affiliation was similarly coded. The most frequent response was "hobby circle" (54 percent, $\alpha = 0.67$). These were used in the analysis weighted by the level of involvement.

Political participation.

We measured this variable by asking respondents whether they had engaged in 10 listed political activities in the past five years. The list included "voted in an election," "contacted politician," "signed petition," and so on.

Intolerance.

Political intolerance was measured with the question, "Concerning how politics and society should be, what would you think if your opinions differed from those you associate with?" Four items were measured on the four kinds of others: family, employers or seniors, intimate fellow workers, and intimate friends. Each response was measured in four-point scales: 1 = *no problem to have a different opinion*, 2 = *not a big problem to have a different opinion*, 3 = *rather wish they had the same opinion*, 4 = *better to have the same opinion*. A higher number of points indicates more intolerant attitudes. A factor analysis (principal component factor method) was conducted using these four items to extract a single factor, with the factor score labeled as intolerance.

Trust and Reciprocity.

(a) Generalized trust: A scale of generalized trust was constructed by adding two items, "Most people are trustworthy" and "Most people will respond in kind when they are trusted by others" ($r = 0.39$). *(b) Generalized reciprocity (cognition):* A scale of generalized reciprocity (cognition) was constructed by adding two items, "By helping someone in trouble today, someone else will help me when I am in trouble someday" and "If you help a person, the world is such that the next time when you are in trouble, someone will help you" ($r = 0.51$). *(c) Generalized reciprocity*

(norm): A scale of generalized reciprocity (norm) was constructed by adding two items, "If you received aid from someone during times of difficulty, you should help that person if he/she is troubled in the future" and "Generally speaking, if you are helped by someone you should aid other people as well" ($r = 0.68$).

Private life orientation.

Using a factor analysis (principal component factor method), a scale of private-life orientation was constructed from the factor score. This factor heavily loaded on items: "I'd rather spend my time enriching my own life than pursing political goals," "A comfortable and affluent life based on expenditure of money is the most important," "Time spent with friends or family is the most important," and "The feeling of fulfillment through work is the most important." These items were all measured in four-point scales: 1 = agree, 2 = somewhat agree, 3 = somewhat disagree, and 4 = disagree. Agreeing with these statements indicates higher private-life orientation. In the following analyses, the factor score of private orientation was constructed so that a larger value represents higher private-life orientation.

ANALYSES

To examine H1a to H1d, a partial correlation analysis was conducted. Table 4.1 shows the results for H1a and H1b. The figures shown are the partial correlation coefficients between the diversity variables and social/

Table 4.1 Partial Correlation Between Network Diversity and Participation

Partial Correlation	*Network Diversity*	*Political Network Diversity*
Social participation (a) formal voluntary organizations	0.19**	0.30**
Social participation (b) informal groups	0.20**	0.12**
Political participation	0.18**	0.21**
Political network diversity	0.64**	

Note. Holding constant for sex, age, years of residence, final education, frequency of political conversation, and frequency of political information access. For Social participation (a), social participation (b) was also controlled for the analysis and vice versa.

**p < .01

Table 4.2 Partial Correlation Between Network Diversity and Participation With Interactions

	Trust		**Reciprocity (Cognition)**		**Reciprocity (Norm)**		**Private-Life Orientation**	
	High	*Low*	*High*	*Low*	*High*	*Low*	*High*	*Low*
Partial correlation with network diversity								
Social participation (a) formal voluntary organizations	0.19	0.20	0.18	0.20	0.19	0.19	0.16	0.20
Social participation (b) informal groups	0.18	0.21	*0.13*	0.25	0.24	0.20	0.23	0.15
Political participation	0.24	*0.13*	0.24	0.15	0.19	0.19	0.19	0.20
Partial correlation with political network diversity								
Social participation (a) formal voluntary organizations	0.34	0.31	0.32	0.33	0.30	0.35	0.31	0.26
Social participation (b) informal groups	0.15	*0.13*	0.17	0.13	0.22	<u>0.09</u>	0.17	*0.09*
Political participation	0.24	0.20	0.21	0.22	0.26	0.18	0.20	0.27

Note. All the correlations are significant at 1% level, except italicized are 5% signifncant, and underlined is 10% marginally significant. Holding constant for sex, age, years of residence, final education, frequency of political conversation, and frequency of political information access. For three variables of participation, partial correlations for each variables are the results after controlling for the other two participation variables as well.

political participation variables, holding constant sex, age, years of residence, education, frequency of political conversation, and frequency of political information access.[3] All coefficients are highly significant, thereby supporting H1a. As shown, these correlations are relatively firm, meaning that network diversity and participation go together, and that social participation is a way of becoming connected to politically powerful positions.

Table 4.1 also shows that network diversity and political network diversity are strongly correlated (r = 0.64), even after controlling for demographic and political variables. This result supports H1b, suggesting that a socially diverse network will significantly increase the chance of accessing a politically influential network.

Table 4.3 Heckman Regression Models Predicting Intolerance With Interaction Variables

		Coef. (B)								
		Model 1	*Model 2*	*Model 3*	*Model 4*	*Model 5*	*Model 6*	*Model 7*	*Model 8*	*Model 9*
			Generalized Trust		*Generalized Reciprocity (Cognition)*		*Generalized Reciprocity (Norm)*		*Private-Life Orientation*	
Variables	Dependent: Intolerance		*Low*	*High*	*Low*	*High*	*Low*	*High*	*Low*	*High*
Demographic variables	sex	0.01	0.02	0.10	0.02	0.20	–0.05	0.29*	0.07	0.13
	age	0.01**	0.01**	0.01**	0.02**	0.01*	0.02**	0.01*	0.01**	0.02**
	years of residence	0.02	0.04	0.03	0.03	0.03	–0.01	0.12+	0.07	0.08
	education	–0.14**	–0.20**	–0.10+	–0.21**	–0.03	–0.10+	–0.21**	–0.18**	–0.10
	size of the city of residence	0.02+	0.01	0.02	0.00	0.03	0.03	–0.02	0.01	0.02
Political variables	ideology (conservative)	0.03*	0.06*	0.03	0.06**	0.01	0.05*	0.03	0.03	0.00
	political talk	0.09**	0.00	0.05	0.01	0.05	0.00	0.08	0.06	0.00
	political information access	–0.15**	–0.24**	–0.14*	–0.25**	–0.07	–0.23**	–0.10	–0.20**	–0.15*
Position generator variable	network diversity	–0.02*	0.00	–0.02+	–0.01	0.00	–0.01	–0.01	–0.02*	0.00
	constant	–0.35	–0.47	–0.88+	–0.50	–0.90	–0.54	–0.99+	–0.51	–0.91
	Number of obs	4027	962	1021	1240	728	1239	773	1073	1089
	Censored obs	2994	631	646	797	469	792	510	722	788
	Uncensored obs	1033	331	375	443	259	447	263	351	301
	Wald chi2	212.49	91.05	64.70	144.14	31.07	97.36	61.64	96.52	41.43
	Prob > chi2	0.00	0.00	0.00	0.00	0.00	0.00	0.00	0.00	0.00

$^{**}p < .01$. $^{*}p < .05$. $+p < .10$.

Table 4.2 shows another partial correlation table, obtained by dividing the sample by the interaction variables. As is shown, there is apparently no systematic difference in the strength of the correlation coefficients, suggesting no systematic interaction with social capital variables and private-life orientation as hypothesized in H1c and H1d.

To test H2a to H2c, we estimated Heckman's two-step regression model to control for the attrition of the sample in the panel data.

Model 1 in Table 4.3 clearly shows that the effect of network diversity reduces political intolerance, even after controlling for demographic variables as well as ideology,[4] political talk, and political information access. This supports H2a.[5] However, the effect of network diversity on intolerance was not very strong. To check the possibility that some multicollinearity causes this effect, such as great correlation between network diversity and political information access, we estimated VIF (Variance Inflation Factor) among independent variables included in Heckman models (VIF is an indicator of multicollinearity, and it is widely accepted that multicollinearity is severe when VIF is over 2.0). However, each VIF of independent variables was under 2.0. Therefore, we excluded the possibility of multicollinearity as a cause of low explanatory power of network diversity.

Returning to Model 1 in Table 4.3, among the demographic variables age shows a positive effect on political intolerance, and education has a negative effect on political intolerance. Among the political variables, conservative ideology and political talk have a positive effect on intolerance, whereas political information has a negative effect. In particular, the positive effect of political talk on intolerance can be interpreted as a manifestation of the dark side of social capital that fortifies borders between in- and out-groups. In other words, the more people talk about politics with family, friends, and colleagues, the more likely they are to share the same social identity, which in turn, leads to lower tolerance.

Models 2 to 9 in Table 4.3 attempt to detect the interaction effects of the intervening variables. The entire sample was divided into two groups based on the scores in the interaction variables: generalized trust, generalized reciprocity (cognition), generalized reciprocity (norm), and private-life orientation. For example, the column "low" in the column of generalized trust means that the model is estimated only for the sample that scored less than the average in the generalized trust scale.

Among the social capital variables, network diversity has a negative effect only in the high subsample of generalized trust, but the effect is only significant at the 10 percent level. This weakly supports H2b for trust. However, network diversity did not have any significant effect on intolerance in each subsample divided on the basis of the scores of generalized reciprocity (both cognition and norm). These results did not support H2b.

A comparison between Models 8 and 9 shows the result of H2c. Clearly, network diversity effectively reduces intolerance when private-life orientation is low. This result supports H2c.

DISCUSSION

As hypothesized, network diversity is a positive function of social participation. Partial correlation analysis shows a close relationship between the access to diverse social networks and participation in intermediary organizations, i.e., revealing how well these organizations function as bridges across a diverse range of positions on the social ladder. We can conclude from these findings that the well-known importance of intermediate organizations for democracy (Kornhauser 1959; Almond and Verba 1963) partly originates from this effect of diversifying social networks. Moreover, as the results have a greater impact regarding politically-related networks, we now realize that network diversity is also tied to the accumulation of social power. That is, the more diverse one's social network, the greater the access to politically powered social positions.

As for political participation, our findings are consistent with those previously mentinoed, i.e., network diversity is positively correlated with involvement in politics. This is apparently contrary to Mutz (2002a) and Costa and Kahn (2003), though the specification in this analysis differs from both of these studies. The former uses dissension with daily political discussants as its indicator of political diversity, and the latter employs demographic diversity. Both effects could be very serious. However, based on the logic of weak ties, our position generator also has an important implication: Having greater diversity of social networks in the extensive social ladder potentially gives a higher probability of obtaining different information/opinion resources (a higher possibility of accessing various weak ties). A diverse social network is thus a useful resource in which to participate even after controlling the variable on political information access (i.e. mass media information resource). Moreover, greater social diversity means potentially more effective routes of influence in the political arena, although more detailed analyses are needed, including analysis using measurements such as upper reachability (the upper limit of one's social network access on the social ladder). If this is, indeed, the case, then our findings differ from past studies, indicating that further research would be worthwhile.

The lack of a strong interaction effect between either the network diversity indices or social/political participation suggests that the relationships are straightforward: Social capital variables do not intervene in the network diversity effect. Our presumption is that the informational (accessible-to-power) effect of the diversity index overrides the effects on the intervening factors. In other words, network diversity is a powerful promotional factor for political participation, irrespective of trust/reciprocity. Indeed, it is another independent source of social capital; i.e., the vertical social network has a positive effect on participation, which somewhat contradicts Putnam's idea of overemphasizing the horizontal relationship (Putnam, 1993).

The effect of network diversity on reducing intolerance is evidence that diverse social networks create open-minded attitudes toward others, which are essential for the functioning of liberal democracy. The effect is not large, as the coefficient of extensity is only 0.02, and even a 10-point increase in social network access to various occupations (within the range of 32) infers a decrease as small as 0.2 in intolerance (within a range of about four). However, the effect still contrasts to that of political talk in strong ties networks, which increases intolerance. These are consequences of the roles of bridging social capital and bonding social capital, respectively.

Moreover, the analyses did not systematically show any significant interaction between social diversity and trust/reciprocity. In this sense, the effect of network diversity is weakly dependent: As the scale of diversity measures the range of vertical accessibility on the social ladder, it may have a different mechanism in intolerance from that working in horizontal networks where trust and reciprocity are important in a Putnamian sense. We need to test this interpretation by using, for instance, some variable on dissension among horizontal political discussants as an indicator of political diversity, as in Mutz (2002a).

As for the interaction between network diversity and private orientation, the hypothesis was supported. That is, those who are politically involved are also sensitive to their network diversity (the more diversity, the less intolerance), most likely due to their open-mindedness in the political arena. On the other hand, for those who are politically detached, diversity had little to do with tolerance, such that they are insensitive to information from a diverse network.

Finally, this study has a number of limitations. To start with, the study is not clear on the scale of the political network from the viewpoint of social stratification theory. That is, we do not include information on the prestige scores of politically-related occupations or executives in voluntary organizations. This lack of knowledge serves as an obstacle to the future development of the analysis because we are unable to construct, for example, an upper reachability scale on the political network. The second limitation is that we do not know the prestige scores of each respondent; we only have measurements of his or her subjective affiliation to social strata or his or her spouse's occupation (the prestige scores of occupation are not necessarily known). Therefore, we are unable to investigate whether the respondent's own position on the social ladder is a determinant of his or her socially diverse access, participation, or intolerance. The third limitation is related to the measurement of intolerance. Although we use the weak version of intolerance, we do not empirically know how it is related to the strong version of intolerance. Also, as the effect on the weak version is not large, further exploration of the concept and improvement in the measurement of intolerance is needed. Overall, we believe that this study contributes to strengthening the bridge between the study of social participation and the study of social networks in sociology and political science.

APPENDIX

Table A4.1 Summary of Position-Generator Variables in the Sample

Accessed Positions	*Prestige Scores**	*Percentage***
Physician	90.1	53.7
Owner of large company	87.3	12.1
Lawyer	87.3	13.8
Congressman	74.9	11.7
Jounalist/editor	63.2	8.5
Teacher (elementary school)	64.6	45.4
Nurse	59.7	53.9
Policeman	57.9	29.0
Computer programmer	54.6	18.5
Owner of a shop	51.3	59.5
Mail carrier	46.2	30.6
Janitor	39.9	20.0
Executive above director in municipal office	60.4	31.2
Executive above director in government departments	67.2	4.7
Member of local assembly	67.2	40.0
Restaurant waiter/waitress	38.1	23.2
Offical of neighborhood association/self-governing body	—	59.9
Official of volunteer group/civic movement group	—	33.2
Official of trade association	—	19.7
Official of labor union	—	15.3
Executive above director in prefectural office	—	11.4
Mayor/village chief	—	19.9
Manager of support group for politicians (*Koenkai*)(Including secretary of assembly members)	—	17.9
People who do not answer		3.5

N = 1,188.
*The data of SSM Survey which were held in 1995 and 1985.
** Joint percentage of those who have access to the given position occupied either by male or female.

NOTES

1. The JES3 data set and its further information is accessible at http://ssjda.iss.u-tokyo.ac.jp/abstract/0530a.html.
2. The correspondence and frequencies of each occupational category in the position-generator variables are shown in the Appendix Table A4.1.
3. Two composite variables, frequency of political conversation and frequency of political information access, were created for the analysis by a factor analysis (principal component factor method) using the items of political conversation and media exposure to political information. The first factor consists of the items "Talk about local politics with family member," "Talk about local politics with friends and colleagues," "Talk about national politics with family members," and "Talk about national

politics with friends and colleagues." Therefore, the factor score is labeled as *frequency of political conversation*. The second factor consists of "Read political articles in newspapers," "Watch political news on TV," and "Read political articles in magazines." The factor score is labeled as *frequency of political information access*.

4. *Political ideology*: Political ideology was measured by the question "We often hear the words 'conservative' and 'liberal' being used. What do you consider your political position to be, on a scale of 0 to 10?" Zero indicates a liberal position and 10 a conservative position.
5. In addition to the analysis shown in Table 4.3, we also estimated Models 1 to 7 using political network diversity instead of network diversity. However, political network diversity did not show any significant effect on intolerance in any model. This may be due to the difference of extensity measurement between those two scales. Political network diversity measures the diversity only in the political arena. It measures the diversity of personal network in political contexts in one's life, but the measurement is constrained only into political context. On the other hand, network diversity measured the diversity of personal network that extends well beyond political contexts. It measures the more general diversity in one's daily life. We assume that this difference explains the different effects of network diversity and political network diversity on intolerance.

REFERENCES

Almond, G. A., and S. Verba. 1963. *The Civic Culture: Political Attitudes and Democracy in Five Nations*. Princeton, NJ: Princeton University Press.

Bobo, L., and F. C. Licari. 1989. "Education and Political Tolerance: Testing the Effects of Cognitive Sophistication and Target Group Affect." *Public Opinion Quarterly*, 53: 285–308.

Costa, D. L., and M. E. Khan. 2003. "Civic Engagement and Community Heterogeneity: An Economist's Perspective." *Perspectives on Politics*, 1: 103–11.

Eliasoph, N. 1998. *Avoiding Politics: How Americans Produce Apathy in Everyday Life*. Cambridge, MA: Cambridge University Press.

Gimpel, J. G., and J. C. Lay. 2005. "Party identification, Local Partisan Contexts, and the Acquisition of Participatory Attitudes." In *The Social Logic of Politics: Personal Networks as Contexts for Political Behavior,* ed. A. S. Zuckerman, 209–27. Philadelphia: Temple University Press.

Huckfeldt, R., J. Morehouse, and T. Osborn. 2001. Disagreement, Ambivalence, and Engagement: The Political Consequences of Heterogeneous Networks. Paper presented to the American Political Science Association annual meeting, San Francisco, 2001.

Ikeda, K. 2004. Social Construction of Reality: An Empirical Study using a Japanese National survey: Focusing on Interpersonal Environment. Paper presented at the International Congress of Psychology (ICP: "The social foundations underlying our understanding of this world," Beijing, 10 August 2004.

———. 2007. *Political Reality and Social Psychology: The Dynamics of the Koizumi Years*. Tokyo: Bokutaku-sha (in Japanese).

———. 2008. "Social Capital and Political Orientation.," In *Japanese attitude and behavior: Dynamics of Japanese society measured by JGSS studies*, ed. I. Tanioka, N. Iwai, and M. Nitta 273–94. Tokyo: The University of Tokyo Press (in Japanese).

Imada, T. 1989. *Social Stratification and Politics*. Tokyo: The University of Tokyo Press (in Japanese).

Inglehart, R. 1977. *The Silent Revolution: Changing Values and Political Styles Among Western Politics*. Princeton, NJ: Princeton University Press.

———. 1990. *Culture Shift in Advanced Industrial Society*. Princeton, NJ: Princeton University Press.

Granovetter, M. 1974. *Getting a Job*. Chicago, IL: University of Chicago Press.

Kornhauser, W. 1959. *The Politics of Mass Society*. London: Routledge & Kegan Paul.

Kwak, N., A. E. Williams, X. Wang, and H. Lee. 2005. "Talking Politics and Engaging Politics: An Examination of the Interactive Relationships Between Structural Features of Political Talk and Discussion Engagement." *Communication Research*, 32: 87–111.

Lin, N., Y. Fu, and R. Hsung. 2001. "The Position Generator: Measurement Techniques for Investigations of Social Capital." In *Social Capital: Theory and Research*, ed. N. Lin, K. Cook, and R. S. Burt, 57–81. New York: Aldine de Gruyter.

McLeod, J. M., D. A. Scheufele, P. Moy, E. M. Horowitz, R. L. Holbert, W. Zhang, W. Zubric, and J. Zubric. 1999. "Understanding Deliberation: The Effect of Discussion Networks on Participation in a Public Forum." *Communication Research*, 26: 743–74.

Mutz, D. C. 2002a. "The Consequences of Cross-Cutting Networks for Political Participation." *American Journal of Political Science*, 46: 838–55.

———. 2002b. "Cross-Cutting Social Networks: Testing Democratic Theory in Practice." *American Political Science Review*, 96: 111–26.

Naoi, Y., and K. Seiyama, K., eds. 1990. *Social Stratification in Contemporary Japan* (4 vol.). Tokyo: The University of Tokyo Press (in Japanese).

Newton, K. 2001. "Trust, Social Capital, Civic Society, and Democracy. *International Political Science Review*, 22: 201–14.

Norris, P. 2000. Making Democracies Work: Social Capital and Civic Engagement in 47 Societies. Paper presented at the European Science Foundation EURSCO conference on social capital: Interdisciplinary perspectives, Devon, September 2000.

Portes, A. 1998. "Social Capital: Its Origins and Applications in Modern Sociology." *Annual Review of Sociology*, 24: 1–24.

——— and P. Landolt. 1996. "The Downside of Social Capital." *The American Prospect*, 26, May–June 1996. http://www.prospect.org/print/V7/26/26-cnt2.html

Putnam, R. D. 1993. *Making Democracy Work: Civic Traditions in Modern Italy*. Princeton, NJ: Princeton University Press.

———. 1995. "Bowling Alone: America's Declining Social Capital." *Journal of Democracy*, 6: 65–78.

———. 2000. *Bowling Alone: The Collapse and Revival of American Community*. New York: Simon and Schuster.

Schulman, M. D., and C. Anderson. 2001. "The Dark Side of the Force." In *Beyond Tocqueville: Civil Society and the Social Capital Debate in Comparative Perspective*, eds. B. Edwards, M. W. Foley, and M. Diani, 112–24. Hanover, NH: University Press of New England.

Simon, B., and B. Klandermans. 2001. "Politicized Collective Identity." *American Psychologist*, 56: 319–31.

Sullivan, J. L., J. E. Piereson, and G. E. Marcus. 1982. *Political Tolerance and American Democracy*. Chicago, IL: University of Chicago Press.

Umino, M., ed. 2000. *A Sense of Fairness and Political Consciousness (Stratification System in Japan 2)*. Tokyo: University of Tokyo Press (in Japanese).
Verba, S., N. Nie, and J. Kim. 1978. *Participation and Political Equality: A Seven-Nation Comparison*. Cambridge, MA: Cambridge University Press.
Walsh, K. C. 2004. *Talking About Politics: Informal Groups and Social Identity in American Life*. Chicago, IL: University of Chicago Press.

Part II

Markets and Social Capital

5 The Context Challenge

Generalizing Social Capital Processes Across Two Different Settings[1]

Bonnie H. Erickson

Interest in social networks and their potential benefits goes back to the origins of sociology and has recently flourished in discussions of "social capital" as the productive aspect of social networks. The "capital" metaphor is a stimulating one because it draws our attention to basic questions: what is useful (capital) about networks, how do people build useful networks, and what profits do they gain from them? At the same time, the social capital metaphor can seem maddening, because the answers to all these basic questions vary from one context to another. Every facet of networks is useful for some things, but useless or even harmful for others, depending on the setting under study. Again depending on the setting, access to social capital arises from different kinds of social location. This variability poses a formidable challenge for research and theoretical generalization. In this chapter, I illustrate one productive path for generalization: the application of the same theoretical arguments to two different contexts, using different operationalizations appropriate for each context.

One of the two contexts is Toronto Local Employment and Trading System (LETS), a community organization with its own currency and banking system, which members use to buy and sell goods and services within the group. The second context is the wider social world and economy in which LETS members participate whenever outside of LETS. Because the two contexts differ but the people studied are the same, differences are clearly due to variations in the contexts and not to differences in the populations compared. This is a more powerful design than the usual kind in which both contexts and their populations differ, as when comparing the role of networks in getting a job in different labor markets. Different kinds of people enter different contexts, so it is usually difficult to tell whether differences between contexts are real effects of the contexts themselves, or are effects of the kinds of people selected into the contexts. Here this perennial problem is neatly sidestepped.

In the next section, I develop a general theoretical argument applicable to both settings, and begin a discussion of how the general argument can be applied by specifying concepts and measures appropriate to each setting. In general, higher social status and greater social participation lead to richer social capital, and greater social capital leads to more of two kinds of profit: money and mastery. In the wider context outside of LETS, status and participation are higher for those in generally advantaged social locations: older people, men, the better educated, and the employed. Within LETS, the relevant forms of status and participation are activities in LETS social interaction foci. In general, one powerful form of social capital is network variety, or the number of different kinds of occupations in which a person knows someone. It is crucial to distinguish the variety of people known outside LETS (which should flow from advantaged position in the wider society, and lead to profits in that wider world) from the variety of people known in LETS (which should flow from LETS activities and lead to profits within LETS). In general, both money and mastery are valuable potential profits. Outside LETS, money is the familiar and widely useful Canadian dollar that can be exchanged for all the goods and services in the standard economy. Mastery is an overall sense of control over one's own life, a psychological resource known to be useful in successfully negotiating wider life, as in getting better jobs or maintaining good general health. Within LETS, money is a special local currency. Mastery takes a special form, the sense of being empowered through LETS, which is a form of special importance and meaning for LETS members.

The crucial combination here is a powerful general theory merged with contextually appropriate versions of the key variables in the theory. In each context, status leads to social capital, which leads to profits. Theory generalizes across contexts, so long as it is properly applied.

The LETS example is also strategic for exploring another theoretical challenge: how do social capital processes in different settings connect? In particular, what are the connections between social capital, its sources, and its profits in specific settings (like LETS), and social capital, its sources, and its profits in the wider society in which a setting is embedded? When discussing this issue in general terms, I refer to the "local" (a specific organization, interaction focus, subculture, or other social setting) and the "global" (the wider society). These terms apply to settings, not people, and should not be confused with the more famous pair of concepts "local" and "cosmopolitan," nor with issues of globalization.

The literature provides a variety of predictions concerning links between local and global settings. On the one hand, some approaches emphasize similarity. Local and global social capitals may be related strongly and spuriously, because the same advantages (including gender or class) that produce good networks in general also produce good networks in local settings. Global and local may be related nonspuriously, because better global networks generate resources that can be used to build better local ones. On the other hand, some discussions emphasize the differences. Networks rooted in a local community build through local activities, and in a local subculture can develop quite differently from networks that range more widely. From the first point of view, people or groups in advantaged social locations relentlessly reproduce their advantages in one setting after another. From the second point of view, reproduction is more partial and conditional because the generally less advantaged may become the more advantaged in some local settings.

Both points of view are correct: global and local are strongly related for some local settings and disconnected for others. Thus we need to examine various local settings to see how local and global capitals are related, how they are each related to different profits, who benefits, and how these relationships are conditional on the type of local setting and wider context. The setting used here has some special advantages. First, this setting allows direct comparison of parallel forms of capitals and important potential profits at the local and global level. Second, the setting is potentially boundary defining in that it is likely to have especially high levels of disconnection between the local and the global. By comparing this setting to others, we can gradually map out the wider space of possible types of groups and types of local–global connections.

THEORETICAL BACKGROUND

Capitals and Profits

First, what do we mean by "social capital"? As a number of analysts (e.g., Newton 1997; Woolcock 1998) have usefully argued, it is important to define social capital as a single variable, not several blended together, and especially not possible causes confounded with possible consequences. A popular target of critical analysis is Putnam's famous definition of social capital as "features of social organization, such as trust, norms, and networks, that can improve the efficiency of society by facilitating coordinated actions" (1993, 167). Trust, norms, and networks are distinct variables that have variable relationships with both each other and possible outcomes; we need to separate such things to theorize and study their relationships (Newton 1997). I take the view that the "social" in social capital refers to social relationships: aspects of social networks that have the potential for yielding profits. The particular kinds of network features that yield profits depend on the kind of profits (as well as on many other factors), so one needs to make a joint choice of the kinds of social capital and profits to be examined.

Here I define social capital in one of its many possible senses: the variety of kinds of contacts in a person's network, and in particular the variety of occupations in which a person knows someone. Although this interpretation is not, by any means, the only useful one, it is especially useful for predicting the two kinds of nonnetwork "profits" that will be central in this chapter. One potential profit is important and material: money. There is abundant reason to predict that people with more diversified contacts will have higher incomes in many settings. Diversified contacts provide a wide variety of information and access to a wide variety of settings and decision makers, including people who allocate jobs, so they are better able to access good jobs with high incomes through their networks (Boxman, De Graaf, and Flap 1991; Granovetter 1995). Employers often want people with diverse networks to do higher-level jobs, which typically include extensive responsibilities for information gathering and working with people, so those with more diverse networks sometimes get better jobs even if they do not find them with the help of network members (Erickson 2001). Some people do not have "jobs" but are freelance entrepreneurs, self-employed, or business owners. All LETS members are independent entrepreneurs within the LETS economy, seeking trading partners in the group. Entrepreneurs often need a diverse network to provide a range of potential clients.

The second kind of potential profit is important and nonmaterial: mastery. Coser (1975) argued persuasively that people with complex role sets develop personal autonomy, or a sense of control over one's own fate, often called internal locus of control or mastery. Later research shows that mastery is a very important psychological resource linked to major life conditions and consequences. Mastery is not a fixed personality trait but a resource responsive to real lived experience of control over life: mastery is thus higher for those more advantaged in each major form of inequality. Mastery is an important predictor of good physical or mental health (e.g., Turner and Roszell 1994). People with greater personal autonomy work their way into more autonomous jobs (Kohn and Schooler 1982); more autonomous jobs are more desirable both for the autonomy itself and for its many correlates, such as higher authority level and income.

The third kind of potential profit is further enrichment of one's network. This form of profit is usually neglected in the social capital literature, which stresses network profits of nonnetwork kinds: trust, income, and so on. But profit in kind is both a plausible possibility and a theoretically interesting concern. Theoretically, the capacity to produce profits in kind is a critical feature of true capital, just as money invested yields more money. Networks can produce profits in kind because people with already better networks develop resources that make it easier for them to add to their networks. They become skilled at making and maintaining relationships, their existing friends introduce them to new friends, or their existing contacts introduce them to voluntary associations or other settings where they can meet new people. Here I investigate the extent to which global social capital (the diversity of a person's totality of accumulated ties outside the local group) goes with local social capital (a person's diversity of ties within the group).

Sources of Local and Global Capital

Individuals can make contacts in settings that are "local" in many senses, including geographic (neighborhoods), ethnic (ethnic communities and enclave economies), or organizational (schools, voluntary organizations, social movements, or firms). Individuals also have global networks made up of all the contacts accumulated through local settings, kinship, introduction by mutual friends, and so on. One way in which these two forms of social capital may connect is through their sources: the more they have the same sources, the more they will be alike, spuriously. The obvious candidates for sources of both kinds of social capital are the major forms of higher social status such as male gender, more mature age, higher education, and working for pay. Higher status provides more chances to make ties, both because people tend to prefer associating with higher-status people (Laumann 1966), and because higher-status people are thought to be more competent in many settings and hence generally gain better access to more powerful roles (e.g., Ridgeway 1997) and their network-building opportunities.

> *Hypothesis 1.* Both local and global social capital are higher for men, older people, the more educated, and those working for pay.

But there is a different argument going back as far as Simmel (1955). Some specific settings revolve around a particular common interest, generating distinctive activities and distinctive definitions of competence, attractiveness, and status, so much so that ranking in the setting may be unrelated to general social ranking or may even invert it. This is perhaps least likely for settings that are seen as important parts of mainstream life, for in such settings global social status will seem relevant and those who have high status will be motivated to take advantage of it. Thus Ridgeway (1997) argues that gender is pervasively important in work-related social interactions and male advantage is continually renewed. Global status is likely to be least important in settings that are decoupled from the mainstream by highly specialized activities and distinctive cultures, especially if the activities call for skills unrelated to general social status or the culture is ideologically opposed to mainstream values and practices. As I explain in the following, these conditions are met in the setting used in this chapter, making it a useful boundary-defining case. This leads to an alternative hypothesis:

> *Hypothesis 1a.* Global social capital is higher for people with higher general status, that is, for men, older people, the more educated, and those working for pay (as in Hypothesis 1). However, local social capital is higher for those more active in the local setting and is unrelated to global status (contrary to Hypothesis 1 for local social capital).

Finally, local and global social capitals are sources for each other. The impact of local on global is partly an obvious compositional effect: ties made in a local setting are part of a person's total network. To avoid confounding the two capitals, this chapter will measure global social capital in terms of ties other than those in the local setting analyzed here. Of primary interest here is the potential for global capital to yield profits in kind in the form of local social capital, and the means by which this may occur. Global social capital may produce local social capital profits by two quite different routes: personal traits or network connections. On the one hand, global capital may enhance personal resources that facilitate building networks in the local setting. Here I explore one especially promising kind of personal trait: mastery. People with diverse overall networks develop enhanced mastery (Coser 1975), which may, in turn, facilitate taking initiative in making contacts in a local setting. On the other hand, global social capital may yield local social capital profits by network means. People are often recruited to local settings through people they know, and recruiters may introduce newcomers to their local networks as well as to the local setting. The extent to which recruiters actually do provide local introductions and new ties depends in part on the newcomer's networking skills (including eagerness and ability to meet new people), skills that grow with the diversity of the newcomer's preexisting network. Thus for those who enter the local setting at the invitation of a member, global social capital translates into local social capital. McPherson has discussed the connection between networks and voluntary association membership in several interesting papers (e.g., McPherson, Popielarz, and Drobnic 1992). Thus:

> *Hypothesis 2.* Global and local social capitals are positively related, even after controlling for possible common sources.

> *Hypothesis 2a.* Global social capital leads to (global) mastery, which in turn leads to local social capital.

> *Hypothesis 2b.* Global social capital is related to local social capital, but only for those recruited to the local setting by a member of the setting.

The Profits That Capitals Yield

As previously argued, social capital generally produces money and mastery. Mastery in its most familiar form, an overall sense of control over one's life, is a general personal resource reflecting one's overall experience of mastery in life as a whole. If, as Coser (1975) argues, mastery grows with the complexity of one's network, it is one's total network that provides the maximum possible complexity and the widest range of life experiences, so it is global social capital that should be most related to global mastery. But local settings can provide their own cultural definitions of the relevant form of mastery, which will grow with setting-specific experiences. For someone in an environmental movement, for example, knowing and working with many fellow activists should generate a sense of being able to do something about environmental issues, and a sense of being in charge of one's political fate. It is well known that members of political groups have a higher sense of political efficacy (Almond and Verba 1965).

> *Hypothesis 3.* Global social capital is related to an overall sense of mastery, and local social capital is related to a sense of mastery within the local arena.

It is also possible that capital at one level can be related to mastery at another, although more weakly than global relates to global or local to local. Local social capital may contribute to a person's general sense of mastery if the local setting is a very important one. This argument is parallel to the "learning generalization" argument that Kohn and Schooler (1982) make for work and personality: The degree of autonomy experienced at work helps shape the person's overall sense of personal autonomy, because work has such an important role in most people's lives. Because the local setting considered here is a voluntary association, just one of many contexts of leisure life for most of the participants, local social capital is not likely to have much effect on global mastery. On the other hand, global social capital may contribute to a local sense of mastery indirectly, through global mastery. General mastery is a generalized personality attribute that will tend to transfer to specific settings unless these are strongly defined as unique. Masterful people tend to feel competent about taking some control in any arena calling for general skills, such as neighborhood associations, but become more hesitant in arenas calling for specific abilities they may not have, such as a tennis competition. Because the setting to be examined in this chapter is distinctive, global mastery is not likely to have much effect on local mastery. In short, spillover between local and global mastery should be slight in this particular case.

> *Hypothesis 3a.* Global and local mastery are very weakly related, or unrelated, when local mastery develops in a distinct social setting.

The second important profit to be considered is money, local or global. When employers are looking for well-connected people to fill higher-level jobs, or when entrepreneurs are trying to make profitable deals, the more varied and wide ranging the network the better; thus global social capital should be much more strongly related to overall income than the more limited local social capital. On the other hand, local exchanges made between people in a setting are shaped by local networks, not by outside ties.

Hypothesis 4. Global social capital is related to overall income, and local social capital is related to income made within the local arena.

Again, the distinctness of the setting suggests that there will be little local–global spillover. People in the group are immersed in local economic processes and indifferent to how much money people make in the rest of their lives, and the specificity of the setting means that financial success within it carries little weight in the general economy.

Hypothesis 4a. Global and local incomes are very weakly related, or unrelated, when local earnings are earned in a distinctive local economy.

The arguments in this section are similar to some made for cultural capital. Although cultural capital in a wider sense is rooted in family background, education, and global social capital, particular settings (or "fields" in the cultural capital literature) have their own forms of cultural capital and their own dynamics that relate cultural capital to success and social capital (Bourdieu 1984; Anheier, Gerhards, and Romo 1995; Erickson 1996).

Comparing Local and Global Processes

In a well-structured local setting with its own social networks, subculture, exchanges, incomes, and sense of mastery, the causal impacts previously discussed should be strong. But the parallel global processes should be clearly weaker, because global processes are agglomerations of many multiple processes. Global social capital has potential implications for income in many different labor markets in which social capital has varying importance, different kinds of network variety are more useful, and average incomes differ. For people in different social locations, different kinds of network diversity will be salient for feelings of mastery. For a corporate lawyer, ties to fellow professionals and client companies may be the root of income and sense of control; for a building contractor, ties to tradespeople and real estate agents would be more pertinent.

Hypothesis 5. Local social capital is more strongly related to its local sources and profits than global social capital is related to its global sources and profits.

RESEARCH METHODS

The Local Setting: Toronto LETS

The local setting examined in this chapter is the Toronto LETS, a community organization with over 700 members. Members can buy and sell goods or services using their own currency ("green dollars") or a mixture of "green" and "federal dollars" (Canadian currency). When one member sells to another, the traders report their transaction to the LETS office, which transfers the agreed number of green dollars from one account to the other. This system is intended to be especially valuable to the poor, since there is no credit limit or interest, and also appeals to more prosperous people who want to conserve cash. A member short of federal dollars can simply go into green dollar negative balance without penalty when in need, and seek ways to earn green dollars and reduce debt later. There are dozens of LETS-type groups in North America, and hundreds around the world.

Not only does LETS have a distinct currency and economy, but it has a distinct organizational culture. LETS Toronto was founded by environmentalists, community activists, and therapists, and the prevailing ideology stresses related themes. For example, during our fieldwork the group newsletter, *The LETS Trader*, had the following masthead announcement: "LETS Toronto's mission is to build a healthy local economy that meets human needs through the use of a new kind of money called green dollars. We aim to bring business and community together, stimulate meaningful work, reduce dependence on cash, foster self-reliance, promote ecological sustainability, and practice local democracy." In the following, I report evidence showing that LETS has recruited those who largely subscribe to these distinct goals and values, providing member, as well as organizational cultural, support for locally determined social capital and the resulting profits.

The Membership Survey

All current members of LETS are listed in the organization's database for recording trades. In the year prior to our survey, February 1995 through March 1996, 590 accounts were current. The initial target sample included all of the 360 accounts showing at least one trade in this period, plus a random sample of 95 of the other 230. Thirty-one of the 455 initial targets turned out to be ineligible because they had left LETS, the Toronto area, or both by the time we tried to reach them in a telephone survey throughout summer 1996. Of the 424 eligible targets, 352 agreed to an interview, for an overall response rate of 83 percent.

Many of the responses showed interest in LETS as an alternative economy. Respondents were asked how important various possible reasons for joining LETS were to them. Many described economic reasons as "somewhat" or "very" important: extra earnings (74.6 percent), saving money (86.2 percent), using and developing skills (69.5 percent), and getting new customers (60.8 percent). There is considerable support for the activist's view of the local green dollar currency, that is, that green dollars should be used as much as possible and valued on par with federal dollars. Seventy-seven percent ask for payment in at least 50 percent green dollars when selling in LETS, 81.2 percent usually get at least 50 percent green, and 86 percent thought that people in LETS should trade for at least 50 percent green. The most popular reason for including some federal dollar component in prices was necessity: people often have to spend federal dollars to trade (as in buying ingredients to make food to sell); 85.4 percent agreed with the statement, "I have to spend federal dollars, so I have to include federal dollars in my prices," and a minority (41.9 percent) agreed with the statement "Green dollars are not as valuable as federal dollars" as a reason for trading at less than 100 percent green. Of the 266 people who could compare their prices in LETS in green plus federal dollars to their prices outside LETS in federal dollars alone, 65.8 percent reported charging the same. Further, the economic activities pursued in LETS were often different from those pursued outside. When asked whether they mainly offered the same kinds of goods and services through LETS as produced in their external job, 53.6 percent said no (*n* = 207, because not all respondents had both external and internal work).

At the same time, members were often interested in LETS for noneconomic aspects of its culture. When asked about the importance of reasons for joining, the percent rating a reason "somewhat" or "very important" was 68.4 percent for "meeting like-minded people," 75.5 percent for "becoming self-reliant," 86.8 percent for "putting your values into practice," 91.7 percent for "to build a better community," 86.7 percent for "to help others," and 78.1 percent for "protecting the environment." These and further results reported in the following indicate that LETS is an alternative subculture with a distinct set of values and practices, a potential basis for distinct accumulation of social capital, and distinctive rewards from social capital.

The telephone survey provided useful measures of the variables in the hypotheses previously developed. Measures of general social status potentially relevant to accumulating global social capital included age, gender, years of education, and employment status. Age ranged from twenty to seventy-nine in years, and was square-rooted to correct skew. Women comprised 60.7 percent of respondents. Years of education ranged from five to thirty. Employment status was determined by whether or not the respondent reported currently working for pay outside of LETS; 81 percent were doing so.

Measures of aspects of LETS participation relevant to accumulating local social capital included length of membership and participation in LETS activities. Length of membership in months was copied from the organization database. Survey respondents reported how often in the past twelve months they had attended three kinds of LETS meetings. Although all meetings include a variety of kinds of activity, each of these three has a different primary focus. Meetings of the first kind, markets and swaps, are the most important venues for economic activity. At markets, LETS members offer goods and services for sale in a day-long community fair open to members of the public, as well as to LETS members. At swaps, LETS members bring things that they no longer want, all the contributions are displayed, and people take what they wish without payment. Markets and swaps include considerable social, as well as economic, activity; people mingle, meet, and talk extensively. But more purely social are meetings of the second type: potluck dinners and other social events. Besides socializing, these events may offer chances to discuss trades or include efforts to get newer members more involved in LETS activities. The third type of meeting is primarily political and organizational: attending meetings of the LETS governing body, the Steering Committee. Such meetings are open to all LETS members, although best attended by those elected to the committee. All of the LETS participation measures were square-rooted to help correct for skew. Like all of the measures specific to LETS, these questions were developed with the invaluable assistance of several volunteers from the LETS community.

To measure social capital, interviewers asked: "We'd like to know about the variety of contacts our members have. I will ask you whether you know anyone at all of a certain kind, for example, whether you know any carpenters. You do not have to know them very well, as long as you have met them and know them by name and by sight or voice. I will ask whether you know anyone IN LETS and then whether you know anyone like that who is NOT IN LETS." Respondents were asked about contacts in thirty occupations chosen to include mainstream work of varied status and type, plus some occupations more common in LETS than in the mainstream. The relatively common mainstream occupations were chosen using the standard "position generator" strategy: these occupations vary from high to low in occupational prestige, and hence vary in the amount and kind of resources to which members of the occupations may provide access (see Lin, Fu, and Hsung 2001 for an extended discussion). LETS members are not a random sample from the mainstream occupational distribution and often pursue relatively unusual occupations, and even members with standard kinds of work in their mainstream economy may pursue alternative kinds of work in LETS. Thus, we consulted with knowledgeable LETS informants to develop a list of occupations especially common among LETS members, to provide a social capital measure relevant to their mainstream and LETS social environments. The thirty occupations (in the order asked) were: a local business owner outside your own company, a manager who runs a business other than your own company, lawyer, doctor, engineer, university or college professor, schoolteacher, professional writer or editor, farmer, child care provider, accountant, bicycle courier, carpenter, computer programmer or technician, homeopath, massage therapist, housecleaner, grocery store owner, hairstylist, astrologer, auto mechanic, plumber, secretary, retail salesclerk, social worker, nurse, gardener or landscaper, insurance agent or broker, psychologist, palm or card reader. Global social capital is the number of occupations in which a person knew someone not in LETS;

local social capital is the number of occupations in which a person knew someone in LETS. Both of these scales have excellent reliability (Cronbach's alpha of .8483 and .8379, respectively).

One form of potential profit from social capital is mastery. To measure global mastery I used five items from the stress process literature, drawing on a prior survey partially reported in Turner, Wheaton, and Lloyd (1995). Respondents reported their degree of agreement or disagreement with these statements: "I have little control over the things that happen to me," "There is really no way I can solve some of the problems I have," "There is little I can do to change many of the important things in my life," "I often feel helpless in dealing with problems of life," and "Sometimes I feel that I am being pushed around in life." Responses were coded so that higher values indicate greater sense of mastery. Scale reliability was very good ($\alpha = .7525$). To measure local mastery, I used two newly developed items. Respondents reported their degree of agreement or disagreement with the statements "Taking part in LETS has helped me to take charge of my life," and "LETS helps me to feel empowered." Higher scale values show higher sense of empowerment and alpha is .8284. The two forms of mastery are quite different, being completely uncorrelated ($r = .010$, n.s.).

The second form of potential profit is money. Global income is the respondent's report of personal income from all sources outside LETS in the past year, reported in fifteen income categories. Local income is reported income in the past year, in green dollars and in federal dollars, gained through LETS. Local income is unrelated to global income: personal income outside LETS is uncorrelated with both LETS green dollar income ($r = -.028$, n.s.) and LETS federal dollar income ($r = -.050$, n.s.).

LETS in Comparative Perspective

To assess the degree to which LETS draws on a distinctive population, I used several measures from a high-quality survey of the general Toronto population conducted in 1990 and 1991 (Turner, Wheaton, and Lloyd 1995), just a few years before the LETS survey. Because the general survey was restricted to ages eighteen to fifty-five, and the LETS respondents range from twenty to seventy-nine, I compared the general survey both to the whole LETS sample and to the sample restricted to those fifty-five or less; because results were very similar, I report results for the whole LETS sample. LETS members were more often women (61 percent vs. 51 percent) and Canadian born (66 percent vs. 53 percent). They were equally likely to be working outside LETS (81 percent in both samples) for similar hours per week (35 for LETS members vs. 38). LETS members were more often self-employed (52 percent vs. 11 percent) but often in a small way, for example, only 28 percent of self-employed LETS members supervised anyone at work. Mean personal income was lower for LETS members (4.13 vs. 5.43 on the fifteen level scale, on which 4 = $15,000 to $19,999 and 5 = $20,000 to $24,999). Mastery (global) was slightly higher in mean level in LETS (20.55 vs. 19.18) and very similar in scale reliability (.75 in both samples). Thus LETS members were, on average, richer in personal than in economic resources, which may help to account for their willingness to adventure in an alternative economy.

LETS groups are widely thought to be politically distinctive, for example, to have spread worldwide in part through networks of environmentalists. To assess this I compared rankings of "goals that are frequently thought of as being important for society" (Tindall 1994, 159) as found in the LETS survey and in surveys of the general public and members of environmental protection movements in British Columbia. This particular comparison is useful because the survey of environmental movement members includes an item not found in general public surveys, "protecting nature from being spoiled and polluted," which got the highest ranking in both the environmentalist and the LETS samples. For items on which they could be compared to the general public of British Columbia, both LETS members and environmentalists gave higher rankings to "progress toward a society where ideas count more than money," "progress toward a less impersonal, more humane society," and "seeing that people have more say in how things get decided at work and in their communities;" they gave lower rankings to "the fight against crime," "maintaining a stable economy," "maintaining a high rate of economic growth," and "maintaining order in the nation." Thus, LETS members are largely environmentalists, proponents of decentralized democracy and self-reliance, and critics of the mainstream economy. Their politics and culture, as well as their economy, include enough shared and distinctive features to potentially support distinct processes for developing social capital and gaining yields from capital.

RESULTS

Given the distinct nature of LETS as a community with its own economy, activities, and shared culture, it seems more likely that global and local social capital have different sources (Hypothesis 1a) than that they stem from the same set of general social statuses (Hypothesis 1). This is indeed the case. Global social capital, the diversity in people's entire networks outside of the local setting, is related to general status but not to participation in the local setting (Table 5.1). As expected, global social capital is greater for those who are older, more educated, or employed in the mainstream economy. Contrary to expectations, women had greater (global) social capital than men. LETS members sometimes remark that LETS women are a particularly feisty lot; perhaps activist, network-building women have recruited each other into this group.

Table 5.1 Predicting Global Social Capital (Multiple Regressions)

Independent Variables[a]	*Model 1*[b]	*Model 2*[c]
Age	.207**	.174**
Gender (female)	.126**	.142**
Education	.119**	.114**
Employed	.151**	.136**
Time in LETS	.095	
Markets and swaps attended		–.052
Social event attended	–.042	
Steering committee meetings attended		.084
Adjusted R^2	.076**	.104**
p level for R^2 difference,		
Model 2 versus. Model 1	.238	
N	322	322

Note. LETS = Local Employment and Trading System.

[a]See text for full description of variables. [b]Prediction using general social status only, standardized regression coefficient. [c]Prediction using general social status and LETS participation, standardized regression coefficient.

*$p < .05$. **$p < .01$.

In striking contrast to global social capital, local social capital has almost no relationship to general status and a very strong relationship to local participation (Table 5.2). Although there is a mild tendency for older people to have less diversified networks in LETS, there is no effect at all of gender, education, or employment, and the set of general status variables has no significant impact as a whole. Meanwhile, local social capital grows vigorously with time in the local setting and participation in local markets, swap meets, social events, and steering committee meetings. LETS is a world of its own in which people build their networks irrespective of their position in the wider world, even though these external positions are quite relevant for the external social capital of the same people.

Another consequence of LETS as a world apart is that mastery has its own local form and local sources (Hypothesis 3 and Table 5.3). I showed previously that local mastery, feeling empowered through LETS, is uncorrelated with general mastery, a sense of control over one's life. Table 5.3 shows that general mastery is not related at all to LETS participation, but is related to general social status and to global social capital. The results for status are a little different from those usually found in the stress process literature (Turner and Roszell 1994). The employed and the more educated

Table 5.2 Predicting Local Social Capital (Multiple Regressions)

Independent Variables[a]	*Model 1*[b]	*Model 2*[c]
Age	–.110**	–.102*
Gender (female)	–.027	.027
Education	.093	.043
Employed	–.026	–.007
Time in LETS	.180**	
Markets and swaps attended		.341**
Social event attended	.107**	
Steering committee meetings attended		.242**
Adjusted R^2	.008	.375**
p level for R^2 difference, Model 2 vs. Model 1	.000	
N	322	322

Note. LETS = Local Employment and Trading System.

[a]See text for full description of variables. [b]Prediction using general social status only, standardized regression coefficient. [c]Prediction using general social status and LETS participation, standardized regression coefficient.

$*p < .05$. $**p < .01$.

have more mastery, as is usually found. But age is not related to mastery (whereas it typically declines with increasing speed with age) and, even more unusual, women have greater mastery in the LETS survey, whereas men have greater mastery in most general population surveys. Again, LETS has somehow recruited an unusual set of women. But the strongest predictor of general mastery is not any of the social statuses, but global social capital. This provides interesting support for Coser's (1975) theory, in which the central claim is that network diversity leads to personal autonomy.

Local mastery, or empowerment through LETS, is not related to global social capital, nor to any of the general social status variables, but only to experiences within LETS. In another interesting confirmation of Coser's (1975) argument, the strongest predictor of local mastery is local social capital. It is also intriguing that participation in markets and swaps is the only form of LETS participation related to LETS empowerment. Because markets and swaps are the major economic fora in LETS, participation in them is analogous to work in the mainstream economy. Thus, work in both economies generates feelings of mastery, though mastery of different kinds.

The second kind of potential yield from social capital, money, also has distinctive global and local patterns (Hypothesis 4 and Table 5.4). Personal

Table 5.3 Social Capitals and Masteries (Multiple Regressions)

Independent Variables[a]	*General Mastery*[b]	*LETS Empowerment*[b]
Age	.016	–.041
Gender (female)	–.153**	–.021
Education	.140*	–.039
Employed	.143**	–.034
Global social capital	.218**	–.032
Time in LETS	–.035	–.011
Markets and swaps attended	.003	.161*
Social event attended	–.018	.017
Steering committee meetings attended	–.027	.001
Local social capital	.045	.269**
Adjusted R^2	.121**	.126**
N	310	315

Note. LETS = Local Employment and Trading System.
[a]See text for full description of variables. [b]Standardized regression coefficients.
$^*p < .05$. $^{**}p < .01$.

income from all sources outside of LETS is related only to external matters, not to LETS experiences. External income is higher for older people and for those employed. Surprisingly, it is not higher for men or for those more educated. Again, LETS women seem unusual. The lack of effect of education, which is quite high on average in this group, may suggest either that: (1) Members have not chosen to maximize their income returns to education but prefer to maximize alternative returns, such as political efforts or qualitatively rewarding work, or (2) Being underemployed has helped to interest them in new ways of adding to their limited incomes, and hence led them to try LETS. Contrary to expectations, global social capital is not related to income. This is probably because the value of social networks is highly dependent on the contexts within which income is gained (Granovetter 1995). In some labor markets, networks add nothing to income. In others, diverse networks do contribute to income, but one needs to specify the particular kind of diversity that pays off in the particular context. Where a clear link between networks and success has been found, the research has been done in specific markets such as the Toronto private security industry (Erickson 2001) or Dutch managers (Boxman et al., 1991). And the measure of network diversity is often specific to the setting, as in Erickson (2001), in which people reported their contacts with others on a list of occupations especially useful to those working in security.

Table 5.4 Social Capitals and Monies (Multiple Regressions)

Independent Variables[a]	*Personal Income*[b]	*Green Dollar Income*[c]	*Federal Dollar LETS Income*[d]
Age	.125*	.038	.088
Gender (female)	–.004	–.091	–.104
Education	.067	–.001	–.002
Employed	.301**	0.19	.137**
Global social capital	.064	–.004	.045
Time in LETS	.008	.073	.069
Markets and swaps attended	–.118	.283**	.270**
Social events attended	–.069	–.032	–.123*
Steering committee meetings attended	.058	–.003	.021
Local social capital	.024	.345**	.264**
Adjusted R^2	.124**	.285**	.204**
N	304	310	304

Note. LETS = Local Employment and Trading System.

[a]See text for full description of variables. [b]Y = personal income from all sources outside LETS in federal dollars, standardized regression coefficient. [c]Y = income earned in LETS in green dollars, standardized regression coefficient. [d]Y = income earned in LETS in federal dollars, standardized regression coefficient.

*$p < .05$. **$p < .01$.

Within LETS, the most important form of income is green dollar earnings, important both because it is culturally central in the group and because it is more extensively earned (although 100 people reported no green dollar earnings in LETS in the previous year, 188 reported no federal dollar income). Green dollar income has nothing to do with general social status, nor with global social capital, but it is clearly linked to local economic activities (participation in markets and swaps) and, even more strongly, to local social capital. Having a diversified network is especially important in this setting because of the difficulty in gaining information needed for exchange. Some information concerns the availability of potential buyers or sellers. Local advertising is quite limited; *The LETS Trader* offers a directory, but most members do not advertise in it and it comes out at long, irregular intervals. Markets are a more effective way to bring potential buyers and sellers together, but 47 percent of respondents had not been to a market or swap in the past year. Besides knowing who a potential exchange partner might be, potential buyers need to know whether the things offered for sale are worth buying. This is especially difficult when many of the offerings are personal services, from alternative medicine to writing, whose quality varies greatly with the ability of the provider. Under these conditions, a person's local network is his or her market just as much as the physical markets are.

Though LETS centers on green dollars culturally, earning federal dollars is also important to buying power outside of LETS and even within it, because many sales include a federal dollar component. As for green dollar income, the most important predictors of federal dollar income are internal to LETS: participation in activities and local social capital (Table 5.4). But unlike green dollar income, federal dollar income shows some effect of external status, with federal income less for women and for those not working in the external economy. Those who are working may have more bargaining power to demand federal dollars, because they can gain federal dollars outside LETS. But this argument cannot apply to women, who earn as much as men in the external economy; perhaps their ideological commitment to the green dollar economy is greater. In any case, the impact of external status on LETS incomes is slight and is confined to incomes not in LETS currency.

According to Hypothesis 5.5, local processes should be stronger than global ones because they are more singular; global results blend and blur results from many different local processes. Comparing Tables 5.1 and 5.2, local social capital is more strongly related to capital's sources (R^2 is .375 for local social capital vs. .104 for global social capital). Comparing the columns in Table 5.4, local social capital has a strong and significant impact on local earnings but global social capital has no significant effect on global earnings. Departing from these results, Table 5.3 shows comparable strength for the impact of local and global processes on masteries. Global social capital has a strong significant impact on mastery as a general personality trait; local social capital has a strong significant effect on feeling empowered through the local setting. This suggests that global diversity may be the actual network basis of global mastery, not just a summary of the various diversities encountered in many different settings.

To this point, the story of global and local levels is a story of differences: global and local social capitals have their own distinct sources and yields. Nevertheless, there is a link between these two arenas: controlling for the sources of both capitals, people with more global social capital also develop more local social capital (Table 5.5, Model 1). Social capital is a "capital" in the sense that ordinary money is; that is, it can yield profits in its own kind: network diversity breeds more network diversity. But how does this theoretically striking result occur? By personal or by network means? Is it because diversity in general networks produces personal qualities that make it easier to make more contacts, or is it because personal recruitment into a setting opens the opportunity for networking skills developed in a wider

Table 5.5 Global and Local Social Capital (Multiple Regressions)

Independent Variables[a]	*Model 1*[b]	*Model 2*[b]
Age	–.137**	–.121*
Gender (female)	–.002	.000
Education	.020	.014
Employed	–.035	–.037
Global social capital	.203**	.178**
Mastery	.031	
Time in LETS	.161**	.163**
Markets and swaps attended	.352**	.357**
Social events attended	.115*	.111*
Steering committee meetings attended	.225**	.230**
Adjusted R^2	.388**	.387**
R^2 difference, Model 2		
Model 1: not significant		
N	310	310

Note. LETS = Local Employment and Trading System.
aSee text for full description of variables. bStandardized regression coefficients.
$^*p < .05$. $^{**}p < .01$.

network to pay off in a local setting? Although this study cannot address all the personal qualities that might link global to local social capital, it can test for one strong possibility: mastery. Previous sections showed that general network diversity does go with mastery, which, in turn, could help people to approach new network-building opportunities with confidence and effectiveness. This is not true: mastery has no effect on local social capital and controlling mastery has no effect at all on the link between global and local social capital (Table 5.5, Model 2). On the other hand, personal recruitment does play a crucial role in the link between global and local social capital. This link is moderately strong and quite significant ($r = .302$, $p <.001$, $n = 143$) for people who first heard about LETS from a LETS member, but small and not significant ($r = .124$, $p <.109$) for others. LETS members who draw people into LETS could also introduce them to their LETS activities and networks. I speculate that the more networking skill people have acquired through practice in working with a diverse general network, the more they can translate such opportunities into further local additions to their social capital. Future research on the mechanisms of this connection is needed.

SUMMARY AND DISCUSSION

LETS members set out to build a different world and, to some extent, succeeded. Social location, social capital, money, and mastery all take special forms within LETS. Most of the LETS variables are unrelated to their theoretical parallels in LETS members' wider social lives. Income in the LETS economy is unrelated to income in the mainstream economy, and feeling empowered through LETS is unrelated to an overall sense of mastery. The one variable that is correlated across contexts (social capital) shows a modest correlation between social capital in LETS and social capital in the rest of life. Although modest, the correlation of local and global social capital is theoretically fascinating, because it shows that social capital can yield profits in itself, just as money in the bank earns interest in more money. This result enhances the appeal of using the "capital" conceptualization. The modesty of this correlation, and the absence of correlations between other variables in their local and global forms, shows that LETS is, indeed, a boundary-defining case. LETS shows that a local context can be quite different from the global context of people's lives as wholes.

The distinctiveness of life in LETS makes it all the more striking that the distinct LETS variables interrelate in the same theoretically coherent way as the parallel but unrelated measures of members' global social lives. In both contexts, social location shapes social capital, which in turn yields profits in mastery. The one real lack of theoretical parallelism lies in money, with LETS incomes related to LETS social capital but general economy incomes not related to global social capital. However, this result makes sense in light of the great variability in social capital's usefulness in different global labor markets. In some labor markets, but not all, relevant forms of social capital do yield higher incomes just as in LETS (e.g., Erickson 2001). The most important difference between the two contexts is the overall strength of the parallel connections: relationships are generally stronger for the local level than for the global. This, too, is theoretically coherent, because the global relationships are the complex combination of many different underlying processes in many settings. Although the local and global differ in concrete operationalizations, they are the same theoretically.

This chapter's approach to theoretical generalization is not the only route to generalizations about social capital. Other routes are possible, and indeed necessary, for other facets of this complex topic. For example, Lin (1999) reviews a number of studies showing that global social capital has much the same sources and effects in different countries. Unlike the research reported in this chapter, these studies used very similar measures that related to each other in very similar ways. The key difference is that all the studies that Lin reviewed concerned status attainment in developed economies, which have quite similar types of occupations and quite similar occupational prestige hierarchies. When comparing similar stratification systems and their processes, one can use similar or identical measures and generalize results. This chapter, on the other hand, focuses on settings with different kinds of stratification. In such cases, one must develop theoretically appropriate measures for each setting to generalize.

NOTES

This research was supported by a grant from Health Canada and by the Centre of Health Promotion, the Centre for Urban and Community Studies, and the School of Graduate Studies at the University of Toronto. An earlier version of this chapter was presented at the Sunbelt XVIII and 5th European International Conference on Social Networks, Sitges, Spain, May 27–31, 1998. I gratefully acknowledge invaluable assistance and advice from Donald A. Lloyd, Irving Rootman, Chantal Hilaire, David Burman, and many members of the LETS community.

REFERENCES

Almond, G. A., and S. Verba. 1965. *The Civic Culture.* Boston: Little, Brown.

Anheier, H. K., J. Gerhards, and F. P. Romo. 1995. "Forms of Capital and Social Structures in Cultural Fields: Examining Bourdieu's Social Topography." *American Journal of Sociology,* 100: 859–903.

Bourdieu, P. 1984. *Distinction.* London: Routledge and Kegan Paul.

Boxman, E. A. W., P. M. De Graaf, and H. D. Flap. 1991. "The Impact of Social and Human Capital on the Income Attainment of Dutch Managers." *Social Networks,* 13:51–73.

Coser, R. L. 1975. "The Complexity of Roles as a Seedbed of Individual Autonomy." In *The Idea of Social Structure: Papers in Honor of Robert K. Merton,* ed. L. A. Coser, 237–62. New York: Harcourt Brace Jovanovich.

Erickson, B. H. 1996. "Culture, Class, and Connections." *American Journal of Sociology,* 102:217–51.

———. 2001. "Good Networks and Good Jobs: The Value of Social Capital to Employers and Employees." In *Social Capital: Theory and Research,* eds. N. Lin, K. Cook, and R. S. Burt, 127–58. New York: Aldine de Gruyter.

Granovetter, M. 1995. *Getting a Job: A Study of Contacts and Careers* (Second Edition). Chicago, IL: University of Chicago Press.

Kohn, M. L. and C. Schoole. 1982. "Job Conditions and Personality: A Longitudinal Assessment of Their Reciprocal Effects." *American Journal of Sociology,* 87: 1257–86.

Laumann, E. O. 1966. *Prestige and Association in an Urban Community.* Indianapolis, IN: Bobbs-Merrill.

Lin, N. 1999. "Social Resources and Status Attainment." *Annual Review of Sociology,* 25: 467–87.

———, Y.-C. Fu, and R. M. Hsung. 2001. "The Position Generator: Measurement Techniques for Investigations of Social Capital." In *Social Capital: Theory and Research,* eds. N. Lin, K. Cook, and R. S. Burt, 57–81. New York: Aldine de Gruyter.

McPherson, J. M., P. A. Popielarz, and S. Drobnic. 1992. "Social Networks and Organizational Dynamics." *American Sociological Review,* 57: 153–70.

Newton, K. 1997. "Social Capital and Democracy." *American Behavioral Scientist,* 40: 575–86.

Putnam, R. D. 1993. *Making Democracy Work: Civic Traditions in Modern Italy.* Princeton, NJ: Princeton University Press.

Ridgeway, C. L. 1997. "Interaction and the Conservation of Gender Inequality: Considering Employment." *American Sociological Review,* 62: 218–35.

Simmel, G. 1955. "The Web of Group-Affiliations." In *Conflict and the Web of Group-Affiliations,* ed. G. Simmel, 125–95. New York: Free Press.

Tindall, D. B. 1994. "Collective Action in the Rainforest: Personal Networks, Collective Identity, and Participation in the Vancouver Island Wilderness Preservation Movement." Unpublished Ph.D. thesis, Department of Sociology, University of Toronto, Toronto, Canada.

Turner, R. J., and P. Roszell. 1994. "Psychosocial Resources and the Stress Process." In *Stress and Mental Health: Contemporary Issues and Prospects for the Future,* eds. W. R. Avison and I. H. Gotlib, 179–210. New York: Plenum.

Turner, R. J., B. Wheaton, and D. A. Lloyd. 1995. "The Epidemiology of Social Stress." *American Sociological Review,* 60: 104–25.

Woolcock, M. 1998. "Social Capital and Economic Development: Toward a Theoretical Synthesis and Policy Framework." *Theory and Society,* 27: 151–208.

6 The Transaction Cost Embeddedness Approach to Studying Chinese Outsourcing

Jar-Der Luo and Yung-Chu Yeh

Since Granovetter (1985; 1992) proposed his embeddedness approach, many studies on Chinese organizations have investigated the role of trust in building and managing networks between manufacturers and their vendors (Hamilton, Zeile, and Kim 1990; Chang and Kao 1996; Luo 1997). In studying small and medium-sized garment firms, specifically those not utilizing modern large-scale assembly lines, "pseudo-familial ties" in the broadest sense were found to be the main source of outsourcing relations (C. H. Chen 1994: 219; 1995; Hamilton and Kao 1990). Because mutual trust is embedded in social connections, maintaining social relationships is thought to be as important as pursuing profit. Network governance of this sort thus relies on reciprocity and social control, rather than formal regulation and authority (Powell 1990). The term "weighted balance of social relations and business interests" precisely describes the art of governing an outsourcing network of this type (C. H. Chen 1994; 1995).

However, network governance of this type is rarely seen in newly developed Taiwanese hi-tech industries. In spite of some variation between different firms, Luo and Yeh (2002) found in interviews with 27 monitor and notebook PC firms that certain common governance structures within hi-tech industries were distinctly different from those of small and medium-sized garment firms. First, the source of the outsourcing relationship in the PC industry does not necessarily involve "simulated familial *guanxi*." (Chen 1994; 219) Partners are recruited mainly from the open market, except for some monitor firms that purchase key parts from fellow members of their conglomerates.

Second, the source of trust in the daily management of PC firms is not rooted in social relations or personal feelings. Instead, trust is gradually built up through the process of cooperation between two firms (Chang and Pan 1997; Luo and Yeh 2002). Similar findings were also observed in the Taiwanese IC industry (D. S. Chen and Jou 1996). The network governance of these industries utilizes more systematic and institutional control mechanisms and performance evaluations. This is very different from the small and medium-sized firms in the garment industry, which tend to complicate relationships with personal feelings, and where it is difficult to restore a relationship once it breaks down.

These hi-tech industries require fairly sophisticated technical skills in the production process, so it is understandable that quality of supplies is the most important criterion in choosing vendors. Many studies have shown that technological considerations form the basis for interorganizational relations in hi-tech industries (Powell 1996; Barley, Freeman, and Hybels 1992; Saxenian 1994). In governing a network, quality control in this industry can be measured by clear and strict industrial standards, and all outsourcing behaviors have formally institutionalized processes to follow (D. S. Chen and Jou 1996; Luo and Yeh 2001). Furthermore, Taiwanese hi-tech firms have generally adopted a globally recognized process of standardization and documentation, known as ISO9000, to manage outsourcing relations (Luo and Yeh 2001), so that these firms are qualified to do OEM/ODM (Original Equipment Manufacturing/Original Design and Manufacturing) jobs for world-famous brands like DELL, Compaq, HP and IBM.

Because network governance of this sort is ruled primarily by institutionalized mechanisms, what room is left for trust relationships? Are the outsourcing actions of the large Chinese hi-tech firms embedded in social relations? In other words, is the embeddedness argument still applicable to an outsourcing system of this sort? This question leads us to review the embeddedness theory.

THEORETICAL BACKGROUND—REVIEWING EMBEDDEDNESS

Based on the argument that economic actions are embedded in social relations, the embeddedness approach has sought to create a dialogue with the Transaction Costs Theory (Granovetter 1985), and especially with Williamson's (1975, 1981) famous argument concerning markets and hierarchies.

The Transaction Cost Approach to Studying Outsourcing

Following the publication of Coase's thought-provoking article in 1937, transaction cost has become a main theme in economic studies on institutions and organizations. If there is no transaction cost, as assumed by those theories that consider only scarcity and competition, then free competition is the most efficient way to allocate economic resources, as neoclassical economists argue. Any restriction on competition, whether in the form of institutions or synergetic relationships, thus has no reason to exist (Coase 1937; North 1990). Because transaction costs do exist and are sometimes vital to economic decision making, institutional studies have become an important area of research in economics.

Among the so-called New Institutionalism economists, Williamson has proposed an important thesis linking organization structure with transaction costs. In his famous analysis of markets and hierarchies, minimizing transaction costs is proposed as the rationale behind organizational structuring (Williamson 1975). In his argument, transaction costs are a result of the bounded rationality and opportunism of actors, and information searching and malfeasance control in transactions become central to this doctrine (Williamson 1981). Markets and hierarchies respectively provide controls for malfeasance in transactions, but also incur costs. An intentionally rational actor will choose the most cost-efficient way to carry out his or her transactions; therefore transaction costs are a determinative factor in deciding where a transaction should be executed—either in market or in hierarchy—and this in turn determines the form of organizational structure (Williamson 1975).

Williamson (1985) extended his argument further by proposing four forms of transaction contracts—classical contracts, neoclassical contracts, relational contracts between two firms, and relational contracts within hierarchies. Each form of contract is accompanied by its most efficient governance structure—market, trilateral, bilateral (or network form), and unified (hierarchical form) governance. The nature of a transaction can be assessed according to its frequency, asset specificity, hazards due to measurement, and the institutional and business environment. These aspects are used to determine the level of uncertainty in conducting the transaction. One of the key factors in choosing a particular form of contract is the minimum cost for controlling uncertainty, and the governance structure is determined accordingly. Outsourcing belongs to a category known as network transactions, which Williamson views as an intermediate form between market and hierarchy (Imai and Itami 1984; Hemmert 1999). A frequent transaction characterized by middle-level asset specification and hazards will usually adopt networks as the preferred governing structure.

Alternatively, this relationship can also be taken as a hybrid form (Williamson 1996), because network governance is a mixed mechanism of market and hierarchy. Searching in markets, bargaining, and signing contracts often feature the use of market mechanisms; standard operation processes, authority systems, and organizational regulations are the key elements of hierarchy mechanisms (Williamson 1996; Powell 1990). Network forms of governance combine these two types.

But why does a similar transaction with the same level of environmental hazard take different forms of governance in different countries? For instance, why did the purchase of automobile parts have different governance structures in the United States and Japan during the 1970s? Granovetter (1985) proposes two penetrating arguments against Williamson (1981): (a) Trust is one of the factors that determine the contract form of a transaction by influencing its associated transaction costs, and (b) trust is necessary for initiating any kind of transaction. Trust was suggested as the intervening variable that mediates between cultural factors and economic actions in Granovetter's embeddedness argument.

Trust in Reducing Transaction Costs

Williamson (1975) identifies opportunism and bounded rationality as the main sources of transaction costs. Trust relationships in outsourcing networks play a significant role in fighting against opportunism. "Goodwill" in an outsourcing relationship helps to avoid or resolve many potential disagreements that can result from conflicts of interest, such as unsatisfactory quality, dealing with special requests like emergent or extra services, fulfilling contracts, and even sharing losses due to accidents (Dore 1992; Powell 1990; Perrow 1992). As Granovetter has observed:

> Yet a hierarchical structure associated with the vertically integrated firm does not arise to meet this "problem" [shirking performance requirements in construction contracts.] I argue this is because the long-term relations of contractors and vendors, as well as embeddedness of those relations in a community of construction personnel, generate standards of behavior that not only obviate the need for but also are superior to pure authority relations in discouraging malfeasance. . . . This phenomenon can be explained in part in investment terms—through a "continuing association both parties can benefit from the somewhat idiosyncratic investment of learning to work together." (Granovetter 1985, p. 498)

With goodwill, lengthy contracts, teams of lawyers, and heavy enforcement by the legal system become unnecessary. For example, Taiwanese small firms consider trust relationships to be a very efficient way of accessing economic resources, whether by forming organizations, building forward and backward linkages, or borrowing capital (Luo 1997). Trust relationships can thus significantly reduce transaction costs in these economic activities.

From Adam Smith on, economists have always hoped that free markets would bring about a free flow of information that would prevent malfeasance by providing the opportunity for rational comparisons on the part of buyers. Unfortunately, even in a mass-production market with homogeneous products, spatial and temporal barriers as well as strategic manipulation for the sake of business competition can make information a valued commodity, to say nothing of those markets with a wide variety of products that differ in function and quality. Because information is a valued commodity, "purchasing" it is worthwhile. The more "secret" and valuable a piece of information is, the higher its worth.

Through observing a bazaar economy in Morocco, Geertz (1978) reminds us how costly and important information searching may be to a transaction.

To start with a dictum: in a bazaar information is poor, scarce, maldistributed, inefficiently communicated, and intensely valued. The search for information that one lacks and the protection of information that one has is the name of the game. At the same time, Geertz also recognizes the value of trust in searching for information when information is so maldistributed. Without alliances, a trader in a Morocco bazaar needs to search for information one shop at a time, and to bargain for a price again and again to understand the market. The transaction costs of information searching of this sort are too high to make trading profitable. Clientellization is, thus, an important strategy for Morocco bazaar traders, as Geertz states:

> Clientellization represents an actor-level attempt to counteract, and profit from, the system-level deficiencies of the bazaar as a communication network—its structural intricacy and irregularity, the absence of certain sorts of signaling systems . . .—by improving the richness and reliability of information carried over elementary links within it. (Geertz 1978, p. 30)

According to Williamson's (1996) argument, the consideration of transaction costs determines the contract form regulating a transaction. Because the function of trust relationships in reducing transaction costs, both in terms of malfeasance control and information searching, is recognized by the embeddedness argument, this view thus can help us to understand the role of trust relationships in the formation of contracts.

Minimum Trust as a Necessary Condition for Transactions

Many scholars have observed the role of trust in reducing transaction costs (Bromiley and Cummings 1995; Creed and Miles 1996). However, to view the institutional mechanisms in a contract as complete substitutes for trust is naive, as Granovetter has argued, because trust is a necessary part of transactions to varying degrees. The causal relationship between transaction efficiency and contract forms should not be overemphasized (Granovetter 1985). In addition to the rational design of a contract for minimizing transaction costs, the necessity of trust as a lubricant to make the contract executable should not be ignored.

In hierarchies, Granovetter (1994) showed that the lack of vertical or horizontal group solidarity leads to the failure of long-term cooperation. He examined the case of the pasar traders of Modjokuto, and found that the high frequency of short-lived alliances among pasar traders is the main obstacle to forming economic organizations. Lack of long-term trust resulted in their failure to integrate their capital and efforts to exploit long-lasting market opportunities. Geertz (1963) called them "entrepreneurs without enterprises" (p. 40). A second example was observed in Estancia in the Philippines, which contrasts with ethnic Chinese living in Southeast

Asia who mobilize strong ties to collect capital and pool human resources to form firms. Granovetter described the local Estancia social structure as follows: "Social systems with a lack of horizontal solidarity, which can arise in various ways, are deficient in the trust required to build enterprises larger than run by individual or families" (1994, p. 16).

In markets, the written form of a contract is never thorough enough to regulate all economic actions in all possible situations. Furthermore, according to Macaulay's (1963) study of business contracts, businessmen will seldom bring a dispute before the courts, even when the legal means to resolve the dispute have been specified in the contract. In other words, a minimum mutual trust is needed on the part of economic actors who face uncertainty in a transaction because institutional mechanisms are unable to protect them completely. In addition, they generally choose to give up this protection so that the trading relationship can continue. Uncertainty is unavoidable, especially in a long-term transaction, so it is necessary to trust the other party not to take advantage of this uncertainty.

In addition to trust, weak ties are also necessary for finding opportunities to start a transaction. Burt (1992) extends Granovetter's (1973) argument on the strength of weak ties in his famous theory on structural holes, in which entrepreneurship is thought of as the ability to discover information about market opportunities, and a person with many weak ties has a better information network for finding such opportunities. Since Schumpeter (1939), entrepreneurship has been considered to be one of the factors influencing economic production. In Schumpeter's definition, entrepreneurs are those persons who can invent new products or new business processes. Casson (1982) modifies this definition by viewing entrepreneurship as the ability to find a gap between demand and supply, and to bridge this gap. Burt (1992) accepts this definition and goes on to point out that the best position to discover a market opportunity is a bridge, because a gap between demand and supply often occurs between two segregated groups. In addition, social relations not only provide necessary information at the right time, but also necessary references critical for increasing both sides' faith in the transaction. Without these social ties, business opportunities may be very difficult to find, and outsourcing relationships are not easily established.

THE RESEARCH METHOD

The Transaction Cost—Embeddedness Analytical Framework

Uncertainty is found at the core of both transaction-cost and embeddedness arguments. Not only is uncertainty unavoidable in any form of contract that makes trust necessary, but also the trust relationship is a good substitute for other arrangements that reduce uncertainty. In Williamson's

(1996) theory, behavioral and environmental hazards, transaction frequency, and asset specificity compose the three main features of a transaction that determine the most efficient contract form (i.e., minimizing its associated transaction costs) for governing the uncertainty in the transaction. Trust is very useful for information searching and malfeasance control, as Granovetter (1985) argued; so all hazards can be effectively controlled in trust relationships. Because trust relationships greatly change the uncertainty of a transaction, a rational actor must take trust into account in designing the form of contract and its associated governance structure.

Thus, the transaction cost-embeddedness approach proposes a new analytical framework to investigate outsourcing transactions. Specifically, social relations are factored into the three aspects of transaction features as explanatory variables, and trust is taken as a mediator that influences governance structure. The analytical process of transaction cost theory is maintained, but the new elements are integrated as follows:

1. Identifying a transaction as the analytical unit. Transaction cost theory takes transactions as its object of study.
2. Describing the process of the transaction. In this study, we followed the IS9000 to categorize these processes into six steps: (a) searching for vendors; (b) reaching a purchase agreement; (c) bargaining on the price; (d) ordering and delivering; (e) monitoring contracts and managing equipment; and (f) evaluating performance and support.
3. Analyzing the uncertainty in each step of the transaction. The uncertainty of the transaction can be measured according to its frequency, asset specificity, hazards due to measurement, and the institutional and business environment.
4. Determining the social relations involved. It is necessary to analyze the different kinds of social relations involved in each step of the transaction process.
5. Identifying institutional mechanisms. What are the institutional arrangements, either market or hierarchy mechanisms, that control outsourcing behaviors for each step? These mechanisms include written contracts, company regulations, industrial community norms, and technological rationale. Whatever procedures are not included among these institutionalized mechanisms constitute the space in which trust can operate.
6. Operationally defining real trust. As defined in this chapter, trust includes two categories—trust due to full control, also known as calculative trust (to use Williamson's 1996 term); and real trust (Granovetter 2002). Real trust can be defined as a psychological state in which an individual is willing to risk losing personal interests because of an expectation that the other party in the transaction will not take advantage of them (Andaleeb 1992; Bromily and Cumming

1995; Rousseau et al. 1998). Unlike trust based on calculation, real trust involves risk. In the following section, we try to operationally define real trust in Chinese *guanxi*.

Operationally Defining Real Trust in Chinese *Guanxi*

Many scholars have proposed a typology of trust. Zucker (1986) defined three types of trust, i.e. process-based, characteristic-based, and institutional-based. Shapiro, Sheppard, and Cheraskin (1992) proposed three categories of trust: deterrence-based, knowledge-based, and identification-based trust (also in Sheppard and Tuchinsky 1996). Combining these typologies, Rousseau et al. (1998) suggest that calculative trust evolves into real trust with development over time, and institutional trust is the foundation for risk-taking behaviors in the initial stage of social relations.

Institutional factors, including legal forms and societal norms, build a person's confidence in the institutional mechanisms that make the other party honest and consistent (Gulati 1995; Creed and Miles 1996). Trust of this sort can be called general trust, because no person in particular is specified as the one being trusted.

Calculative trust quantifies a person's confidence in the other party in terms of a rational calculation of personal costs and benefits. Calculative trust is based on familiarity with the other party resulting from frequent interaction, a process in which there are repeated games involving power, hostages, and cost-benefit analysis (Williamson 1996). Real trust comes from benevolent social interactions. Both types of trust are, thus, embedded in a social relational context, and can be called dyad trust. Real trust is the focus of embeddedness theory. How can we observe real trust in the process of an outsourcing transaction? This question leads us to define real trust operationally.

The Chinese concept of *guanxi* differs from the Western notion of social ties in at least two ways. First, Chinese are particularistic and treat different categories of *guanxi* in different ways (Fei 1948; Luo 2005). This can also be termed "relationalism" (Ho and Chiu 1998; Hwang 2000; Ho et al. 2001). Second, there is a special type of *guanxi* called "familiar *guanxi*," which is absent from Western culture. There are three types of *guanxi* in the Chinese egocentric social network, as shown in Figure 6.1—i.e., simulated familial *guanxi*, familiar *guanxi*, and weak *guanxi* (Hwang 1987; Luo 2005, 2006). Three different moral standards and behavioral patterns apply for the three categories: simulated familial *guanxi* follow the "rule of need"; familiar *guanxi* fit the "rule of favor exchange"; and weak *guanxi* fall under the "rule of equity" (Hwang 1987; Luo 2006). In each category of *guanxi*, we can find behavior indicating the presence of real trust.

By definition, simulated familial *guanxi* are the trustworthiest relationships in Chinese society, and most evidence confirms this view (Wang and Liu 2003).

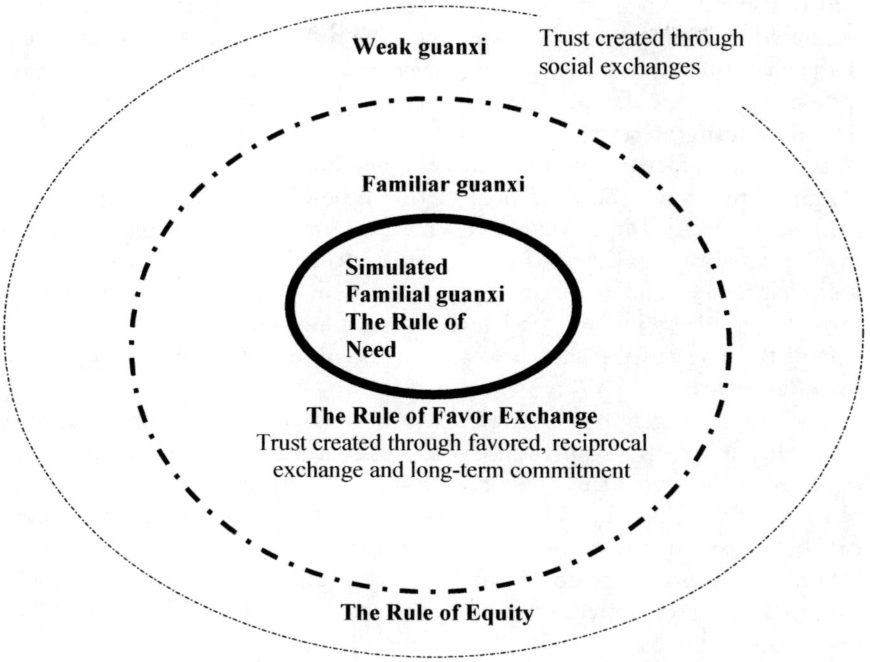

Figure 6.1 The three categories of Chinese *guanxi* and real trust in each category.

However, in our study we find no ties of this type in the outsourcing networks of the hi-tech industry. Weak *guanxi* are often built up in the process of good cooperation in outsourcing relations. Before reaching a purchase agreement, a manufacturer always asks its potential vendors to provide a small quantity of their product to check their quality control in mass production. In this step of evaluating performance, the quality of a vendor's product and service are key to keeping a business going. The vendor's trustworthy behavior is the base on which the manufacturer builds its trust. The "encapsulated interest account of trust" (Hardin 2001, p. 3) explains this sort of trust well. This theory states that, in caring for each other's interests, one party shows trustworthy behavior in repeated exchanges, and the other side thus gradually builds trust in him or her. However, trust of this sort is calculative rather than real trust.

There is also some evidence of real trust in weak *guanxi*, that is, in behaviors of social exchange. As Blau (1964) argues, unlike in economic exchanges, a person engaging in social exchanges cannot expect instant rewards, and thus needs to believe in the goodwill of the other party that will result in future reciprocity. Social exchange in the outsourcing process is best seen in the "good service" of vendors. A vendor's extra service may include overtime work for emergent orders, joint R&D (resource and development), and rendering help in crisis management. These extra services cannot be regulated by contracts or the manufacturer's regulations. Vendors may render such good services due to their lower power status. This kind of behavior may signal calculative trust only, because vendors use "good service" to gain long-term interests.

If the manufacturer reciprocates the vendor's goodwill, it is definitely a sign of real trust. Because help of this type offered by a manufacturer cannot be specified in a written contract, exchanges of this sort inevitably involve risk, and real trust is thus required to believe that the other party will reciprocate. The manufacturer gives up using power to force vendors to provide "good service"; instead, it chooses to show goodwill in the expectation of future return. Real trust can thus be observed in the reciprocity of manufacturers.

Social exchanges may occur between two firms, but favor exchanges exist only between two persons, who in general are high-ranking executives from the two firms. Favor exchange is a kind of social exchange, but differs from social exchange in several ways. First, favor exchanges can be classified under the name of brotherhood. Second, both sides in a familiar *guanxi* need to satisfy the real needs of the other party, and cannot ask for recompense because they are like brothers. Third, familiar *guanxi* are, above all, instrumental exchange relations, so the favor-taker needs to remember the debt in his or her "favor account." Although the favor-giver must not mention it again, the favor-taker needs to remember to return the favor as soon as the opportunity arises. Thus, it is exchange under the name of friendship. Last, most favors are for specific personal needs, which include face-giving and face-saving behaviors, as well as providing urgently needed practical assistance. The arguments made by both the strength of strong ties (Krackhardt 1992) and social exchange theories (Blau 1964) help explain the existence of real trust in Chinese familiar *guanxi*. Favor exchange among high-ranking managers is always a sign that real trust exists in their transactions.

A review of the embeddedness argument leads us to understand how a firm utilizes trust relationships to reduce uncertainty in a transaction. There are always some institutional mechanisms to reduce uncertainty. Some are written in document form, such as contracts, company regulations, and formal business processes (defined as the formal mechanisms in Table 6.1); some are not, for example, industrial community norms and technological rationales (defined as informal mechanisms). We question to what extent these institutional mechanisms control uncertainty in a transaction. The uncontrolled part is where trust comes into play. Rousseau et al. (1998) have made a similar observation: "In a sense, trust is not a control mechanism but a substitute for control, reflecting a positive attitude about another's motives" (p. 399). In the following study we analyze uncertainty in a network form of contract, and how a firm can combine institutional mechanisms and trust relationships to control this uncertainty.

Table 6. 1 The Six Steps in the Outsourcing Process and Governance Mechanisms

Searching for vendors	
Uncertainty	Unable to find a proper vendor.
Formal mechanisms	A formal standard process of searching for vendors. A list of evaluation items and evaluation criterion.
Informal mechanisms	A standard industrial measurement to measure the quality of samples.
The role of social relations	Social relations with minimum trust function here as a reference and a recommendation.
Reaching a purchase agreement	
Uncertainty	Unable to regulate the vendor's behavior.
Formal mechanism	A formal agreement to write down obligations of each side.
Informal mechanisms	Industrial community norms generally offer fairly standard terms along the lines of this type of agreement.
The role of trust	Calculative trust may help both sides avoid overly detailed regulations.
Bargaining price	
Uncertainty	The risk of high price
Formal mechanisms	A standard procedure to evaluate the cost structure of the vendor.
Informal mechanisms	The vendor's cost plus a certain percentage profit as the price. Price-down every quarter.
The role of trust	Real trust between the two sides' representatives can make the bargaining process smoother.
Ordering and delivering	
Uncertainty	The risk of stopping assembly lines.
Formal mechanisms	Orders are formal contracts.
Informal mechanisms	Quarterly or even monthly demand predictions should be made by the manufactures. One to several vendors as supplementary suppliers.
The role of trust	A good relationship is helpful in persuading vendors to work overtime during times of increased operation, as well as to give first priority of supply during times of normal operation. Maintaining this good relationship requires real trust.
Monitoring contracts and managing equipment	
Uncertainty	The risk of poor quality of supply.
Formal mechanisms	A formal standard procedure of quality control. If the ratio of qualified products in the sample is lower than a certain percentage, the entire batch of supplies will be returned to the vendor.

(continued)

Table 6.1 The Six Steps in the Outsourcing Process and Governance Mechanisms (continued)

Searching for vendors	
Monitoring contracts and managing equipment	
Informal mechanisms	A standard industrial measurement to measure the quality of supply. Manufacturer keeps the molds and tools, but provides safeguard for vendors.
The role of trust	Calculative trust can save costs by using fewer samples, but benevolent actions with real trust help the vendor improve its production technology and management skills.
Evaluating performance and support	
Uncertainty	The risk of poor service in the long run.
Formal mechanisms	A standard procedure to evaluate vendors' performance periodically.
Informal mechanisms	Switching orders to the supplementary suppliers according to the vendor's service. The partnership relation may even be temporarily suspended.
The role of trust	Real trust helps provide technological support, joint R&D, and coordinated growth pace. In addition, real trust between the two sides' executives is usually able to provide solutions that will resolve any unpleasantness or discord.

Note. R&D = resource and development.

Data Sources

To answer the aforementioned question, we investigated two large manufacturers. One is a world-famous brand that produces computer peripherals and mobile phones; the other is the world's second-largest producer of CD drives. We also included 11 different vendors in our survey. In each case, several interviews were conducted with the relevant managers for the manufacturers and vendors, the purpose being to fully understand the control mechanisms in each step of the outsourcing process. Eventually a total of 31 interviews were conducted in the mainland cities of Dongguan and Suezhou, as well as in the Taiwanese city of Xinzhu. Before the interviews, we first collected ISO9000 documentation from one of the vendors, and analyzed hundreds of pages of documents required by this globally accepted business process. Table 6.1 is a map of the ISO9000 outsourcing process.

We focused on several questions in the in-depth interviews for each step: (a) What is the institutionalized mechanism controlling outsourcing actions for each step? (b) Is there any industrial norm or technological rationale controlling these actions? (c) To what extent do trust relationships operate in the contract? (d) In what circumstances do contract laws allow trust relationships to exert influence? (e) How is transaction cost influenced by the operation of trust relationships in this network governance? In the following section, we adopt the viewpoint of the manufacturers to analyze their outsourcing processes, transactional uncertainty, the formal and informal institutional mechanisms used to control the uncertainty, and the role of trust in their outsourcing.

WHERE IS TRUST POSSIBLE?

Searching for Vendors

Two departments in the manufacturer's organization are involved in this step. The procurement department takes charge of collecting the name list of potential vendors, whose product samples are sent to the R&D department. The R&D department examines the sample quality according to a standard industrial measurement, and certifies the reliability of vendors who meet the standard. A team of investigators is then organized to evaluate the qualified vendors' financial health, their R&D ability, production capacity, and factory efficiency. There are quantitative measurements for these evaluations. The best vendor is then generally chosen.

Social relations among high-ranking executives and R&D managers are helpful in this step. Because evaluating potential vendors is a costly process, very few firms among hundreds or even thousands of possible vendors are considered. As many studies show, weak ties with minimum trust function here as a reference and a recommendation (Burt 1992; Granovetter 1995).

Reaching a Purchase Agreement

When the potential vendor is selected as a partner, an agreement of cooperation is usually signed before a formal alliance is formed. In the very beginning, a comparatively small quantity of supplies is delivered. As this alliance grows over time, the manufacture may increase orders according to the development of their relationship. In this agreement, such things as quality requirements, principles that guide pricing, periodical discounts, predicted demand for the next year, and delivery methods are typically regulated. In Taiwan's hi-tech industry, industrial community norms generally offer fairly standard terms along these lines. However, many unexpected situations can occur, such as sharp increases or decreases in demand, huge variations in market price, unexpected accidents, quality control problems, and so on. Trust relationships may help both sides avoid overly detailed regulations. For example, punishment clauses may or may not be included. In the ODM agreements of a manufacturer (referred to here as CDRA Firm) with its American buyers, the punishment was precisely regulated, but in the agreements with its main metal molding vendor (referred to here as CDRA-PERJB Firm), good relations made the addition of such punishment clauses in their contracts unnecessary. This practice can be based on calculative trust, because the manufacturer holds long-term interest in the vendor and has various methods to guarantee its conducted behavior.

Bargaining Price

Price bargaining continues along the entire life cycle of a component. In terms of community norms in Taiwan's hi-tech industries, price is lowered almost every quarter according to the following four factors: (a) increasingly lower costs; (b) disparity between supply and demand; (c) new technology and the appearance of new competitors; and (d) terms of payment. Generally the vendor submits its cost structure for review; if the manufacturer approves the cost, they then add a certain percentage profit to the final price.

Trust relationships can smooth out the bargaining process. If a buyer trusts the vendor, the vendor's cost analysis will be approved more quickly and both parties can easily agree on a price. In the absence of such a relationship, the cost comparisons made by the manufacturer between a particular vendor and its competitors may continue to create new tensions.

Without a good relationship, price bargaining always becomes a tense negotiation process for the manufacturer and vendors, and sometimes ends in the breakup of established ties. The smooth negotiation process is based on both long-term cooperation between the two firms and friendship between the two negotiation representatives. In addition to calculation of long-term interests, real trust in familiar *guanxi* also plays a certain role in bargaining prices.

Ordering and Delivering

The predicted annual demand is often stated in the previously mentioned partnership agreement, and quarterly or even monthly predictions are usually made by the manufacturers to allow vendors sufficient time to make appropriate preparations. However, the most important contracts are those orders offered on a daily basis. Following the schedules laid out by the production department, the procurement department issues orders to vendors each day. Vendors follow these orders and deliver the required quantity to a given location. One main vendor generally receives these orders, along with one or more vendors functioning as supplementary suppliers to guarantee nonstop supply to assembly lines.

However, the market uncertainty within hi-tech industries is so high that occasionally there may be variations of up to 50 percent from the original forecast, and key components can go out of stock overnight. A prediction of demand that is too high produces costly inventory, but a prediction that it too low exposes a firm to the risk of stopping assembly lines. A good procurement manager takes the responsibility for keeping the assembly lines running, because the losses incurred as a result of stopping the production process are intolerably high. A good relationship between the manufacturer and the vendor is extremely helpful in persuading vendors to work overtime during times of increased production, as well as to gain first priority of supply during times of normal operation. As stated, the good service of vendors may signal only calculative trust, but the reciprocal behaviors of the manufacturer definitely show goodwill and real trust.

Monitoring Contracts and Managing Equipment

The quality control (QC) and production departments play the most important roles in this step. Once the supplies are delivered to the manufacturer's storage facility, samples will be randomly chosen by the QC to check quality. Measurements of quality follow the technological standards of the industry—if the ratio of qualified products in the sample is lower than a certain percentage, the entire batch of supplies will be returned to the vendor.

Trust can save significant costs by using fewer samples than in the regular procedure. Full trust in a vendor's quality may even render this QC process unnecessary, so supplies can be sent directly to the assembly line. On the other hand, uncertainty regarding the quality of a vendor's supplies may result in the manufacturer selecting a higher percentage of each order from that vendor for sampling. In even more extreme cases, a QC team may be dispatched to the vendor's factory to oversee operations on an ongoing basis. This trust is generally based on a long history of good product quality, so it is calculative.

The problem of managing equipment comes from asset specificity. Williamson (1985) has stated that specific investment is always a serious problem in any relational contract between firms. Who invests and controls specific equipment? Is there any safeguard installed, as stated in Williamson's (1985) hostage model in relational contract form III? Following the community norm, molds and tools are generally invested in by vendors, but are stored by the manufacturer. A hostage is required unless the manufacturer can take advantage of its greater power to exempt itself from this obligation. However, there are exceptions in the relation between the manufacturer and its main metal molding vendor. In their joint R&D project, the vendor invests in all molds and tools, and the manufacturer guarantees that it will purchase a certain quantity at a higher price at the beginning of the project. Trust relationships make this guarantee reliable.

Trust relationships are also useful for a vendor when its supplies repeatedly fail to pass the buyer's QC standards. Without real trust, the buyer only needs to follow the regulations to punish the vendor. In such a case, the buyer may show goodwill and dispatch a QC team to help the vendor improve its production technology and management skills. Both sides try to pinpoint where the problems are occurring. Without real trust between both sides, benevolent actions may not occur, and cooperation may be endangered.

Evaluating Performance and Support

An evaluation of a vendor's overall performance is required as part of the manufacturer's standard outsourcing procedure. The buyer may switch orders to other vendors if satisfactory improvements have not been made. The partnership relation may even be temporarily suspended due to irresolvable differences.

Rewards are certainly a result of good performance. A larger quantity of orders and more technological support are generally offered to good vendors. As the buyer designs new products, good vendors may subcontract more parts and even join the design team. Joint R&D is a significant indication of better cooperation. Long-term cooperation requires good coordination. For example, the manufacturer we studied grew very quickly—it took only a few years for it to grow from a medium-sized firm to one of the three largest in the world. Good vendors, like its main plastic supplier, helped sustain the manufacturer's pace of growth.

A trust relationship is very helpful in this coordination process because high-ranking managers on both sides often become involved in negotiations. Informal and friendly talks are usually able to provide solutions that will resolve any unpleasantness or discord. The real trust embedded in familiar *guanxi* plays an extremely important role in this process.

WHY IS TRUST NECESSARY IN CHINESE TRANSACTIONS?

Minimum Trust Necessary to Initiate a Transaction

Building a partnership relationship is not only an issue of technique, quality control, and price, but in Chinese eyes also an issue of personality, good fit, and benevolence. Examining samples and knowing the vendor's brand name are generally not enough. Further information concerning the vendor's reputation, culture, and the behavior of its leadership are also necessary. A trustworthy middleman is, therefore, very useful. As stated, high-ranking executives and R&D managers often play this role. Under the endorsement of these middlemen, the minimum trust necessary to start the costly procedure of investigating the vendor is established.

The Importance of Social Exchange

For the Chinese, giving favors, and thus saving credits in others' "favor accounts," is the best hedge against future uncertainties. For the manufacturer, the main goal of supply management is keeping inventory as low as possible and never taking the risk of stopping assembly lines. However, the market for hi-tech products is so volatile that real orders often differ hugely from earlier estimates of demand. At such times, the manufacturer needs the good service of its vendors. If demand far exceeds forecasts, then the vendor is called on to provide the extra labor needed to meet the targets for timely delivery. If it falls far short of expectations, then the vendor is expected to absorb the surplus of material inventory due to the manufacturer's faulty forecasts. In exchange for this service above and beyond contract requirements, the manufacturer usually offers favors to the vendor in the areas of price bargaining and technological assistance.

As described in the previous section, there are some practices in the outsourcing process that are not included in written contracts, company regulations, or industrial community norms. These practices create the possibility for flexible operations. In an unstable and changing business environment, having such flexibility is vital. Why do manufacturers often prefer to give favors to a vendor and then expect a voluntary return during times of need, rather than using their power to coerce vendors into providing such good service? One reason is information asymmetry. Some vendors have specific state-of-the-art technology, which can be an area that the manufacturer is unable to fully control. By offering favors first, the manufacturer cultivates the goodwill of the vendor, which creates an expectation that the vendor will be responsible in its dealings with the manufacturer by sharing information in its areas of expertise.

Trust Fits With the Chinese Emphasis on Favor Exchange Over Use of Power

The third reason that trust is necessary in Chinese transactions is that many Chinese have a keen sense of the uncertainty of life. There is an old Chinese proverb that luck stays on the east bank of a river for thirty years, but moves to the west bank for the next thirty years. In other words, those who are powerful today will not always be in that position. Applied to business, the vendor may someday become powerful and hold the key resources necessary for the survival of the manufacturer.

Even for unequal partners, although the exercise of power can force the weaker side to comply, overreliance on power may cause vendors to exit. "Changing partners is like divorce," said one purchase manager, because changing procedures is always costly. When a vendor decides to quit, its good service disappears, and its behavior may even become untrustworthy. It takes several months to find and switch orders to a reliable new partner.

It may take several more months to make cooperation as efficient as before. Because the process is so costly, the powerful side (in most cases, the manufacturer) needs to show benevolence to win vendors' loyalty.

The powerful side can take advantage of vendors in flexible operations and reject their requests for favors, especially in the process of price bargaining. However, usually a partnership of this sort will not be long lasting. The breakdown of the partnership may lead to revenge by the vendor in the future. The powerful side often gives favors to maintain a good image and minimize future uncertainty, even in outsourcing relationships that are slated to end for other reasons.

Building Up an Egocentric Trust Network

Apart from extra services provided and favors exchanged, friendship between high-ranking executives of the various partners is also vital to the cooperation of their firms. What motivates executives to make friends for the sake of their companies? Executives build familiar *guanxi* not only for present transactions, but also for the possibility of future cooperation, and even to gain personal favor exchanges in the future. As stated, in the Chinese view, familiar *guanxi* are generally considered the best way to protect against future uncertainty. A Chinese executive attempts to build up his or her egocentric network of familiar *guanxi* by taking advantage of current opportunities for cooperation. In the transactional process, the executive can observe his or her partners' personality, and include those with trustworthy and benevolent traits in his or her personal network. Good personal relations not only help the executive to gain more cooperative opportunities for their company, they also help them develop the egocentric network that is so vital for their career advancement. The executive may mobilize these resources to achieve individual goals by means of personal cooperation. This kind of relationship may last a long time, even longer than the ties between the executive's firms, and can cover a wide diversity of fields including joint investment, transactions for personal purposes, knowledge sharing, mediation of key persons, and so on.

CONCLUSIONS AND DISCUSSIONS

Conclusions

After a detailed review of the outsourcing process within Taiwan's hi-tech firms, our main findings can be stated as follows:

1. Formal contracts, business processes that follow IS9000 standards, company regulations, industry technological standards, and community norms all play an important part in network governance of

relational contracts. However, trust still functions as a lubricant in economic exchange and communication. As summarized in Table 6.1, in the searching process, weak *guanxi* provide the minimum trust needed to initiate investigation of a vendor's qualifications. In signing an agreement and during the bargaining process, trust makes cost analysis easy and punishment clauses unnecessary. In the ordering process, trust allows both sides to be flexible and willing to coordinate with each other. In the monitoring process, faith in a vendor's quality helps reduce costs and the effort required to check quality. In managing equipment, trust relationships make joint R&D possible and the use of safeguards on specific investments unnecessary. In evaluating a vendor's performance, close interaction between executives on both sides helps to settle disputes. Although trust relationships are not the only governance mechanism in Taiwan's hi-tech firm network, they are, without doubt, a vital one.

2. Industry technological standards are extremely strong in hi-tech industries, as one commonly used slogan within this community illustrates—"no quality, no deals." Some sociologists put undue emphasis on the importance of trust relationships and social control in network forms of transaction, as Powell (1990) stated in his paper "Neither Market nor Hierarchy":

   > Network forms of exchange, however, entail indefinite, sequential transactions within the context of a general pattern of interaction. Sanctions are typically normative rather than legal. . . . In markets the standard strategy is to drive the hardest possible bargain in the immediate exchange. In networks, the preferred option is often one of creating indebtedness and reliance over the long haul. . . . Reciprocity is central to discussion of network forms of organization. (pp.301, 304)

   However, in our findings, trust relationships cannot be viewed as the only factor, or even the most important one, in controlling outsourcing processes. The written contract, a firm's internal management procedures, as well as trust relationships are all relevant. The governance structure of outsourcing in the Taiwanese hi-tech industry is a combination of market, hierarchy, and network mechanisms.

3. Because the highest possible transaction costs result from stopping assembly lines, hedging against this uncertainty becomes the main task of procurement managers. Long-term contracts can be used to purchase the minimum required amounts of key components, and good relations with key vendors are the main mechanism for acquiring extra supplies during times of increased operations. A manufacturer often creates indebtedness by offering reasonable prices when the market is on the buyer's side, but asks for first priority in return from the vendors when key components are out of stock. In highly

uncertain markets like the one for electronic components, fierce fluctuation and periodical business cycles constitute the best reasons for building good relations with key vendors.

4. Real trust, defined in terms of social and favor exchanges, can still be found in Taiwan's high-tech industry. This has to do with a Chinese cultural awareness of uncertainty and the function of good relations as a safeguard against such uncertainty. In addition, Chinese culture also emphasizes harmony, so most Chinese prefer to exchange favors instead of relying on brute power. Last, executives frequently engage in social exchanges not only on behalf of their companies, but to build up their own egocentric social network as well. Given that we have found that real trust plays an important role in a globally competitive industry with high technology requirements, we expect that more trust is needed in transactions involving labor, knowledge, and services in other industries with a high level of uncertainty as well.

Limitations

This chapter has a number of limitations that should be pointed out. Its purpose is to analyze the role of trust relationships in network governance, so we do not investigate how these trust relationships are built. Social relations are helpful in searching for potential vendors, but trust between the buyer and the vendor is generally not rooted in these social relations. The saying "no quality, no deal" indicates that trust relationships are developed through successful cooperation and satisfaction with product quality. Calculative trust is tied up with real trust in this trust development process. The buyer generally tries to collect relevant information that will increase the dependence of the vendor on itself and decrease its dependence on the vendor so that the vendor's behavior can be more effectively predicted and regulated. Even deterrence methods may be employed, if necessary, to make the vendor comply. At the same time, the buyer often shows generosity to the vendor, and asks the vendor to reciprocate in times of need. Different buyer strategies determine different ways of utilizing these two types of trust.

In this study, two kinds of behavior are identified as signals of calculative trust, i.e., trustworthy behavior based on long-term interest and the social exchange of the powerless side. On the other hand, two indicators demonstrate real trust: (a) when the powerful side gives up using power but engages in social exchanges, and (b) when executives of both sides exchange favors to keep familiar *guanxi* with each other. By employing these indicators, we can roughly analyze how different kinds of trust function in various steps of outsourcing. However, the Chinese generally mix these two types of trust, so it is difficult for observers to clearly distinguish one from the other.

The Chinese are calculative in social exchanges. As stated, favor exchange in familiar *guanxi* aims at resource-saving and risk-hedging needs, although it is conducted under the name of brotherhood. In a sense, it can be reduced to the calculative variety. But time is the key for distinguishing between calculative and real trust. Favor exchanges are often for the purpose of unknown opportunities to cooperate in the future. The Chinese may engage in favor exchanges to hedge against bad luck in the future. Even more, the Chinese sometimes save the repayment of favors for the following generations. When the time period of an exchange lasts more than 30 or even 100 years, nothing can be predictable and calculation becomes useless. This is a subject beyond the scope of this chapter, and must await future studies that explore these complex issues.

Our data is limited. Both manufacturers are based in northern Taiwan and set up their factories in the Mainland. One is a CD-drive producer and the other has a CD-drive department, which is the focus of our study. There are many common practices, as stated, but also some differences. For example, one manufacturer's contract is more detailed than the others,' so that the manufacturer employs more formal mechanisms. However, the most important difference between the two cases is their strategy. The one with a detailed contract focuses its searching efforts on low-cost vendors, and the other puts more emphasis on the R&D ability of vendors. The CD-drive producer gives those with good R&D ability better treatment, so a rough contract leaves more room for unequal treatment. Future studies need to include cases based in different locations and in various industries so that cultural and industrial comparisons are possible.

Close relations with vendors may cause negative effects. On the one hand, closure raises social capital (Coleman 1990), but on the other hand, it may exclude new ideas and competition. The manufacturers notice the danger and establish mechanisms to reduce its damage. For example, the sourcing departments keep searching for new vendors and the quality control departments keep monitoring product quality. The buyers and executives cannot make decisions alone. However, closure is still possible and structural data can detect it. Unfortunately, our survey focused on dyadic relations so that there is a limitation to conclusions on the possible damage caused by closure. Future studies should include more data from the entire industry.

After examining the role of trust in each step of the outsourcing processes, we have found the network governance of Taiwanese hi-tech firms to be a mixture of market bargaining, legal contracts, company regulations, industry technological standards, community norms, power maneuvers, and trust relationships. The method of governance also varies, depending on the buyer's trust in different vendors. This chapter explores only a small part of this complex issue. More studies on the detailed processes controlling transactional uncertainty are needed in the future.

NOTES

Thanks go to Taiwan's NSC for financial support via Projects NSC93–2412-H-007–003 and NSC91–2416-H-155–014.

REFERENCES

Andaleeb, S. S. 1992. "The Trust Concept: Research Issues for Channels of Distribution." *Research in Marketing*, 11: 1–34.

Barley, S., J. Freeman, and R. Hybels. 1992. "Strategic Alliances in Commercial Biotechnology." In *Networks and Organizations*, eds. N. Nohria and R.G. Eccles, 311–347. Boston: Harvard Business School Press.

Blau, P. 1964. *Exchange and Power in Social Life*. New York: Wiley.

Bromiley, P., and L. L. Cummings. 1995. "Transactions Costs in Organizations With Trust." *Research on Negotiation in Organization*, 5: 219–47.

Burt, R. 1992. *Structural Holes: The Social Structure of Competition*. Cambridge, MA: Harvard University Press.

Casson, Mark C. 1982. *The Entrepreneur: An Economic Theory*. Oxford, NY: Martin Robertson.

Chang, W. A., and C. S. Kao. 1996. "State and Business—An Analysis of the Rise of the Semiconductor Industry in Taiwan." Paper presented at International Conference of Economic Governance and Flexible Production in East Asia sites in Tsing-Hua University, 3–6 October 1996.

———. and M. L. Pan. 1997. "Flexible Production and Subcontracting Networks." Paper presented at Annual International Conference of Institute of East Asian Economics and Societies sites in TungHai University, Taiwan, 21–22 March 1997.

Chen, C. H. 1994. *Subcontracting Networks and SocialLlife*. Taipei: Lien-Jin Press.

———. 1995. *Financial Networks and Social Life*. Taipei: Lien-Jin Press.

Chen, D. S. and S. C. Jou. 1996. "Patterns of Inter-Organizational Relations in Technology and Capital Intensive Industries." Paper presented at International Conference of Economic Governance and Flexible Production in East Asia sites in Tsing-Hua University, 3–6 October 1996.

Coase, R. H. 1937. "The Nature of the Firm." In *The Nature of the Firm*, ed. O. W. a. S. Winter, 18–33. New York: Oxford University Press, 1993.

Coleman, J. 1990. *Foundations of Social Theory*. Cambridge, MA: Harvard University Press.

Creed, D., and R. Miles. 1996. "Trust in Organizations." In *Trust in Organization*, eds. R. M. Kramer and T. Tyler 16–38. London: Sage Publication.'

Dore, R. 1992. "Goodwill and the Spirit of Market Capitalism." In *The Sociology of Economic Life*, eds. M. Granovetter and R. Swedberg, 159–180. Boulder, CO: Wesview Press.

Fei, H. T. 1948. *Peasant Life in China*. London: Routledge and Kegan.

Geertz, C. 1963. *Peddler and Princes*. Chicago: University of Chicago Press.

———. 1978. "The Bazaar Economy: Information and Search in Peasant Marketing." *American Economics Review*, 68: 28–32.

Gulati, R. 1995. "Social Structure and Alliance Formation Patterns: A Longitudinal Analysis." *Administrative Science Quarterly*, 40: 619–52.

Granovetter, M. 1973. "The Strength of Weak Tie." *American Journal of Sociology*, 78: 1360–80.

———. 1985. "Economic Action and Social Structure: The Problem of Embeddedness." *American Journal of Sociology*, 91: 481–510.

———. 1992. "Economic Institutions as Social Constructions: A Framework for Analysis." *Acta Sociologica*, 35: 3–11.

———. 1994. "Business Groups." *The Handbook of Economic Sociology*, eds. N. Smelser and R. Swedberg 453–475. Princeton, NJ: Russell Sage Foundation

———. 1995. "Coase Revisited: Business Groups in the Modern Economy." *Industrial and Corporate Change*, 4: 130–93.

———. 2002. "A Theoretical Agenda for Economic Sociology." In *The New Economic Sociology: Development in an Emerging Field*, eds. F. G. Mauro, C. Randall, P. England, and M. Meyer, 35–60. New York: Russell Sage Foundation.

Hamilton, G. G., W. Zeile, and W. J. Kim. 1990. "The Network Structures of East Asian Economies." In *Capitalism in Contrasting Cultures*, eds. R. S. Clegg and S. G. Redding 105–129. New York: Walter de Gruyter.

———. and C. S. Kao. 1990. "The Institutional Foundations of Chinese Business: The Family Firm in Taiwan." *Comparative Social Research*, 12: 135–51.

Hardin, R. 2001. "Conceptions and Explanations of Trust." In *Trust in Society*, ed. K. S. Cook, 3–39. New York: Russell Sage.

Hemmert, M. 1999. "Intermediate Organization Revisited: A Framework for the Vertical Division of Labor in Manufacturing and the Case of the Japanese Assembly Industries." *Industrial and Corporate Change*, 8: 487–517.

Ho, D. Y. F., S. Q. Peng, and S. F. Chan. 2001. "An investigative research in teaching and learning in Chinese societies." In *Multiple Competencies and Self-Regulation Learning*, eds. C. Y. Chiu, F. Salili, and Y. Y.Hong, 215–244. Beijing: Information Age.

Ho, D. Y. F. and C. Y. Chiu. 1998. "Collective Representations as a Metaconstruct: An Analysis Based on Methodological Relationalism." *Culture and Psychology*, 4(3): 349–69.

Hwang, K. K. 1987. "Face and Favor: The Chinese Power Game." *American Journal of Sociology*, 92: 944–74.

———. 2000. "Chinese Relationalism: Theoretical Construction and Methodological Considerations." *Journal for The Theory of Social Behavior*, 30: 155–80.

Imai, K., and H. Itami. 1984. "Interpenetration of Organization and Market: Japan's Firm and Market in Comparison With the U.S." *International Journal of Industrial Organization*, 10: 285–310.

Krackhardt, D. 1992. "The Strength of Strong Ties: The Importance of Philos in Organizations." In *Networks and Organization*, eds. N. Nohria and R. G. Eccles, 216–239. Boston: Harvard Business School Press.

Luo, J. D. 1997. "The Significance of Network in the Initiation of Small Businesses in Taiwan." *Sociological Forum*, 12(2): 297–319.

———. 2005. "Particularistic Trust and General Trust—A Network Analysis in Chinese Organizations: Toward a Theory of Trust in Chinese Organizations." *Management and Organizational Review*, 3:437–58.

———. 2006. "Chinese Renmai—Ego-Centric Trust Network." *Research in Relational Management*, 3: 1–24.

——— and K. Yeh. 2001. "The Role of Trust in the Governance Structure of Subcontracting System—Taking Taiwanese Hi-Tech Firms as Examples." Paper presented at International Sunbelt Social Network Conference, Budapest, 25 April, 2001.

——— and K. Yeh. 2002. "From Family Business to Business Family: Transformation of Taiwan's Organizational Networks." *Hong Kong Journal of Sociology*, 3: 71–94.

Lyons, B., and J. Mehta. 1997. "Contracts, Opportunism and Trust: Self-Interest and Social Orientation." *Cambridge Journal of Economics*, 21: 239–57.

Macaulay, S. 1963. "Non-Contractual Relations in Business: A Preliminary Study." *American Sociological Review*, 28: 55–67.
North, D. C. 1990. *Institutions, Institutional Change, and Economic Performance*. Cambridge, MA: Cambridge University Press.
Perrow, C. 1992. "Small-Firm Networks." In *Networks and Organizations*, eds. N. Nohria and R. G. Eccles 445–470. Boston: Harvard Business School Press.
Powell, W. W. 1990. "Neither Market nor Hierarchy: Network Forms of Organization." *Research in Organizational Behavior*, 12: 295–336.
———. 1996. "Trust-Based Forms of Governance." In *Trust in Organizations*, eds. R. M. Kramer and T. R. Tyler, 51–67. London: Sage Publication.
Rousseau, D. M., S. B. Sitkin, R. Burt, and C. Camerer. 1998. "Not So Different After All: A Cross Discipline View of Trust." *Academy of Management Review*, 20(3): 393–404.
Saxenian, A. 1994. *Regional Advantage: Culture and Competition in Silicon Valley and Route 128*, Cambridge, MA: Harvard University Press.
Schumpeter, J.A. 1939. *Business Cycles*, New York: McGraw-Hill.
Shapiro, D., B. H. Sheppard, and L. Cheraskin. 1992. "Business on a Handshake." *Negotiation Journal*, 8(4): 365–77.
Sheppard, B. H., and M. Tuchinsky. 1996. "Micro-OB and the Network Organization." In *Trust in Organizations*, eds. R.M. Kramer and T. Tyler, 140–165. London: Sage Publication.
Wang, S. G., and X. Liu. 2003. "The Base of Trust." In *Trust in China Society*, eds. Y. F. Zheng and S. Q. Peng, 209–249. Beijing: China City Publication Press.
Williamson, O. 1975. "Transaction-Cost Economics: The Governance of Contractual Process." *Journal of Law and Economics*, 22(2): 233–61.
———. 1981. "The Economics of Organization: The Transaction Cost Approach." *American Journal of Sociology*, 87: 548–77.
———. 1985. *The Economic Institutions of Capitalism*. New York: Free Press.
———. 1996. *The Mechanisms of Governance*. New York: Oxford University Press.
Zucker, L. 1986. "Production of Trust: Institutional Sources of Economic Structure." *Research in Organizational Behavior*, 8: 53–111.

7 Constructed Network as Social Capital

The Transformation of Taiwan's Small and Medium Enterprise Organization

Chieh-Hsuan Chen

This chapter explores the economic action and social action in the transformation of Taiwan's small and medium enterprises. According to overall observation in the fieldwork, transformation is related to complicated social action. Therefore, enterprise focuses not only on economic capital formation but also on concentrating social capital cultivation. Social capital plays an important role in transferring social resources while business faces external challenges. To more deeply understand the relationship between social capital and enterprise action in the transformation process, we first discuss organization activity and network activity in Taiwan's small and medium businesses.

There are two activities categories that exist in Taiwan's small and medium enterprises. One is organization activity; the other is network activity. Both types of activities undergo transformations when facing changes in the domestic and external managing environment. The entrepreneurs continuously redefine their organization and network activities, thus creating various strategies and models for enterprises' transformation. In our field study of Taiwan's small and medium enterprises, we found that many entrepreneurs further expand the range and category of their organization activity by adjusting and changing for network activity, such as managing spontaneous networks and developing constructed networks (to be defined below). The most important concept is that in this process manufacturers are continuously changing the definition of resources; they also extend many constructed ways and transferring activities of social resources. We consider it a dynamic structural quality in Taiwan's industry economy. This chapter uses a social capital perspective to analyze the two activities, and clarify some fundamental problems of small and medium enterprises in their transformation of globalization challenges.

The argument in this chapter can be summarized as follows: first, we discuss how Taiwan's small and medium firms face global challenges and the need to upgrade or transform. Second, this upgrading and transformation require redefining and reconfiguring the organization of production. Third, in contrast to the routinized organizations where networks among firms (the central plant and satellite plants) follow practices guided by the existing institutional field—the spontaneous networks that mimic social relations in this institutional fields—the transformed production organization must adapt to other practices expected in other institutional fields, which may contain a hybrid of economic and social relations that cross institutional borders. Fourth, this chapter demonstrates how such transformation takes place in the organizational setting, moving from spontaneous (institutionally expected) networks to constructed (adaptation to multiple institutional expectations) networks. Fifth, this does not deny the contribution of social relations or social capital in constructed networks. Rather, it emphasizes the simultaneous significance of economic and social networks.

REDEFINING AND RECONFIGURING THE ORGANIZATION OF PRODUCTION

From our long-term study of Taiwan industry, the major issue in enterprise transformation and social changing is the definition of organization and network. What is enterprise organization? What are firms? What is a network among firms? If you have a clear definition, you can have further and specific action. Each transformation of enterprises and society forces actors to question what the enterprise is and what society is. The redefinition of the firm's organization means that their operation models will change entirely in the future. There are several samples in the development history of sociological knowledge. In his argument of "the nature of the firm," Coase (1990) begins with the transaction cost economy, which enables people to have different recognition and operating concepts (Williamson 1975, 1985) about the existing meaning of the firms. In reexamining "corporate concept," Peter Drucker (1986), the father of modern management philosophy, enables us to sense the importance of management for changing the management models of the firm's organization. We discover from the sociologist Coleman's (1990) theory of the "corporate actor" the huge scope of the change in the modern social structure. We thus have new understanding about social activity (Coase 1990). To redefine the firm's organization means that the actors have new ability to organize. Coase, Drucker, and Coleman are thus contributors to the notion that organizational changes are key to firms redefining and reconfiguring the organization of production (organizational changes depend on how the entrepreneurs redefine and reconfigure the organization of production). As researchers, we observe how the interviewed actors define and interpret their organization and network. It will be a good indicator for us to judge their transformation.

Only by clearly defining the meaning can precise actions result; redefining an organization's position in its own industry helps it to focus and allocate resources more efficiently. Only when there is the possibility for a new definition of meaning is there the possibility for new actions. How can this redefining of organization be possible? The key point is that the actor needs to have the ability to define and interpret. The most outstanding practitioner of the theory is the CEO of Taiwan Semiconductor Manufacturing Company Limited (TSMC), Morris Chang. Through his redefinition of so-called "OEM" (original equipment manufacturing), he created a new management and development model in the semiconductor industry. When he was with Texas Instruments, he noted a trend toward semiconductor circuit-designing firms. Compared to the United States, the specialized force cultivated by Taiwan's education system had a special trait—a high level of discipline. The labor force—from foremen, team leaders, directors, and plant managers, to engineers—was well suited to the manufacture of semiconductors. Combining the two could create an unprecedented OEM model (interview record E033P21b). This is an example in which the actor has to possess the ability to reorganize according to the reality. Morris Chang integrated the three relevant factors: a boom in the U.S. semiconductor circuit-designing market; Taiwan's highly disciplined education system that offers specialization and a high-quality labor force; and the manufacturing ability in Taiwan's industrial sector that allowed TSMC to be established, which initiated a new direction for the semiconductor industry. In other words, Chang's redefinition that led to reorganization of the industry was that, instead of integrating organization to design, manufacture, and assemble components, he was the first one to envision a single foundry in charge of manufacturing only. This unprecedented redefining of the industry led to reorganization—investment in and construction of a foundry.

To take the lead in the industry is not a simple task. However, the example of TSMC's OEM illustrates the fact that Taiwanese manufacturers, whose organizational forms have a competitive advantage in the future, must proceed with a new interpretation of their own industry. In a fast-changing society and industry environment with drastic upgrades in technology, the organization activity of the firms is a continuous process of new interpretation and adjustment. That is the only way that they can acquire a developing advantage. This phenomena occurred not only in the high-tech semiconductor industry, it also occurred in the traditional textile industry in the case of Everest Textile Co., Ltd.

Our 2003 study of Taiwan's textile industry confirmed our viewpoint that traditional industry is not as some scholars believed: an organization form that cared only about personal relationships (D.-S. Chen 2003; Luo 1998). From our interview with Everest Textile, we can see that it had transformed itself into a knowledge-intensive learning organization. General manager Ching Chuan Yeh's far-reaching positioning and interpreting of textile industry development demonstrates how an entrepreneur can lead an organization's transformation through intensive acquisition of knowledge while, at the same time, encouraging the transfer of social resources to transform employees from traditional physical laborers to knowledge workers. If we view this from the perspective of the transformation of Taiwanese industry and society, the social meaning of the Everest case study is an even better example than TSMC and deserves further analysis.

Our observation of Everest's transformation revealed three important concepts. The first is that entrepreneurs facilitated the reinterpretation of the textile industry. General manager Ching Chuan Yeh pointed out that the "Taiwan textile industry is not about the ability to do but how you do it." When Everest was considering its own transformation, it learned directly from the top American firm of the same line of business, Millicant Textile Company, which successfully transformed itself through learning. Like Everest, Millicant Textile Company was a traditional industry, but it was able to transform itself into a knowledge-intensive company, as Everest hoped to. Everest truly understood the meaning of "knowledge society" as proposed by Peter Drucker (1993), and turned the knowledge team into the company's organization activity. If we view it from Everest's angle, the organization transformation depends first on the entrepreneur's ambition, energy for learning, and vision. As Ching Chuan Yeh pointed out, "Men's quality and ambition decide everything." The fight for victory drives people to search for information. Ambition motivates employees' passion. This is difficult for others to imitate. If one wants to break the lines of division in an organization, one has to share information with others. People grow together after they have shared, and are inclined to continue in an unselfish way (interview record T040P25). We can therefore say that ambition, energy for learning, and vision will lead to reinterpretation and redefinition of organizations.

The second important concept is that organization activity is totally transformed after absorbing knowledge. The company's internal operation is a system of balancing human resources. Yeh stated, "It is the system's problem. Later we learned that when problems happened not to blame people but the system. We should find out what the problem is in the procedure system" (interview record T040P25). Whether applying "systematic procedure thinking," "teamwork," or "performance balance analysis," these all demonstrated Everest's breakthrough beyond the limitations of a traditional personal relationship operating model to form its own original internal operating system that utilized newly developed management knowledge. Everest's organization development absorbs and applies a series of strategic tools learned from other industries, such as global operating, product modularizing, cooperating, and work distribution. The operating and market strategies previously applied to machinery and high-tech industries have now been adopted by Everest as actual activities in managing. Everest's knowledge acquisition is transformed into organization activity that results in increasing profits by upgrading employee quality.

The third concept is that a knowledge working team should be created in the firm through transferring social resources to make the virtualized organization operation possible. Everest foresaw the knowledge society in its early development period, and utilized many and any outside training centers, educational groups, and government and academy resources to maintain continuous and intensive on-the-job training. When the employees become mature, the on-the-job-training gradually changes from outside educational institutions to internal educators. The percentage of outside educational institutions is only 10 percent compared with the 90 percent of internal educators. What makes Everest's on-the-job-training unique is not its courage to undertake unprecedented investment in human resources, but its utilization of social resource transferring to promote company growth. When a company's on-the-job training transfers from external into internal, it means that the knowledge work in the company is complete. Yeh stated, "We are now searching for internal lecturers. There are four or five people to prepare handouts for one subject. These people may be from different departments and they have to lecture to other departments and give them assignments to share the knowledge. They are naturally together and become close friends" (interview record T040P25). Everest created a unique learning culture; even the illiterate senior worker on the basic production line shares and acquires knowledge. Knowledge leads to an upgrade in the employee's quality. It also affords an opportunity to reorganize and create new groups and networks among workers.

This chapter does not take Everest as a representative sample of the traditional textile industry. During our recent investigation of Taiwan's small and medium enterprises, we sensed that the organization ability of small and medium enterprises needed to upgrade (C.-H. Chen 2006). The premise for upgrading organization ability is that the entrepreneurs must have vision to position enterprise management and development. In other words, the entrepreneurs should have the ability to reinterpret organization development and move the interpretation to organization activity. Finally, to summarize: upgrading as the environment changes is important. One important way to upgrade Taiwan's small and medium firms is to redefine or reinterpret the process of production. Redefining and reinterpretation become possible when entrepreneurs turn their attention to knowledge building. The path begins with knowledge learning and redefining, then reorganization, and finally, organization upgrading.

NETWORKS AMONG FIRMS IN THE EXISTING INSTITUTIONAL FIELD

The previous examples of TSMC and Everest give us a remarkable lesson: the integration of management knowledge and other professional knowledge enables firms to cross the borders of countries and cultures to perform the transfer of international resources (C.-H. Chen 1998). The foundation of transferring is knowledge. The most valuable item to transfer is also knowledge. Therefore, transferring knowledge within the world is the important factor for fundamentally changing the modern firm's social nature. In other words, in contrast to schools, which are organizations that produce knowledge, firms have to take more profound and thorough actions to facilitate knowledge learning and creativity. Because the firms are the body for creating knowledge as well as learning, the concept of the firm goes beyond just products. If what Drucker (1993) said about knowledge society is possible, the firms' social nature has to change from what Weber (1978, 1982, 1988) called "labor organization" to "knowledge organization." At this time, the major change in the society happens not only because the development of the knowledge organization itself, but because of the development would continuously change the social resources transferring method and format. Because firms are so important to social development, we have to reexamine the nature of the firm discussed in economics (Coase 1990; Williamson 1975, 1985, 1994).

If the existence of firms can embody the creative transferring from natural resources and human resources to social resources (C.-H. Chen 1998), then the social meaning of the existence of firms is not only, as Coase (1990) said, simply to lower the transaction cost in the market. If we view it from a purely economic perspective, the firms, as a producing unit of industry, business, and finance, have an important role in decreasing the transaction cost. However, as a motor of social development, the firms' social function has to be interpreted differently. Weber was the first to recognize the important social meaning in the emergence of firms. Weber (1982) considered the birth of rational modern capitalism as based on the new system developed from rational labor organization as a core. If we take Weber's labor organization as that of the modern firms, then the emergence of firms must have a certain social foundation. Weber's (1978, 1982, 1988) argument states that the emergence of rational labor organization has to combine many conditions to become possible, including propriety of materials, rational markets, labor, laws, technology, and the commercialization of economic life. In other words, the emergence of rational labor organization that developed from modern capitalism is based on the justification of Western society. From our viewpoint, Weber's study of modern Western capitalism illustrates that the emergence of rational labor organizations opens a new way for Western civilization to create "social resources." Following Weber's approach, we can here define "social resources" as the various results made in the institutional field.

The emergence of Western rational labor organization enables a new way for Western society to transfer resources, totally different combination formats of land, labor, and capital. Natural resources and human resources can create new social resources by new organization integration. Weber's approach was fully developed by the later social economist Schumpeter (1989,

1993). From our viewpoint, Schumpeter's most important contribution is not just the concept of entrepreneurs and entrepreneurship, but in redefining enterprise. Schumpeter theorizes that enterprise is a new combination of the dispersed factors in the society. Thus, entrepreneurs play an important function in performing these new combinations of factors. In other words, the fundamental function of entrepreneurs is to create enterprises. We learned from Weber's rational labor organization and Schumpeter's enterprises concept that the firm's existence is not just an economic phenomenon, but is also, more importantly, a social phenomenon. We can say that if there are no firms there is no capitalist society, and modernization is impossible. For modern society, firms provide a method of resources integration that cannot be found in traditional society. The study of firms should become the major issue of sociological study (DiMaggio 2001). In this approach, Coleman's (1990) research on the firms as modern corporate actors is straightforward and captures this core issue of modern social structure.

Weber's and Schumpeter's arguments clearly point out that the firm is a new form of combining social relationships and social resources. However, because they do not have the concept of "networks among firms," they cannot concretely describe the social meaning of the firms' existence. They go backward to discuss capitalism, the vast system concept. We pointed out from the previous TSMC and Everest examples that firms no longer exist as labor organizations, but as knowledge organizations. This point is not the only difference between our understanding and Weber's and Schumpeter's ideas about firms' social nature. From the angle of social resources creation and transferring, and contrary to the traditional handicraft industry, the firms as new organization actors are a kind of network action themselves. From the firm network activity dimension, we better understand why Badaracco (1991) would distinguish migratory knowledge from embedded knowledge. The firms' creating and acquisition of knowledge, and their traits of organization activity and network activity are perfectly reflected in public "migratory knowledge" and private network "embedded knowledge." Thus, the firms' progression from labor organizations to knowledge organizations reflects the network as a critical factor.

The firms play a unique "social resources transferring" role in modern society. We can analyze the firms' existence and development from not only the organization angle, but also from a network perspective (Alter and Hage 1993). Network analysis is important to the firm's behavior not only because of network scholars' thoughts on the flow of resources (Dubois and Hakansson 1997; Easton and Araujo 1997; Lomi and Grandi 1997), the flow of information (Lipparini and Sobrero 1997; Lutz 1997; Holland and Lockett 1997), and the advantages provided by trust (Ring 1997; Laat 1997; Casson and Cox 1997). The more important idea is that networks among firms demonstrate the practices of the institutional field.

Here we illustrate the situation by the "conspicuous credibility" concept I proposed in the book *Monetary Network and the Structure of Daily Life*

(C.-H. Chen 1995). "Conspicuous credibility" means some kind of social credit; people use ritual or symbolized objects to demonstrate the asset volume to achieve quasi-capital power in the market field (C.-H. Chen, 1995, pp. 278–79). We learn from the operation of Taiwan's small and medium enterprises in the real world that conspicuous credibility is necessary in the entrepreneurs' strategic operation. Because they are sensitive to and recognize the pressure from the environment when starting a business, the market and the present industrial network repulse and criticize newcomers. The entrepreneurs' conspicuous actions thus have the purpose of gaining market share or getting a foothold in the market. The targets they are trying to convince differ in their traits. Those targets are possibly the banks that want to finance capital, the prospects that can place orders, competitors, suppliers from whom to buy raw materials, and employees. From the entrepreneurs' show-off activity to construct their own credibility, the formation of the firms is different from the birth of people in their nature. The entrepreneurs have to clearly understand that without the acceptance by their existing market as system environment, and by other firms existing as organization environment, it is difficult for firms to succeed. For example, product quality is very good but is not accepted by the market, or the manufacturers that do business with the firm extend the accounts receivable. These illustrate the disadvantageous environment of market and industry network that newly established firms have to face.

When we break down the formation and development of Taiwan's firms into two different stages of analysis, we find that firms need various forms of conspicuous credibility strategy to manage and operate. We can reach one simple conclusion from the investigating procedure—successful entrepreneurs clearly know the importance of conspicuous credibility and know how to perform conspicuous activity to help their enterprises compete in the capital leverage stage. The entrepreneurs know who their conspicuous targets are, which firms they need to convince, and what is the limit of their conspicuous credibility. The situation illustrates that the formation of the firms is the formation of the firms' activity. The firms ensure their position in the market through their activity, and other related firms' are acquainted with their existence (Podolny 2005). Thus, as corporate actors, the nature of firms' activity is network oriented. The firms form networks by activity. There are two compasses that enable the firms' existence: networks as an activity unit and corporate organizations as another activity unit. It is meaningless to overemphasize the production system of manufactures as the base of the network (Biggart and Hamilton 1997). Once a firm has survived, it already has two factors at the same time. The point is then the relationship between the corporate organization activity unit and the network activity unit.

Realizing the importance of the network, contemporary sociologists start from the network point of view to study the structure in each life area (Fisher 1982; Wellman and Berkowiz 1988; Mizruchi and Schwartz 1987;

Knoke 1990; Castells 1996). In this chapter, the most important issue is the study of network applications to economic life and economic activity. It is obvious from the works of White (1970, 1992), Burt (1982, 1992, 2005), Granovetter (1974, 1992), Jarillo (1993), Ebers (1997a, 1997b) and Watts (2003) that interpersonal social networks derived from Granovetter's embedded perspective are more dominant in interpreting economic activity. From my personal perspective, this is the correct direction to develop, but if the network study of economic activity is overly influenced by Granovetter's embedded perspective and confuses the analysis of economic network and social network in economic life, it will limit the study of economic sociology. We want to clearly point out that because network activity is an indispensable factor, how we correctly reposition the relationship of social network and economic network is an important management concept.

After we clearly distinguish economic networks from social networks, we can understand the completely different social traits of the two networks. The economic network is a network that is linked by transaction activity among purely economic organizations (such as purely profit-making firms). The forming and connecting of economic networks is constrained by an economic principle, profit making. In other words, the development of the economic network is not the goal, but economic gain is. The nature of an economic network has to be distinguished from that of a social network. In our view, a social network can itself be the purpose of its existence. Thus, regardless of the social network's social-linking foundation, as long as interaction exists, its own characteristics can reveal its existing value. Constructing social networks within the social life compass does not need high-level calculating, or even cost concept. But in economic activity, acquiring valuable information costs you a certain amount (Stigler 1983; Arrow 1984). How to pay the least amount to receive the most value needs to be constrained by the marginal benefit effect principle.

In what kind of situation do entrepreneurs have to construct social networks within the social transferable compass? When the social network is not only served as a supporting system of social life and social existence for an entrepreneur, and is expected to become a useful resource for economic activity. In other words, on the one hand, entrepreneurs take the social network as the goal of their social life to fulfill their own lives, but on the other hand, they want to employ the social network as a means of achieving the goal of transferring it to become an economic resource. Under this premise, it is necessary to consider this principle when constructing social networks. Judging from the principle, we can explain how the different developing models of economic network and social network influence their managing performance in the firms' economic activity. Because the firms need to construct social networks within the social transferable compass, we need to clarify in what situation the firms need social resources transferring, and what social resources the firms need. If the firms do not need new social resources transferring, it is not, in fact, necessary to expand the social network unless these social networks are constructed for social life itself and have nothing to do with economic purpose.

During our ten-year study of over 500 of Taiwan's major industries, including textile, petroleum chemicals, machinery, and electronic information, we found that entrepreneurs especially need social resources transferring in three specific situations: establishment of a new firm, a firm in crisis, and a firm in transformation. Thus, construction of social network does have importance.

Regarding the first situation when the firm is established, actors planning to start their own businesses need the transferring of social resources most. The resources include acquiring investment information, establishing land or buildings, recruiting employees, financing capital, understanding the related legal issues, acquiring approval from each related government agency, acceptance of the market, receiving identification from clients, eliminating local resistance to the factories (if the plant is set up in industrial zone there are no problems), and how to overcome criticism from competitors. During this stage, the entrepreneurs need to proceed in what Schumpeter called the integration of various social factors. The construction of the social network has economic value. Through studying the start-up process of many of Taiwan's small and medium enterprises, we observe that the transfer from the social network of friends and relatives into the resources to establish business is the critical factor in the formation of enterprises. Saxenian's (1998, 2006) study on entrepreneurs of Chinese origin in Silicon Valley also provides support for this fact. What is needed most during the business start-up period is the transfer of social resources as a whole. The resources are in each system life area; the entrepreneurs have to be involved in all areas to acquire these useful resources. The social network creates extremely strong supporting functions. Whether the factories can be set up or not totally depends on the resources in the economic compass. The entrepreneurs' social network is necessary for acquiring resources outside the economic system.

The second situation is when the firms' existence is in crisis. There are many different situations in which firms can experience a survival crisis. However, from the study data of Taiwan's small and medium enterprises, no matter in which organization dimension the problems occur, they are reflected in financing when the firms cannot pay their bills. To get through the difficult time, the firms need a much greater transfer of their social resources than usual, especially the social resources regarding financial leverage. Again, this shows the importance of social resources to the firms. The Chinese saying, "Finance people in urgent situations, but not in poor," reflects the fact that the social network is an effective option when firms need capital in an emergency. The small and medium enterprises maintain a friendship relationship with other firms for the economic purpose of providing an immediate support network in times of crisis. One entrepreneur stated that he has several friends in the same industry; they treat him well not only because they are friends but also because they know that he is the sole owner of his company and totally in control of financial operations. If they have financing difficulties in the future, he will be a very important financial resource (interview record T906P25). Every entrepreneur needs to construct and maintain social networks to respond to any possible urgent situations. Compared to the beginning stage when entrepreneurs are starting their own business, the social network they need for solving crises is in special fields, especially the network that can be helpful in financial assistance.

The last situation is when the firms are facing the pressure of transformation. The firms in various industries have different transformation problems. Some need transformation in organization, some in products, some in technology, some in investment. From our point of view, the building of the firm's vertical organization development or horizontal organization expansion, the adjustments of organizational operations to maintain a current competitive advantage, keep a current profit, or simply continue to exist are all types of activity for transformation. Thus, they need to employ an unusual social network and to utilize social networks and their reconstruction. From our field study, we found that no matter what transformation the enterprises needed to acquire new investment channels, new technology, new knowledge in organizational management, or new products, the acquired resources cannot come solely from the organization internally. Once the firms consider transformation, the traits of the social resources they employ and transfer are different from their daily operation. As I mentioned before in the Everest example, the firms have to search for useful resources and transfer them to be employed in their own organization. At this time, the social resources that the firms need are not the same as when they were established, and not like the specific style that they need when they encounter crisis, but pretty subjective choices to meet their own needs. As for the forming of the choices, social network plays an indispensable role.

From this discussion we can understand that distinguishing economic networks from social networks does not mean social networks are not important in economic activity. By nature, social networks are not purely economic activity. They can help the firms transfer social resources in the aforementioned three situations. Therefore, we not only need to understand the firms' network activity but also their correct position in economic networks and social networks. The routinized organizations where networks among firms, the central plant, and satellite plants follow practices guided by the existing institutional field highlight the difficult challenge for entrepreneurs to manage networks in their business activity. Under- or overemphasizing social networks will harm the development of organizational capability (Chandler 1977, 1990; Lazonick and Mass 1995). This is why I discuss the redefining and reconfiguring of the organization of production as a priority. Second, we must grasp the network approach of firms and make a distinction between economic and social networks in different business contexts.

SPONTANEOUS NETWORK (INSTITUTIONALLY EXPECTED) AND CONSTRUCTED NETWORK (MULTIPLE INSTITUTIONAL EXPECTATIONS)

After clarifying social networks and economic networks, we can return to studying the basic dimension of the economic network of Taiwan's small and medium enterprises. For the firms, the construction of economic network capability demands organizational capability. We can clearly see from Taiwan's production satellite networks that, in the long term, whether it is the vertical relationship between the center plant and satellite plants or among horizontal plants, the transaction relationship foundation is still based on several economic factors such as product lead time, quality, and reasonable price. The firm's network as an activity unit is like the firm's organization as an activity unit. We can observe the economic network by the performance of its activity. If we look at the vertical structure of each industry, it is clear that the firms in the industry have various levels of economic networks. Deciding which firms can enter at which level depends on the firms' organizational capability. The organizational capability and the economic network are always in a dynamic balancing-competing situation. Under these premises, it is worth investigating the general structures of the development of the economic networks of Taiwan's small and medium enterprises, what we refer to here as "spontaneous network" and "constructed network" development.

"Spontaneous" means the network constructs the firms as activity units. The production satellite network in Taiwan from the 1970s to the '90s is representative of a spontaneous network. From the textile, petroleum chemicals, machinery, and electronic information industries, we can see the production of the end product for domestic need or for exporting results in different networks. The four levels of firms that we observed in the earlier period are family businesses, small factories, small and medium plants, and large plants. Through professional work distribution, the modes of production, semiproduct composition, components production, conversion, and finished products are done within each level. The various firms form an actual activity unit during the process of constructing specific products. No end product would be produced without the activity unit. The unique feature of Taiwan production is that most export products are not made by a single firm. They are all produced by coherent networks. Even the semiconductor industry is produced in this manner (interview record E041P21). We mentioned previously that Taiwan's small and medium enterprises are based on two activity units. One is the firm itself; the other is the economic network among the firms.

The spontaneous network thus means that the firm uses its organizational capability to participate in the network production.

Compared to spontaneous networks, constructed networks are not linked by end-product producing activity among the firms. The network construction does not have to be related to end-product production, but to the firms' strategies of organization developing and profiting. "Constructed network" refers to the network that the firms construct to develop their own organization capability. There are many strategic alliances and exchanges of property or shares in Taiwan's computer and semiconductor industries that can be referred to as constructed networks. We suggest that spontaneous networks are always economic networks and constructed networks are always social networks. In fact, spontaneous networks are intrinsic components of the production or performance of the firm, yet constructed networks are extrinsic to production and performance. Theoretically speaking, we can define spontaneous networks as routine, expected networks in the local institutional field, and state that constructed networks create opportunities for redefining and reconfiguring production and performance. Therefore, constructed networks must adapt to other practices expected in other institutional fields, which may contain a hybrid of economic and social relations that cross institutional borders. In other words, constructed networks must adapt to multiple institutional expectations.

According to Piore and Sabel's (1984) study of industrial production transformation and Best's (1990) *New Competition Age*, the change in global consumption and production models changed Taiwan's exporting structure. It enabled Taiwan's constructed networks to develop and spontaneous networks to adjust toward management. The development process of Taiwan's production satellite networks is network linked by producing export products. There are very flexible relationships among the firms. At the time that Taiwan's export products were low value added, and labor intensive, the coherent network management was involved in personal relationships and was also part of the social network. For example, the quality control staff could make a deal orally with the boss of related firms. But with the emergence of China and Southeastern Asia, Taiwan's low-value-added, labor-intensive products were replaced. Taiwan moved toward higher quality and value-added products. The networks of each industry also headed for systemized management models. From 1989 to 1991, many center plants began to make regulations for satellite firms to further regulate the business between them and minimize the interference of personal relationships.

Taiwan's production networks grew from loose spontaneous networks to management-style networks. Clearly defining business systems to expel personal and social network interference provides objective standards to judge whether satellite firms are suitable or not. The criteria can include delivery time, quality, and price. Once regulations are set and implemented, the satellite network becomes network activity. By moving from loose style to management style, the economic network becomes professional and further expels social networks, enabling the economic network to become more independent and have room to develop. It is, thus, clear that economic networks and social networks are opposites—one will replace the other. In fact, economic networks are "better" than social networks and, from the organizational managerial point of view, the latter needs to be replaced by the former. This is a central and important theme for this chapter. What I am arguing, then, is that Granovetter's (1974, 1992) embeddedness proposition is true only when social networks have not yet been replaced by economic networks. Under this premise, the upgrading of the organizational capability of the firms in the satellite network becomes much more important. With the regulating network management and increase of professionals in the business, the entrepreneurs have to backtrack and upgrade their economic dimension in managing the enterprises. Spontaneous network management makes the firms' organization activity and network activity among the firms unite in a new relationship that upgrades the firms' organizational capability and network capability.

The need for spontaneous networks to upgrade capability illustrates that the nature of the firms' activity is the collective behavior of networks. When the management of center plants forces satellite plants to upgrade, it also forces themselves to upgrade. From the end-product angle, all satellite plants can be thought of as a "virtualized production line." During our nearly three-year study of the transformation of small and medium enterprises, we found that many center plants encounter problems in helping the satellite plants to upgrade. Taiwan's small and medium enterprises develop to the stage that network management becomes the vital issue, and learning from other firms within the network becomes an important problem. Production and management knowledge thus becomes a resource for many small plants. The development of spontaneous network management opens up the learning energy of the small and medium enterprises. The transfer of social resources is organized by way of seminars, training, and social activity. The systemized spontaneous network illustrates an international economic structure changed in one way, and also that Taiwan's small and medium enterprises are changing their structure. The firm's network activity moves toward professional production, spontaneous networks in the existing network activity move to repulse social network interference and achieve managing resources to transfer to professional production. If spontaneous networks represent the relationship between the center plant and the satellite plants, I am saying that such relationships used to be social, rather than economic. Upgrading results in replacing social with economic relationships, but the networks are still spontaneous.

I mentioned previously the difference between spontaneous networks and constructed networks. Taiwan's small and medium enterprises are involved in the organization and network activity categories at the same time, and also need to manage the dual network activity. Taiwan's competitive advantage is in production (C.-H. Chen 2006). Most economic sociologists concur

(Hamilton and Biggart 1997; Orru 1997; Saxenian 1998; Hamilton 1998; Feenstra and Hamilton 2006). This is the reason why I discussed spontaneous networks and their transformation. Through the development of spontaneous networks, the firms' organizational capability develops. We can see the effect of the network structure in times of financial crisis. However, the firms linked by production are able to adapt to changes in social resources. I have observed that many labor-intensive small and medium plants were shut down after the former production network deconstructed because they did not facilitate the development of the constructed network and use the network to develop another production satellite network, or other transinvestment opportunities.

The T9 plant is an example; it worked on cotton textile production networks for a long period and neglected the study of the filament and knitting industries. When it sensed that the cotton industry in Taiwan was declining, it tried to expand its production network and still maintain its profit. It then entered the filament network and knitting network (interview record T906P25). The same situation also occurred in other industries. One home electronic appliances entrepreneur pointed out that the Taiwan home electronic appliances market was saturated. The players in the industry tend to go for the information industry market, and vice versa (interview record M116P25). A large construction firm in central Taiwan invested in high-tech business because the real estate market was in recession. The high-tech business doubled the revenue of the construction firm. These examples illustrate spontaneous networks as a foundation for expanding professional production. It is necessary for developing the direction of the firms. However, constructed networks are the key for the firms to change the industry. Braudel (1992) considered this the secret of capitalism's success. But a constructed network is more difficult than a spontaneous network in activity. How does one develop it?

How does a firm switch to another industry, and how can they choose a good industry to switch to? The question is similar to the situation of when the firm is starting business. How does one get information about good investments and transformation? The social network is important in this situation for the firms. In the spontaneous network of professional production the social network is repulsed, but it is indispensable in the constructed network strategy. The social network becomes the indicator to the firm's management of management capability in a conflicted situation. There are many production networks of small and medium enterprises that expanded from the existing network. As a typical example, our research subject, the Chia-Fu sponge firm, switched from sponge production to plastic injection for the information industry. Because it imported sponges and plastic raw materials, it could expand to a production network. But expanded investment was not related to its current network, so they needed to use personal relationships. How does one define social network in business management? How does one make professional management capability work with, and not in conflict with, a personal network? In other words, how do we manage social networks? This is the main point of discussion: spontaneous networks are economic and constructed networks are social. But in the transformation, firms need to move from spontaneous to constructed networks, so social networks assume more significance in the process and they are not expelled or repulsed by economic networks.

We have discussed the fact that spontaneous networks develop toward professional production and repulse social networks to enforce their professionalism. But constructed networks have to include social networks, because the social resources that the firms need depend on the society changing. The firms transfer the resources they need and employ different network strategies according to their development. However, when spontaneous networks move toward systemized managing, the firm's network professional is still the mainstream and the foundation of the entire economic network. To set up a constructed network is to upgrade the organizational capability for supporting both types of networks. In the firms' view, without a good spontaneous network it would be difficult for a constructed network to expand, and without constructed network development, it would be difficult for a spontaneous network to upgrade. Both networks are indispensable to the future development of Taiwan's small and medium enterprises.

CONSTRUCTED NETWORKS AS SOCIAL CAPITAL: SIMULTANEOUS SIGNIFICANCE OF ECONOMIC AND SOCIAL RELATIONS

Based on the previous discussion, this section explores a more significant issue: how constructed networks serve to upgrade the global competitive advantage for Taiwan's small and medium businesses. Observation from my fieldwork has shown that the successful exporting businesses in Taiwan are able to create a globally based social capital and economic capital. These cases have demonstrated an interesting problem: why do constructed networks become social capital? According to the previously mentioned characteristic of economic networks, constructed networks obviously belong to the category of economic networks. Therefore, I need to explain the resulting dilemma. According to spontaneous networks, if a company can survive in the market environment, it is the result of a successful transfer of a social network into an economic network. Under this situation, spontaneous networks are undoubtedly social capital as defined by Lin (2002). To achieve their economic goals, most small and medium businesses use social networks as a transfer instrument. But if constructed networks are fully oriented toward establishment in the global field, how can they be viewed as social capital?

From a broader perspective, constructed networks are simultaneously playing both roles, as economic capital and as social capital. Table 7.1 explains this point more clearly.

Table 7.1 Two Types of Networks in Taiwan's Small and Medium Enterprises

Two Types of Networks in Taiwan's Small and Medium Enterprises		
Conditions	Spontaneous Network	Constructed Network
Transfer field	Local	Global
Transfer foundation	One institutional field	Multiple institutional fields
Transfer instrument	Social network	Organizational capability
Transfer function	Economic capital	Social capital and economic capital

Table 7.1 shows the different types of networks in Taiwan's small and medium businesses in the past two decades. The spontaneous networks developed in local society; in contrast, the constructed networks often occurred in global society. Spontaneous networks can transfer social resources in one institutional field, but constructed networks must transfer social resources among different institutional environments in different countries or societies. If we check the transfer instruments in these two networks, spontaneous networks transfer resources through social networks and constructed networks depend on organizational capability. Finally, we see businesses forming spontaneous networks to create economic capital, but also constructed networks for social capital and economic capital. In terms of globalization, all businesses must develop globally based social capital to upgrade their competitive advantage. For this reason we need to discuss constructed networks as social capital.

Table 7.1 provides a simple comparison of the different structures and characteristics of two networks. On the one hand, in business transformation these two networks must be clearly distinguished from each other; on the other hand, they need to be combined. When a business makes a decision for its networking types, it considers the developing situation. But the key point is that creating globally based social capital is more difficult than locally based social capital. Therefore, paying more attention to constructed network formation is crucial for the transformation of businesses. But why does a business in the process of creating a constructed network need to consider economic capital and social capital at the same time? The major reason is that a business that wants to achieve institutional leverage in different countries and societies needs support in the form of personal trust. Globally based social capital is the proper mechanism for creating personal trust across different institutional settings. Taking all of these arguments into account, we can say that any business in transformation that hopes to obtain a global competitive advantage will be particularly serious in their accumulation of globally based social capital and the creation of successful constructed networks.

CONCLUSION

In my interview with TSMC, Morris Chang pointed out that in his view, doing OEM in Taiwan's semiconductor development is "mainstream," not "niche." Reflecting back to the first section, this is a very visionary interpretation in industry development. We see the structure development trend of the entire structure through this interpretation. To define an industry-managing format such as TSMC's "OEM" as mainstream indicates that if you have the overall control over composing possible forms of important international and domestic factors, then you can achieve the conclusion. We see that many firms are continually searching for a niche over a long period in the development process of Taiwan's small and medium enterprises. The more important issue is why different entrepreneurs have totally different interpretations of industry and firm organization. How do the entrepreneurs catch the trend of the mainstream to make the niche they find during their continuously searching for niches? The transformation pressure faced in this process provides a good opportunity to learn.

The research and interpretation of the future development of the firms' industry is directly linked with the firms' organization activity and network activity. Theoretically speaking, both the activity unit of corporate organization and of the network are important to the country's economic development of industry. The former is "organizational capability" development; the latter is "network capability" development. If the firms do not have good organizational capability development, it will be difficult to upgrade the entire network capability, and vice versa. TSMC and Everest, one in the advanced high-tech industry and the other in a traditional industry, both illustrated the fact that if Taiwan's spontaneous networks upgrade to the most competitive network in the world, firms in the network need to continuously upgrade their organization competence, because the coherent network will not be formed by domestic firms under the development of the constructed network. We can see this trend in many American and Japanese firms that have become coherent plants for domestic semiconductor plants. Once the transfer of social resources takes place in the international areas, the constructed network development of Taiwan's small and medium enterprises plays a role in upgrading spontaneous networks. Otherwise, Taiwan's production advantage for some industries will fade out. The question of to what stage the constructed network can expand depends on the organizational capability and world vision of the entrepreneurs and professional managers.

NOTES

This article was submitted for Tunghai University's 2004 Conference on the International Social Capital Conference: Institutions, Organizations and Communities

REFERENCES

Alter, C., and J. Hage. 1993. *Organizations Working Together.* London: Sage.

Arrow, K. J. 1984. *The Economics of Information.* Cambridge, MA: Belknap Press of Harvard University Press.

Badaracco, J. L. 1991. *The Knowledge Link: How Firms Compete Through Strategic Alliances.* Boston, MA: Harvard Business School Press.

Best, M. H. 1990. *The New Competition: Institutions of Industrial Restructuring.* Cambridge, MA: Harvard University Press.

Biggart, N. W. and G. G. Hamilton. 1997. "On the Limits of a Firm-Based Theory to Explain Business Networks: The Western Bias of Neoclassical Economics." In *The Economic Organization of East Asian Capitalism,* eds. M. Orru, N. W. Biggart, and G.G. Hamilton, 33–54. Thousand Oaks, CA: Sage.

Braudel, F. 1992. *The Perspective of the World: Civilization and Capitalism 15th-18th Century, Vol. 3.* Berkeley, CA: University of California Press.

Burt, R. S. 1982. *Toward a Structural Theory of Action: Network Models of Social Structure, Perception, and Action.* New York: Academic Press.

———. 1992. *Structural Holes: The Social Structure of Competition.* Cambridge, MA: Harvard University Press.

———. 2005. *Brokerage and Closure. An Introduction to Social Capital.* New York: Oxford University Press.

Casson, M., and H. Cox. 1997. "An Economic Model of Inter-Firm Networks." In *The Formation of Inter-Organization Networks,* ed. Mark Ebers, 174–196. New York: Oxford University Press.

Castells, M. 1996. *The Information Age: Economy, Society and Culture: The Rise of the Network Society, Vol. 1.* Oxford, UK: Blackwell.

Chandler, A. D. 1977. *The Visible Hand: The Managerial Revolution in American Business.* Cambridge, MA: Belknap Press of Harvard University Press.

———. 1990. *Scale and Scope: The Dynamics of Industrial Capitalism.* Cambridge, MA: Belknap Press of Harvard University Press.

Chen, C. H. 1995. *Huobi wangluo yu shenhuo jiegou: Difang jinrong, zhongxiao giye Taiwan shisu shehui zhi zhuanhua* (Monetary Network and the Structure of Daily Life: Local Finances, Small and Medium-sized Enterprises, and the Transformation of Folk Society in Taiwan). Taipei: Linking.

———. 1998. *Taiwan chanye de shehuixueyanjiu* (Sociological Research on Taiwan's Industries). Taipei: Linking.

———. 2006. "Toward World Number One: The Formation of Vertical Integration in Taiwanese Firms." Paper presented at Conference on Branding with Innovation: Taiwanese firms in the Age of Globalization, Tunghai University, June 16–17, 2006.

Chen, D. S. 2003. *Making it Integrated: Organizational Networks in Taiwan's Integrated-Circuit Industry.* Taipei: Chun-Hsueh Chu-Pan Yu-hsien Kung-Ssu.

Coase, R. H. 1990. *The Firm the Market and the Law.* Chicago, IL: University of Chicago Press.

Coleman, J. S. 1990. *Foundations of Social Theory.* Cambridge, MA: Belknap Press of Harvard University Press.

DiMaggio, P., ed. 2001. *The Twenty-First-Century Firm: Changing Economic Organization in International Perspective.* Princeton, NJ: Princeton University Press.

Drucker, P. F. 1993. *For the Future: The 1990s and Beyond.* New York: Truman Talley Books/Plume.

———. 1986. *Innovation and Entre-Preneurship: Practice and Principles.* New York: HarperBusiness.

Dubois, A., and H. Hakansson. 1997. "Relationships as Activity Links." *The Formation of Inter-Organization Networks*, ed. Mark Ebers, 43–65. New York: Oxford University Press.

Easton, G., and L. Araujo. 1997. "Inter-Firm Responses to Heterogeneity of Demand over Time." In *The Formation of Inter-Organization Networks*, ed. Mark Ebers, 66–94. New York: Oxford University Press.

Ebers, M. 1997a. "Explaining Inter-Organizational Network Formation." In *The Formation of Inter-Organization Networks*, ed. Mark Ebers, 3–40. New York: Oxford University Press.

———. (ed.) (1997b) *The Formation of Inter-Organizational Networks.* New York: Oxford University Press.

Feenstra, R. C., and G. G. Hamilton. 2006. *Emergent Economies, Divergent Paths: Economic Organization and International Trade in South Korea and Taiwan.* New York: Cambridge University Press.

Fisher, A. C. 1982. *To Dwell Among Friends.* Chicago, IL: University of Chicago Press.

Granovetter, M. 1974. *Getting A Job: A Study of Contacts and Careers.* Chicago, IL: University of Chicago Press.

———. 1992. *The Sociology of Economic Life.* Boulder, CO: Westview Press.

Hamilton, G.G. 1998. "Asian Business Networks In Transition or What Alan Greenspan Does not Know About The Asian Business Crisis." Paper presented at International Conference on Business Transformation and Social Change in East Asia, Tunghai University, May 22–23.

———. and Biggart, N. W. 1997. "Market, Culture, and Authority: A Comparative Analysis of Management and Organization in the Far East." In *The Economic Organization of East Asian Capitalism*, eds. M. Orru, N. W. Biggart, and G. G. Hamilton, 111–150. Thousand Oaks, CA: Sage.

Holland, C. P., and G. Lockett. 1997. "Mixed Mode Operation of Electronic Markets and Hierarchies." In *The Formation of Inter-Organization Networks*, ed. Mark Ebers, 238–262. New York: Oxford University Press.

Jarillo, J. C. 1993. *Strategic Networks: Creating the Borderless Organization.* Oxford, UK: Butterworth-Heinemann.

Knoke, D. 1990. *Political Networks: The Structural Perpective.* New York: Cambridge University Press.

De Laat, P. 1997. "Research and Development Alliances: Ensuring Trust by Mutual Commitments." In *The Formation of Inter-Organization Networks*, ed. Mark Ebers, 146–173. New York: Oxford University Press.

Lazonick, W., and W. Mass. 1995. *Organizational Capability and Competitive Advantage* (Edward Elgar Reference Collection). London: Edward Elgar.

Lin, N. 2002. *Social Capital: A Theory of Social and Action.* New York: Cambridge University Press.

Lipparini, A., and M. Sobrero. 1997. "Co-Ordinating Multi-Firm Innovative Processes: Entrepreneur as Catalyst in Small-Firm Networks." In *The Formation of Inter-Organization Networks*, ed. Mark Ebers, 199–219. New York: Oxford University Press.

Lomi, A., and A. Grandi. 1997. "The Network Structure of Inter-Firm Relationships in the Southern Italian Mechanical Industry." In *The Formation of Inter-Organization Networks*, ed. Mark Ebers, 95–110. New York: Oxford University Press.

Luo, J. D. 1998. "The Savings Behavior of Small Investors—A Case Study of Taiwan." *Economic Development and Cultural Change*, 46(4): 771–89.

Lutz, S. 1997. "Learning Through Intermediaries: The Case of Inter-Firm Research Collaborations." In *The Formation of Inter-Organization Networks*, ed. Mark Ebers, 220–237. New York: Oxford University Press.

Mizruchi, M. S., and M. Schwartz, eds. 1987. *Intercorporate Relations: The Structural Analysis of Business*. New York: Cambridge University Press.

Orru, M. 1997. "The Institutional Logic of Small-Firm Economies in Italy and Taiwan." In *The Economic Organization of East Asian Capitalism*, eds. M. Orru, N. W. Biggart, and G. G. Hamilton 340–367. Thousand Oaks, CA: Sage Publications.

Piore, M. J., and C. F. Sabel. 1984. *The Second Industrial Divide: Possibilities for Prosperity*. New York: Basic Books.

Podolny, J. M. 2005. *Status Signals: A Sociological Study of Market Competition*. Princeton, NJ: Princeton University Press.

Ring, P. S. 1997. "Processes Facilitating Reliance on Trust in Inter-Organizational Networks." In *The Formation of Inter-Organization Networks*, ed. Mark Ebers, 113–145. New York: Oxford University Press.

Saxenian, A. 1998. "Building a Transnational Technical Community: The Silicon Valley-HsinChu Connection." Paper presented at International Conference on Business Transformation and Social Change in East Asia, Tunghai University, May 22–23.

———. 2006. *The New Argonauts: Regional Advantage in a Global Economy*. Cambridge, MA: Harvard University Press.

Schumpeter, J. A. 1989. *Business Cycles: A Theoretical, Historical and Statistical Analysis the Capitalist Process*. New York: Porcupine Press.

———. 1993. *The Theory of Economic Development*. New Brunswick, NJ: Transaction Publishers.

Stigler, G. J. 1983. *The Organization of Industry*. Chicago, IL: University of Chicago Press.

Watts, D. J. 2003. *Small Worlds: The Dynamics of Networks between Order and Randomness*. Princeton, NJ: Princeton University Press.

Weber, M. 1978. *Economics And Society*. Berkeley, CA: University of California Press.

———. 1982. *General Economic History*. New York: Dover Publications.

———. 1988. *The Agrarian Sociology of Ancient Civilizations*. New York: Verso.

Wellman, B., and S. D. Berkowiz, eds. 1988. *Social Structures: A Network Approach*. New York: Cambridge University Press.

White, H. C. 1970. *Chains of Opportunity: System Models of Mobility in Organizations*. Cambridge, MA: Harvard University Press.

———. 1992. *Identity and Control: A Structural Theory of Social Action*. Princeton, NJ: Princeton University Press.

Williamson, O. E. 1975. *Markets and Hierarchies: Analysis and Antitrust Implications*. New York: The Free Press.

———. 1985. *The Economic Institutions of Capitalism: Firms, Markets, Relational Contracting*. New York: The Free Press.

———. 1994. "Transaction Cost Economics and Organization Theory." In *The Handbook of Economic Sociology*, eds. N. J. Smelser and R. Swedberg, 77–107. Princeton, NJ: Princeton University Press.

Part III

Social Capital in Communities

8 Production and Returns of Social Capital

Evidence from Urban China

Nan Lin, Dan Ao, and Lijun Song

PURPOSES

Social capital, or resources embedded in social networks, and its effect on attainment in the labor market has been extensively studied and documented in the literature (Lin 1999b). Initial evidence came from community studies (Lin, Ensel, and Vaughn 1981; Marsden and Hurlbert 1988). Attempts have been made to estimate this effect from national samples (e.g., De Graaf and Flap 1988; Angelusz and Tardos, forthcoming). This chapter makes a contribution to this growing literature with data from a national sample of urban residents in China. We examine the production of social capital, or what factors determine the variation of social capital among the sampled respondents; and the returns to social capital, or the effects of social capital on several attainment measures, including positions in the occupational hierarchy, supervisory responsibility, and wage. The chapter begins with a general introduction to social capital as a concept and theory, its measurements, and the processes of its production and returns that allow individuals to attain better jobs. Data from a recent survey conducted in a national sample of cities in China will be analyzed to illustrate these processes.

DEFINITION AND THEORY OF SOCIAL CAPITAL

In the broadest sense, social capital consists of elements of social structure (Coleman 1990). A more precise definition has been offered by Lin (1982, 1999a, 2001)[1] and Bourdieu (1983/1986)[2] as resources embedded in social networks. It may be measured operationally as the quantity or quality of resources, actual (i.e., mobilized) or virtual (e.g., perceived or accessed), embedded in one's networks.[3] A theory of social capital then follows this definition: *investment in social relations for expected returns* (Lin 2001). Investment in social relations produces social capital, which in turn generates expected returns. Social relations, in general, are dictated by the positions of the actors in the hierarchical or stratification structure and by their locations in social networks. Within these structural constraints, actors make choices in the retention and reciprocal relations with certain others; these choices represent investments of each actor's time and efforts. Social capital, then, consists of resources embedded in such invested relations. Such capital is expected to generate returns. Empirical investigation and verification focuses on the extent of actual realization of any returns.[4]

Much empirical work has verified the instrumental returns to social capital in the labor market. Cumulative evidence confirms that open networks and diversity in social capital brings about better information (Granovetter 1973; Burt 1992), better control (Burt 1992), or more influence (Lin 1982) resulting in relative advantages on the job market (Flap 1991; Erickson 2001), and in economic organizations (see review in Burt 2000). Yet much of the research focuses on returns to social capital rather than the production of social capital (see exceptions in Flap 1999 and Flap and Völker 2004). This chapter attempts to integrate the study of the production and returns of social capital, using a nationwide survey of urban residents in China. The next section proposes a model for such an integrative study.

PRODUCTION AND RETURNS OF SOCIAL CAPITAL: A DYNAMIC PROCESS

The theory of social capital not only captures both the social and capital elements but also reminds us that social capital must be viewed as both an endogenous and an exogenous variable in research. As an endogenous variable, it is necessary to investigate what factors lead to differential social capital—the production of social capital. As an exogenous variable, research must address the consequences that social capital may lead to—the returns to social capital.

Modeling the production and returns processes should recognize simultaneously the need to frame in concepts, applicable to multiple societies, and at the same time the need to reflect the reality of each society under study. An illustration of this process for urban China is presented in Figure 8.1. It depicts the hypothesized relations between a set of factors that lead to inequality of social capital, where social capital is the endogenous variable; as well as the attainment consequences of social capital, where social capital is the exogenous variable. We identify a number of contributing factors for the production of social capital. Two other types of capital, human capital and political capital, are included. The link between human capital and social capital has long been identified in the literature. For some, social capital is expected to facilitate human capital (Bourdieu 1983/1986; Coleman 1988). That is, broadened social contacts and accessed resources provide further opportunities to access and accumulate human capital. Coleman's study of parental networks and school cohesion suggests such a link. Bourdieu speculates that networks among the elites afford further reproduction of human capital. At the same time, human capital may be expected to facilitate social capital. Increased human capital should provide better positioning in the labor market, thus providing more social ties to richer and more diverse resources. Further, human capital should also offer resources and opportunities to participate in social activities, including participation in voluntary organizations. The intricacy and reciprocal relationships between human capital and social capital, although complicated,[5] nevertheless anticipates that human capital will play a significant role in the production of social capital.

The link between political capital and social capital gains significance in any political economy, where political or party identity constitutes a capital in that its investment brings about valuable resources embedded in such connections. In the case of China, the one-party system and the long-standing command economy (Walder 1986; Bian 1994) have long dictated political influence in the attainment process. Although the command system has undergone changes in the past decade, since the mid-1990s the overwhelmingly urban work force has remained occupied in the public and state sector (state-owned enterprises contributed more than half of the GDP in 2004).[6] A significant portion of the labor force still prefers to work in this sector for the relative job security, wage, compensation, and pension that it offers.

The Communist Party apparatus penetrates beyond the public sector. It is active in large-scale private and joint venture enterprises as well.

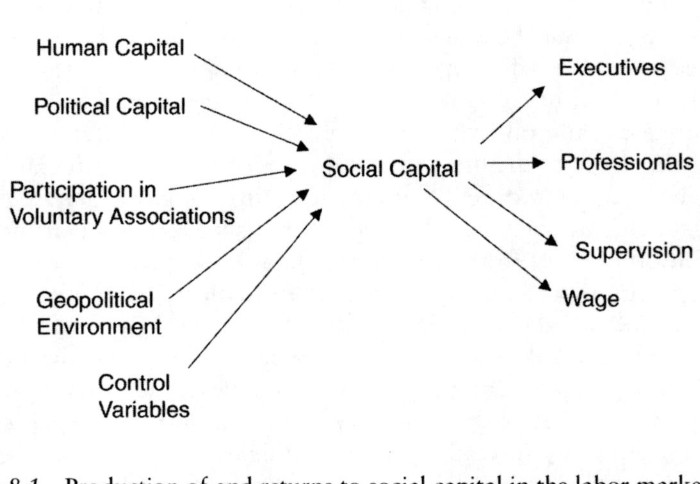

Figure 8.1 Production of and returns to social capital in the labor market.

Being a member of the Communist Party, therefore, ought to offer structural opportunities to access ties or other party members with better resources in the hierarchy. We also expect that the effect of political capital holds in other societies, where it finds different expressions.

Another factor is the emergence of civil engagement or networking in urban China. As China undergoes significant economic and social reforms, nongovernmental organizations have begun to emerge. Although the number remains limited and participation stays relatively low, these groups offer opportunities for connections to others that were previously not available. During the prereform period and even much of the early phase of the reform period (1978–early 1990s), networks for urban Chinese tended to be restricted to extended families, work units, neighborhoods, school ties, and political and governmental connections. However, as the economy diversifies and housing is privatized, movements into different economic sectors and more diversified work and residential settings have become possible. As a result, the contexts for networking have extended significantly, and awareness of and participation in nongovernmental associations and activities have increased. Such emerging connections should offer greater diversity in the individual's social capital.[7]

Finally, we explore the effect of the geopolitical forces in the ecological context. In most societies, cities assume geographic and political significance, due to their critical roles and locations in political, economic, and geographic hierarchies. In China, cities are clearly designated in three categories: those directly administered by the central government, those cities that are provincial capitals, and other cities. Beijing, Shanghai, Tianjin, and Chongqing are not only large in population, but also assume critically important political and/or economic significance in the northern, eastern, and central regions. They are under direct central government jurisdiction. All personnel and budget are under state control and allocation; as a result the cities are usually given priority in construction and developmental funding, and their workers enjoy higher rankings and benefits relative to their counterparts in other cities. Similarly, provincial capitals are focal administrative and political centers in different regions, and in most cases are the most important economic and financial hub of the province. Again, workers enjoy relative advantages in pay, bonuses, and other benefits (e.g., health services, housing, transportation) over workers in other cities in the province. The relative locations afford different opportunities to network with others with better power, wealth, and status—all valuable resources.

At the same time, the rise of the private sector and the penetration of foreign-invested capital and firms have complicated the previous orderly hierarchy among the cities. In the core (state-administered) cities, the penetration of foreign-invested capital and firms has gained momentum in the past decade, and provides a counterweight or alternative in the labor market for workers. More and more, workers now have the option of moving to the foreign-invested sector, despite the security offered by the state sector, for higher wages and greater chances for mobility. In the provinces, the private, small-sized firms have become pervasive, although the public sector (the state and collective firms) still holds the advantage in firm size and employment opportunity. Self-employed enterprises are catching on. It is rather in the peripheral (other) cities, where the penetration of the foreign-invested firms is few in number and size, that the public sector remains the dominant force in the labor market. The question of how these complex forces—the state sector, the foreign-invested sector, and the private sector—interplay across the different types of cities deserves research attention, especially during this transforming period. Nevertheless, we would expect that the geopolitical locations provide a macrostructural source of inequality in social capital.

Having better social capital should subsequently enhance returns in the labor market. We expect this relationship to hold, even after other significant factors are accounted for. Here we also expect human capital, political capital, networking activities, and the geopolitical environment to be important factors. Although these resources contribute to the acquisition of social capital, we expect that social capital, once acquired, will add to returns beyond the contributions from these resources. That is, social capital has the capacity of reproducing itself—social ties enhance more social ties, and thus produce even richer and more diverse resources. This reproduction assumes a momentum unaccounted for by human, political, and regional capital, and adds to the returns in the labor market. In certain societies, social capital of a political nature may assume exceptional significance, as in the case of China. Connections to cadres in higher positions may afford access to greater political influence, which may contribute to labor market outcomes as well. Thus, the measurement of social capital must be dictated in each society by the relevant and valuable resources embedded in social networks.

We now turn to examining these processes with a national sample of currently or previously employed adults residing in urban China.

DATA

The targets of the survey were adults, ranging in age between 21 and 64, currently or previously employed, registered and residing in urban cities. The sampling plan was a multistage systematic probability sample. At the initial stage, households in all urban cities were sequenced. The basic unit of sampling at this stage was a clustering of 19 consecutive households. The desired sample size was determined to be 3,535 to provide adequate subsamples for possible subgroup (gender, region, and so on) analyses. An interval was thus established and a random start number was drawn.

Starting from the top of the list of all households by cities, clusters of households were sampled, resulting in 184 clusters from 167 cities.[8]

At the second stage, all qualified respondents in each sampled household were identified, and the one whose birth date was closest to June 30 was designated as the sample respondent. A personal interview was conducted by professional interviewers between November 2004 and March 2005. After up to three attempts with each designated respondent and further sampling from adjacent households, if previous households failed to yield respondents, the response rate was about 40 percent. The relatively low response rate was due to several factors. We held the sampled respondents rigidly and without replacement. Respondents who could not be contacted and interviewed after the initial attempt and follow-ups were counted as lost. We also found that more and more urban residents in China are becoming less willing to be interviewed, and we made no effort to force their participation. The effects of the low response rates are difficult to estimate. It is difficult to find the appropriate census data from the sampled cities for currently or previously employed adults, aged 21 to 64. However, as we show later in the article, comparison of sample characteristics with Chinese census data was made to whatever extent possible. Strong correspondence in key parameters assures us that the sample provides credible estimates for the population under study. To further ensure against possible sample biases, the study incorporated critical control variables in all analyses.

The total sample size was 3,529. The sample was, approximately, evenly distributed between men (49.4 percent) and women (50.6 percent). This is consistent with the Chinese census (51.5 percent of 2005 urban residents are men). The average age was 39. The average number of years of education was 11.4. This is a higher number than the 2004 one percent national survey data for the urban population, where the average number of years of education was 9.4 for urban residents aged six and over. However, because we are focusing on employed adults only, an elevation of education should be expected.

The median income was in the range of RMB$10,000–14,000 per annum.[9] The 2005 national survey showed a median of RMB$10,493 for urban residents. For sectors of work unit, our survey showed that 56.4 percent of the respondents were in the state sector, and 8.8 percent were in the collectives. The 2005 one percent national survey showed that the corresponding percentages were 57.9 and 7.1 respectively. We, therefore, conclude that the study sample of employed urban residents shows a high degree of representation of the national parameters. Table 8.1 presents some characteristics of the study sample.

Also note that about 7 percent of the respondents worked for work units in state-administered cities (i.e., Beijing, Shanghai, Tianjin, and Chongqing); another 12 percent in provincial capitals;[10] and the remaining respondents, 82 percent, in other local cities.

Table 8.1 Summary of Sample Characteristics (Percent or Mean)

	Total (N = 3,529)	*Male (n = 1,743)*	*Female (n = 1,786)*	*Significance Test*[a]
Age	39.3	39.6	39.0	0.06
Age [b]	29.1	29.0	29.2	0.57
Education				
Secondary or lower	29.4%	25.8%	32.9%	
High school	25.2	24.8	25.5	
Associate college	26.1	25.3	26.9	
College and graduate	19.1	23.9	14.5	
Previous job experience				
No previous job	55.3%	52.9%	57.6%	
Held a previous nonexecutive/professional job	32.0	33.3	30.7	
Held a previous executive/ professional job	12.5	13.5	11.4	
Tenure (years)	10.2	10.7	9.7	0.00
Party member	21.9%	29.8%	14.1%	0.00
Voluntary organization participation	10.5%	11.5%	9.6%	0.06
Voluntary organization participation[b]	4.8%	5.1%	4.5%	0.47
Location of work unit				
State-administered city	6.7%	6.7%	6.8%	
Provincial capital city	11.6	10.3	12.8	
Other cities	81.7	83.0	80.4	
Sector of work unit				
State	56.4%	59.6%	53.2%	
Collective	8.8	6.9	10.7	
Shareholding	11.8	12.9	10.8	
Private	18.6	17.1	20.0	
Hong Kong/Macao/Taiwan	1.0	0.9	1.2	
Foreign/joint	1.1	1.2	1.0	
Other	2.3	1.5	3.1	
Present/last occupational group				
Executives	6.7%	10.0%	3.5%	

(continued)

Table 8.1 Summary of Sample Characteristics (Percent or Mean) *(continued)*

	Total *(N = 3,529)*	*Male* *(n = 1,743)*	*Female* *(n = 1,786)*	*Significance Test*[a]
Professionals	23.6	21.1	25.9	
Technicians	2.0	1.4	2.6	
Administrators	13.5	16.5	10.5	
Sales/service	26.8	20.2	33.2	
Workers	26.6	29.6	23.3	
Farmers	0.9	0.8	1.0	
Supervision in present/last job				
No supervision	75.7%	67.3%	83.9%	
Supervising someone who did not supervise	12.2	15.0	9.5	
Supervising someone who supervised	12.1	17.7	6.6	
Annual income of present/ last job				
(Chinese Yuan) Less than 6,000	24.1%	16.1	31.9%	
6,000–10,000	24.2	21.4	27.0	
10,000–14,000	21.3	22.6	20.1	
14,000–24,000	21.5	26.8	16.3	
24,000 and more	8.8	13.1	4.7	

[a]The significance levels for t tests on the equality of means for men and women. [b]At the time of finding the current/last job.

RESEARCH DESIGN

Following the previously explained articulation, we formulated two conceptual models: one for the production of social capital and another for the returns to social capital. To conserve space, the two models are integrated and presented in Figure 8.1. Human capital, political capital, networking activities, and the geopolitical environment (type of city where the work unit was located) are considered significant contributing factors for the production of social capital. It is conceivable that such relationships are reciprocal; for example, human or political capital enhances networking activities and networking activities enhance human and political capital.

We make no assumption or test of the casual patterns among them for the present study. They are simply considered exogenous to social capital.

For returns to social capital, we considered a variety of attainment variables including holding an executive or professional job, being a supervisor, and earning a higher wage. The measurements show that social capital was measured at the time that respondents were considering their current/last job; thus a temporal sequence was imposed between social capital and the outcome variables. Not shown in the figure are direct effects from the ultimate exogenous variables (i.e., human and political capital, networking activities, and the geopolitical environment and control variables) on the outcome variables that are allowed in the analyses. We make no argument that effects of these variables are completely mediated through social capital. Instead, we expect them to exert direct effects on the outcome variables, while social capital contributes as added value to the returns, even after their direct and indirect effects through social capital are accounted for.

MEASUREMENT OF KEY VARIABLES

Social Capital

Social capital was measured using the position-generator items (Lin and Dumin 1986; Lin, Fu, and Hsung 2001). We asked each respondent, "Do you know anyone among your relatives, friends, or acquaintances that has one of the following jobs? ('Knowing' means that you and the person can recognize and greet each other. If you know several persons that have a particular job, please name the person that comes to mind first.)" A list of 21 jobs then followed: nurse, writer, farmer, lawyer, middle-school teacher, housemaid, janitor, personnel manager, administrative assistant, hairdresser, accountant, security guard, production manager, operator in a factory, computer programmer, receptionist, taxi driver, professor, policeman, hotel bellboy, and CEO in a large corporation (see the list in Table 8.2).

Two sets of these position-generating items were included in the survey: (a) the present time, to capture current social capital; and (b) prior to the time the respondent began their present/last job, to capture social capital prior to the current/last job. Detailed information (such as gender, relationship to the respondent, and so on) in regard to each accessed occupation was only obtained for the current social capital.[11] In this study, *only prior social capital was examined*, to ascertain with a degree of confidence the possible temporal sequence of social capital and current job attainment.

Three indexes were generated from the 21 occupations: (a) *extensity*—the number of occupations a respondent could access, (2) *upper reachability*—the highest occupational prestige score among accessed occupations, and (3) *range*—the difference between the highest and lowest accessed occupational prestige scores.[12] Table 8.2 shows the distribution of general social capital prior to the current/last job by gender.

Table 8.2 Position Generator and Differential Access to General Social Capital (Prior to the Current/Last Job)

Position (Standard International Occupational Prestige Scale)	*Respondent Accessing*			
	Total (N = 3,529)	*Men (n = 1,743)*	*Women (n = 1,786)*	*Significance Test**
Professor (78)	18.1%	22.0%	14.3%	0.00
Lawyer (73)	21.7	25.3	18.3	0.00
CEO (70)	23.6	27.1	20.2	0.00
Production manager (63)	26.0	29.7	22.3	0.00
Middle-school teacher (60)	62.3	64.4	60.2	0.01
Personnel manager (60)	33.4	36.8	30.1	0.00
Writer (58)	6.9	7.9	6.0	0.03
Nurse (54)	43.6	42.5	44.7	0.19
Computer programmer (51)	14.7	17.5	11.9	0.00
Administrative assistant (49)	14.8	17.5	12.1	0.00
Accountant (49)	54.6	55.1	54.1	0.55
Policeman (40)	38.4	44.5	32.4	0.00
Farmer (38)	68.3	70.2	66.5	0.02
Receptionist (38)	13.1	13.9	12.4	0.18
Operator in a factory (34)	36.2	39.3	33.1	0.00
Hairdresser (32)	24.8	22.4	27.0	0.00
Taxi driver (31)	32.7	36.0	29.4	0.00
Security guard (30)	29.8	34.5	25.2	0.00
Housemaid (23)	12.9	11.8	14.0	0.05
Janitor (21)	20.0	19.6	20.3	0.60
Hotel bellboy (20)	19.3	22.4	16.3	0.00
Summary Indices				
Extensity				
Mean	6.1	6.6	5.7	0.00
SD	4.4	4.6	4.1	
Range of scores	0–21	0–21	0–21	
Range				
Mean	33.3	34.9	31.7	0.00
SD	16.4	16.3	16.4	
Range of scores	0–58	0–58	0–58	
Upper reachability				
Mean	63.7	64.9	62.5	0.00
SD	11.8	11.7	11.9	
Range of scores	20–78	30–78	20–78	

*The significance levels for t tests on the equality of means for males and females

Table 8.3 Factor Structure of Access to General Social Capital (Prior to the Current/Last Job)

Factor	*Sample* *(N = 3,529)*	*Men* *(n = 1,743)*	*Women* *(n = 1,786)*
I	2.50	2.50	2.49
II	0.37	0.37	0.38
III	0.12	0.12	0.13
Factor loadings on Factor I *			
Upper reachability	0.898	0.898	0.896
Extensity	0.879	0.879	0.877
Range	0.959	0.958	0.958
Factor scoring on Factor I *			
Upper reachability	0.360	0.360	0.360
Extensity	0.352	0.352	0.352
Range	0.384	0.384	0.385

*Principal Component Analysis, minimal eigenvalue of 1 and varimax rotation

A factor analysis, as shown in Table 8.3 (principal component and varimax rotation), yielded a single factor solution. A factor score based on the three indexes was thus constructed for each respondent. We also performed the factor analysis for men and women separately. Because the factor solution and patterns were essentially the same, the same factor-scoring procedure was used for all respondents.

Political Social Capital

We also listed three types of cadres in the position generator—(a) the leading cadre in the work unit; (b) the leading cadre of the supervising work unit; and (c) the regular civil servant or worker—to represent political social capital in China. The rank scores assigned to the three political positions are: the leading cadre of the supervising work unit (3), the leading cadre in the work unit (2), and the regular civil servant or worker (1). Three indexes were generated from the three political occupations: (a) *extensity*—the number of political occupations a respondent could access, (b) *upper reachability*—the rank score of the highest accessed political position, and (c) range—the rank score difference between the highest and lowest accessed political occupations. Table 8.4 shows the distribution of political social capital prior to the current/last job by gender and a factor analysis based on

Table 8.4 Position Generator and Differential Access to Political Social Capital (Prior to Current/Last Job)

Position (Rank Score)	*Respondent Accessing Total (N = 3,529)*	*Men (n = 1,743)*	*Women (n = 1,786)*	*Significance Test[a]*
Leading cadre of the supervising work unit (3)	29.6%	33.4%	25.8%	0.00
Leading cadre in the work unit (2)	53.6	58.1	49.2	0.00
Regular civil servant or worker (1)	44.1	47.6	40.7	0.01
Summary Indices				
Extensity				
Mean	1.3	1.4	1.2	0.00
S. D.	1.1	1.1	1.1	
Range of scores	0–3	0–3	0–3	
Range				
Mean	0.6	0.7	0.5	0.00
S. D.	0.8	0.8	0.8	
Range of scores	0–2	0–2	0–2	
Upper reachability				
Mean	1.5	1.7	1.4	0.00
S. D.	1.2	1.2	1.2	
Range of scores	0–3	0–3	0–3	
Factor Analysis				
I	2.75	2.76	2.74	
II	0.22	0.21	0.23	
III	0.03	0.03	0.03	
Factor loadings on Factor I[b]				
Upper reachability	0.940	0.941	0.937	
Extensity	0.990	0.990	0.990	
Range	0.942	0.945	0.937	
Factor scoring on Factor I[b]				
Upper reachability	0.342	0.341	0.343	
Extensity	0.360	0.359	0.362	
Range	0.342	0.342	0.342	

[a]The significance levels for t tests on the equality of means for men and women. [b]Principal Component Analysis, minimal eigenvalue of 1 and varimax rotation

the three indexes. Men have a relative advantage over women in accessing better political social capital.

Again, as shown in Table 8.4, the factor analysis resulted in a single factor solution. A factor score was then generated to measure political social capital for each respondent. No differences in factor loadings and scoring are found between the male and female subsamples.

Human Capital

Two measures were used to indicate human capital: (a) education, measured on a four-level scale (secondary or lower, high school, associate college, and college and graduate); and (b) tenure, measured by the number of years the respondents have/had worked in their present/last jobs (this variable is then logged).

Political Capital

This is indicated by membership in the Communist Party (1 = *member* and 0 = *not a member*).

Previous Job Experience

We aggregated the respondents into three groups in terms of previous jobs: (a) no previous job, (b) previously held a nonexecutive/professional job, and (c) previously held an executive/professional job. "No previous job" was used as the reference (missing) category; the other two categories became dummy variables.

Location of Work Unit

The cities where the respondents currently work were categorized into three levels: state-administered cities (Beijing, Tianjin, Shanghai, and Chongqing); provincial capital cities; and others.

Participation In Voluntary Associations

In the questionnaire, we asked each respondent if she or he participated in any of a list of voluntary associations: (a) academic, cultural; (b) medical, health; (c) religious; (d) athletic; (e) social services; (f) international; (g) economic, commercial, business; (h) clans; (i) alumni; (j) professional; or (k) other public benefits. Each response was coded as a dummy variable (1 = *yes* and 0 = *no*) and a sum total was calculated. We noted that the extent of participation in voluntary associations in China was low, averaging less than two participations. We thus decided to use a dummy variable, participation versus no participation.

Control Variables

The control variables included: (a) age (this variable is centered in this study) and (b) gender (1 = *male* and 0 = *female*).

Attainment Variables

Three attainment variables were considered here: (a) holding an executive/professional position, (b) having supervisory responsibility, and (c) earning a higher wage.

Holding an Executive or Professional Position

Each respondent's current/last job in the dataset was coded using 1995 Chinese Standard Classifications of Occupations (CSCO). As shown in Table 8.1, we categorized the jobs into seven occupational groups: (a) executives, (b) professionals, (c) technicians, (d) administrators, (e) sales/service, (f) workers, and (g) farmers. They were then grouped into three types of jobs: (h) executives, (i) professionals, and (j) other.

Being a Supervisor

Supervision was measured as a three-level ordered variable: 0 = *no supervision*; 1 = *supervising someone who did not supervise*; and 2 = *supervising someone who also supervised.*

Earning a Higher Wage

The final return variable is the annual income for the current/last job, which contained 27 categories. We adjusted the medians of the 27 income categories in accordance with the Consumer Price Index (CPI) published by the National Bureau of Statistics of China, standardized relative to 1990, that has an index weight of 100. We then took the logarithm of the CPI-adjusted medians.

Analytic Procedure

Following the model as specified in Figure 8.1, analyses were conducted in two phases. In the first phase, to account for the process of the production of social capital, the two measures of social capital—general social capital and political social capital—were used as the endogenous or dependent variables. The selected exogenous or independent variables were entered into each equation, including measures for human capital (education levels, previous job experience); political capital (party membership); networking activities (participation in voluntary associations); and the geopolitical environment (city location of the work unit). Control variables, including age, age squared (to account for nonlinear effects), and gender (male) were also entered.

In the second phase, we examined the returns to social capital. Equations were constructed for returns in the labor market, including holding a professional or executive job, being a supervisor, and wage. Entered into each equation were all the exogenous variables mentioned previously for the first phase, as well as the two types of social capital—general social capital and political social capital. Tenure—number of years in the current/last job (logged)—was an additional variable entered as another measure of human capital. For the wage equation, types of jobs and supervision were entered to reflect the fact that wage is dictated by these career locations.

The equations constructed were dictated by the nature of each endogenous variable. For social capital and wage as interval variables, we employed the ordinary least squares equations. For types of jobs (being an executive or professional), we used the multinomial logit regression, with "other jobs" as the missing or reference group for comparisons. For supervision as an ordinal variable (with three levels), we conducted the ordinal logit regression analysis.

Because the data set is a cross-sectional one, causal attributions are tentative at best. We tried to frame various variables in time sequences in the measurements (e.g., age, participation in voluntary associations, and social capital were measured relative to the time of entering into the current/last job[13]). However, we could not rule out the possibility that some of the exogenous variables interact or reciprocate in relations. Of particular concern were the interactions between gender and other variables, as gender turned out to be significant in almost all equations. We were also interested in the interactions between types of cities and other variables; thus we explored the interactions between gender and types of cities with other exogenous variables for all equations by conducting additional separate analyses for men and women, and types of cities separately. By comparing the coefficients of each key exogenous variable between the male and female subsamples and among the three types of cities, we could estimate if a significant interaction existed. We would then report any significant comparisons.

In the case of comparisons across the three types of cities, uneven distributions of subsample sizes and limited subsample size for the core state-administered cities (about 7 percent) made significant tests unreliable. We examined the relative normalized coefficients and their corresponding standard errors and made substantive interpretations.

Table 8.5 Determinants of General Social Capital (Prior to the Current/Last Job) Ordinary Least Squares Regression)

	General Social Capital
Age[a]	0.042***
Age squared[a]	–0.001***
Male gender	0.153***
Education (ref: Less than high school)	
High school	0.231***
Associate college	0.410***
Bachelor degree and above	0.650***
Previous job experience (ref: Previous job)	
No previous job	–0.218***
Had a previous executive/professional job	0.134**
Location of work unit (ref: Other cities)	
State-administered[b]	0.130**
Provincial capital	0.018
Party member	0.015
Participation in voluntary association[a]	0.414***
Constant	–0.971***
Observations	3300
Adjusted R^2	0.11

*Significant at 10%. **Significant at 5%. ***Significant at 1%. [a]ATT: At the time when R acquired the current/last job. [b]State-administered cities: Beijing, Tianjin, Shanghai, and Chongqing

PRODUCTION OF SOCIAL CAPITAL: FINDINGS

General Social Capital

Table 8.5 shows the ordinary least-squaring regression model that predicts the differential access to prior general social capital. In these models, age and participation in voluntary associations have been adjusted to their statuses at the time when the respondent was looking for the current/last job. Table 8.1 shows the distribution of these variables prior to the present/last jobs.

The results show that access to general social capital (prior to current/last job) was significantly related to: (a) human capital (higher education and having a previous job, especially when the previous job was an executive or professional position); (b) being a man; (c) participation in voluntary organizations; and (d) working in state-administered cities.

Additionally, age (between the ages 21 to 64) has a general modest negative effect on access to general social capital (due to the negative function of Age Squared).

We also examined data on men and women separately, and found that the only factor that might interact with gender was previously holding an executive/professional job. When we entered the interaction between gender and previous executive/professional experience (both centered) into the equation in Table 8.5, it did not yield a significant effect.

When we conducted separate analyses for each type of city, we found that the effects of being a man and having previous executive experience were more salient in the state-administered cities, whereas the effects of both high school and college education, and previous job experience were more salient in the other cities. The only salient variable for provincial capitals was party membership. Again, these tentative findings support the earlier observation that general social capital is somewhat richer and perhaps more relevant in the state-administered cities and other cities, in comparison with that in provincial capitals.

Table 8.6 Determinants of Political Social Capital (Prior to the Current/Last job) (Ordinary Least Squares Regression)

	Political Social Capital
Age [a]	0.018*
Age squared [a]	–0.000
Male gender	0.093***
Education (ref: Less than high school)	
High school	0.261***
Associate college	0.532***
Bachelor degree and above	0.749***
Previous job experience (ref: Previous job)	
No previous job	–0.202***
Had a previous executive/professional job	0.091*
Location of work unit (ref: Other cities)	
State-administered[b]	0.088
Provincial capital	–0.016
Party member	0.234***
Participation in voluntary association[a]	0.080
Constant	–0.763***
Observations	3404
Adjusted R-squared	0.14

*Significant at 10%. **Significant at 5%. ***Significant at 1%. [a]ATT: At the time when R acquired current/last job. [b]State-administered cities: Beijing, Tianjin, Shanghai, and Chongqing.

Political Social Capital

Table 8.6 shows the Ordinary Least-squaring Regression model that predicts the differential access to prior political social capital. Results indicate that prior political social capital was significantly affected by (a) being older in age; (b) being a man; (c) human capital (higher education and having a previous job); and (d) being a party member.

We also estimated these models for men and women separately, and found that political social capital was similarly determined by these independent variables for men and women. Separate analyses for types of city suggested that the effects of being a man, having a high school education, having previous work experience, and participating in voluntary associations were more salient in the state-administered cities, yet the effects of college education and party membership were more salient in other cities. Now a pattern begins to emerge. For the state-administered cities, acquisition of political social capital seemed to rely more on human capital (education and previous work experience) and networking, but in the other cities education and political assets seemed to be more important. There was still no salient pattern for acquiring political social capital in the provincial capitals.

RETURNS TO SOCIAL CAPITAL: FINDINGS

As discussed earlier, three attainment variables were examined: (a) holding an executive/professional position, (b) having supervisory responsibility, and (c) earning a higher wage.

Having an Executive or Professional Position

Table 8.7 presents the multinomial logit equations that predict which respondents were more likely to hold an executive or professional position. The reference (missing) category is all other jobs. To summarize, the results show that having an executive position is determined by (a) being older in age; (b) being a man; (c) having a higher level of education and having a previous job, especially an executive/professional job; (d) being in the private sector; (e) being a party member; and (f) having better political social capital. Note that being in a state-administered city or a provincial capital provided no advantage to becoming an executive. Rather, it was being a man, having a college education, previous job experiences, being in the private sector, and having political assets (i.e., party membership and political social capital) that enhanced the probability of being an executive.

Also shown in Table 8.7 are the results for being a professional. We summarize that the chances of being a professional, compared to all other jobs, are related to: (a) being older; (b) being a woman; (c) having higher

Table 8.7 Multinomial Logistic Regression on Executive, Professional, and Other Types of Jobs (Reference Category: Other Jobs)

	Executive Jobs	*Professional Jobs*
Age	1.059***	1.024***
Age squared	1.000	1.001
Male gender	1.869***	0.593***
Education (ref: Less than high school)		
High school	1.130	4.121***
Associate college	2.586***	17.708***
Bachelor degree and above	3.706***	23.115***
Previous job experience (ref: Previous job)		
No previous job	0.451***	2.048***
Previous executive job	3.242***	6.199***
Tenure (logged)	1.002	1.269***
Location of work unit (ref: Other cities)		
State-administered[a]	0.636	0.383***
Provincial capital	1.040	0.936
Sector of work unit (ref: State)		
Collective	1.449	0.664*
Shareholding	0.977	0.549***
Private	2.073***	0.792
Hong Kong/Macao/Taiwan	0.371	0.408
Foreign	1.183	0.512
Other	2.434*	0.174**
Party member	2.714***	0.988
Participation in voluntary association	1.339	1.122
General social capital[b]	0.913	1.090
Political social capital[b]	1.394***	1.072
Observations	3252	
Likelihood ratio chi^2 (42)	1244.76	
Pseudo R^2	0.2460	

*Significant at 10%. **Significant at 5%. ***Significant at 1%.

[a]State-administered cities: Beijing, Tianjin, Shanghai, and Chongqing. [b]ATT: At the time when R acquired current/last job.

education; (d) having previous executive/professional experience; (e) working longer at the current/last job; (f) not working in a state-administered city; and (g) being in the state sector. Professional jobs were thus more likely to be held by women, and these jobs were more concentrated in the state sector. On the other hand, these jobs were distributed across all cities, not just those that are state administered.

We examined the samples for men and women separately, and entered a possible interaction between gender and being in a state-administered city (centered). It yielded no significant results. Comparisons across the three types of cities showed that the only salient factor for becoming an executive in the state-administered cities is party membership. In the other cities, salient factors included age, being a man, high school and college education, previous job experience, being a party member, and having better political social capital. In the provincial capital, becoming an executive was associated with age, college education, having previously been an executive, and having better political social capital. There appears to be a trend that both human capital and political assets were significant in provincial capitals and other cities. In the state-administered cities, only political assets made a difference.

For becoming a professional in the state-administered cities, high school and college education and having been an executive in a previous job had salient effects. In the other cities, becoming a professional was more saliently associated with being a woman, having high school or college education, and having previously been an executive. In the provincial capitals, becoming a professional was associated with being older, having college education, and having been an executive in a previous job. In other words, becoming a professional was associated primarily with better human capital, and was quite similar in all types of cities.

Being a Supervisor

Supervision, as an ordered dependent variable, calls for ordinal logistic regression. Before estimating such a model, the first step is to test the assumption of proportionality. It turned out that the approximate likelihood-ratio test of proportionality of odds across response categories ($\chi^2(21) = 61.03$, Prob. > $\chi^2 = 0.0000$) is significant, which means that the assumption of proportionality is violated. In this case, we used the generalized ordinal logistic regression, which relaxes the proportional odds assumption and allows the effects of the explanatory variables to vary with the point at which the categories of the dependent variable are dichotomized. Consequently, no assumption of proportional odds (ordinal regression model) needs to be made. Table 8.8 presents the results from the generalized ordinal logistic regression. Two pairs of comparisons are made here: supervision versus no supervision; and supervision level 2 versus supervision level 1 and no supervision.

Table 8.8 Generalized Ordinal Logistic Regression on Supervision[a]

	Any supervision (2) and (3) vs. none (1)	*Supervision over two or more levels (3) vs. no supervision (1) or supervision over just one level (2)*
Age	1.029***	1.058***
Age squared	0.999***	0.999
Male gender	2.191***	2.189***
Education (ref: Less than high school)		
High school	1.046	1.316
Associate college	1.677***	1.741***
Bachelor degree and above	1.740***	2.126***
Previous job experience (ref: Previous job)		
No previous job	0.506***	0.682***
Previous executive job	1.348**	1.231
Tenure (logged)	1.038	0.865**
Location of work unit (ref: Other cities)		
State-administered[b]	0.971	0.429***
Provincial capital	1.201	1.048
Sector of work unit (ref: State)		
Collective	0.901	0.989
Shareholding	1.180	1.454**
Private	1.877***	1.745***
Hong Kong/Macao/Taiwan	2.146*	1.604
Foreign	1.167	1.953
Other	1.712*	3.348***
Party member	2.236***	2.089***
Participation in voluntary association	1.207	1.347*
General social capital[c]	1.289***	1.443***
Political social capital[c]	1.057	1.042
Observations	3301	
LR $\chi^2(42)$	614.50	
Pseudo R^2	0.1265	

(continued)

Table 8.8 Generalized Ordinal Logistic Regression on Supervision[a] *(continued)*

*Significant at 10%. **Significant at 5%. ***Significant at 1%. [a]Supervision: (1) = No supervision; (2) = Supervising someone who did not supervise; and (3) = Supervising someone who supervised. [b]State-administered cities: Beijing, Tianjin, Shanghai, and Chongqing. [c]ATT: At the time when R acquired current/last job.

To summarize the results, being a supervisor is determined by: (a) being older; (b) being a man; (c) having a college education; (d) having had previous jobs, especially executive jobs; (e) being in a shareholding, private, Hong Kong–Macao–Taiwan, or other firm; (f) being a party member; and (g) having better general social capital. Again, note that being in a state-administered or provincial capital city did not increase the probability of being a supervisor.

Additional examination of the samples for men and women suggested a further possible interaction between gender and being in a state-administered city. When we added this interaction (centered) into the equation in Table 8.8, it did not yield a significant effect. Analyses for each type of city suggested that being a man; having a college education; having had previous jobs, especially having previously been an executive; and having better general social capital were all significant. In addition, in the other cities, age, tenure, and being a party member were also helpful. For the provincial capitals, party membership also mattered. Human capital and social capital is thus associated with being a supervisor in all cities, but in the noncore cities party membership helped as well.

Having a Higher Wage

Table 8.9 displaces the findings from the OLS regression on the annual income. All previously analyzed exogenous and endogenous variables are in the equation, including types of jobs (i.e., professional, executive, or other) and supervision. We can summarize that having a higher income is associated with: (a) being younger; (b) being a man; (c) having a higher level of education; (d) having had previous jobs, but not necessarily executive level; (e) tenure; (f) being a professional or executive in the current job; (g) being a supervisor; (h) being in the state, private, or foreign sector; (i) being in a state-administered or provincial capital city; and (j) having both better general and political social capital.

We again examined the samples of men and women separately, and entered the possible interaction between gender and party membership (variables centered) into the equation. The interaction was not significant. In comparing across cities (also reported in Table 8.9), we found that in the state-administered cities, being a man, having a high school education, working in a foreign or Hong Kong-Macao-Taiwan firm, having tenure, and having better social capital were all associated with better

Table 8.9 Ordinary Least-Squares Regression on Annual Income by Types of Cities[a]

	Whole Sample	*Core Cities[b]*	*Provincial Capitals[b]*	*Other Cities[b]*
Age	–0.007***	–0.160*	–0.295***	–0.066***
Age squared	–0.000***	–0.011	–0.004	–0.075***
Male gender	0.232***	0.246***	0.138***	0.149***
Education (ref: Less than high school)				
High school	0.075**	0.132*	–0.046	0.050**
Associate college	0.246***	0.003	0.096	0.158***
Bachelor degree and above	0.405***	0.128	0.197***	0.218***
Previous job experience (ref: Previous job)				
No previous job	–0.086***	0.029	–0.030	-0.074***
Previous executive job	0.015	–0.033	0.014	–0.001
Tenure (logged)	0.088***	0.200**	0.282***	0.087***
Location of work unit (ref: Other cities)				
State-administered[c]	0.460***	—	—	—
Provincial capital	0.113***	—	—	—
Sector of work unit (ref: State)				
Collective	–0.228***	–0.056	–0.015	–0.098***
Shareholding	0.078**	0.034	0.120***	0.016
Private	0.198***	0.112	0.177***	0.091***
Hong Kong/Macao/Taiwan	0.048	0.136**	0.039	–0.005
Foreign	0.448***	0.150**	0.015	0.054***
Other	0.035	0.057	0.045	–0.002
Party member	–0.003	0.101	–0.035	–0.003
Participation in volunteer association	0.060	0.105	0.102**	0.011
General social capital[d]	0.039***	0.146**	0.099*	0.030
Political social capital[d]	0.035**	0.011	0.079	0.047**
Job status				
Other job (reference)				
Professional	0.118***	0.007	0.034	0.058***
Executive	0.158***	0.061	-0.016	0.084***

(continued)

Table 8.9 Ordinary Least-Squares Regression on Annual Income by Types of Cities[a] *(continued)*

	Whole Sample	*Core Cities[b]*	*Provincial Capitals[b]*	*Other Cities[b]*
No supervision (reference)				
Supervision (level 1)[e]	0.218***	0.097	0.150***	0.092***
Supervision (level 2)[e]	0.280***	–0.032	0.136***	0.131***
Constant	7.944***	12.175***	9.654***	10.856***
Observations	3199	218	375	2606
Adjusted R^2	0.23	0.23	0.31	0.22

*Significant at 10%. **Significant at 5%. ***Significant at 1%. aLOG of CPI-adjusted median value of 27 income categories (base year: 1990). bStandardized coefficients are reported in the models for different types of cities. cCore (state-administered) cities: Beijing, Tianjin, Shanghai, and Chongqing. dATT: At the time when R acquired current/last job. eSupervision: Level 1 = supervising someone who did not supervise; Level 2 = Supervising someone who also supervised.

income. In the provincial capitals, being younger, being a man, having a college education, working in the shareholding or private sector, having tenure, being a supervisor, participating in voluntary organizations, and having better social capital were significant. For the other cities, the only salient factors were having a college education and having a professional/executive job. Here we see that in the core cities and provincial capitals, wage was affected by human capital, networking, and social capital; whereas in other cities education and occupational positions seemed to be the only salient factors. We should note that another advantage in the core (state-administered) cities is that of working in a foreign/Hong Kong–Taiwan–Macao firm. In the provincial capitals, the private sector enjoys somewhat of an advantage in receiving better wages. No such advantage is apparent in the peripheral (other) cities.

SUMMARY AND DISCUSSION

As can be seen in the summary in Table 8.10, the data are quite rich and many interesting findings have emerged. We briefly summarize the effects of certain key variables, and comment on the general effects of geopolitics, as represented by the location of the work-unit cities.

First, significant factors for the production of general social capital include being older, being a man, having a high school education or higher, having previous job experience, being active in civic engagement or networking (participation in voluntary associations), and working in

Table 8.10 Summary of Findings

	Dependent Variable					
Predictor	*General Social Capital*	*Political Social Capital*	*Professional*	*Executive*	*Supervision*	*Income*
Age	–*	+	+	+	+	–
Male	+	+	–	+	+	+
Education						
High school	+	+	+			+
Associate college	+	+	+	+	+	+
Bachelor degree and above	+	+	+	+	+	+
Job experience	+	+	–	+	+	+
Previous job as executive/ professional	+	+	+	+	+	
Tenure			+			+
Location	Core		Cap./ Other			Core/ Cap.
Sector			State	Private	Private/ share/HK	Private/ share/ foreign
Party member		+		+	+	
Participation in voluntary association	+					
General social capital					+	+
Political social capital				+		+
Professional						+
Executive						+
Supervision						+

*For age range 21–64.

state-administered cities. That is, human capital and networking activities contribute to the inequality in general social capital. It is also clear that inequality in general social capital is associated with being in a core city (a state-administered city). Political capital (being a party member) provides no significant advantage. On the other hand, for political social capital (access to cadres at various levels) human capital is helpful, but being a party member is important as well.

What, then, are the effects on returns in the labor market of having differential general and political social capital, as well as human and political capital, networking activities, and residing in a geopolitically significant city? Consistent results show that general social capital enhances the chances of becoming a supervisor and having a better income, but political social capital promotes the chances of becoming an executive and having a better income.

The data suggest that, in China, there are different career paths and returns in the labor market. One path is to become a professional. Becoming a professional is affected more significantly by human capital (high school education, previous job experience), and not as significantly by social capital networking activities. This path is more open to women. Becoming an executive or supervisor not only requires better education (college) and previous job experience, but also political resources (being a party member). Further, social capital, either general social capital or political social capital, becomes significant. This path is more open to males. The inequality of gender is clearly reflected in these two types of careers. Note in Table 8.1 that, although both men and women had substantial college education, the men had a significant advantage in getting college degrees. In part, the paths chosen by men may thus be determined by their advantage in human capital. However, men additionally access better resources in their networks; these become added assets as they advance their careers in becoming an executive or supervisor. As shown in Table 8.9, either path seems to generate better wages, but again we note that having better social capital offers an additional advantage. It is thus not surprising that men continue to carry an advantage in achieving a better income.

Also note that, interestingly, it is college education that provides better returns, whereas even high-school education enhanced having better general social capital and political social capital. These different patterns suggest that social capital is acquired earlier on in one's educational experience, perhaps through the establishment of social connections during the high school years and beyond. It is also true that early experiences in civic engagement (participation in voluntary organizations) also help in acquiring better social capital. As one moves on in occupational careers, a high level of human capital (college education) becomes necessary for getting better jobs (e.g., becoming a professional, executive, or supervisor) and better pay.

Finally, some comments on the effects of the location of work units. Interpretations of the effects must go beyond merely statistical significance, as it is affected by subsample size. For example, in many cases the coefficients for the peripheral cities are statistically significant, simply because of the large subsample size. Rather, interpretations must be based on the relative magnitudes of the normalized coefficients across the three types of cities. Being in a particular location does make a difference in terms of the production and returns of social capital. In this study, the significance of geopolitics is represented by the location of the work unit, specified in the three types of cities in China. State-administered cities are the core political and economic cities. They are designated by the central government for their geopolitical-economic significance and provided with enormous amounts of financial, economic, communication, educational, and other resources. Residents also receive greater benefits in better housing, transportation, communication, hospitals, education, and, most important, choices in jobs, work units, and benefits. Alternative economic opportunities are also provided by the penetration of foreign-invested firms (also those from Hong Kong, Taiwan, and Macao). At the second tier are the provincial capitals. These are core cities for the provinces, where regional resources are invested and concentrated. A thriving private sector is emerging that provides an alternative to the public sector. In comparison, the peripheral (other) cities do not see, as of yet, penetration of foreign-invested firms, nor a thriving and pervasive private sector. Instead, they still largely rely on the public sector (the state- and collective-work units) for employment in the labor market.

Interestingly, social capital per se does not significantly differentiate across the different types of cities. Workers in the peripheral cities enjoy as many and diverse connections as those in the core cities. It is the returns to social capital that differ among the locations. Using wage as the ultimate returns indicator, it was clear that the workers in the core cities and provincial capitals benefit from their social capital, whereas those in the peripheral cities do not. Penetration of foreign-invested firms in the core cities has enriched the labor market, and has also enriched the embedded resources in social networks for many workers. The opportunity for accessing better resources in their networks becomes an added advantage. These connections turn into an advantage in the return of wages. In the provincial capitals where foreign-invested firms are few, the rise of the private sector has also provided somewhat of an advantage for workers to access and use their social capital. It is the peripheral (other) cities that lack both foreign investment and a thriving private sector; this lack constrains the returns to social capital. The relative structural opportunities and constraints across the three types of cities are in sharp contrast.

NOTES

An earlier version of this chapter was delivered as the keynote address at the III International Seminar on Regional Development, "Territory, Social Capital, and Regional Development," organized by the Graduate Program on Regional

Development of the University of Santa Cruz do Sul, October 17–20, 2006, in Santa Cruz do Sul, Rio Grande do Sul state, Brazil. Data used in this chapter were drawn from the thematic research project "Social Capital: Its Origins and Consequences," sponsored by Academia Sinica, Taiwan, through its Research Center for Humanities and Social Sciences, and the Institute of Sociology. The principal investigator of the project is Nan Lin.

1. Lin (1982) defined it as "resources accessible through one's direct and indirect ties" (p. 132).
2. Bourdieu (1983/1986) defined it as "the aggregate of the actual or potential resources which are linked to possession of a durable network of more or less institutionalized relationships of mutual acquaintance and recognition" (p. 248), and conceived it operationally as "the sum of resources, actual or virtual, that accrue to an individual or group by virtue of possessing a durable network or more or less institutionalized relationships of mutual acquaintance and recognition" (Bourdieu and Wacquant 1992, p. 119)
3. Although it is clear in the theoretical formulations that social networks are the basis for social capital, but not social capital themselves (Bourdieu 1983/1986; Lin 1982), subsequent statements have blurred the distinctions. Coleman (1988; 1990) states that "social capital inheres in the structure of relations between persons and among persons. It is lodged neither in individuals nor in physical implements of production" (1990, p. 302). Putnam (2000) equates social capital to features of social organization "such as networks, norms, and trust—that facilitate coordination and cooperation for mutual benefit." In his conceptual synthesis, Portes (1998) argues that social networks must be considered as the core of the concept. Elsewhere, Lin (1999a) has argued that a network-based theory of social capital provides the necessary theoretical foundation for a systematic development of the concepts and research programs.
4. Research programs investigate two types of expected returns: instrumental or expressive. Instrumental returns are gains of resources resulting from social relations and embedded resources, or for success and attainment in market competition; expressive returns are retention or preservation of resources, or for social solidarity. This chapter addresses instrumental returns in the labor market.
5. See, for example, Flap and Boxman's study (2001) of vocational graduates seeking their initial careers in the Netherlands, showing that social capital may be even more important than human capital as a resource in the entry into the labor market for such a labor group.
6. According to the McKinsey report (November 2004), the state and collective enterprises dominated critical and urban sectors of financial/banking, foreign trade, land development, large-scale construction projects, and the offerings on the stock market.
7. For some scholars (e.g., Putnam 2000), civil engagement or participation in voluntary associations is seen as social capital. However, from our perspective where social capital refers to embedded resources, civil engagement becomes network opportunities that may lead to greater or more diverse embedded resources (see Lin 2006).
8. The actual distribution of clusters is as follows:

Shanghai	5 clusters	95 households/respondents
Beijing	4 clusters	76 households/respondents
Chongqing	4 clusters	76 households/respondents

Tianjin	3 clusters	57 households/respondents
Wuhan	3 clusters	57 households/respondents
Shengyang	2 clusters	8 households/respondents
Guangzhou	2 clusters	38 households/respondents
Chendu	2 clusters	38 households/respondents
159 other cities	1 cluster each	19 households/respondents each.

9. The exchange rate at the time was about RMB (Chinese Yuan) $8.00 = US$1.00.
10. There are 27 provincial capitals in China. The study sample included respondents from 18 provincial capitals.
11. For each job, we asked each respondent (a) if they knew such a person, (b) the nature of their relationship with that person, (c) whether they knew that person through their spouse, (d) the sex of the person, (e) how long they had known each other (in number of years), and (f) how intimate they were to each other (very intimate, intimate, so-so, not intimate, and not at all intimate).
12. For occupational prestige, we applied the Standard International Occupational Prestige Scale constructed by Harry B. G. Ganzeboom and Donald J. Treiman (1996).
13. The variable, "political capital," was not adjusted to the time when the respondent took the current/last job, due to lack of information on the year when the respondent joined the Party.

REFERENCES

Angelusz, R., and R. Tardos. Forthcoming. "Assessing Social Capital and Attainment Dynamics—Position Generator Applications in Hungary, 1987–2003." In *Social Capital: An International Research Program*, eds. N. Lin and B. H. Erickson, 394–420. (Oxford: Oxford University Press)

Bian, Y. J. 1994. *Work and Inequality in Urban China*. Albany, NY: State University of New York Press.

Bourdieu, P. 1983. "The Forms of Capital." In *Handbook of Theory and Research for the Sociology of Education*, ed. J. G. Richardson 241–58. Westport, CT.: Greenwood Press, 1986.

Burt, R. S. 1992. *Structural Holes: The Social Structure of Competition*. Cambridge, MA: Harvard University Press.

———. 2000. "The Network Structure of Social Capital." In *Research in Organizational Behavior*, eds. R. I. Sutton and B. M. Staw, 345–423. Greenwich, CT: JAI Press.

Coleman, J. S. 1988. "Social Capital in the Creation of Human Capital." *American Journal of Sociology*, 94: S95–S121.

———. 1990. *Foundations of Social Theory*. Cambridge, MA: Harvard University Press.

De Graaf, N. D., and H. D. Flap. 1988 "With a Little Help from My Friends." *Social Forces*, 67: 452–72.

Erickson, B. H. 2001. "Good Networks and Good Jobs: The Value of Social Capital to Employers and Employees." In *Social Capital: Theory and Research*, eds. N. Lin, K. S. Cook, and R. S. Burt, 127–158. New York: Aldine de Gruyter. (Oxford University Press)

Flap, H., and E. Boxman. 2001. "Getting Started: The Influence of Social Capital on the Start of the Occupational Career." In *Social Capital: Theory and Research*, N. Lin, K. S. Cook, and R. S. Burt, 159–81. New York: Aldine de Gruyter.

——— and B. Völker. 2004. *Creation and Returns of Social Capital: A New Research Program*. London and New York: Routledge.

Flap, H. D. 1991. "Social Capital in the Reproduction of Inequality: A Review." *Comparative Sociology of Family, Health and Education*, 20: 6179–6202.

———. 1999 "Creation and Returns of Social Capital: A New Research Program." *La Revue Tocqueville*, 20: 5–26.

Ganzeboom, H. B. G., and D. J. Treiman. 1996. "Internationally Comparable Measures of Occupational Status for the 1988 International Standard Classification of Occupations." *Social Science Research*, 25: 201–39.

Granovetter, M. 1973. "The Strength of Weak Ties." *American Journal of Sociology*, 78: 1360–80.

Lin, N. 1982. "Social Resources and Instrumental Action." In *Social Structure and Network Analysis*, eds. P. V. Marsden and N. Lin, 131–45. Beverly Hills, CA: Sage.

———. 1999a. "Building a Network Theory of Social Capital." *Connections*, 22: 28–51.

———. 1999b. "Social Networks and Status Attainment." *Annual Review of Sociology*, 25: 467–87.

———. 2001. *Social Capital: A Theory of Structure and Action*. London: Cambridge University Press.

———. 2006. "Social Capital." In *Encyclopedia of Economic Sociology*, eds. J. Beckert and M. Zagiroski, 604–12. London: Rutledge.

——— and M. Dumin. 1986. "Access to Occupations Through Social Ties." *Social Networks*, 8: 365–85.

———, W. M. Ensel, and J. C. Vaughn. 1981. "Social Resources and Strength of Ties: Structural Factors in Occupational Status Attainment." *American Sociological Review*, 46: 393–405.

———, Y. C. Fu, and R. M. Hsung. 2001. "The Position Generator: Measurement Techniques for Investigations of Social Capital." In *Social Capital: Theory and Research*, eds. N. Lin, K. S. Cook, and R. S. Burt 57–81. New York: Aldine de Gruyter.

Marsden, P. V. and J. S. Hurlbert. 1988. "Social Resources and Mobility Outcomes: A Replication and Extension." *Social Forces*, 66: 1038–59.

Mckinsey Quarterly. 2004. "Spurring Performance in China's State-owned Enterprises," November 24.

Portes, A. 1998. "Social Capital: Its Origins and Applications in Modern Sociology." *Annual Review of Sociology*, 22: 1–24.

Putnam, R. D. 2000. *Bowling Alone: The Collapse and Revival of American Community*. New York: Simon & Schuster.

Walder, A. G. 1986. *Communist Neo-Traditionalism: Work and Authority in Chinese Industry*. Berkeley: University of California Press.

9 The Distribution and Return of Social Capital in Taiwan

Chih-Jou Jay Chen

INTRODUCTION

This chapter examines how social capital is distributed among individuals in a society, how it is accessed, and how and to what extent it affects status attainment. This study defines social capital as resources accessed through one's social networks. The cliché, "It's not what you know but who you know that matters" prescribes social networks as a panacea for many things, from everyday problems to securing better jobs. The nature and effects of social capital have been extensively studied in the literature in which empirical evidence was initially drawn from community studies before being extended to national samples (Lin 1999; Lin and Dumin 1986; Lin, Ensel, and Vaughn 1981; Marsden and Hurlbert 1988; De Graaf and Flap 1988).

This study is based on data from a national survey conducted in Taiwan in 2004, modifying the measurement methodology in advancing the concept of social capital, and thus contributing to this ever-growing field of study. The chapter begins with a review of social capital as a concept and theory, its conceptualization at the micro- and macrolevels, followed by its measurements and the many processes of its production and returns for individual attainment.

Social capital is in vogue in contemporary social sciences. Over the past two decades, it has come to prominence as a theoretical perspective that captures the contributions of social relations and presciently explains a wide variety of individual and collective behaviors, ranging from life chances and well-being of individuals to economic growth and political participation in societies (see reviews in Portes 1998; Woolcock 1998; Lin 1999, 2001a). Originally it was a concept that described the relational resources embedded in personal ties useful for the development of individuals in community social organizations (Jacob 1961; Loury 1977). That concept was then applied to a wide range of social phenomena, including family relations (Coleman 1988), social mobility and labor markets (Chen 2006; Lin, Ensel, and Vaughn 1981; Marsden and Hurlbert 1988), relations and performance of firms (Burt 1992), and public life in contemporary societies

(Putnam 1993). As the research enterprise of social capital grew, it gained manifold varieties of theoretical perspectives and practical applications. As such, scholars were concerned that the concept had become the Wild West of academic work or a catch-all and cure-all symbol (Burt 2005; Lin 2000; Portes 2000).

The central proposition of social capital theory is that networks of relationships constitute valuable resources, providing their members with "the collectivity-owned capital, a 'credential' which entitles them to credit, in the various senses of the world" (Bourdieu 1986, p. 249). Social capital refers to the social relations and resource advantages of both individuals and communities (Coleman 1988; Portes 2000). However, the research enterprise of social capital is seriously divided depending on whether individual or collective advantage is the focus. At the individual level, social capital refers to returns that emanate from individual network connections. A transition occurs as the concept transforms from an individual asset to a community or national resource. This refers to an attribute of the community itself. This conceptual stretch, initiated by Putnam (1993, 1995), focuses on the "stock" of social capital possessed by communities and even nations, and the consequent effects on their development. Thus, work focused on communal social capital has been based on the assumption that connections between actors promote public goods to the benefit of the entire network.

As a result, social capital has been conceptualized at both the micro- and macrolevels, i.e., an individualistic approach and a collective or communal approach. Insofar as the individualistic approach is concerned, Lin points to a network theory of social capital and defines social capital as "resources embedded in social networks accessed and used by actors for actions" (2001b. p. 25). On the other hand, for the macrolevel approach, Putnam (1993, p. 167) sees social capital as a collective asset: "Social capital here refers to features of social organization, such as trust, norms, and networks, which can improve the efficiency of society by facilitating coordinated action." Despite their diverse origins, analysis levels and styles of accompanying evidence, there is a point of general agreement between these two representative perspectives. Social structure defines a certain kind of capital that can create advantages for individuals or groups pursuing their own ends. Furthermore, individuals and their relations form the basis of social capital, which may have microconsequences both for individuals and for collectivity.

This study takes an individualistic approach and aims to identify the differential access and returns of social capital. Research programs carried out in North America, Europe, and East Asia have demonstrated that social capital significantly affects labor market outcomes. Yet there remain a number of questions that necessitate assessment and clarification. This chapter targets two critical questions: (a) the inequality of access to social capital (who has access to better or poorer embedded resources); and (b) the return from access to social capital for individual attainment. Further, how can these relationships be tested for possible mutual causations or reciprocal effects? These questions represent some of the cutting-edge issues to be examined in this chapter.

HOW SOCIAL CAPITAL WORKS: ACCESS AND MOBILIZATION

Social capital is the resources embedded in social networks. There are two theoretical approaches describing the process of how social capital is expected to generate returns in the process of status attainment. One process focuses on the access to social capital—i.e., resources accessed in one's general social networks. In this process, social capital is conceived in terms of its potential capacity—the pool of potentially mobilizable resources embedded in one's social networks, which along with human capital (education, experiences) and initial positions (parental or prior job statuses) are expected to affect attained statuses such as earnings, occupational status, employment sectors, or authority positions. Another process focuses on the mobilization of social capital in the status attainment process—the use of a specific social contact and its resources. In this process, social capital is defined in terms of its actual use—the mobilization of a particular contact and its resources. The assumption is that contact status, along with human capital and initial positions, will have important impact in the status attainment process (e.g., the job-search process; Lin 2001b).

Accessed social capital and mobilized social capital are two independent types of social capital in the process of status attainment. One interesting question is the extent to which accessed social capital influences the mobilization of higher social capital. If at all possible in current research, both types of social capital should be measured and closely examined, because neither is perfectly adequate for capturing the linkage between social capital and status attainment.

The problem with regard to data concerning accessed social capital lies, on the one hand, in imperfect measurements of the pool of resources of the entire networks of social capital. On the other hand, relying on data on a particular tie (say, in the job-searching process) is even riskier because it misses much of the invisible returns to social capital (Lin forthcoming). For example, in job-search research, the strength of the tie that leads to a job cannot alone predict attributes of that particular job. One has to know the whole network in which the job seeker is embedded (Montgomery 1992; Granovetter 1995). Aggregate measures of personal networks, such as constraint (Burt 1992) or heterogeneity and extensity (Lin 2001b), better capture a network's capacity to transfer nonredundant information and exert influence. It is the nature of social resources embedded in a network, instead of a particular tie or its bridging property, which conveys advantage and reaches someone with the type of resource required for one to fulfill his/her instrumental objectives (Lin et al. 1981). Granovetter (1985) also emphasizes the need to examine one's overall embeddedness in a relevant network to understand his or her ability to undertake an economic action.

Therefore, for developing cross-sectional and standardized measures of social capital, it is more straightforward to focus on measuring the potential access of individuals to social capital (Van der Gaag and Snijders 2004). This study measures social capital within the access perspective, and thus defines social capital as the collection of all potentially available resources embedded in one's networks. In this respect, the measurement of access to social capital has been pursued following several methodological paths, including name generator, position generator, network size, and resource generator. To focus on the distribution of individual social capital and its returns on status attainment, this study employs the position generator methodology to measure social capital embedded in wider networks beyond the few close ties where people are safely and intimately embedded.

Measures of Social Capital: The Position Generator

The position generator, initiated and continually refined by Nan Lin and associates (Lin and Dumin 1986; Lin, Fu, and Hsung 2001), measures a person's access to a sample of structural positions (mainly occupations, or authorities, work units, class, or sector) through social relationships. Respondents are asked whether they know anyone in each of a set of hierarchical positions ranging from high to low, and to indicate contacts, if any, in each of the positions. In the literature, occupation is mainly used as an indicator of structural positions in position-generator methodology. This approach is theoretically meaningful because occupation plays a dominating role in modern societies and serves as a good indicator of one's social status, role, and resources. For example, from the position-generating responses one can construct measures of (a) *extensity* or heterogeneity of accessibility to different occupations (number of occupations accessed); (b) *range* of accessibility to different hierarchical occupations (the distance between the highest and lowest accessed occupations); and (c) *upper reachability* of accessed social capital (the highest prestige occupation accessed; Lin 2001b; Lin, Fu, and Hsun 2001).

As reviewed by Lin (1999), there has been consistent evidence that social network resources are positively correlated with labor market outcomes such as job prestige and income. That is, the results of social capital models suggest that individuals with better social capital do better in the labor market. However, it deserves a closer examination to determine whether this result reflects causality or merely social homophily (the tendency for similar people to associate with each other). Mouw (2003) criticizes the measurement of social capital on the grounds that much of the effect (i.e., any association between the contact's occupational status and respondent's postcontact attained occupational status) is due to the homogeneity effect, not the contact's influence. That is, Mouw argues that it is the similarity between the contact's occupation and the respondent's attained occupation—the selection of the contact, rather than the contact's superior status, that is positively affecting respondent's superior attained status.

Although research has already shown that the position generator is strongly related to important causes and consequences, there is sufficient room for modification in its measurement and operationalization. To ascertain the causal sequence of social capital in the process of status attainment, the time framework of the contacts needs to be specified. For this research project, two sets of position generator items were included in the survey: (a) occupations accessed in the present time, to capture current social capital, and (b) occupations accessed prior to the time the respondent took the present job, to capture social capital prior to the current job. This study focuses on the latter—*prior social capital*—to measure one's accessed social capital at the time when he/she started his/her current job. As a result, the possible temporal sequence of social capital and current job attainment can be ascertained and the causal relations assessed.

DATA AND MEASUREMENT

Data used in this study were drawn from the thematic research project "Social Capital: Its Origins and Consequences" sponsored by Academia Sinica, Taiwan, through its Research Center for Humanities and Social Sciences, and the Institute of Sociology. This project called for a two-wave, three-site survey to be conducted between the periods 2004 to 2005 and 2006 to 2007. The three sites selected were Taiwan, mainland China, and the United States. These sites were selected to capture two different political regimes (state socialism in mainland China and capitalism in Taiwan and the United States) and two different cultural groups (Chinese in Taiwan and mainland China and Anglo-Saxons in the United States). A panel design allowed some preliminary tests of alternative causal and reciprocal effect.

This study investigates data from that part of the project's Taiwan survey conducted in 2004. Instruments of that survey were administrated in interpersonal interviews with respondents in an islandwide stratified (levels of urbanization) probability (by district and household) sample of adults between the ages of twenty-one to sixty-four. The total sample size was 3,281, of which 13 percent were housewives, 8 percent were either unemployed or students, and 4 percent were retired. The study sample consisted of 2,292 respondents, including those who were currently employed with complete answers on all measurements in the analysis, and excluding housewives, those retired, or those not currently participating in the labor force. Table 9.1 presents the summary of sample characteristics. Because this study focused on those who were currently employed and excluded those who were outside the labor market (with housewives the largest deleted group, consisting of 13 percent of the respondents), the study sample consisted of more men than women (59 percent to 41 percent). The respondents' average age was forty, with an average of ten years tenure with current job. Regarding education, 44 percent of the respondents had advanced degrees (associate college or higher), and only 23 percent received secondary education or lower. The average monthly income was in the range of NT$30,000 to NT$40,000 (about US$900 to US$1,200).

The key position-generator question used in this study was: "At the time when you were starting your current job, did you know anyone that had one of the following jobs?" Twenty-two occupations were sampled from a full list of all occupations to represent different levels of occupational prestige, for which this study followed the Standard International Occupational Prestige Scale (SIOPS) constructed by Harry B. G. Ganzeboom and Donald J. Treiman (1996). The sampled occupations have prestige scores ranging from 85 (legislator) to 20 (hotel bellboy) and can be roughly grouped into three hierarchical groups: the upper class (high-status professionals such as professors, lawyers, CEOs, legislators, and production managers), the middle class (middle-level professionals such as middle school teachers, personnel managers, writers, nurses, computer programmers, administrative assistants, accountants, and policemen), and the lower class (farmers, receptionists, operators in a factory, hairdressers, taxi drivers, security guards, janitors, and hotel bellboys). These positions and their relative rankings are shown in Table 9.2.

Three indexes were constructed from the position-generator items: (a) extensity, number of positions accessed; (b) range, the difference between the highest and lowest prestige scores among accessed positions; and (c) upper reachability, the prestige score of the highest accessed position. These were indicators of social capital capacity. As shown in Table 9.2, the average number of accessed positions was 7.4 out of twenty-two sampled positions, with the highest prestige score among accessed positions being 62 and the average range of prestige scores between the highest and lowest accessed positions about 35. A comparison between men and women shows that there was no statistically significant difference between men and women in terms of these three indexes. Unlike China, where men had significantly better social capital than women on all three dimensions of social capital (Lin 2001b; Lin this volume), Taiwan is shown to be a more equal society in terms of gender difference in the access to social capital (see also Lin, Fu, and Hsung 2001).

The most accessible position was farmer (59 percent of the respondents), followed by accountant, operator in a factory, and personnel manager. The next cluster of accessed positions included hairdresser, middle school

Table 9.1 Summary of Sample Characteristics (Percent or Mean)

	Total (N = 2,292)	*Men (n = 1,352)*	*Women (n = 940)*	*Significance Test*[a]
Age	40.17	40.84	39.22	0.000
Age[b]	32.73	33.12	33.18	0.016
Education				
Secondary or lower	22.7%	22.4%	23.2%	0.054
High school	33.2%	35.4%	30.2%	
Associate college	21.2%	20.8%	21.7%	
College and graduate	22.9%	21.4%	24.9%	
Tenure (years)	9.5	10	8.7	0.000
Urban degree				0.026
Core	26.7%	24.9%	29.4%	
Town	58.5%	59.99%	57.4%	
Rural	14.8%	15.9%	13.2%	
Voluntary org. participation	46.6%	49.9%	41.9%	0.000
Voluntary org. participation[b]	25.4%	25.7%	25.0%	0.719
Occupational status [c]	0.000			
Self-employed	18.3%	22.2%	12.8%	
Service class	15.2%	16.9%	12.8%	
Others	66.4%	60.9%	74.5%	
Occupational status[b]	0.000			
Service class	10.3%	11.3%	8.7%	
Self-employed	5.1%	6.5%	3.0%	
No previous job	20.1%	20.7%	19.1%	
Others	64.6%	61.5%	69.1%	
Monthly income of present job (20 groups) [d]	6.47	7.05	5.64	0.000
Ethnic group				0.009
Minnan	75.8%	73.52%	79.0%	
Haka	14.0%	15.5%	11.8%	
Mainlanders	10.3%	11.0%	9.1%	
Supervision in present job				
No supervision	64.2%	57.7%	73.6%	
Supervising someone who did not supervise	20.3%	23.2%	16.2%	
Supervising someone who supervised	15.5%	19.2%	10.2%	

[a]The significance levels for t tests or chi-square tests for males and females. [b]ATT: at the time of finding the current job. [c]Service class, including professionals, administrators and managers; higher-grade technicians; supervisors of nonmanual workers. [d]The monthly income in the questionnaire has 20 categories (in Taiwanese NT$): (1) no income; (2) under 5,000; (3) 5,000–10,000; (4) 10,000–20,000; (5) 20,000–30,000; (6) 30,000–40,000; (7) 40,000–50,000; (8) 50,000–60,000; (9) 60,000–70,000; (10) 70,000–80,000; (11) 80,000–90,000; (12) 90,000–100,000; (13) 100,000–120,000; (14) 120,000–140,000; (15) 140,000–160,000; (16) 160,000–180,000; (17) 180,000–200,000; (18) 200,000–250,000; (19) 250,000–300,000; and (20) 300,000 and more.

Table 9.2 Position Generator and Differential Access to General Social Capital (Prior to Current Job)

Position (Standard International Occupational Prestige Scale)	*Respondent Accessing* Total (N = 2,292)	Men (N = 1,352)	Women (N = 940)	Significance Test*
Legislator (85)	13	15	10	0.000
Professor (78)	25	25	26	0.791
Lawyer (73)	16	18	13	0.000
CEO (70)	25	26	24	0.133
Production manager (63)	28	32	23	0.000
Middle school teacher (60)	44	44	44	0.744
Personnel manager (60)	48	48	48	0.843
Writer (58)	6	7	5	0.248
Nurse (54)	39	34	46	0.000
Computer programmer (51)	36	37	35	0.258
Administrative assistant (49)	33	33	32	0.469
Accountant (49)	53	50	57	0.000
Policeman (40)	38	40	34	0.001
Farmer (38)	59	62	55	0.001
Receptionist (38)	29	28	29	0.465
Operator in a factory (34)	52	55	47	0.000
Hairdresser (32)	46	38	59	0.000
Taxi driver (31)	30	34	25	0.000
Security guard (30)	39	42	34	0.000
Housemaid (23)	27	22	33	0.000
Janitor (21)	30	30	32	0.242
Hotel bellboy (20)	27	33	17	0.000
Summary indices				
Extensity				
Mean	7.43	7.55	7.27	0.206
SD	5.22	5.37	4.99	
Range of scores	0–22	0–22	0–22	
Range				
Mean	35.47	36.12	34.52	0.059
SD	20.34	20.32	19.59	
Range of scores	0–65	0–65	0–65	
Upper reachability				
Mean	62.07	62.56	61.38	0.150
SD	19.23	19.46	18.88	
Range of scores	0–85	0–85	0–85	

*The significance levels for t tests on the equality of means for men and women.

teacher, security guard, nurse, policeman, computer programmer, and administrative assistant. The third cluster, accessed by less than one-third of the respondents, included janitor, production manager, receptionist, taxi driver, professor, housemaid, hotel bellboy, CEO, lawyer, and legislator. The least accessible position was writer, accessed by only 6 percent of the respondents (Table 9.2).

Although there appears to be no significant gender difference in the three indexes of social capital, gender difference in accessing certain positions exists and reveals a discernible pattern. Although women had better access to female-dominated occupations like nursing, accounting, hairdressing, and domestic services, men in the power structure had overall advantage in accessing both privileged positions (e.g., legislators, production managers, and lawyers) and male-dominated occupations (e.g., policemen, farmers, factory operators, taxi drivers, security guards, and bellboys). Thus, men had an advantage in reaching positions similar to or better than those acquired in the prestige hierarchy. Women who were disadvantaged in accessing many of the positions were probably compensated by the traditional household roles played, such as health care for family members, personal beauty care, and housework. Such roles and the social resources they accessed may well have been useful for their individual well-being, but may not have been as useful for gains in the labor market. Thus, it is important to make a separate gender analysis of the sources and returns of social capital if possible.

Table 9.3 Factor Structure of Access to General Social Capital (Prior to Current Job)

Factor	*Sample (N = 2,292)*	*Men (n = 1,352)*	*Women (n = 940)*
I	2.509	2.583	2.601
II	.311	.316	.304
III	.098	.100	.095
Factor loadings on Factor I*			
Upper reachability	.919	.919	.918
Extensity	.900	.897	.905
Range	.967	.966	.969
Factor scoring on Factor I*			
Upper reachability	.355	.356	.353
Extensity	.348	.347	.348
Range	.373	.374	.372

*Principal Component Analysis and varimax rotation

To assess whether the three measures of social capital can be considered as a cluster of a single dimension of "access to social capital," the factor analysis yielded a single factor solution and almost identical patterns and coefficients for men and women (Table 9.3). The results strongly suggest a single dimensionality among the three indices for access to social capital. When restricting solutions for factors with eigenvalues greater than 1, the factor loading of the three variables on the single factor were all very high (.96, .91, and .89). As a result, a factor score was computed with differential weights assigned to the three indices (.35 for extensity, .37 for range, and .36 for upper reachability). Because separate factor analyses for males and females result in identical patterns, the same scoring weights were used to construct a general social capital score for all respondents.

Research Design

This study formulates two conceptual models: one for access to social capital and another for returns to social capital. Human capital, associational activities, and socioeconomic environment (urbanization degree of one's residence) are hypothesized to significantly contribute to the production and return of social capital. For returns to social capital, this study examines three dimensions of labor market outcomes: occupational positions, authority in the workplace, and economic well-being.

The occupational structure, people's mobility in terms of occupation, is the key to an understanding of social stratification and class differentiation. The occupational status reflects the position of the individual within the system of work organization and economic structure. This study refers to the well-known Erikson, Goldthorpe, and Portocarero (EGP) class schema commonly used in cross-national research on social stratification (Erikson, Goldthorpe, and Portocarero 1979; Erikson and Goldthorpe 1992), collapsing its class schema into a three-category occupational classification as follows: (a) service class consisting of professionals, administrators, managers and high-grade technicians, and supervisors of nonmanual workers; (b) self-employed (petty bourgeoisie), referring to small proprietors with and/or without employees; and (c) workers, including farmworkers, manual and nonmanual workers. The EGP class schema is based on occupations and on the employment relations of industrial employment structure. The starting point of the division of social classes is threefold: employers, self-employed workers, and employees. Starting from this threefold hierarchical classification, professional workers with specialized knowledge and expertise are described as members of the "service class," who exchange not only effort for wages but make a much more diffuse commitment to service to their employers for a more general and long-term prospect of compensation and career development. In the advanced capitalist economies this "service relation" was secured largely through the institutions of the hierarchical corporation, the internal labor market, and the bureaucratic career (Goldthorpe

1982, 2000). This study considers this threefold class schema as a reflection of important social cleavages in Taiwan.

Conceptually, EGP class schema is not constructed around any single hierarchical principle from which a regular ordering of the classes could be derived. However, it is possible, for particular analytical purposes, to produce an ordering by reference to external criteria such as SIOPS and a number of occupational scales. Erikson and Goldthorpe (1992) conducted a mapping between the categories of the occupational scales and those of the EGP class schema. They showed that the service class consistently ranked above all others, and those of nonskilled workers in industry and agriculture consistently ranked below all others. As such, the service class is considered to be a valid indicator of occupational attainment in social status.

In addition to occupational positions, this study examines the effects of social capital on being a supervisor and earning a higher wage in the labor market. As discussed in the previous section, the social capital was measured at that juncture when respondents were starting their current jobs; thus a temporal sequence was imposed between social capital and the variables of labor market outcome.

After constructing a social capital score for all respondents, the factors that facilitated or hindered access to social capital were scrutinized. Several groups of structural variables were identified to help explain the production and returns of social capital, including age, gender, education, ethnicity, occupational status, urbanization of residence, participation in voluntary associations, and current job tenure. First, education as a key feature of human capital enhances one's labor market opportunities and consequently affects one's access to social capital. Schools are an important source for building lifelong connections and friendships, on which social capital is based. This is particularly applicable to those who attend university or MBA programs where identification with their alma mater and dynamic alumni networks are vital sources of social capital. In this study, education was measured on a four-level scale (secondary or lower, high school, associate college, and college and graduate). Second, employment reflects the respondent's social status and the opportunities for further social contacts in daily life. This study used occupational status as an indicator that was categorized into four groups: service class, self-employed, other jobs, and no previous job. Ethnicity in Taiwan used to play a key role in social cleavage; previous studies on social stratification in Taiwan suggested that ethnicity channeled people into different employment sectors (i.e. whether public, private, or self-employed). Mainlanders in Taiwan (those who themselves or whose parents or grandparents fled mainland China in 1949 following the Nationalist defeat in the Chinese Civil War) presumably have a narrower kinship network than native Taiwanese, who usually have a wider kinship network through their extended families. Thus, "kinship capital" as a result of ethnicity may affect one's access to social capital.

The urbanization of residence, reflecting the socioeconomic environment in which the respondents were situated, was categorized into three levels: core cities, town, and rural areas.

Age is included in the analysis representing general life experience and accumulation of social skills. In this study, age refers to the respondent's age when he/she started his/her current job. Research findings indicate that wages increase with age up to a point (usually in the mid- to late thirties) and then decrease as ages rise. This may well be true when it comes to accessing social capital as well. For those who are active in work, family, and social life, social capital may rise and fall with age, peaking in mid-life (Erickson 2004). Thus a variable of age-squared is included to test whether social capital or income will increase with age, albeit at a decreasing rate. A control variable in this study is whether the respondents were participating in voluntary associations, both when they started their current jobs and when they were interviewed. One-fourth of the respondents reported that they participated in one or more voluntary associations when they started their current jobs, and 47 percent were currently participating in voluntary associations when interviewed. Such associational activities might be important in providing diversified contacts that differ from those accessed at work and in schools. Indeed, this variable may independently contribute to one's access to social capital. Finally, gender is included because in social life men and women may function under different social norms and, thus, be offered different opportunities that affect their access to social capital. Marital status and having young children in the household were originally included in data analyses, but revealed no significant effects on access to social capital and attainment; they were thus not included in this study.

INEQUALITY IN ACCESS TO SOCIAL CAPITAL

Table 9.4 shows the parameter estimates of the determinants of access to social capital, for the whole sample and separately for men and women. In these models, social capital, age, and participation in voluntary associations were measurements at the time when the respondent was starting his/her current job. Taking into account other variables in the model, there was no gender difference in access to social capital; urbanization of residence was also not related to access to social capital. A related study in China shows that men and those who worked in state-administered cities had better access to social capital (see Lin et al. this volume). Additionally, ethnicity had no significant effect on access to social capital. For both men and women access to social capital was contingent on age (with a curvilinear pattern, i.e. a diminishing effect), education level, participation in voluntary associations, and having a previous job. Education and participation in voluntary associations were two powerful sources of social capital, verifying that school experiences and association activities led to numerous contacts with diversified others. Access to social capital was hindered for those who did not change jobs, because there were fewer chances to know a diverse range of contacts.

Men and women differed on one factor relating to access to social capital. Men benefited from having previous service-class jobs (e.g., executive/

Table 9.4 OLS Estimates of the Determinants of Access to General Social Capital (Prior to Current Job)

	Total	*Male*	*Female*
Age [a]	.069***	.066***	.087***
Age squared [a]	–.001***	–.001**	–.001**
Ethnic group (ref: Minnan)			
Haka	.100+	.086	.109
Mainlanders	–.027	–.025	–.013
Education (ref: High school)			
Secondary or lower	–.473***	–.350***	–.656***
Associate college	.386***	.346***	.438***
Bachelor degree and above	.629***	.580***	.675***
Male gender	.062		
Participation in voluntary association [a]	.236***	.231***	.234***
Previous occupational status (ref: Other jobs)			
Service class	.152*	.204*	.090
Self-employed	.119	.172	–.060**
No previous job	–.201***	–.176**	–.203**
Urbanization of residence (ref: Rural)			
Core cities	–.061	–.056	–.074
Town	–.041	–.002	–.077
Constant	–1.646***	–1.592***	–1.914***
Observations	2292	1352	940
Adjusted R^2	.201	.172	.249

Note. OLS = Ordinary Least-Squares.
+$p < 0.1$. *$p < 0.05$. **$p < 0.01$. ***$p < 0.001$.
[a]ATT: At the time when R acquired the current job.

professional jobs), and women did not. Women with previous self-employed jobs were in a relatively disadvantageous position for access to social capital. This suggests that executive/professional networks only facilitated men's access to social capital, and self-employed jobs further hindered women's access to social capital. It is also worth noting that women relied more on education than men in gaining better access to social capital.

Differential Returns to Social Capital

The next analytic issue assesses the effects of social capital on social inequalities, namely inequalities of social status, power, and economic well-being. In correspondence, three indicators were used in this assessment: (a) holding a service-class or self-employed occupation, (b) authority in the workplace, and (c) monthly income. These variables were taken as a sequential set of status attainment and labor market outcomes: an individual first entered an occupational group, occupied a job position in a given hierarchical structure, and earned an economic return. The analyses focused on each of these attainment variables as endogenous (dependent) variables in the sequence.

The first analysis mainly assesses the effects of capital and control variables on landing in one of the occupational groups, which are categorized into three classes: (a) service class, accounting for 15 percent of the respondents, and includes professionals, administrators, managers, and high-grade technicians, and supervisors of nonmanual workers; (b) self-employed (petty bourgeoisie), accounting for 18 percent of the respondents, referring to small proprietors with and without employees; and (c) workers/farmers, accounting for 67 percent of the respondents, including farmers, and manual and nonmanual workers. Because there are three groups, multinomial logistic regressions were employed to estimate the odds-ratio likelihood of being a particular occupational class given these exogenous variables. It follows from Table 9.5 that, given the control that other variables exert, social capital significantly enhanced the chances of being in the service class, relative to being workers/farmers. That is, net of the other variables in the model, the chances of holding a service-class occupation rose with social capital. Likewise, all the human-capital variables increased the chances of holding a service-class occupation. Education (particularly holding a university or graduate degree), experience in the present job, and prior service-class working experience all accompanied greater chances of being employed at the service-class level. Age, ethnicity, and urbanization of residence were not significantly related to being in the service class relative to being in the farmers/workers class, whereas gender (being a man) significantly enhanced the probability of entering the service class. Taking into account other variables in the model, participation in voluntary associations showed no significant effect on being in the service-class level, but significant effect on being in self-employed occupations relative to being in the workers/farmers class. Thus, on the whole, the impact of social capital on moving on to the service class was substantial, even after careful controls for human capital, age, ethnicity, residence urbanization, and gender.

Table 9.5 Parameter Estimates of Multinomial Logistic Model for Determinants of Occupational Status

	Service Class	*Self-employed*
Age	1.100	1.365***
Age squared	.999	.997***
Tenure (logged)	1.323**	1.214**
Ethnic group (ref: Minnan)		
Haka	.658+	.782
Mainlanders	1.181	1.168
Education (ref: High school)		
Secondary or lower	.091***	1.118
Associate college	3.268***	.700*
Bachelor degree and above	9.974***	.778
Male gender	1.642**	1.912***
Participation in voluntary association	1.062	2.003***
General social capital [a]	1.317**	1.067
Previous occupational status (ref: Others)		
Service class	18.98***	3.256***
Self-employed	1.978	2.364***
No previous job	2.684***	.732+
Urbanization of residence (ref: Rural)		
Core cities	1.266	1.028
Town	1.301	.940
–2LL	1028.646***	
Observations	2292	
D.f.	32	

Note. The reference group for outcome variable is "workers/farmers." Because there are zero cells in some variable categories, equations for men and women separately are not applicable.
$^{+}p < 0.1$. $^{*}p < 0.05$. $^{**}p < 0.01$. $^{***}p < 0.001$.
[a]ATT: At the time when R acquired current job

The second indicator of labor market outcomes is authority in the workplace. Authority in the workplace is one form of power that identifies the relative ranking between any pair of positions. This study uses supervision in the workplace as an indicator of authority. The questionnaire asked the respondents: "At your current job do you supervise someone?" If the answer was positive the next question pertinently inquired: "Do any of those under your supervision supervise someone else?" The respondents were then accordingly grouped into three categories: (a) upper-level supervisors, supervising someone who also supervised others; (b) lower-level supervisors, supervising someone who did not supervise anybody; and (c) those who did not engage in supervision of any sort. Although this is an ordinal variable to which ordinal logistic regressions can be applied, some regression models violated the parallel regression assumption, and thus multinomial logistic regressions are used (Long and Jeremy 2003). Table 9.6 shows the results pertaining to being upper-level supervisors and lower-level supervisors (relative to no supervision), indicating that gender, social capital, human capital, and urbanization of residence had substantial effects on authority in the workplace. Holding other variables constant, the chances to become an upper-level supervisor rose with being a man, his/her social capital, education, current job tenure, and living in an urbanized area, whereas the chances of becoming a lower-level supervisor were not significantly related to the urbanization of residence and advanced degrees (associate college and above). Age, ethnicity, participation in voluntary associations, and previous occupational status were not related to one's authority in the workplace.

Table 9.6 also shows the equations for men and women separately and revealed noteworthy results. For both men and women, social capital and current job tenure significantly facilitated one's chances of being a supervisor in the workplace. Education, however, benefited men and not women. Being a supervisor in the workplace was mainly contingent on social capital and current job tenure for women, whereas for men education played an additional important role.

Finally, Table 9.7 presents the estimates of the determinants of income. The measure of income includes twenty categories of current personal average monthly income, coded from 1 to 20. The lowest income group is "no income," and the highest income category is "NT$300,000 or more," so all monthly incomes above NT$300,000 are top coded. As presented in Table 9.7, controlling for other variables in the model, mainlanders tended to make more money than Minnan, and men tended to earn more than women. When samples for men and women were examined separately, few differences revealed themselves between men and women as to the variables contributing to one's income. The factors that had no significant effects on income for men and women include being Haka (relative to Minnan) and participation in voluntary associations. Both men and women's incomes rose with age until mid-life and then leveled off. All human-capital variables

Table 9.6 Parameter Estimates of Multinomial Logistic Model for Supervision

	Total		*Men*		*Women*	
Supervisors	*Upper Level*	*Lower Level*	*Upper Level*	*Lower Level*	*Upper Level*	*Lower Level*
Age	1.106+	1.054	1.124+	1.065	1.041	1.075
Age squared	.999+	.999	0.999	0.999	0.999	0.999
Tenure (logged)	1.543***	1.480***	1.656***	1.552***	1.539**	1.41**
Ethnic group (ref: Minnan)						
Haka	1.026	1.043	1.088	1.091	0.904	0.945
Mainlanders	1.300	1.376+	1.377	1.415	1.155	1.328
Education (ref: High school)						
Secondary or lower	.510**	.665*	0.41**	0.596*	0.81	0.888
Associate college	2.960***	1.252	3.713***	1.278	1.756+	1.232
Bachelor degree and above	2.637***	1.225	3.15***	1.474+	1.943+	0.886
Male gender	2.539***	1.891***				
Participation in voluntary association	1.074	.987	1.2	1.123	0.997	0.791
General social capital [a]	1.997***	1.438***	2.145***	1.403***	1.812***	1.552***
Previous occupational status (ref: Others)						
Service class	1.189	1.032	1.426	1.053	0.795	1.149
Self-employed	.932	.777	0.757	0.68	2.28	0.964
No previous job	.772	.911	0.851	0.85	0.504+	1.091
Urbanization of residence (ref: Rural)						
Core cities	1.748*	1.183	1.673	1.076	1.942	1.408

(continued)

Table 9.6 Parameter Estimates of Multinomial Logistic Model for Supervision (continued)

	Total		*Men*		*Women*	
Supervisors	*Upper Level*	*Lower Level*	*Upper Level*	*Lower Level*	*Upper Level*	*Lower Level*
Urbanization of residence (ref: Rural) (continued)						
Town	1.712*	1.140	1.612	1.148	1.995	1.098
–2LL	447.922***		326.697***		90.86***	
Observations	2292		1352		940	
D.f	32		30		30	

Note. The reference group of the outcome variable is "those who are not supervisors."
$^{+}p < 0.1$. $^{*}p < 0.05$. $^{**}p < 0.01$. $^{***}p < 0.001$.
[a]ATT: At the time when R acquired current job.

increased income: higher educational levels, current job tenure, and current employment in service class or self-employment (relative to farmers/workers) all went with higher income. Nevertheless, women tended to benefit more from education than men in income attainment, whereas men tended to benefit more from current job tenure and social capital than women in income attainment. Living in urban core cities improved men's, but not women's, incomes.

Table 9.7 OLS Estimates of the Determinants of Income

	Total	*Men*	*Women*
Age	.260***	.302***	.189***
Age square	–.003***	–.004***	–.002***
Tenure (logged)	.433***	.585***	.218***
Ethnic group (ref: Minnan)			
Haka	.115	.068	.293
Mainlanders	.356*	.387+	.339+
Education (ref: High school)			
Secondary or lower	–.985***	–1.021***	–1.02***
Associate college	.640***	.500**	.845***
Bachelor degree and above	1.229***	1.051***	1.422***
Male gender	1.173***		
Participation in voluntary association	.159	.162	.173
General social capital[a]	.430***	.482***	.335***
Occupational status (ref: Others)			
Service class	1.418***	1.558***	1.264***
Self-employed	.867***	.929***	.688***
Urbanization of residence (ref: Rural)			
Core cities	.520***	.698**	.270
Town	.323*	.320+	. 031+
Constant	–1.311+	–1.103	.196
Observations	2292	1352	940
Adjusted R-squared	.363	.315	.350

Note. OLS = Ordinary Least Squares.
+$p < 0.1$. *$p < 0.05$. **$p < 0.01$. ***$p < 0.001$.
[a]ATT: At the time when R acquired current job.

Most important, access to social capital significantly affected current income levels. That is, holding other variables in the model constant, better social capital consequently caused higher income for both men and women. As noted in the previous section, the measure of social capital in the model was measured at the time when the respondent started his/her current job, with a temporal sequence followed by labor market outcomes (income, occupational status, and supervision). Therefore the significant causal effect of social capital on income can be asserted.

DISUSSION AND CONCLUSION

This study first examines a critical issue in social capital research—inequality in social capital—investigating the extent to which social capital is unequally distributed across social groups in Taiwan. It used position-generator methodology to measure social capital and yielded informative findings from surveys conducted in Taiwan. It found that there is no gender difference in access to social capital. That is, in Taiwan, men had no significant advantage over women in the average number of accessed positions, the highest prestige among accessed positions, and the range of prestige scores between the highest and lowest prestige scores of accessed positions. Even taking into account other variables, the regression model showed that gender is not associated with access to social capital. Nevertheless, gender differences in accessing certain positions do exist and reveal a discernible pattern. Although women had better access to female-dominated occupations, men had overall advantage in accessing both privileged positions and male-dominated occupations. It is most likely that women who were disadvantaged in accessing many of the positions were compensated by the traditional female-oriented positions better accessed by women. Thus, men and women have different "kinds" of social capital because of their advantage or disadvantage in structural positions and social networks. That is, despite different kinds of positions accessed by men and women, the three indicators (extensity, range, and upper reachability) amounted to similar quantitative scores for men and women overall.

A previous study in Taiwan also found that although men tended to access more positions, there was no significant difference between men and women in terms of upper reachability (the highest prestige score) and the range of scores (Lin, Fu, and Hsung 2001). Compared with studies conducted in China where males had significantly better social capital than females on all three indicators (Lin 2001b; Lin et al. this volume), the overall inequality in social capital is not associated with gender in Taiwan. This may imply that Taiwan has a more open and diversified society that allows women to access just as many social positions as men. Despite the fact that positions accessed by men and women are qualitatively different, their prestige scores are not quantitatively different.

The key determinants of access to social capital are human capital and networking activities. It is clear that human capital induces social capital because better-educated individuals tend to move in social circles rich in resources. Education facilitates access to social capital, probably because schools teach students valuable social skills, including language and communication abilities, which are crucial for networking abilities. Also, friendships made during school are usually long-lasting and tend to become one's core source of social capital. It is also noteworthy that college education brings far better returns to social capital, whereas high school education also helps with accessing social capital. This tends to suggest that social capital is acquired and accumulated earlier in one's schooling experience. Following one's school life, early experiences in civic engagement (participating in voluntary associations) further improve the acquisition of better social capital that may not be accessible in the workplace and through one's kinship ties.

Following the issue of access to social capital, this study examines the extent to which inequality in social capital contributes to social inequality across social groups. To ascertain the causal sequence, a time framework is specified for the contacts by identifying social capital accessed at the present time and social capital accessed prior to the current job. With the position-generator instrument and three attainment variables—occupational groups, authority in workplace, and monthly income—this study explores these mechanisms for attainment in the labor market in Taiwan. Taking other variables into account, social capital, indeed, affects one's chances of moving into the desirable service class (professional and managerial occupations), taking supervisory positions in workplace, and earning a higher income.

This fundamental finding confirms that social capital exerts a profound effect on status attainments beyond that accounted for by personal resources. Thus, this study makes a contribution to knowledge in the ongoing research of social stratification and social mobility, and to the theory of social capital itself where research in this field has been carried out in multiple political economies in North America, Europe, and Asia and have involved scholarly theses from academics emanating from diversified nations and cultures.

REFERENCES

Bourdieu, P. 1986. "The Forms of Capital." In *Handbook for Theory and Research for the Sociology of Education*, ed. J. G. Richardson, 241–58. New York: Greenwood Press.

Burt, R. S. 1992. *Structural Holes: The Social Structure of Competition*. Cambridge, MA: Harvard University Press.

———. 2005. *Brokerage and Closure: An introduction to Social Capital*. New York: Oxford University Press.

Chen, C-J. J. 2006. "Elite Mobility in Post-Reform Rural China." *Issues & Studies, 42*: 53–83.
Coleman, J. S. 1988. "Social Capital in the Creation of Human Capital." *American Journal of Sociology,* 94: S95–S121.
De Graaf, N. D., and H. D. Flap. 1988. "With a Little Help from My Friends." *Social Forces,* 67: 452–72.
Erickson, B. H. 2004. "The Distribution of Gendered Social Capital in Canada." In *Creation and Returns of Social Capital: A New Research Program,* ed. H. Flap, 27–50. London: Routledge.
Erikson, R. and J. Goldthorpe. 1992. *The Constant Flux. A Study in Class Mobility in Industrial Nations.* Oxford, UK: Clarendon Press.
———, Goldthorpe, J. H., and Portocarero, L. 1979. "Intergenerational Class Mobility in Three Western European Societies: England, France and Sweden." *British Journal of Sociology* 30: 415–41.
Ganzeboom, H. B. G. and D. J. Treiman. 1996. "Internationally Comparable Measures of Occupational Status for the 1988 International Standard Classification of Occupations." *Social Science Research,* 25: 201–39.
Goldthorpe, J. H. 1982. "On the Service Class: Its Formation and Future." In *Social Class and the Division of Labour,* eds. A. Giddens and G. Mackenzie, 162–85. Cambridge, UK: Cambridge University Press.
———. 2000. *On Sociology.* New York: Oxford University Press.
Granovetter, M. 1985. "Economic Action and Social Structure: The Problem of Embeddedness." *American Journal of Sociology,* 91: 481–510.
———. 1995. "Afterword 1994: Reconsiderations and a New Agenda." In *Getting a Job* (2nd ed.), ed. M. Granovetter, 139–82. Chicago, IL: University of Chicago Press.
Jacobs, J. 1961. *The Death and Life of Great American Cities.* New York: Vintage Books.
Loury, G. C. 1977. "A Dynamic Theory of Racial Income Differences." In *Women, Minorities and Employment Discrimination,* eds. P. A. Wallace and A. Lamond (eds) 153–86. Lexington, MA: Lexington Books.
Lin, N. 1999. "Social Networks and Status Attainment." *Annual Review of Sociology,* 25: 467–87.
———. 2000. "Social Capital: Social Networks, Civic Edgemont, or Trust?" Paper presented at the Workshop on Social Capital, University of Trento, Italy, Oct. 19–20.
———. 2001a. "Building a Network Theory of Social Capital." In *Social Capital: Theory and Research,* eds. N. Lin, K. Cook, and R. S. Burt, 3–30. New York: Aldine de Gruyter.
———. 2001b *Social Capital: A Theory of Structure and Action,* New York: Cambridge University Press.
———. (forthcoming) "A Network Theory of Social Capital," in D. Castiglione, J.W. van Deth and G. Wolleb (eds) *Handbook on Social Capital,* Oxford: Oxford University Press.
——— and M. Dumin. 1986. "Access to Occupations through Social Ties." *Social Networks,* 8: 365–85.
———, Y. C. Fu, and R. M. Hsung. 2001. "Position Generator: A Measurement for Social Capital." In *Social Capital: Theory and Research,* eds. N. Lin, K. Cook, and R. S. Burt, 57–84. New York: Cambridge University Press.
———, W. M. Ensel, and J. C. Vaughn. 1981. "Social Resources and Strength of Ties: Structural Factors in Occupational Status Attainment." *American Sociological Review,* 46(4): 393–405.
Long, J. S., and F. Jeremy. 2003. *Regression Models for Categorical Dependent Variables Using Stata, Revised Edition.* College Station, TX: Stata Press.

——— and Hurlbert, J. S. 1988. "Social Resources and Mobility Outcomes: A Replication and Extension." *Social Forces*, 66(4): 1038–59.

Montgomery, J. D. 1992. "Job Search and Network Composition: Implications of the Strength of Weak Ties Hypothesis." *American Sociological Review*, 57: 586–96.

Mouw, T. 2003. "Social Capital and Finding a Job: Do Contacts Matter?" *American Sociological Review*, 68(December): 868–98.

Portes, A. 1998. "Social Capital: Its Origins and Applications in Modern Sociology." *Annual Review of Sociology*, 22:1–24.

——— 2000. "The Two Meanings of Social Capital." *Sociological Forum*, 15: 1–12.

Putnam, R. 1993. *Making Democracy Work: Civic Traditions in Modern Italy*. Princeton, NJ: Princeton University Press.

——— 1995. "Tuning In, Tuning Out: The Strange Disappearance of Social Capital in America." *Political Science and Politics*, 28: 664–83.

Van der Gaag, M. P. J., and T. A. B. Snijders. 2004. "Proposals for the Measurement of Individual Social Capital." In H. Flap and B. Völker (eds), *Creation and Returns of Social Capital*, 199–218. London: Routledge.

Woolcock, M. 1998. "Social Capital and Economic Development: Towards a Theoretical Synthesis and Policy Framework." *Theory and Society*, 27: 151–208.

10 Social Capital in Communities, Development and Integration

The Four Village Case Study in Hungary, 2000

Róbert Tardos

INTRODUCTORY NOTES ON BEHALF OF A COMPARATIVE PERSPECTIVE

Research on social networks and social capital can receive an important impetus from the inclusion of comparative perspectives. Differentiation of contexts can provide new and incisive illumination to findings that are hard to interpret within the frameworks of standard assumptions. Variation of settings is available, and need not be artificially produced. Existing cultural, institutional, and territorial differences among cases provide a strategic research site for the formulation and testing of comparisons, which may often be conducted in an experiment–like fashion.

In its earlier history social network analysis (SNA) was not exemplary regarding these points, though one should note some important exceptions with an explicitly comparative design in these early decades, from Laumann-Pappi (1976) on. Recent decades have witnessed greater incorporation of comparative perspectives, including important volumes focusing on social networks that explicitly seek to transcend limited cultural frames (such as Wellman 1999 or Lin, Cook, and Burt 2001). Of particular interest are projects with an explicitly comparative objective. For example, the successive International Social Survey Programme modules on social support, although they unfortunately exclude familiar techniques of SNA research such as network generators, nonetheless provide a range of data on basic ties of family, work, and social associations that allow a spectrum of comparative analyses.[1] The number of studies that embrace several countries drawn from differing cultural contexts has also grown. Variation in the range and composition of various types of ties is of interest in its own right. Such interest only grows if different mechanisms of access and mobilization of social capital are also involved.[2]

An important set of lessons along these lines is that both strong and weak ties may exhibit varying degrees of efficiency, depending on the type of existential constraint that the ties are exposed to. Moreover, these constraints often depend crucially on context. Based on our typical experiences with urban postindustrialism, we tend to identify strong ties as expressive and homophilous, whereas we tend to think of weak ties as instrumental and heterophilous. These assumptions may, in fact, be correct in any given circumstance. However, what is needed is analysis covering a considerable spectrum of settings in a number of different countries. In raising the problem of patronage, Flap (1990) suggests that the case is sometimes more complicated even with regard to contemporary mainstream settings. A closer examination of these mechanisms provides in itself one motive for calling for increased comparative efforts. Such efforts would be expected to generate theoretical and practical findings and insights in areas ranging from social mobility studies to community development.[3]

Cross-cultural perspectives do not necessarily assume the application of cross-national designs. One country can offer a variety of settings rich in network implications (see Erickson 2004 for an interesting example of regional comparison in the case of Canada). Although this point may be true even for countries in the highest zone of economic development, it is especially the case for countries comprised of regions that are more heterogeneous in their historical, economic, and sociocultural backgrounds.[4] A small country like Hungary, even with its relatively homogeneous landscape with respect to ethnicity, religion, and language, is not an exception. In Hungary, territorial characteristics related to settlement type and regional differentiation affect levels of social cohesion, and these characteristics get increased attention when it comes to the distribution of public funds for infrastructure development. Furthermore, in an atmosphere of frequently heated competition for parliamentary and government positions, an increasingly salient regional ecology of electoral behavior (with respect to voter turnout and party preferences) gets increasingly foregrounded. The stability and coherence of these regional features (not a national peculiarity, of course) is, again, a reason for deeper scrutiny.

The four village case study in 2000 was initiated from concerns such as those just described. It was preceded by a study of Cultural-Interaction Stratification (or CIS, in the second half of the 1980s), and a Project on Contextual/Social Network Influences on Political Participation in the second half of the 1990s, both of which applied an SNA approach within a national framework (using representative samples). Our objective this time was to take a closer look, even if such a village-oriented view might entail a strong restriction on the domain of our investigation. In addition to social network and social capital interests, our approach was also motivated by community traditions in the study of electoral behavior (as exemplified by pieces of the Lazarsfeld-school implicitly anticipating some features of the SNA-approach, such as Katz and Lazarsfeld 1955). As an especially significant feature, our analytic design introduced an explicitly comparative focus. On the potentially negative side, our multicase strategy may have detracted to some degree from the sharpness of the qualitative picture that is characteristic of single-case studies. However, this lack is compensated for by a definite enhancement of analytic possibilities.[5]

SUBSTANTIVE TOPICS OF THE STUDY[6]

Although they are less in the limelight, small communities fulfill an important role in social cohesion. Although somewhat archaic in aspects of system integration, these very characteristics may serve as a kind of buffer for a considerable segment of the population, particularly during times of economic breakdowns. The last one-and-a-half decades of Hungarian transformation, with massive life changes in its wake, presents a case for the assessment of this role. Earlier strategies of concentrated industrialization heavily pushing the rural labor force from villages to urban areas entailed a considerable downgrading of longer-term rural perspectives.[6] As a kind of vicious circle, diminishing population manifested itself as a sign of erosion of living conditions and presented a motive, in the token of economic rationality and the improvement of general standards, for shifting a number of functions of communal provision (education, health, and so on) toward larger territorial units. Although settlements of low to medium size on the verge of rural and urban infrastructure were not really able to fill these gaps, the small settlements on the bottom of the population scale not only lost an increasing number of requisites of self-sustenance but various accessories for maintaining local identity, and in a broader sense, social integration as well.

The change of system at the turn of the 1980s and 1990s brought important changes in these respects. Institutions of local self-government, along with other requisites of pluralistic democracy, were introduced, accompanied by a degree of economic decentralization (although a significant share of income tax was left at the local level, this proportion declined considerably later on). Economic changes were of no less importance with their direct or indirect implications. Although the "transformational recession"[7] taking place in the first half of the nineties drastically reevaluated the viability of domestic production, in its worst period crowding out almost one-third of jobs from the labor market, this shift took place in a rather differentiated way across regions and territorial units, striking the less-developed eastern part of the country much harder than the western and especially the central parts, and rural areas significantly more than urban ones. However, the latter developments were, in a certain sense, offset by the political event of land compensation, allocating certain amounts of estates to small producers (mediated by a mechanism of partial pecuniary restitution). Although unemployment rose most steeply in the countryside, a reverse trend of migration began from urban to rural areas, based on the relatively easy access to land with its opportunity for daily subsistence, plausible for those who had previously left agriculture for an urban living and were now pushed back after losing (typically unskilled, industrial) jobs. This safety-valve capacity of rural areas proved most vital during the period of most pronounced hardship, but is, in fact, a matter of longer-term concern. Even after a period of economic recovery, the level of employment in Hungary continues to be rather low in either a temporal or a cross-country comparison.[8]

Although a steady extension of legal categorization of settlements as towns has largely increased the official rate of urban population, some one-third of citizens still belong to villages, not to speak of the significantly higher proportion of legally urban settlements that are poorly equipped with the important ingredients for urbanization. The number of small villages with less than one thousand inhabitants amounts to one-half of the territorial units, and still comprises nearly 10 percent of the total population. In many respects on their own, their day-to-day coping depends, to a large degree, on their capacity for maintaining inner cooperation and building outer linkage with regard to labor market positions, opportunities for local investment, or access to means of budgetary redistribution by central authorities. At this time, I do not go into the complications implied by differing interpretations and the stricter or wider uses of the term "social capital" (for a more detailed treatment see Angelusz and Tardos 2001); but one can relate several aspects of social capital to these capacities as embedded resources attached to either individuals and their groups or the respective communities as a whole. Whether we speak of social network resources, embeddedness, or cohesion, it relates to aspects of social integration of special importance to localities on the periphery.

Although the relationship of social capital and community development may be more or less clearly conceived in the previous frames, the inclusion of the term "social integration," as exhibited in the title of this study, may appear more doubtful. The relationship of the terms "social capital" and "social integration" depends, to a large extent, on the choice of a stricter or broader interpretation of social capital. Components like investment, mobilization, and return (emphatic elements of the former conception) are regarded as advisable in treating this issue on a theoretical plane; however, strategic aspects of research suggest the plausibility of a more comprehensive approach that embraces group-level perspectives as well. A key issue of our study concerns the relative benefits of various types of social ties related to social integration, with a view to the possible drawbacks of social capital as well (see Portes 1998). Although bridging and linking ties are widely regarded as beneficial and densely knit, bonding ties are considered more problematic in this respect, capable of harming social integration on a larger plane. Our study focuses on the prevalence of various types of ties among various settings, and their implications for the welfare of the members of the respective communities as a whole.

The problem of territorial differences or regional embeddedness, in a wider sense, has been a matter of longer interest. The aforementioned CIS-project[9] found that following a more traditional pattern of community-wide relationships of familiarity, rural people had a relatively large pool of ties of wider acquaintanceship. More or less coherent regional differences have also been pointed out, related to different historical paths and current geographical positions, the room of commerce and tourism, labor market positions, and migration. Although a general finding based on temporal comparisons ranging from the 1980s to the 1990s pointed to a shift in background factors of access to social network resources centering on the increased role of the economic (wealth) factor among other (cultural, political) types of capital, this trend manifested itself more unanimously in the western, rather than the eastern, part of the country. Also, the western region was found to be better equipped with contacts, especially of the "weaker" type of wider acquaintanceship related to a meso level (see Angelusz and Tardos 1991).

Regarding the criteria of selection of localities included in the sample, two dimensions—regional characteristics (more-and less-developed parts of the country) and level of electoral participation—were elected for this purpose. Steady high and low voter turnout was chosen not only because of the easy access to such data, but for conceptual considerations related to the connection of civic participation and social integration, even if it does not share the former factor's direct inclusion to the components of social capital (as in Putnam 2000). Although the character of causality between political participation and social integration is not unambiguous, and the necessity of high voter turnout as a prerequisite of democracy is also regarded as questionable by a number of political scientists and sociologists (see, e.g., van Deth 2000),[10] it is generally acknowledged that a lasting separation of a considerable segment of the population from wider civic issues is a negative symptom in this regard (as stressed by Lijphart 1997 in the context of electoral participation, or Halpern 2005 as to social capital).[11]

The lasting observation has been made on the basis of territorial election statistics in Hungary that, other than the largest cities, it is the smallest villages that display the highest level of electoral participation (in spite of their clearly less-advantaged populations). The situation is similar in both parts of the country, as those characteristics of the villages are even more salient in the more developed western, rather than the eastern, region. This is the case not only with regard to municipal, but national elections as well. It is assumed that denser communication on community affairs and a closer interface between local leaders and ordinary citizens contribute to a stronger sense of civic responsibility in these small settlements.

The next sections give an account of the design, the methods applied, and the substantive findings of the study. After a basic characterization of the four villages (including their positions on some network features), a comparison will analyze access to social capital with special emphasis on differences in types of tie. Following these findings, the chapter treats the mobilization of social resources, stressing their differential use among various contexts. Other target variables besides earnings have also been included, such as labor activity (having a job), local esteem/reputation, and electoral participation at the national and municipal levels. This composition of indicators implies a distinction between outcomes of primarily instrumental and expressive/integrative character, an explicit focus of this study.[12]

DESIGN AND METHODS

The survey of the four village study took place in early spring 2000 by means of face-to-face interviews on a sample of more than 700 persons.[13]

As a central feature, the sample was formed on a 2 × 2 analytical design based on the total adult population of four minivillages from two regions of Hungary. The choice of these microsettings was a deliberate decision, having to do with research antecedents concerning political behavior and social capital. As indicated, the repeated observation of a U-shaped pattern of electoral participation was a motive of first importance. By beginning with these two aspects, a fourfold typology was developed. The 200 or so interviews designated for each place reached a quantity that permitted a range of quantitative analyses, although this number was still small enough to make possible, at least in principle, a saturated sample based on the whole populations.

As to the first dimension, our criterion was participation during three national elections, selecting from the pool of villages with a turnout higher than 80, respectively lower than a 60 percent rate each time. As to the regional aspect, two counties were chosen from the western and eastern border territories of the country that differ in many respects (with Austria neighboring on the one side, Ukraine and Romania on the other). As a point of importance for the sampling procedure, the county in the western part has a host of settlements of the targeted size (mostly situated in valleys of a hilly countryside), and the eastern one is predominantly a lowland territory with larger settlements as a rule. Also, the former county, as a whole, exhibits a more intensive electoral participation than the latter one, so it was easier to find a village with high turnout of the given size in the western part and one with a low rate at in the eastern one, while finding their counterparts was more difficult in both regions.

Table 10.1 sums up the features of design with sample sizes reached by the survey.

Due to the fact that willingness to respond is relatively high even today (or at least at the time of the survey) in the countryside in Hungary (which

Table 10.1 The Scheme of the Two-dimensional (2*2) Sample Design

	Regional Embeddedness	
Level of Civic Participation	*Western Region*	*Eastern Region*
High	*"West-High"* *(n = 170)*	*"East-High"* *(n = 225)*
Low	*"West-Low"* *(n = 114)*	*"East-Low"* *(n = 227)*

Note. "Normal cases" = West-High and East-Low. "Deviant cases" = West-Low and East-High
N: The number of adult respondents of the villages.

applies especially to relatively isolated rural locations), the response rate was satisfactory on the whole, amounting to an average of more than 75 percent. Nonresponse moved between 17 percent and 30 percent, moderate enough to approach a saturated outline of total networks. As a substantive trait of the rates of coverage, the two high-participation cases also exhibited the highest response rates (both presumably related to the level of social integration in one way or another).[14]

The interviews took about one hour, with little variation by settlements. Applying a multistranded approach of social network resources, several techniques were used.[15] Of the standard approaches, the Fischer and McAllister (1978)/GSS name-generator[16] and the Lin and Dumin (1986) occupational position-generator[17] techniques were utilized as best adapted to the national setting and the objectives of the project.[18] Besides its methodological advantages, this simultaneous application was justified by substantive reasons, our intention to include microlevel core ties (targeted by the former method) and mesolevel wider acquaintanceship contacts (closer to the latter method).

Following our former measurements of social network resources on the individual level, further indicators were also included (such as contacts through association membership or mail networking). A composite measure of social network resources was formed, again similarly to the given research antecedents.[19] However, with different ties and their benefits in the focus, the emphasis will shift this time to the distinct types of relationships. Three indicators stand out hereby: two out-degree measures, produced by the position-generator and the name-generator instruments; and an in-degree measure by the latter instrument, permitted by the saturated-sample approach applied. Nexus diversity, the position generator-based index most widely used in our analyses, is based on a summation of occupations contacted one way or another.[20] In addition to these practical reasons, more substantive reasons also play some part, such as the emphasis on network diversity/heterogeneity as emphasized by Erickson (1996) and Lin (2001) in a number of contexts, with the theoretical framework of the synthesizing work.

Another improvement of this case study (from a substantive point of view as well) was the inclusion of a larger number of social capital-related variables. An assessment of local reputation (based on several aspects of esteem and excellence) is close to the character of in-degree ("authority") measures.[21] Referring to specific foci of ties, a next set of variables involved indexes like the extensity of kin and family ties, residential status (seniority), and local/global embeddedness (based on measures of horizontal mobility). These individual attributes were added by structural variables derived by complex analyses (based on individual and household-level measures) like community network centrality; and additionally, variables that describe neighborhood contexts (in some cases the primary basis of clique-like formations).

As to the procedures of data analysis, sets of simple correlations are used along with more sophisticated multivariate techniques for an assessment of the magnitude of influence of various social capital-related indicators. Optimal scaling (CATREG) regression analysis has been applied (capable of handling variables of various levels of measurement, categorical among them). Target variables like earnings, local reputation, or electoral participation, and the indexes related to them are described in more detail regarding instrumental and expressive outcomes of mobilization of social capital.

FINDINGS

The Four Cases—A General Profile With Some Background Characteristics

The settlements selected lag somewhat behind the rural average with regard to most economic and cultural indicators, and have an older age composition, generally characteristic of villages of this size. However, they also largely differ one from another, with the case West-High well above the others.

The community West-High stands out on almost all indicators of socioeconomic development, even in a broader comparison of rural settlements in Hungary. Its favorable geographic conditions, such as closeness to both the county center and the Austrian border, are decisive factors in its urban-like opportunities. Also, after an era of neglect of the Western border region during waves of state-controlled industrialization, a former handicap has now reversed. Less subject to the breakdown of the state industry at the beginning of the nineties, this case was not hit as hard by the economic hardships of that period. The rate of unemployment was as low as 3 percent at the time of the survey, coupled with a 46 percent level of employment that was also exceptional for rural areas. With a regional center in the close vicinity (once a remarkable commercial settlement with a considerable Jewish population) and Burgenland also accessible on the other side of the border, a range of employment opportunities presents itself, although perhaps not all of them legally settled. As shown by the respective blocks of Table

Table 10.2 An Overall Review of the Salience of Individual- and Community-Level Assets Related to Social Capital in the Four Communities

Types of of assets			West-High	East-High	West-Low	East-Low
1.Individual-level social network resources						
A. General ego-network measures	**By types of ties,** measured by different generator techniques, and expressed in an	Extended network range – **nexus diversity** (position generator)	+++	+		
		Core network range (name		+++		
		Composite index of social network resources	+++	++		
B. Specific foci (kinship, territorial contacts, closer and wider connections)	**Kinship** ties**	Local kinship ties (number of relatives)		+++		++
		Outside kinship ties	+++			+
	Travel contacts***	Travel contacts in the vicinity (frequency)		++	+	++
		Travel contacts at a longer distance	+++	++		
	"Global" (vs. local) embeddedness	Based on data of outside (domestic and foreign) and closer contacts	+++		++	
2. Community-level properties derived from individual- and household-level data						
A. Based on the distribution of individual core network range scores	**Differentiation/ Inequality******	Variance		+		
		Skewness			++	
		Kurtosis			++	
B. Describing the configuration of community networks constituted by between-household ties		Core-periphery Gini			+	
	Cohesion****	Density	++	++		
		Inclusiveness	+	++		
	Clustering, structuration*****	Clustering coefficient	+			
		Transitivity	+	+		
		Reciprocity		+		+
	Centralization measures based on out-degree,	Out-degree centrality	++			
		Betweenness centrality	+	++		
		Eigenvalue centrality			++	+
C. Voluntary local associations, institutions of social support	Occurrence of **associations** and rates of membership*****	Functional associations (farmers' circle, women's circle, etc.)	+++			
		Leisure circles (local cultural, sports clubs)	+++			
	Institutions of **local reciprocity*******	House-building support	++	++		
		"Potlatch"-like exchanges		++		++

* Lin-Dumin and GSS/Fischer-McAllister types of network generator techniques, and composite indexes including these some further measures, see Table A10.1.1 in the Appendix for more details.
** See in TableA10.1.2 in the Appendix.
***See Table A10.1.3 in the Appendix.
****See Table A10.1.4 in the Appendix, based on Ucinet, Netminer, and SPSS computations.
***** See Table A10.1.5 in the Appendix for more details.
****** +: $p < .05$, ++: $p < .01$, +++: $p < .001$.

10.2 and the subsidiary table in the Appendix, travel patterns clearly reflect these chances for horizontal mobility. Even though a large part of available jobs are still related to agriculture, the weight of tertiary sector is also high, especially in a comparison with the other cases. Although the gravity of economic activity shifts from agriculture to other spheres, subsidiary agricultural production of small farms (household plots) is still ubiquitous as a second or third leg of the inhabitants' sustenance. It is a special feature of this community, a source of heterogeneity not unique in this region, that it has a Lutheran religious minority of about one-fourth of the population. Religious activity is highest among the four cases including the majority denomination, Catholic. As a whole, from some angles of tradition the village resembles the rural population of the wider region of Austria and Slovenia.

As compared to the former case, the situation of the village West-Low is less favorable in almost all respects, but is better than the two eastern ones, especially the East-Low case. In matters of infrastructure and a number of cultural aspects, it occupies second place out of the four settlements. Age structure, however, is especially unfavorable, with 62 percent of the adult population above fifty years. The recent decade witnessed a rapid population decline. This demographic feature, which goes back to a longer period, is reflected by the low number of closer family and, even more, kinship ties (as seen in the respective tables). The positive West-High employment experience does not extend to this case. The proportion of active wage earners is only 24 percent, slightly above that in the eastern cases. Due to the somewhat greater distance from the regional center and the western border as well, the geographic–economic conditions of this settlement are less advantageous. Although territorial contacts of the inhabitants are rather limited, a relatively new feature has been the purchase and renovation of houses left behind in the wake of population loss by foreign buyers (German and Austrian pensioners, making use of the still relatively cheap housing estate in the Hungarian countryside and the natural attractions of this landscape, with its hillsides and vineyards). In contrast with the former case, religious pluralism is less present, Catholics being a large majority. Church attendance is just a little behind that of the former case. Village administration takes place within strongly centralized frames. Characteristically, this was the only village out of our cases to present one candidate only, the incumbent, for the post of mayor in the previous municipal elections.

On the other side of the country, the economic and cultural conditions of the settlement East-High are most affected by the general circumstances of the eastern region. If taking only these circumstances into account, the high civic participation of this case might be a difficult fact to explain. Although higher than those for its East-Low counterpart, the educational and infrastructural indicators do not exceed the scores for the settlement West-Low. The unemployment rate is at 20 percent (not unique for the region), a proportion not less then the rate of active wage earners with legally settled jobs providing standard social security, rather than casual jobs of a "grey" type. Being a terminal node at the Rumanian border, railroad employment was a traditional feature of its occupation structure that was badly affected by the downsizing of such activities in recent decades. Its administrative function as a border site, although not without relevance for local activities, has no decisive role from an economic point of view. Agricultural production, although it is of a subsidiary character in the majority of cases, is more significant; in fact, it is a basic pillar of sustenance for the bulk of households. The rate of those producing for the food market in some way stands out among the four cases. It is not without historical interest that a part of the populations stems from an eighteenth-century wave of South German settlers. Although not salient, some manifestations of that tradition are present even now. This ethnic background is exceptional in the region, having its expression in the majority religious denomination of Catholic. The remaining part of the population is of Protestant origin, closer to the general religious profile of the region. Religious activity is far less intensive than in the western counterparts. The pluralistic character of the community manifests itself even more strongly with party preferences. Although the voters of the three other cases tend to present a right-conservative political preference in agreement with the general tendency of rural areas, the village East-High provides a stronghold for the left-wing forces as well, a tendency probably not unrelated to its varied (present or past) employment profile. An approximate balance of party preferences is observed across the elections, commuting between left and right according to the general current.

East-Low is, doubtlessly, the least developed of the four cases. The proportion of those with a high school degree is not more than 10 percent. Half of the adult population is attached to traditional agricultural production, with an employment rate even lower than in the previous case. Although its surroundings with the river Tisza might offer favorable opportiunities, these are actually offset by natural disasters (frequent floods) in the recent years. The distance from the regional center is, again, a bad point. The closeness to the Ukrainian border, in turn, yielded some chances in the field of grey (black) economy, such as small-scale informal trade with petrol, tobacco, and produce of the region. Infrastructural and household equipment indicators are especially poor. Almost half of the houses were without bathrooms at the time of the study; the rate of households with a car was no more than 20 percent. From the aspect of religious denomination, the village is rather homogenous, close to the regional Protestant profile. Religious activity is quite low across denominations. Data indicating a large number of relatives outside the village (such as the capital) evidence attempts of mobility by means of migration. This chance of exit lost much of its earlier significance due to the decreased demand of labor and increased travel costs of commuting. The net balance of migration in the last decades has resulted in some shift of the ethnic composition of the population; although not salient by a segregated pattern, the rate of Roma population (by some assessments about one-fifth of the inhabitants) has reached the highest level among the four cases.

Access to Social Network Resources

As outlined, the four village case study applied a large set of indicators related to social capital with regard to resources both on the individual and the community level. Classic ego-network techniques were applied on the individual level along with some simpler indicators pointing to specific foci of network resources, from kinship to the range of outside contacts. Although distinct in an operational sense, these two subsets are clearly interrelated substantively. On the whole, a stronger emphasis of kin relationships may underlie a stronger tendency of core network orientation, yet that of travel contacts indicates a higher degree of nexus diversity, as shown by name-generator techniques with the former aspect, and position-generator techniques with the latter. In a differentiation according to the various lines, local kinship and limited outside contacts (remaining in the frames of the vicinity) point to homophilous, more distant ties of kinship, and travel contacts to a more heterophilous composition of ties.

As shown by the upper block of Table 10.2 summarizing respective results in a condensed form (shown in more detail in the Appendix by Tables A10.1.1–A10.1.4), the cases West-High and East-High presented the highest scores of resources with practically all individual-level indicators. This fact is actually a principal finding of the survey. When selecting the four cases, high and low electoral participation was one criterion of choice that assumed a certain relationship between community-level social capital and electoral (or, more broadly, civic) participation. Although not underwriting the conception of electoral participation as a constitutive element of social capital, some correlation was certainly hypothesized between these notions.[22]

However, a distinction by types of ties and specific foci yields a more diffentiatiated picture for the two outstanding cases. The village West-High displays high scores for extended ties, and the strong features of East-High relate to core network resources. As subsidiary indicators, longer distance travel contacts and outside embeddedness join the former, dense kinship, and spacially close contacts join the latter traits, in congruence with the basic observations. The socioecological differences between the two villages outlined previously in the context of level of urbanization may help to explain this divergence, and the following presentation of outcome factors will throw more light on the implications of these characteristics.

The two "low" cases stand out with regard to a few points only. Being relatively well connected due to its geographic situation, the inhabitants of the settlement West-Low have a relatively large range of outer (including foreign) contacts. The case of East-Low displays high scores concerning local kinship ties, not the least on account of a relatively large birthrate and the maintenance of a traditional system of reciprocity.

Although the interrelationship of individual-level and group-level resources related to social capital is a complicated issue,[23] it is the two "high" cases, again, that stand out most in regard to community attributes assessed by various ways. The data at hand taken together, from (total network) density measures to the numbers and memberships of associations or mutual aid on local occasions of house-building,[24] suggest a higher degree of cohesion within these two communities, even if further investigations by in-depth interviews with key figures in the villages revealed tendencies of disintegration at these places as well.

The patterns exhibited are shaded by more specific indicators. As to the prevalence of core network resources with the East-High case, although not quite self-evident,[25] this is true for out-degree and in-degree measures as well. The two villages on the lower end of the spectrum also present some higher scores, although less generally. In agreement with the civil manners of the western region, the inhabitants of West-Low follow their ("high") counterpart in the neighborhood in sending a much higher amount of greeting cards than either case of the eastern region. In turn, again matching a more general pattern, the two villages from the east side exhibit the highest scores related to manifestations of local patronage.

Findings of structural analyses based on the inclusion of total networks are more or less congruent with the previously-described picture above, and contain some further features as well. Measures of cohesion (density, inclusiveness) present themselves as highest for the two "high" cases, which also applies to the indicators of degree of clustering, crystallized structuration of between-household ties, including transitivity and centralization characteristics. Measure of reciprocity stands out in turn, with the two east cases agreeing with a pattern indicated earlier. Finally, inequality of social network resources (based on the distribution of individual measures, as well as the structural indicator core/periphery Gini coefficient) is most marked in the West-Low village, coupled with a similar pattern of eigenvalue centralization that suggests a status-directed pattern of relationships (appearing, in fact, with the East-Low counterpart also). Although inequality of social resources alone is less of a problem (see Blau 1994 with regard to intergroup contacts), its coupling with a high degree of centralization suggests a strong consolidation between various resources and a rigid hierarchical tendency in this setting.

Instrumental and Expressive Gains of Social Capital

In agreement with a decisive line of findings of the literature (such as Lin 2001 regarding the instrumental and expressive gains of social capital), research into the mobilization of social network resources in Hungary on a national plane has also found significant relationships with regard to extended ties (nexus diversity) on the one hand, and instrumental gains such as personal earnings on the other (Angelusz and Tardos 2008). The question arises: if this were true for the given cases, will an abundance of dense core ties (with a view to the East-High case) prove a benefit at all?

Table 10.3 An Overview of Outcomes, With Social Network Resources as Independent Variables, for the Four Cases (Symbols Above: Referring to Level of Significance* of Correlation; Symbols Below: Referring to Level of Significance* of Regression Coefficients)

Dependent Variables (Composite Indexes)	Independent Variables	Measure of Variables	**West-High**	**East-High**	**West-Low**	**East-Low**
1. **Instrumental** benefits (index of income and job position)**	Nexus diversity	Extended network range (position generator)	++ +++	+++ +++	++	+++ +++
	Local hub position	Core ties range (out-degree)		++ +	 ++	 ++
	Local authority position	Core ties range (in-degree)		++		 +
2. **Expressive-**reputational benefits (index of local reputation and civic involvement)***	Nexus diversity	Extended network range (position generator)	+++ ++	+++ +++		++ +++
	Local hub position	Core ties range (out-degree)		++	 +	+
	Local authority position	Core ties range (in-degree)	+++ +	+++ +++	+ +++	+++ +++
3.1. Electoral **participation** (as a criterion indicator for the design of the study)****	Nexus diversity	Extended network range (position generator)	+++ ++	+++ +++		++ +++
	Local hub position	Core ties range (out-degree)	+++ +++	++	 +	
	Local authority position	Core ties range (in-degree)		++	 +	
3.2. Electoral participation—the influence of individual social network resources*****	General social network position	Composite index of individual social network resources	+++ +++	+++ +++		++ ++
3.3. Electoral participation—household-level models of social network and contextual influences	Local seniority	Aggregated residential status (duration of living in the community)	+ +++		 +++	 +++
	Global-local embeddedness	Aggregated index based on outside (versus local or vicinity) contacts	 +++	++ +++		
	Local network centrality	Relational score based on core network data matrix computed for households			+++	
	Local neighborhood (spatial proximity)	Terrritorial segments(streets, blocks) inside the communities	++	+++	+++ +++	+++ +++

*+ $p < .05$. ++$p < .01$. +++p , .001.
**See Table A10.2.1 in the Appendix.
***See Table A10.2.2 in the Appendix.
****Composite index based on retrospective data of turnout on three national and local elections and attitudes toward electoral participation (correlation and regression coefficients for respondents 26 years and above); see Table A10.2.3- Table A10.2.5 in the Appendix more details.
*****Based on nexus diversity (PG), core ties range (NG), association membership, and mail networking (greeting cards, etc.) extensity.

Constructing composite indexes to obtain a general view, an array of assets were involved by means of factor-analytic techniques. Two factors emerged clearly: one that embraces personal earnings and the possession of a steady job (as mentioned, the latter a scarce asset in most villages), the other contains indicators of local reputation (having a name as the owner of various personal properties) and civic involvement (as measured by the intensity of participation in past national and municipal elections). Although the former is clearly an index of instrumental benefits, the latter, which has to do with local status and esteem, comes closer to expressive ones. The following analyses were carried out for both composite indexes by means of correlation and regression-type techniques. Table 10.3 (which summarizes the respective findings, detailed in Tables A10.2.1 to A10.2.5 in the Appendix) also contains a special panel related to civic involvement, a subcomponent of the latter index, with a view to its role in the design of the study and its assumed function in social integration.

The observations display a certain unity of effects alongside important differences regarding the distinct cases. As revealed by the upper panel of the table, the findings for the four villages confirm the general existence of a strong relationship between nexus diversity and instrumental benefits related to earnings[26] and jobs, although this is much less true for network positions based on closer ties (regarding either out-degree or in-degree aspects). One further result is still in line with general assumptions. Benefits of expressive nature are closely related to core tie measures, in particular the in-degree measure that can be conceived as mirroring one's position of local authority; this is especially observable with the East cases. Although assets of group esteem are of no directly tangible gain they are still of worth, especially among traditional contexts as in the villages in question. As a parallel tendency, instrumental gains in the East-High case, differing from the general pattern, turn out to be closely related to core ties range as well. A kind of "strength of strong ties" under these conditions implies the presence of (typically kinship-based) paternalistic relationships, with special regard to the often-informal provision of scarce local assets like jobs.

The findings concerning civic participation involve a broader set of components of social embeddedness. Some of these involve the classic dimension of local and cosmopolitan population (Merton 1949), or with some shift of emphasis, "old" and "new" segments of population (Laumann and Pappi 1976). The West-High case displays a notable combination of factors that enhance civic involvement. Although the role of outer contacts is in correspondence with the salience of wider acquaintenceship in several respects, this influence of cosmopolitan orientation does not preclude a similar effect of local seniority, presenting itself as a more intensive civic participation by residents with a longer past in the given

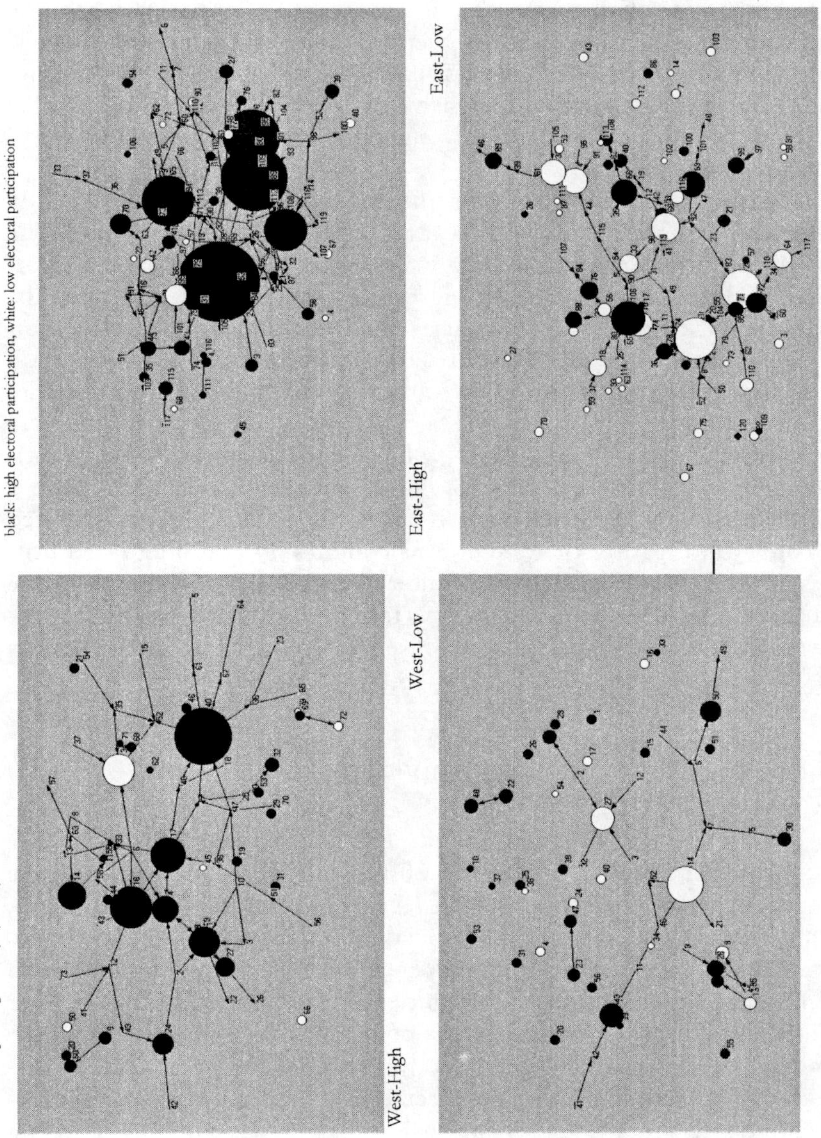

Figure 10.1 Local centrality and network location of families with high and low electoral participation.

milieu. Although it would be hard to generalize using these findings alone, the parallel work of these two tendencies seems to result in a kind of balance in the given case that contributes to social integration. As to the East-High case, the role of micronetwork centrality (concerning either hub or authority positions) stands out with regard to participation; those most prominent regarding local interactions tend to be more active in civic affairs. The two cases, generally less equipped with social resources and less integrated by a structured inclusive network of ties, in turn, display a tendency of influence in the local neighborhood, a contextual factor of sheer spatial proximity.

The network characteristics of the four communities are visually highlighted in Figure 10.1 with regard to electoral participation. The networks outlined derive from data matrices by means of a name-generator technique, transposed by an aggregation on the level of households. (Nodes in black signify generally active households; those in white indicate those that are nonactive with regard to electoral participation).

The chart suggests the role of connectedness, and the close interdependence of network centrality, influence, and a motive to participate, especially in the two "high" cases, a finding also supported by quantitative analyses, as indicated by the lower panel of Table 10.2. With a view to the other pole, a sparser web of relationships is clearly exhibited as a contextual feature that conditions community and microlevel processes as well. A case of negative influence can even be observed in the West-Low village, with an absentee pattern presented by some of its centrally located actors suggesting the presence of a "deviant" model in this context.

A SHORT SUMMARY WITH REFERENCE TO COMMUNITY DEVELOPMENT

Several different findings from the 2000 four village case study have pointed to the cooccurrence of high levels of social network resources, community-level manifestations of social capital, and active civic involvement. The real proof of these interdependencies depends, nonetheless, on the future evolution of these communities. Future manifestations of their viability should reveal whether larger pools of social capital at either the individual or the group level are really conducive to some kind of sustained development. For example, it remains to be seen whether the prevalence of dense core network relationships in the East-High case, with a degree of paternalism and strong tendencies toward centralization that today aid in the survival of a large segment of the population in times of hardship, will prove to be a trap later on, inhibiting the inclusion of this village in developmental processes that require a larger horizon. In fact, how the balance of inner cohesion and marked outer embeddedness will be maintained later on in the West-High case is a matter of future developments as well. Furthermore, the question also arises as to whether future events will confirm a more problematic development, including deterioration of conditions, with regard to the two "low" cases.

Territorial statistics may yield some preliminary answers to these questions.[27] As explained at the outset, demographic developments are of crucial importance in these cases at the rural periphery. Following a long tradition, the natural growth of population (deriving from the difference in the numbers of births and deaths) has been negative for all four villages in the last one-and-a-half decades. However, the data display remarkable differences among the cases. Between 1990 and 2001, population loss was much more moderate in the two "high" cases (and in fact, a deceleration took place in comparison with earlier decades). This trend continued between 2002 and 2004. To point out the different sources of this tendency in the two positive cases: There was a higher birth rate in the East-High settlement, and a lower death rate in West-High. The balance of migration followed a similar pattern, with a more moderate loss for the two "high" cases both before and after the time of our survey. In fact, a moderation of population loss is good news in an ambivalent manner, because fulfilling certain functions of communal self-maintenance presumes some minimal population size, and a reversal of the trend toward population loss, or even a halt to it, has not yet taken place.

Infrastructural developments play a vital role. New construction, especially in the West-High case, is rather high, which is a promising sign. Telephone lines are now more or less ubiquitous (except in the East-High case), as well as the general diffusion of cellular phones. Cable television has reached saturation in West-High, and a partial introduction has taken place in East-High. Broadband Internet access has just made its appearance in West-High and East-High, although coverage remains much lower than in other parts of the country.

Employment opportunities more or less follow the earlier pattern, with relatively enviable opportunities in the western region and in the West-High case in particular. A change with regard to the eastern region can, however, be observed. Whereas East-High led East-Low in unemployment before 2000, this has recently reversed, with a remarkable reduction in the former and a slight increase in the latter case. Concerning related economic tendencies, similar trends manifest themselves in the number of enterprises, the rate of entrepreneurial activities, the number of taxpayers, income levels, and taxes (with West-High in the most enviable position, followed by West-Low and East-High; East-Low is well at the bottom in all these respects). Future tendencies, of course, are not separable from the general course of the economy and the direction of regional-territorial development in Hungary, with many issues still open.

APPENDIX

Table A10.1.1 Basic Data of SC Components for the Cases of the 2000 Four Village Study and Comparable Indicators of the 1997–98 National Studies

2000 Four Village Case Study	Composite Index of Socal Network Resources (Factor-Score)	Core Ties Range (3-Situation Name Generator)				Nexus Diversity (Occupational Position Genrator)			Complementary Measures Of Social Network Resources			
		Out-Degree Measures		In-Degree Measures							Kinship Patron Roles	
		Number of Different Persons Mentioned	Number of Total Mentions	Number of Mentions by Different Persons	Number of Total Mentions	Range - Number of Occupations Mentioned (Out Of 24)	Support Potential (Number of Contacts Likely to Help in Case of Need)	Close-Ness (Number of Contacts on a First Name Basis)	Association Membership, Number	Mail Networking – Sending Greeting Cards	Number of "God-children"	Occurrence of "Best Man" Role at Wedding Ceremonies
West-High	.41	2.53	4.21	1.75	3.17	13.65	9.64	9.01	.68	9.25	1.78	.41
West-Low	–.19	2.44	5.85	1.39	3.57	10.06	5.83	5.95	.20	7.25	1.42	.32
East-High	.09	3.27	6.89	1.93	4.11	10.11	7.45	7.99	.05	4.71	1.56	.51
East-Low	–.31	2.47	4.61	1.57	3.11	9.27	5.42	5.87	.08	4.13	2.49	.55
Total	.00	2.73	5.40	1.70	3.50	10.67	7.09	7.27	.23	5.96	1.88	.47
1997–98 National Survey												
Villages	—	3.57	5.68	—	—	11.35	6.70	—	.43	5.88	1.80	.89
Towns	—	3.78	6.27	—	—	11.90	7.20	—	.44	6.24	1.34	.81
Budapest	—	3.98	6.33	—	—	10.55	5.90	—	.50	7.29	1.01	.72

Table A10.1.2 Number of Close Family and Kin Relationships, the Latter by Residential Locations (Means)

Settlement	Close Family Ties		Number of Relatives (Beyond Close Family)				
	Number of Children	Number of Siblings	In the Village	In the County Center	In Budapest (Capital)	Abroad	Total Kin
West-High	1.55	1.41	2.24	4.46	.50	.12	7.32
	170	170	170	170	170	170	170
West-Low	1.60	1.38	1.04	.60	.92	.42	**2.98**
	106	106	106	106	106	106	**106**
East-Hjgh	1.86	1.59	4.67	.44	2.37	.70	8.19
	227	227	227	227	227	227	227
East-Low	1.80	1.79	3.12	.59	3.34	.70	7.75
	225	225	225	225	225	225	225
Total	1.73	1.58	3.10	1.45	2.02	.52	7.09
	728	728	728	728	728	728	728

Table A10.1.3 Travel Frequencies by Destinations for the Adult Populations of the Four Villages (Means, 4-Point Scales Each, Except Index of Travels Abroad, 1 = Never . . . 4 = Last Month)

Settlement	Neighboring Villages	Neighboring Towns	County Center	Budapest (Capital)	Near Abroad	Remote Abroad	Index of Travels Abroad
West-High	3.33	2.84	3.77	2.25	1.94	1.50	2.94
	169	170	170	157	170	169	169
West-Low	3.61	3.06	3.10	2.04	1.58	1.39	2.36
	104	106	106	100	106	105	105
East-Hjgh	3.66	3.56	2.62	2.23	1.74	1.23	2.20
	223	225	225	218	225	224	224
East-Low	3.62	3.56	2.74	2.24	1.67	1.17	2.02
	227	227	227	221	227	226	226
Total	3.56	3.32	3.00	2.21	1.74	1.30	2.34
	723	728	728	696	728	724	724

Table A10.1.4 Community Network Properties Based on Household-Level and Individual-Level Ties (UCINET6, Netminer, SPSS)

Measures		West-High	East-High	West-Low	East-Low
UCINET6/Network measures (between-household ties constituting community networks)					
Cohesion	Density	.0251	.0116	.0094	.0067
Centralization by measures of network centrality	Out-degree centralization	7.41%	5.87%	5.79%	2.29%
	Betweenness centralization	1.80%	3.97%	0.19%	0.29%
	Eigenvalue centralization	63.82%	49.16%	91.01%	83.00%
Differentiation/ Inequality	Core-periphery Gini-coeff.	0.662	0.554	0.705	0.577
Netminer 2.0/Analysis measures (between-household ties constituting community networks)					
Cohesion	Density	.0014	.`0016	.0009	.0007
	Inclusiveness	0.767	0.929	0.571	0.708
Clustering, structuration	Clustering coefficient	0.727	0.551	0.679	0.565
	Transitivity	0.193	0.137	0.077	0.031
	Reciprocity	0.216	0.393	0.207	0.337
Centralization (based on measures of network centrality)	Out-degree centralization	7.02%	5.63%	6.44%	2.72%
	Betweenness centralization	1.80%	5.78%	0.187%	0.287%
SPSS/Explore measures (indivdual-level ties)					
Differentiation/ inequality based on individual-level out-degree scores	Variance	2.061	2.716	2.059	1.887
	Skewness	.784	.664	1.309	.509
	Kurtosis	.283	.740	2.260	–.112

Table A10.1.5 Participation in Local Associations and Institutions of Local Reciprocity, by the Four Cases (Percentage)

		West-High	East-High	West-Low	East-Low
Associations functional	Farmers'circle membership	28	3	5	10
	Citizens' guard membership	11	6	0	3
	Fire guard membership	16	3	4	53
leisure	Women's circle female	99	0	9	0
	Local cultural circle memb.	10	0	0	0
	Local sports club membership	48	2	0	0
	Elderlies' day	40	0	38	1
Local reciprocity	House-building support deliv.	27	20	14	5
	Wedding food gift receipt	61	90	68	84

Table A10.2.1 Correlations Between Types of Tie and Various Kinds of Benefits, by the Four Cases (Pearson R Coeff)

		Nexus Diversity PG-range	Local Hub Position (NG-Core Ties Out-Degree)	Local Authority Position (NG-Core Ties Out-Degree)	Nexus Diversity PG-Range	Local Hub Position (NG-Core Ties Out-Degree)	Local Authority Position (NG-Core Ties Out-Degree)
		West-High			East-High		
Instrumental benefits	Pearson Corr.	.430(**)	.113	.121	.279(**)	.223(**)	.209(**)
	Sig. (2-tailed)	.000	.144	.115	.000	.001	.002
Expressive benefits	Pearson Corr.	.216(**)	–.004	.190(*)	.317(**)	.218(**)	.441(**)
	Sig. (2-tailed)	.005	.954	.013	.000	.001	.000
Electoral participation	Pearson Corr.	.279(**)	.288(**)	.058	.350(**)	.217(**)	.217(**)
	Sig. (2-tailed)	.001	.000	.485	.000	.006	.006
		West-Low			East-Low		
Instrumental benefits	Pearson Corr.	.270(**)	.152	.155	.263(**)	.072	–.046
	Sig. (2-tailed)	.005	.121	.113	.000	.277	.493
Expressive benefits	Pearson Corr.	.107	–.049	.238(*)	.178(**)	.151(*)	.278(**)
	Sig. (2-tailed)	.277	.615	.014	.007	.023	.000
Electoral participation	Pearson Corr.	.064	.161	.170	.216(**)	.052	.060
	Sig. (2-tailed)	.549	.126	.108	.009	.531	.474

*Correlation is significant at the 0.05 level (2-tailed).
**Correlation is significant at the 0.01 level (2-tailed).
VG: Name generator instrument of social network measurement
PG: Position generator instrument of social network measurement

Table A10.2.2 Regressions of Various Kinds of Benefits Depending on Various Types of Tie, Controlling Age, Sex, and Education, by the Four Cases (Optimal Scaling Categorical Regression Analysis)

West-High	Instrumental benefits			Expressive benefits			Electoral participation		
	Beta	F	Sig	Beta	F	Sig	Beta	F	Sig
Nexus diversity (PG range)	.157	6.140	.001	.351	22.751	.000	.276	9.362	.000
Local hub (NG utdegree)	–.048	.679	.411	–.054	.624	.431	.400	26.701	.000
Local authority (NG in-degree)	–.041	.467	.495	.196	8.114	.000	.070	.899	.409
Age	–.503	66.544	.000	.435	37.860	.000	.164	3.728	.027
Sex	–.274	23.734	.000	–.089	1.689	.188	.031	.185	.831
Education	.132	3.877	.010	.120	2.786	.065	.137	2.368	.126
Adj. R^2	.489			.241			.250		
East-High	Instrumental benefits			Expressive benefits			Electoral participation		
	Beta	F	Sig	Beta	F	Sig	Beta	F	Sig
Nexus diversity (PG range)	.224	15.01	.000	.249	14.166	.000	.475	38.320	.000
Local hub (NG utdegree)	.121	4.672	.010	.116	3.462	.064	–.077	1.106	.334
Local authority (NG in-degree)	.095	2.576	.079	.366	43.799	.000	.094	1.531	.220
Age	.005	.008	.992	.068	1.670	.191	.059	.686	.505
Sex	–.149	6.545	.000	.345	37.998	.000	.138	3.384	.037
Education	.389	42.594	.000	–.029	.225	.636	.069	.793	.500
Adj. R^2	.319			.404			.212		
West-Low	Instrumental benefits			Expressive benefits			Electoral participation		
	Beta	F	Sig	Beta	F	Sig	Beta	F	Sig
Nexus diversity (PG range)	.069	.532	.468	.069	.643	.425	–.102	.916	.341
Local hub (NG utdegree)	.207	6.389	.003	.154	3.335	.040	.223	4.262	.017
Local authority (NG in-degree)	–.076	.785	.459	.388	20.118	.000	.206	3.879	.025
Age	–.368	14.949	.000	.366	13.551	.000	.052	.245	.622
Sex	–.200	6.209	.003	–.219	6.850	.002	.050	.227	.797
Education	.266	6.845	.010	.253	6.318	.014	.251	5.560	.021
Adj. R^2	.367			.304			.305		
East-Low	Instrumental benefits			Expressive benefits			Electoral participation		
	Beta	F	Sig	Beta	F	Sig	Beta	F	Sig
Nexus diversity (PG range)	.290	17.11	.000	.275	14.821	.000	.446	27.732	.000
Local hub (NG utdegree)	.133	4.287	.006	.048	.516	.473	–.033	.174	.677
Local authority (NG in-degree)	–.164	6.411	.012	.215	10.863	.000	.121	2.328	.129
Age	–.094	2.297	.103	–.004	.003	.997	.121	2.387	.096
Sex	.041	.369	.544	.224	12.668	.000	.209	6.381	.000
Education	.142	3.948	.048	–.119	3.236	.073	.130	2.292	.132
Adj. R^2	.165			.141			.181		

PG: Position generator instrument of social network measurement
NG: Name generator instrument of social network measurement

Table A10.2.3 Electoral Participation Depending on a Composite Measure of SC, Socioeconomic Resources, and Neighborhood Belonging (CATREG Optimal Scaling; Standardized Regression Coefficients and Importance Coefficients)

	Pooled Sample		West-High		East-High		West-Low		East-Low	
	Beta	Imp.	Beta	Imp.	Beta	Imp.	Beta	Imp.	Beta	Imp.
Social Capital – composite index*	.27	.38	.28	.42	.35	.68	.15	.14	.39	.52
Socioeconomic resources**	.12	.16	.33	.53	.12	.16	.22	.27	–.11	.00
Neighborhood belonging***	.25	.46	.15	,05	.17	.16	.34	.59	.35	.49
Adjusted R^2	.23		.24		.19		.16		.28	

Table A10.2.4 Household-Level Correlations Between Electoral Participation* and Social Capital-Related and Contextual Variables, by the Four Cases (Pearson R Coeff, Resp. Optimal Scaling Correlation Coeff.)

		West-High	East-High	West-Low	East-Low
Local seniority*	Pearson Corr.	.250	.102	.074	.177
	Sig. (2-tailed)	.035	.317	.617	.089
Global/local embeddedness*	Pearson Corr.	.174	.336	.106	.150
	Sig. (2-tailed)	.149	.001	.473	.151
Local network centrality**	Pearson Corr.	.106	.076	.075	–.025
	Sig. (2-tailed)	.379	.457	.610	.813
Local neighborhood (spatial proximity)***	Optimal Scaling Corr.	.224	.263	.395	.379
	Sig. (2-tailed)	.912	.000	.000	.000

Table A10.2.5 Household-Level Regressions of Electoral Participation* Depending on Social Capital-Related and Contextual Variables, by the Four Cases (Optimal Scaling, Categorical Regression Analysis)

	West-High			East-High		
	Beta	F	Sig.	Beta	F	Sig.
Local seniority*	.386	9.923	.000	–.110	1.218	.301
Global/local embeddedness*	.337	7.377	.000	.401	14.638	.000
Local network centrality**	.154	1.757	.182	.061	.395	.675
Local neighborhood (spatial proximity)***	.239	4.150	.005	–.108	1.156	.336
Adj. R^2		.081		.081		

	West-Low			East-Low		
	Beta	F	Sig.	Beta	F	Sig.
Local seniority*	.323	5.954	.002	.232	5.301	.007
Global/local embeddedness*	.040	.091	.765	.069	.404	.527
Local network centrality**	.500	14.418	.000	–.169	2.727	.071
Local neighborhood (spatial proximity)***	.388	8.898	.000	.321	8.805	.000
Adj. R^2		.226			.089	

*Aggregated indexes based on individual scores of household members (related to electoral participation and further variables).
**Score based on households' community network position (Pajek – Centers).
***Nominal variable based on households' territorial location inside the villages.

NOTES

The case study coauthored by Robert Angelusz was sponsored by the Hungarian National Science Foundation (OTKA) in the frames of the project "Social Network and Contextual Influences in Civic Participation" (1999–2002); later secondary analyses were related to the next OTKA-project "Intersection—Consolidation and Cultural Blocks in the Hungarian Society" (2003–6). Fieldwork of the case study was carried out under the aegis of the Research Group for Communication Studies of the Hungarian Academy of Sciences at Eotvos Lorand University.

I express special thanks to Professor Tang for his thoughtful remarks, during the 2004 Conference in Taichung, that have called for a significant amendment of my original text with a more detailed explication of some issues implied by the topic. Organizing a series of high-level critique for the papers presented was, among others, a feature of the event worth following.

I also express my gratitude for the editors' thorough critiques to an earlier version of this chapter, which certainly contributed to its improvement in several respects.

1. For such a collection of analyses with contributions by students at the University of Szeged, Hungary, see Utasi (2004).
2. See the pertinent chapters of Lin (2001) or Ruan et al. (1997) on experiences from Taiwan and mainland China.
3. See Breiger's remarks on the frequent lack of specification of "distinct kinds of social structure in different empirical settings" (1991, pg. 99).
4. Raising the significance of localities for social research from a network perspective, White (1992) speaks of a tendency of shying away from this field due to complexities that are difficult to handle.
5. Referring to Ragin's formulation related to comparative analysis (1987), our research design attempted some balance of qualitative and quantitative analysis by the joint application of cross-case and within-case analysis.
6. See Szelényi (1983) on processes of industrialization and urbanization under state socialism.
7. See Kornai (1994) on the causes and depth of recession after the change of regime.
8. Köllö (2001) analyzes, in detail, nonemployment segments of the Hungarian labor force, with special regard to rural territories.
9. See Angelusz and Tardos (2001).
10. When speaking about a country with a young democracy, the question of whether high electoral participation is a sign of some survival of monolithic political socialization or the manifestation of some drill presenting itself among changed circumstances may sound reasonable. Hungary, however, is not the best example for such a pattern. The first election under the new multiparty system in 1990 witnessed a relatively low voter turnout (remaining somewhat below two-thirds of the electorate); interestingly, it grew to a certain degree later on, differing from the experiences of several other countries in the region with similar history. It seems that Hungarians, in general, were not too slow to get acquainted with the option of absence and were occasionally ready to make use of this freedom.
11. The "paradox of voting," referring to the apparent lack of personal interest in acts of larger-plane voting with implications of free-rider gains, is also hard to resolve without involving elements of social integration, whether based on selective incentives as mediated by control mechanisms of dense social networks (as explained by Coleman 1990), "turnout cascades" of small-world network models (as by Fowler 2005), or less-sophisticated patterns of normative influences as shown by analysis of patterns of everyday political interactions by Huckfeldt and Sprague, 1995.

12. See Lin (2001) on the pivotal significance of this axis with regard to mobilization of social resources.
13. A limited amount of in-depth interviews were carried out as well, partly in the exploratory phase of the study, partly in the wake of the survey, taking into consideration some of the results in selecting the interviewees.
14. The application of name-generator and reputation techniques among other social capital-related instruments (potentially embracing inhabitants not covered by the surveys as well) permitted a qualitative control of the samples. These types of questions were particularly useful in mapping the most conspicuous voids among the relatively small number of absentees: Those renowned for their property and innovative habits (with all probability, several of them belonging to the ranks of the most successful local entrepreneurs) were most reluctant to be interviewed, especially in the eastern countryside.
15. See van der Gaag and Snijders (2004).
16. Regarding this technique, researchers applied the earlier set used in the 1997–98 waves of the national surveys, a mixture of the GSS-instrument (starting from a core discussion situation) and a simplified version of the multisituation Fischer and McAllister (1978) method. In more detail, this adaptation was based on three situations of confiding (GSS core discussion question), companionship ("those most available for leisure, hobby programs, going out, etc.") and support ties ("those most helpful in case of need around the house and the like"), followed by a sociodemographic attribute generator for all members of the ego network and with a complementary set of specific items ranging from the character of ties to religious and political affiliations.
17. The adoption of the position generator basically followed the setup of the original instrument. In its first application with the CIS project, it was of particular consideration concerning the concrete occupations of the roster applied to not only represent various levels of the social hierarchy, but also the different types of skills distinguished by our scheme. This consideration did not require a remarkable divergence from the original version that already contained some diversity in the given sense. In later stages during the nineties, some modification of the occupational roster took place to reflect the shift toward positions closer to the market, entailed by the recent socioeconomic transformation (with a roster of 24 occupations with newer items such as entrepreneur or banker). The position generator instrument of the 1997–98 national survey, on which the similar technique of the four village study was modeled, is exhibited in greater detail by Angelusz and Tardos (2007). Some follow-up questions were produced out of the basic parts of the occupation roster, such as the estimated number of acquaintanceships in the given categories and greeting habits relative to the respective partners (the use of first names or some more formal alternative).
18. In addition to the immediate plausibility of the two approaches applied in connection with the analytical foci of this study, it may also be noted that the latest attempt at grasping social capital, the resource generator (see van der Gaag and Snijders 2004), was not available at the time of the survey.
19. See Angelusz and Tardos (2001) for more details. To sum it up briefly, the combined index was based on an unrotated principal component analysis factor analysis for the total sample, again resulting in a solution with occupational nexus diversity in its center with the highest loading (for each case, except for the West-Low one with mail networking in this position, as shown by distinct analyses).
20. The stress on the simple measure applied is justified by its close connection with other position generators measures, but also by the lack of renovated occupational prestige scores required by these other types of measures in Hungary, since the end of the eighties (with a change of system in between).

21. A feature widely used by the classic Laumann and Pappi study (1976) of community networks.
22. Remaining within these frames, there is an undeniable connection with the emphases by Putnam (2000).
23. Under certain conditions, the possession of social capital by individual actors may present a kind of zero-sum game; the exploitation of structural holes among unconnected population segments is an example.
24. On this still existing though declining practice, see Sik (1988).
25. The aggregate scores of in-degree measures are smaller for the individual villages than the out-degree ones for two reasons: mentions as bases of out-degree scores contain to a degree outside contacts as well; on the other hand, they refer to a certain number of nonrespondents who are definitively not in the position to return these references.
26. A decomposition of the position-generator measure, however, reveals in these cases that nexus resources related to various segments of occupations are of varying instrumental value; contacts with nonmanual occupations are more beneficial than manual ones, "trendy" occupations imply more gains than traditional ones. On the general tendencies displayed by national surveys in Hungary see Angelusz and Tardos (2007). Among the cases in question, these tendencies are more accentuated in the East-High village, suggesting a more prestige-oriented pattern here in correspondence with a more sharply stratified character of its system of social interactions.
27. These comparisons are based on the data collected by Vécsei (2004).

REFERENCES

Angelusz, R., and R. Tardos. 1991. "The strength and weakness of weak ties." *Research Review* 3: 7–23.

———. 2001. "Change and Stability in Social Network Resources: The Case of Hungary under Transformation." In *Social Capital: Theory and Research,* eds. N. Lin, K. Cook and R. Burt, 297–323. New York: de Gruyter.

———. 2008. "Assessing Social Capital and Attainment Dynamics." In *Social Capital. Advances in Research,* eds. N. Lin and B. Erickson, 394–420. New York: Oxford University Press.

Blau, P. 1994. *Structural Contexts of Opportunities.* Chicago: University of Chicago Press.

Breiger, R. 1991. "Toward an Operational Theory of Community Elite." In *Explorations in Structural Analysis,* ed. R. Breiger, 97–175. New York: Garland.

Coleman, J. 1990. *Foundations of Social Theory.* Cambridge, MA: Harvard University Press.

Erickson, B. 1996. "Culture, Class, Connections." *American Journal of Sociology* 102: 217–51.

———. 2004. "The Distribution of Gendered Social Capital in Canada." In *Creations and Returns of Social Capital,* eds. H. Flap and B.Völker, 27–50. London: Routledge.

Fischer, C., and L. McAllister. 1978. "A Procedure for Surveying Personal Networks." *Sociological Methods and Research* 7: 131–48.

Flap, H. 1990. "Patronage: An Institution in Its Own Right." In *Social Institutions: Their Emergence, Maintenance and Effects,* eds. M. Hechter, K. D. Opp, and R. Wippler, 226–43. New York: de Gruyter.

Fowler, J. 2005. "Turnout in a Small World." In *Social Logics of Politics,* ed. A. Zuckerman, 269–87. Philadelphia, PA: Temple University Press.

Halpern, D. 2005 *Social Capital.* Malden, MA: Polity Press.
Huckfeldt, R., and J. Sprague. 1995. *Citizens, Politics and Social Communication.* New York: Cambridge University Press.
Katz, E., and P. Lazarsfeld. 1955. *Personal Influence.* New York: Free Press.
Kornai, J. 1994. "Transformational Recession: The Main Causes." *Journal of Comparative Economics,* 19(1): 19–63.
Köllő, J. 2001. "The Patterns of Non-Employment in Hungary's Least Developed Regions." Budapest: *Budapest Working Papers on the Labour Market. Institute of Economics—Budapest University of Economics 2001.*
Laumann, E., and F. Pappi. 1976. *Networks of Collective Action.* New York: Academic Press.
Lijphart, A. 1997. "Unequal Participation: Democracy's Unresolved Dilemma." *American Political Science Review,* 1: 1–13.
Lin, N. 2001. *Social Capital: A Theory of Social Structure and Action.* New York: Cambridge University Press.
——— and M. Dumin. 1986. „Access to Occupations through Social Ties." *Social Networks* 8: 365–86
———., R. Burt, and K. Cook, eds. 2001. *Social Capital: Theory and Research.* New York: de Gruyter.
Merton, R. 1949. "Patterns of Influence: A Study of Interpersonal Influence and of Communications Behavior In a Local Community." In *Communications Research 1948–1949,* eds. P. F. Lazarsfeld and F. Stanton, 180–219. New York: Harper & Brothers.
Portes, A. 1998. "Social Capital: Its Origins and Applications in Modern Sociology." *Annual Review of Sociology,* 24: 1–24.
Putnam, R. 2000. *Bowling Alone. The Collapse and Revival of American Community.* New York: Simon and Schuster.
Ragin, C. 1987. *The Comparative Method: Moving Beyond Qualitative and Quantitative Strategies.* Berkeley: University of California Press.
Ruan, D., L. Freeman, X. Dai, Y. Pan,and W. Zhang. 1997. "On the changing structure of social networks in urban China." *Social Networks,* 19: 75–89.
Sik, E. 1988. *Az örök kaláka* [Living practice of reciprocity with rural housebuilding]. Bp.: Gondolat
Szelényi, I. 1983. *Urban inequalities under state socialism.* Oxford, London: Oxford University Press.
Utasi, Á., ed. 2004. *Kapcsolatok nemzetközi metszetben* [Connections from a cross-cultural angle] Budapest, Hungary, MTA PTI (Institute of Political Sciences; the Kingston Academy of Sciences).
van der Gaag, M. and T. Snijders. 2004. "Proposals for the Measurement of Individual Social Capital." In *Creations and Returns of Social Capital,* eds. H. Flap and B. Völker, 199–218. London: Routledge.
van Deth, J. 2000. "Interesting but Irrelevant. Social Capital and the Saliency of Politics in Western Europe," *European Journal of Political Research* 37:115–47.
Vécsei, P. 2004. *Főbb társadalmi, demográfiai és migrációs folyamatok és egyenlőtlenségek alakulása 1960 és 2001 között.* [Major social, demographic and migration processes and inequalities between 1960 and 2001] Budapest: VÁTI (Institute for Urban Planning).
Wellman, B. ed. 1999. *Networks in the Global Village. Life in Contemporary Communities.* Boulder, CO: Westview Press.
White, H. 1992. *Identity and Control. A Structural Theory of Social Action.* Princeton, NJ: Princeton University Press.

11 Distinctiveness and Disadvantage Among the Urban Poor

Is Low Network Capital Really the Problem?

Jeanne S. Hurlbert, John J. Beggs, and Valerie A. Haines

Although the study of poor populations enjoys a long history in sociology and economics, Wilson's (1987, 1991a, 1991b, 1993; Elliott et al. 1996) discussion of "social isolation," "the underclass," and the "ghetto poor" renewed social scientists' focus on the "the truly disadvantaged" (Wilson 1987; see also Tienda 1991; Katz 1993). For Wilson, social isolation represents a structural property, which he defines as "the lack of contact or of sustained interaction with individuals and institutions that represent mainstream society" (1987: 60). With this articulation, Wilson provided a powerful orienting concept for understanding the dynamics of concentrated poverty—a concept that focuses attention squarely on network capital.

Theoretical work on network capital starts from two premises. The first premise is that network capital constitutes "capital" because it is an asset that can aid in the accomplishment of ends (e.g., finding a job, escaping concentrated urban poverty). The second premise is that network capital is "social capital" because it inheres in social structure. Portes's (1998) definition of social capital sets out the two elements of network capital that we use to frame our assessment of Wilson's (1987) concept of social isolation and, through it, what has become the standard sociological picture of the urban poor: "Social capital is decomposable into two elements: first, the social relationship itself that allows individuals to claim access to resources possessed by their associates [the structure element of network capital] and second, the amount and quality of those resources [the resource element of network capital]. (1998:1)"

Network capital can take the forms of closure, range, and resources obtainable from network associates (Bourdieu 1986; Coleman 1990; Portes 1998; Burt 2005). In describing the distinctiveness and disadvantage of the urban poor, Wilson (1987) contends that their networks demonstrate restricted range, and therefore fail to transcend geographic and social boundaries. He also argues that these networks offer fewer instrumental resources[1] (i.e., resources that are useful in such goal-oriented actions as job-finding) than networks of individuals in the general population do. But Wilson's goal is not only to *describe* differences in network capital between the urban poor and more "mainstream" individuals, but also to *explain why* the urban poor are disadvantaged or socially isolated. The core of his explanation links the two elements of network capital: Restricted geographic range of their networks and their separation from mainstream institutions constrain access of the urban poor to instrumental resources—particularly job-finding resources.

For Wilson (1987), then, the key to understanding the distinctiveness and disadvantage of the urban poor lies in understanding their lack of network capital. For Wilson, as for Portes (1998), this means considering both the structure element of network capital (restricted geographic range, particularly a lack of connection to individuals living "in the more stable areas of the city or in the suburbs;" (Wilson 1987: 60); and a lack of connection to mainstream institutions) and its resource element (lack of access to mainstream individuals and instrumental resources).[2]

Granovetter's (1982) discussion of poverty also echoes this distinction between the structure and resource elements of network capital. Although he focuses on the prevalence of weak ties,[3] he argues that poor individuals' networks lack this aspect of range (structure element) and therefore the access to instrumental resources (resource element) that weak ties enable (see also Mouw 2002; Smith 2000).

This portrayal of the urban poor enjoys so much currency that many sociologists classify it as something "everyone knows" about stratification. However, some empirical evidence calls the efficacy of weak ties into question (see, for example, Murray, Rankin, and Magill 1981; Bridges and Villemez 1986). Other theoretical arguments and empirical evidence show that the context of job searches (and matches) affects the types of ties and/or network structures that benefit searchers (see Mouw 2002; Greenbaum 1982), and suggests that certain aspects of restricted range might actually *promote* instrumental action.

Sanders, Nee, and Sernau's (2002) research on Asian immigrants provides one example of the latter. Focusing on the provision of such resources as informal information and "vouching," Sanders et al. document the "somewhat ironic" pattern that "reliance on family- and ethnic-based social networks has properties of a social closure process, yet such a strategy expands the minority group's opportunities in the larger social system" (2002, 306). These findings call into question Wilson's (1987) and Granovetter's (1973) arguments that low network capital, in the forms of restricted range and limited access to instrumental resources, explain distinctiveness and disadvantage among the urban poor. The historical and ongoing discrimination against African Americans (see, for example, Feagin and McKinney 2003) and the barriers African Americans face when using informal search methods (see Holzer 1987) underscore the importance of exploring that possibility.

We do this by asking: is low network capital really the problem? To address that question, we test two central propositions (outlined in the following) from Wilson's (1987) and Granovetter's (1982) portrayal. Our test of those propositions, which uses data on a group of urban poor individuals and a comparison group of residents of nearby, middle-class neighborhoods in a midsized, southern city in the United States, addresses three key conceptual and methodological limitations that fettered previous empirical assessments of Wilson's and Granovetter's representations.

Because the conceptual foundation of the propositions that we test and the importance of our methodological refinements become clear when we review more fully Wilson's (1987) and Granovetter's (1982) arguments about network capital and social isolation, we begin there. Next, we operationalize key components of the propositions. Our analysis begins by assessing the distinctiveness of residents of urban poor areas on the two forms of network capital that Wilson and Granovetter use to characterize social isolation. First, we compare their network capital to those of residents of nearby middle-class areas. Then, because Wilson and Granovetter seek to explain *why* residents of urban poor areas suffer disadvantage, we examine the determinants of these forms of network capital among the urban poor. We ask how individual characteristics of the urban poor affect the structure element of network capital and then move to the focal point of this stage of our analysis, asking how the structure element affects the resource element. In our discussion, we consider the implications of our findings for future studies of network capital and social isolation among the urban poor.

NETWORK CAPITAL AND SOCIAL ISOLATION

A key aspect of Wilson's (1987, 1991a, 1991b) social isolation argument is the link between economic isolation (poverty and welfare dependence, loss of economic capital, high rates of unemployment and underemployment) and social isolation. As Wilson stresses, "The issue is not simply that the underclass or ghetto poor have a marginal position in the labor market similar to that of other disadvantaged groups, it is also that their economic position is uniquely reinforced by their social milieu" (Wilson 1991b: 12; see also Quane and Rankin 1998).

The disadvantages of that social milieu include lack of access to quality schools, marriageable partners, and conventional role models. But lack of access to jobs and job networks rank among the most central and consequential characteristics of social isolation. Evidence that "employed black men seem to be more dependent on finding jobs through informal methods than any other group" (Reingold 1999, p. 19; see also Holzer 1987; Holzer, Ihlanfeldt, and Sjoquist 1994) underscores the potential consequences of this isolation from job networks.

Granovetter's (1973, 1974) study of job finding clarifies these consequences. Among the workers in his sample who found jobs through personal contacts, those who used weak ties (friends of friends, acquaintances) secured better jobs than those who used strong ties (close friends, relatives). Granovetter attributed the "strength" of weak ties to their association with network range. Because weak ties are more likely than strong ties to occur in wide-ranging networks or network sectors (see also Campbell, Marsden, and Hurlbert 1986), Granovetter postulated that weak ties are more likely than strong ties to (a) connect job searchers to dissimilar individuals who can reach diverse parts of the social structure (see Campbell et al. 1986), and (b) provide access to the nonredundant information that arguably improves job search outcomes.

Granovetter (1982) later extended the argument to contend that, because reliance on strong ties and lack of access to weak ties inhibits success in instrumental action, the prevalence of weak ties affects the flow of resources among individuals. Granovetter then reasoned that, at the macro level, weak ties provide important conduits for the flow of information: Where strong ties predominate and weak ties are rare, social structures will be fragmented and information will diffuse slowly.

To clarify the implications of this argument for poor populations, Granovetter drew on ethnographic evidence. Stack (1974) and Lomnitz (1977) showed that poor individuals develop and maintain elaborate exchange networks consisting primarily of strong ties (particularly kin). Granovetter concluded that

> the pervasive use of strong ties by the poor and insecure is a response to economic pressures; they believe themselves to be without alternatives, and the adaptive nature of these reciprocity networks is the main theme of the analysts. *At the same time, I would suggest that the heavy concentration of social energy in strong ties has the impact of fragmenting communities of the poor into encapsulated networks with poor connections between these units; individuals so encapsulated may then lose some of the advantages associated with the outreach of weak ties.* This may be one more factor that makes poverty self-perpetuating. (1982: 116–17; emphasis added)

This quotation captures the tight link between Wilson's (1987) and Granovetter's (1982) arguments. Although Wilson focused on the broader concept of range and Granovetter highlighted one aspect of that construct—the distribution of weak ties—they present a remarkably univocal representation of the network capital of the urban poor. Both argue that poor individuals rely on low-range networks for such vital resources as food, clothing, shelter, financial assistance, and social support (see also Hogan, Hao, and Parish 1990; Taylor and Chatters 1986; Smith 2000; Wilson and Tolson 1990).

The argument that networks of restricted range provide some types of assistance is not at issue. Dense, homogeneous networks and the strong ties that disproportionately constitute them routinely provide social support in the general population (see, for example, Beggs, Haines, and Hurlbert 1996; Hurlbert, Haines, and Beggs 2000, 2001; Lin and Ensel 1989; Haines, Hurlbert, and Beggs 1996). But, as social resources research shows, these kinds of networks and ties do not typically provide instrumental resources. To the extent that networks of the urban poor offer *only,* or at least primarily, restricted-range sectors (see Mouw 2002)—as Wilson (1987) and Granovetter (1982) argue—then low network capital, in the forms of restricted range and limited instrumental resources, is in fact the problem.

We assess the accuracy of that portrayal by testing two of its central propositions, specifying them with arguments from social resources theory. Social resources theory is uniquely suited to this task because it shares with social isolation theory a focus on the question of how social networks affect access to instrumental resources—it simply frames the question in the general population, rather than the urban poor.[4] The first proposition regards distinctiveness of the urban poor: relative to those of residents of middle-class areas, their networks evidence restricted range (structure element of network capital) and offer fewer instrumental resources (resources element of network capital). The second proposition is that the distinct structure of their networks helps explain their disadvantage: restricted range constrains access to instrumental resources.

TESTING WILSON'S AND GRANOVETTER'S PROPOSITIONS

We provide a more complete test of Wilson's (1987) and Granovetter's (1973) portrayals by overcoming three key limitations of previous studies. The first limitation is that they either confounded the structure and resource elements of network capital (see Fernandez and Harris 1992) or failed to distinguish between them explicitly (see, for example, Green, Tigges, and Browne 1995; Reingold 1999), obscuring potentially important relationships between the two elements of network capital.

The second limitation of previous studies is that their data relied on name generators that disproportionately tap strong ties (and the dense networks in which they typically occur; Fernandez and Harris 1992; Green et al. 1995; Browne and Tigges 1999; Green, Tigges, and Diaz 1999; Green, Hammer, and Tigges 1999a, Tigges, Browne, and Green 1998; Reingold 1999; see also Rankin and Quane 2000). Name generators, which elicit the names of alters, tap bounded portions of respondents' networks with the type of name generator setting the boundary.[5]

Campbell et al. argue that relying solely on the kinds of name generators that previous studies used

> will result in a bias toward understating network range, particularly when small numbers of alters are included [as was true for most data used in previous studies] or when the relational content used to generate names is intense [as was true of the name generators used]. For instance, diversity measures are biased downward if strong portions of a network, comprised of persons highly similar to one another and to the focal actor, are sampled. (1986:103)

These studies, therefore, *could* test whether the urban poor rely primarily on strong ties and restricted range (dense) network sectors. But because the presence of strong ties in a network neither precludes the existence nor determines the prevalence of weak ties (see Campbell et al. 1986), one must measure both to test Wilson's (1987) and Granovetter's (1982) arguments that restricted range underlies the distinctiveness and disadvantage of the urban poor. We do this by including a name generator designed to tap the prevalence of friends-of-friends and acquaintances—disproportionately weak ties that are more likely to occur in wide-ranging network sectors than in their restricted-range counterparts.

The third limitation of previous studies is that they failed to recognize that because range "is a multidimensional and complex concept" (Campbell et al. 1986, p. 97), testing Wilson's (1987) and Granovetter's (1982) arguments requires conceptualizing and measuring those multiple dimensions. We meet that requirement by tapping not only the geographic range and density dimensions that Wilson and Granovetter highlight, but also three additional aspects that social resources research shows affect access to instrumental resources: diversity, size, and voluntary organization integration.

By distinguishing explicitly between the structure and resource elements of network capital, by using name generators that tap the prevalence of weak and strong ties, and by expanding the conceptualization and measurement of restricted range, our analysis of the distinctiveness of the urban poor (proposition 1) can explore whether Wilson's (1987) and Granovetter's (1982) arguments about restricted range hold not only for the aspects they identified but also for the aspects that we use social resources theory to incorporate. And when we assess the effects of the structure element of network capital on the resource element (proposition 2), we can ask what aspects of restricted range prove most consequential for which instrumental resources. By exploring the distinctiveness and disadvantage of the urban poor in this way, we provide a more definitive answer to the question, "Is low network capital, in the forms of restricted range and limited instrumental resources, really the problem?" We now turn to our operationalization of the two elements of network capital that Wilson and Granovetter use to characterize social isolation of the urban poor.

The Structure Element

The first two aspects of restricted range that we tap come directly from Wilson's (1987) and Granovetter's (1982) portrayals of network capital of the urban poor. Beginning with restricted geographic range, we include geographic concentration of network members and the proportion of network members who are neighbors. We tap the density dimension by measuring respondents' restricted access to weak ties in three ways: the emotional closeness to network members (alters), the extent to which alters are kin,[6] and the extent to which alters are not acquaintances and friends-of-friends.

Turning to the aspects of restricted range suggested by social resources theory, the first—restricted network diversity—can encompass a wide range of network characteristics. Lin emphasizes the importance of identifying "locally meaningful measures of social capital" (2002, 63). We focus on two locally meaningful measures: religious homophily and age homophily.[7] We chose religious homophily because, in addition to the fact that churches have historically been central in African American communities, our data suggest that they may play a pivotal role in combating social isolation. In our focal urban poor area, we found a higher prevalence of ties to individuals in higher-income areas than Wilson's (1987) analysis would predict. Anecdotal evidence suggests that some of those ties are maintained in churches. If so, then religious homophily may provide a key indicator of low network capital: Not having ties to individuals of a different religion may limit access to instrumental resources. We focus on age homophily because younger and older individuals may provide different kinds of resources. If that is true, then lower age homophily would indicate more network capital. However, lower age homophily can reflect the presence of high proportions of kin in a network, indicating lower, rather than higher amounts of network capital. That fact impedes the development of predictions for this aspect of range (see the following).

Our second expanded measure of restricted range is restricted network size. The third is restricted voluntary organization integration, which we tap with the extent to which respondents do not share voluntary organization memberships with network members (see Beggs and Hurlbert 1997). Social resources research shows that the voluntary organization context of ties can increase access to instrumental resources (Beggs and Hurlbert 1997). If the urban poor are isolated from mainstream institutions and their members, as Wilson (1987) suggests, then they should exhibit less voluntary organization integration in their networks than individuals in higher socioeconomic strata do.

The Resource Element

Wilson's (1987, 1991a, 1991b) arguments point to three central aspects of this element of network capital. We tap the first, restricted access to employment resources, in two ways: lack of employed individuals in respondents' networks (see also Fernandez and Harris 1992; Rankin and Quane 2000; Tigges et al. 1998) and restricted access to individuals who respondents perceive could assist in finding jobs.[8] Turning to the second aspect, we define restricted access to mainstream individuals as lack of (a) more educated alters (see also Fernandez and Harris 1992; Rankin and Quane 2000; Tigges et al. 1998) and (b) alters who own their own homes. Finally, we tap restricted access to individuals with communication and transportation resources with the prevalence of network members who lack (a) phones and (b) working vehicles.

Analytic Strategy and Predictions

In the first stage of our analysis, we assess the distinctiveness of residents of poor urban areas by comparing their levels of network capital (the structure and resource elements) to those of residents of nearby middle-class areas (see the following). Drawing on the arguments of Wilson (1987) and Granovetter (1982; see also Tigges et al. 1998), we predict that residents of poor urban areas will have lower levels of network capital in the forms of range and embedded instrumental resources than residents of middle-class areas.

In the second stage of our analysis, we focus on *explaining* the disadvantage among residents of poor urban areas by predicting their levels of network capital. First, we explore how individual-level factors predict network capital, in the form of range. We then ask how restricted range affects access to instrumental resources. Drawing on Wilson's (1987, 1991a, 1991b, 1993) and Granovetter's (1982) arguments and on social resources theory, we predict that lower-status individuals (those with less education and income, women[9]) will be embedded in networks with more restricted range than higher-status individuals. Those who are working (full-time or part-time) should evidence less restricted range than those who are not working. Given the history of discrimination against African Americans, we predict that their networks will exhibit less network capital in the form of range than the networks of whites.[10]

The work of Wilson (1987, 1991a, 1991b, 1993) and Fernandez and Harris (1992) suggests that individuals who are not currently married or living with a partner will have lower levels of this form of network capital than those who are married or living with a partner (but see Tigges et al. 1998). The effects of age on the structure element of network capital are difficult to predict. Wilson's (1987) arguments suggest that older individuals may represent a more stable segment of the urban poor population that enjoys higher levels of network capital because it is less socially isolated. However, because the elderly are more likely than younger individuals to experience restricted mobility and financial resources, it is also possible that they will have less network capital than younger individuals. We think the latter is more likely, and therefore predict that older individuals will evidence lower network capital. Turning to the effects of the structure element on the resource element of network capital, Wilson's (1987) arguments suggest that individuals with lower levels of network capital in the form of range will have lower levels of network capital in the form of instrumental resources: the restricted range of their networks will limit access to instrumental resources.

The one exception to all of these predictions is age homophily. As we noted previously, the predictions for this measure are ambiguous. We therefore do not predict its effects for any stage of the analysis and perform two-tailed, rather than one-tailed, tests for this measure.

SAMPLE, DATA, AND MEASURES

Sample

The data used in these analyses come from a 1995 study of residents of a mid-sized Southern city in the United States. This city contained nearly 220,000 residents in 1990; 14,662 of them resided in the focal urban (poor) area (U.S. Bureau of the Census 1992). Area residents and others in the city define this as a "social neighborhood" (see Tienda 1991). We included in our operational definition the central block groups of the area (e.g., those that do not border middle-class areas).

Our definition mirrors conventional definitions of urban poor or "underclass" areas, such as the one that classifies them as areas in which at least 40 percent of residents fall below the poverty line (Bane and Jargowsky 1988); in our focal area 52.5 percent of residents lived in poverty around the time of our survey.[11] Consistent with other definitions and characteristics of urban poor areas, we also found high proportions of single-parent families (70.1 percent of the households with children were single parent), low levels of labor force attachment (48.6 percent of residents were not in the labor force and 10.7 percent were unemployed), and low levels of educational attainment (50.1 percent of individuals 25 or more years old and 48.5 percent of those between the ages of 18 and 24 had failed to complete high school). In 1990 the population of the focal area was 92.1 percent Black, with high proportions of youth and elderly (as reflected in the dependency ratio of 81.9). As in many such areas (see Gramlich, Laren, and Sealand 1992), this section of the city once housed a vibrant African American community that included many middle-class residents. During the 1960s and 1970s, the area experienced decline, as many of these middle-class residents and the businesses that they supported left the area—exactly the scenario that Wilson (1987) describes.

We collected data through telephone interviews with residents of this area and adjacent areas (including middle-class areas), using random-digit dialing to select the sample.[12] U.S. Census (1992) data indicated, however, that as many as 30 percent of households in some sections of the focal area lacked telephones. Because poverty rates stood higher in these than in other sections, we clearly needed to represent these households in the sample. We therefore constructed a supplemental sample of area households that lacked telephones. To do so, we identified block groups with high proportions of nontelephone households. We then sent teams of field contacts to designated blocks in these areas, selected through randomization techniques. Interviews with residents of sampled nontelephone households were conducted by cellular telephones, which the field contacts provided.[13] This method thus ensures that nontelephone households are represented in the sample, with methodological comparability to the main sample.

The effective sample size for the focal urban poor area was 311 (of whom 120 came from nontelephone households); for the middle class area it was 201. Comparing statistics describing our sample to comparable figures from the 1990 census indicates that our data represent the focal area well.[14]

Data

To measure respondents' network capital, we used three name generators and a series of name interpreters. The first name generator, which modified the name-eliciting question used in the 1985 General Social Survey, taps routine confidants of respondents (see Burt 1985; Marsden 1987; Bailey and Marsden 1999) by asking them to name up to five individuals with whom they discussed important matters in the six months prior to the interview. To tap the routine associates of respondents, we followed Fischer (1982) and asked respondents to name up to five individuals with whom they socialized routinely. Both of these name generators tap relatively strong ties (Beggs et al. 1996; Marsden 1987; Munch, McPherson, and Smith-Lovin 1997; Bailey and Marsden 1999; McPherson, Smith-Lovin, and Brashears 2006). To ensure that we measured the prevalence of weak ties, we included a third name generator that asked respondents to name up to five individuals whom they knew well enough to call up on the phone but did not know well—individuals they would call "friends-of-friends or acquaintances" (see Granovetter 1973, 1974). This name generator tends to tap weaker ties than the other two.[15] The networks that we examine include all nonredundant alters elicited by these three name generators (maximum possible = 15).

The name interpreter questions gathered information about the personal characteristics of the named alters (including age, race, education, home ownership, whether they were employed, whether they had phones, and whether they had cars) and the characteristics of the relationship between the respondent and each alter (including how close the respondent felt to each alter, whether each alter was the same religion as the respondent, and his or her geographic distance from the respondent). From this information, we constructed our measures of the structure and resource elements of network capital.

Measures

Structure Element of Network Capital

Restricted geographic range

We measure geographic concentration as the proportion of alters who live less than 30 minutes from the respondent.[16] Our measure of the proportion of alters who are neighbors comes from respondents' reports of whether (1) or not (0) each alter is a neighbor.

Density (restricted access to weak ties)

To tap emotional closeness between ego and alters, we asked respondents whether they felt especially close (1), somewhat close (.5), or not close at all (0) to each alter. To measure the proportion of network members who are kin, we used respondents' reports of whether (1) or not (0) each alter was a relative. We tap restricted access to acquaintances/friends of friends by calculating the proportion of network members who were not named in response to the acquaintance/friend-of-a-friend name generator.[17] Higher values on all three indicate more restricted range.

Restricted network diversity

Using respondents' reports, we measure religious homophily as the proportion of alters who share ego's religion. We use respondents' reports of each alter's age (in years) to measure age homophily. We calculate it as the average of the absolute age difference between the respondent and each alter, then reverse the sign of the resulting value.

Restricted network size

We measure restricted network size as the total number of nonredundant alters named in response to our three name generators; we multiply the measure by –1 to reverse the sign (so that it indicates restricted size).

Restricted voluntary organization integration

We use respondents' reports of whether (1) or not (0) each alter belonged to a church or a club/organization to which the respondent also belonged, calculating the measure as the proportion of network members with whom respondents do not share voluntary organization memberships.

Resource Element of Network Capital

Employment resources

Our measure of the proportion of network members who are employed comes from respondents' reports of whether (1) or not (0) each alter was employed. We also use respondents' reports of whether (1) or not (0) network members could provide job-finding assistance. For both measures, lower values signal more limited employment resources and therefore lower network capital in the form of instrumental resources.

Mainstream individuals

We construct our measure of the average education of network members from respondents' reports of the highest grade of school or college that each alter completed. We also use respondents' reports of the proportion of network members who own their own homes.

Communication and transportation resources

We measure the proportion of network members whom respondents reported as having telephones and working vehicles, respectively, with lower proportions signaling less of these instrumental resources.

Individual Characteristics

We measure age and education of respondents in years. Race is measured as African American (1) and other (0).[18] To measure marital status, we include a series of dummy variables. We coded the first as (1) for separated, widowed, and divorced respondents, (0) otherwise; the second is coded (1) for never married respondents, (0) otherwise. The reference category includes respondents who are currently married or living with a partner. We measured family income with a series of categories, which we recoded to their midpoints (and logged).[19] We measure employment status with two dummy variables. We code the first (1) for individuals who are employed full time, (0) otherwise; we code the second (1) for individuals who are employed part time, (0) otherwise. Those who are not employed constitute the reference category. Means and standard deviations for all variables (for the full sample) appear in the first two columns of Table 11.1.

Table 11.1 Comparison of Residents of Urban Poor and Adjacent Middle-Class Areas on Network Capital and Individual Characteristics

	STANDARD DEVIATION[a]	*MEAN FULL SAMPLE*	*MEAN URBAN POOR*	*MEAN, MIDDLE CLASS*
A. STRUCTURE ELEMENT OF NETWORK CAPITAL				
RESTRICTED RANGE				
Restricted Geographic Range				
Geographic concentration	.270	.841	.832	.854
Proportion neighbors	.344	.351	.349	.352
Density (Restricted Access to Weak Ties)				
Proportion close	.212	.778	.785	.770
Proportion kin	.291	.275	.296 *	.247
Proportion not acquaintances	.225	.761	.750	.775
Restricted Diversity				
Religious homophily	.417	.504	.554**	.440
Age homophily[b]	6.802	-9.451	-10.049*	-8.667
Restricted network size	2.357	-4.409	-4.046**	-4.885
Restricted voluntary organization integration	.340	.736	.780**	.320
B. RESOURCE ELEMENT OF NETWORK CAPITAL				
Employment Resources				
Proportion employed	.314	.765	.716**	.829
Could assist in finding job	.383	.323	.305	.346
Mainstream individuals				
Average education	2.371	14.156	13.196**	15.377
Proportion homeowners	.397	.507	.408**	.637
Communication/Transportation resources				
Proportion with phones	.331	.838	.753**	.950
Proportion with working vehicles	.318	.817	.743**	.914

(continued)

Table 11.1 Comparison of Residents of Urban Poor and Adjacent Middle-Class Areas on Network Capital and Individual Characteristics (continued)

	STANDARD DEVIATION[a]	*MEAN FULL SAMPLE*	*MEAN URBAN POOR*	*MEAN, MIDDLE CLASS*
C. INDIVIDUAL CHARACTERISTICS				
Age	15.446	40.882	41.125	40.563
Education	2.784	13.851	12.842**	15.175
Male	.474	.338	.308	.377
African American	.496	.565	.904**	.120
Separated/Widowed/ Divorced	.418	.225	.238	.208
Never married	.496	.435	.492**	.361
Married	.466	.317	.250**	.404
Family income (Logged)	.950	9.888	9.422**	10.499
Employed – Full time	.500	.513	.379**	.689
Employed – Part time	.309	.106	.138*	.066
N	423	240	183	240

[a] Full sample.

[b] Two-tailed t-tests. The signs for the original age homophily and network size measures were reversed (see text), so that they tap restricted range. Among the urban poor network size was 10.049; for the middle class it was 8.667.

* $p < .05$, ** $p < .01$.

ANALYSIS PROCEDURES

In the first stage of our analysis, we use *t*-tests to assess the distinctiveness of the urban poor on the structure and resource elements of network capital. In the second stage of our analysis we use ordinary least squares regression to explore the determinants of disadvantage—low network capital—among residents of poor urban areas. We first explore the effects of individual characteristics on the structure element of network capital. We then ask whether restricted network range constrains access to instrumental resources by regressing our measures of the resource element of network capital on our indicators of the structure element and individual characteristics. To ensure that none of our independent variables was sufficiently correlated to affect the estimation of coefficients, we examine estimates of colinearity (tolerance estimates). Tolerance levels never fell below .4, indicating that colinearity did not affect our results.

RESULTS

Assessing the Distinctiveness of the Urban Poor

Our comparison of levels of network capital between residents of poor urban areas and residents of surrounding middle-class areas begins with the structure element (Table 11.1, Panel A, 3rd and 4th columns). Although we do find significant differences that support our first proposition about network capital, none of these differences appears for restricted geographic range, the aspect that Wilson (1987) suggested is key. Further, only one measure of the density dimension (restricted access to weak ties) supports the proposition that residents of poor urban areas exhibit lower levels of these forms of network capital. Consistent with Wilson's (1987) and Granovetter's (1982) arguments, residents of urban poor areas describe networks with significantly higher proportions of kin than residents of middle-class areas do.

The results for the expanded measures of restricted range suggested by social resources theory provide stronger support for Wilson's (1987) and Granovetter's (1982) propositions about the distinctiveness of the urban poor. We find mixed results for restricted diversity: networks of residents of urban poor areas evidence greater religious homophily but lower age homophily than networks of residents of middle-class areas. If, as we suggest, the latter difference owes to the higher proportions of kin in networks of residents of urban poor areas, that finding is not surprising. Consistent with our predictions, residents of urban poor areas describe significantly smaller networks. Networks of residents of urban poor areas demonstrate significantly less voluntary organization integration than residents of middle-class areas, supporting Wilson's and Granovetter's arguments.

We find stronger support for the resource element of our first proposition about network capital (Table 11.1, Panel B). Starting with employment resources, networks of residents of urban poor areas offer significantly fewer employed alters. We also find significant differences in access to mainstream individuals that support the distinctiveness proposition for both average education and levels of home ownership among alters. The distinctiveness of the urban poor also appears in restricted access to communication and transportation resources (significantly lower proportions of network members who have phones and working vehicles).

Taken together, these findings for the structure and resource elements of network capital provide strong support for Wilson's (1987) and Granovetter's (1982) first propositions. Relative to residents of middle-class areas, the urban poor exhibit low network capital in the forms of restricted range (structure element) and instrumental resources (resource element). We now ask what factors explain that disadvantage in network capital.

Explaining the Structure and Resource Elements of Network Capital of the Urban Poor

We begin to address this question by exploring how individual-level factors affect the structure element of network capital of the urban poor (see Table 11.2).

Beginning with the determinants of restricted geographic range (Panel A), the effects of age, education, and income all support the predictions about levels of this form of network capital that we drew from social isolation theory. We find greater geographic concentration of network members among older than among younger individuals. We also find less geographic concentration among individuals with part-time employment than among the unemployed. Networks of more educated individuals contain a lower proportion of neighbors than those of less-educated individuals. Individuals with higher family incomes have lower proportions of neighbors than less-affluent individuals do.

Turning to our measures of the density aspect (restricted access to weak ties, Panel B), we find that older individuals have higher proportions of alters to whom they are close and higher proportions of kin in their networks than younger individuals do. Men have lower proportions of network members to whom they are close and lower proportions of kin than women do. African Americans evidence higher proportions of kin than whites do. Individuals who are separated, widowed, or divorced have a lower proportion of friends-of-friends/acquaintances in their networks than married individuals do. These effects also support the predictions that we drew from Wilson's (1987) and Granovetter's (1982) arguments that the urban poor are distinct in their low network capital on the density aspect of restricted range.

We next examine the determinants of our expanded aspects of restricted network range—diversity, size, and voluntary organization integration. We find mixed effects of age on restricted diversity (Panel C). Older individuals describe networks of significantly higher religious homophily but significantly lower age homophily. The effect on religious homophily supports our predictions; the effect on age homophily may owe to the prominence of kin—particularly children—in older individuals' networks. African Americans describe networks of significantly greater religious homophily than whites do. Compared to their married counterparts, individuals who never married describe networks of greater age homophily. These effects support the predictions that we drew from Wilson's (1987) and Granovetter's (1982) arguments and from social resources theory regarding the low network capital of the urban poor on these dimensions of network range.

Turning to voluntary organization integration (Panel D, first column), we find that persons with higher family incomes and full-time workers share voluntary organization memberships with a higher proportion of network members than persons with lower family incomes and those who lack employment.

Table 11.2 Predicting the Structure Element of Network Capital of the Urban Poor[a]

A. RESTRICTED GEOGRAPHIC RANGE:	*Geographic Concentration*	*Proportion Neighbors*
Individual Characteristics		
Age	.003*	-.001
Education	.005	-.025**
Male	-.031	.058
African American	-.028	.025
Separated/Widowed/ Divorced[b]	-.078	-.052
Never Married[b]	.011	.003
Family Income	.028	-.052*
Employed:		
Full time	-.031	.022
Part time	-.134*	-.097
Intercept	.469	1.182
R^2	.057	.077
N	240	240

B. DENSITY (RESTRICTED ACCESS TO WEAK TIES):

	Proportion Close	*Proportion Kin*	*Proportion Not Acquaintances*[c]
Individual Characteristics			
Age	.003**	.004**	.0004
Education	.005	.004	.022
Male	-.064*	-.085*	.004
African American	.071	.203**	-.004
Separated/Widowed/ Divorced[b]	.048	-.073	-.099*
Never married[b]	.014	-.075	-.053
Family income	-.006	-.036	-.033
Employed:			
Full time	.027	-.017	-.035
Part time	.077	-.038	.040
Intercept	.589	.332	.819
R^2	.084	.101	.064
N	240	240	240

(continued)

Table 11.2 Predicting the Structure Element of Network Capital of the Urban Poor[a] (continued)

C. RESTRICTED DIVERSITY:	*Religious Homophily*	*Age Homophily*[d]
Individual Characteristics		
Age	.005**	-.179**
Education	.005	.108
Male	-.043	1.245
African American	.336**	.259
Separated/Widowed/ Divorced[b]	-.062	.511
Never Married[b]	-.015	2.059*
Family income	-.049	.949
Employed:		
Full time	-.033	-.048
Part time	.055	-.036
Intercept	.491	-14.562
R^2	.082	.213
N	240	240

D. ADDITIONAL EXPANDED MEASURES, RESTRICTED RANGE

	Restricted Voluntary Organization Integration	*Restricted Network Size*
Individual Characteristics		
Age	-.002	-.012
Education	.003	-.155**
Male	.081	.083
African American	-.054	1.491**
Separated/Widowed/Divorced[b]	-.015	.579
Never married[b]	.019	.349
Family income	-.061*	-.168
Employed:		
Full time	-.094*	.136
Part time	-.021	.129
Intercept	1.439	-1.945
R^2	.067	.125
N	240	240

[a] Unstandardized OLS regression coefficients.
[b] Dummy variable; reference category is married/living with partner.
[c] Proportion of network members who are not acquaintances or friends-of-friends.
* $p < .05$; ** $p < .01$.
[d] Two-tailed significance tests; * $p < .05$; ** $p < .01$.

These findings also support the predictions that we drew from the combined arguments of Wilson (1987) and Granovetter (1982) and social resources theory regarding low network capital in terms of restricted voluntary organization integration. We find two significant effects of individual characteristics on network size (Panel D, second column). More-educated individuals and whites describe significantly larger networks than less-educated individuals and African Americans do, further supporting our predictions.

We now move to the focal point of this stage of the analysis by exploring our second proposition about network capital of the urban poor—that the restricted range of the networks of residents of urban poor areas (structure element) constrains access to instrumental resources (resource element; Table 11.3). Model 1 contains only individual characteristics as explanatory variables; in Model 2 we add our measures of low network capital in the form of restricted range.[20]

Beginning with employment resources (Panel A) we find that net of individual characteristics restricted range does reduce access to instrumental resources. Having a lower proportion of acquaintances (density aspect) decreases the number of network members whom respondents perceive as able to provide job-finding assistance. Among our expanded measures, greater religious homophily (diversity aspect) and restricted voluntary integration both decrease access to employed network members. We find one exception to this pattern. Age homophily exerts a significant, positive effect on this outcome (the perceived number of network members who could assist in finding a job). That finding may reflect the association between low age homophily and the prominence of kin in networks.

Turning to network capital in the form of connections to mainstream individuals (Panel B), we find further support for Wilson's (1987) and Granovetter's (1982) second proposition about network capital of the urban poor. Both of our measures of restricted geographic range decrease the proportion of network members who own homes; having a higher proportion of neighbors also decreases the average education of network members. These effects support Wilson's arguments concerning the geographic concentration of the networks of the urban poor (structure element of network capital) constraining access to resources that could aid in such activities as job-finding (resource element of network capital).

Two of our measures of density (restricted access to weak ties) also exert significant effects: having a higher proportion of kin in the network decreases the average education of network members and having a lower proportion of acquaintances decreases the proportion of network members who own homes. One measure of the diversity dimension of restricted range, religious homophily, decreases the proportion of network members who own homes. Having a lower proportion of network members with whom the respondent shares voluntary organization memberships also reduces access to more-educated network members.

Finally, when we examine communication and transportation resources (Panel C), we find a significant effect of restricted geographic range: having

Table 11.3 Predicting the Resource Element of Network Capital in the Urban Poor[a]

A. EMPLOYMENT RESOURCES

	PROPORTION EMPLOYED		*COULD ASSIST IN FINDING JOB*	
	Model 1	*Model 2*	*Model 1*	*Model 2*
INDIVIDUAL CHARACTERISTICS				
Age	-.002	-.001	-.001	.000
Education	.015*	.010	-.011	-.011
Male	.104**	.122**	-.079	-.056
African American	-.168**	-.119	-.032	-.080
Separated, widowed, divorced[b]	.002	.001	.048	.018
Never married[b]	.088	.092	-.043	-.058
Family income	.019	-.001	.072*	.057*
Employed:				
Full time	.096*	.086*	.159**	.150**
Part time	.071	.060	.202**	.191**
STRUCTURE ELEMENT OF NETWORK CAPITAL				
Restricted Geographic Range				
Geographic concentration		-.057		-.061
Proportion Neighbors		-.074		-.112
Density (Restricted Access to Weak Ties)				
Proportion Close		-.024		.131
Proportion kin		.005		.221
Proportion not Acquaintances		.064		-.221*
Restricted Diversity				
Religious homophily		-.095*		-.036
Age homophily[c]		.004		.009*
Restricted network size		-.016		-.001
Restricted voluntary organization integration		-.143*		-.046
Intercept	.452	.805	-.238	.173
R^2	.133	.184	.090	.170
N	240	240	240	240

(continued)

Table 11.3 Predicting the Resource Element of Network Capital in the Urban Poor[a] (continued)

B. MAINSTREAM INDIVIDUALS

	AVERAGE EDUCATION		*PROPORTION HOME OWNERS*	
	Model 1	*Model 2*	*Model 1*	*Model 2*
INDIVIDUAL CHARACTERISTICS				
Age	.031**	.031**	.011**	.010**
Education	.255**	.243**	.003	.004
Male	.425	.535*	-.164	-.140
African American	-1.210**	-1.050*	.114	.135
Separated, widowed, divorced[b]	.109	-.063	-.034	-.072
Never Married[b]	.551	.461	-.063	-.056
Family income	.515**	.311*	.102**	.089**
Employed:				
Full time	.030	-.071	.133**	.110*
Part time	.107	.008	.178**	.149*
STRUCTURE ELEMENT OF NETWORK CAPITAL				
Restricted Geographic Range				
Geographic concentration		.339		-.194**
Proportion neighbors		-.956**		-.120*
Density (Restricted Access to Weak Ties)				
Proportion close		.656		.058
Proportion kin		-.834*		.065
Proportion not acquaintances		-.462		-.164*
Restricted Diversity				
Religious homophily		-.157		-.103*
Age homophily[c]		.011		-.002
Restricted network size		-.004		-.008
Restricted voluntary organization Integration		-1.137**		-.100
Intercept	4.429	7.616	-1.121	-.665
R^2	.241	.299	.302	.365
N	229	229	240	240

(continued)

Table 11.3 Predicting the Resource Element of Network Capital in the Urban Poor[a] (continued)

C. COMMUNICATION AND TRANSPORTATION RESOURCES

	PROPORTION WITH PHONES		*PROPORTION WITH WORKING VEHICLES*	
	Model 1	*Model 2*	*Model 1*	*Model 2*
INDIVIDUAL CHARACTERISTICS				
Age	.006**	.006**	.002	.002
Education	.002	-.001	.020*	.016
Male	-.087	-.064	.004	.030
African American	-.047	-.042	-.052	-.065
Separated, widowed, divorced[b]	-.046	-.061	.006	-.025
Never married[b]	.075	.076	.057	.061
Family income	.116**	.097**	.118**	.105**
Employed:				
Full time	.060	.052	.087*	.073
Part time	.066	.054	.109*	.071
STRUCTURE ELEMENT OF NETWORK CAPITAL				
Restricted Geographic Range				
Geographic concentration		.021		-.092
Proportion neighbors		-.171**		-.146*
Density (Restricted Access to Weak Ties)				
Proportion close		.032		.139
Proportion kin		.046		.035
Proportion not acquaintances		-.060		.041
NETWORK—EXPANDED RANGE MEASURES				
Restricted diversity				
Religious homophily		-.046		-.028
Age homophily[c]		.001		.001
Restricted network Size		-.002		-.000
Restricted voluntary organization integration		-.104		-.136*
Intercept	-.605	-.219	-.740	-.423
R^2	.127	.157	.166	.223
N	240	240	240	240

a Unstandardized OLS regression coefficients.

b Dummy variable; reference category is married/living with partner.

c Two-tailed tests; * $p < .05$, ** $p < .01$.

* $p < .05$; ** $p < .01$.

a greater proportion of neighbors in the network decreases the proportion of network members who have phones and working vehicles. Thus the greater the degree to which alters are concentrated in the neighborhood, the less likely ego is to have access to these forms of social capital.

Lower voluntary organization integration also decreases the proportion of network members who have working vehicles. Once again, then, the effects support the expectations that we drew from Wilson's (1987) and Granovetter's (1982) arguments about network capital of the urban poor and from social resources theory.

Our findings for employment resources, mainstream individuals, and communication and transportation resources show that for the urban poor, restricted network range constrains access to instrumental resources. Examination of the differences in R^2 between Model 1 and Model 2 for each set of equations in Table 11.3 shows the structure element of network capital to be an important determinant of the resource element. Net of individual characteristics (Model 1), the structure element uniquely contributes between 19 percent and 32 percent of the explained variance in embedded instrumental resources in these models.[21] The one exception is the equation predicting the proportion of respondents' network members who could help with job search. There network structure accounts for 67.7 percent of the explained variance.

DISCUSSION AND CONCLUSIONS

We assessed the accuracy of Wilson's (1987, 1991a, 1991b, 1993) and Granovetter's (1982) portrayal of social isolation among the urban poor by asking: is low network capital really the problem? We did so by testing two propositions from their representation. The first was that the urban poor evidence distinctiveness in both the restricted range of their networks (the structure element of network capital) and their limited access to instrumental resources (the resource element of network capital). The second was that the restricted range of their networks helps explain the second aspect of their disadvantage, their lack of access to instrumental resources. To test these propositions, we used not only measures of restricted range highlighted by Wilson and Granovetter, but also additional aspects that social resources theory suggested.

Beginning with the first proposition, our analysis of distinctiveness on the structure element of network capital yields two important conclusions. First, it suggests that restricted range does distinguish the urban poor from their middle-class counterparts. It also offers an important qualification by suggesting that the aspects of restricted range on which Wilson (1987) and Granovetter (1982) focus—restricted geographic range and density (lack of weak ties)—may not be as central to the distinctiveness of the urban poor as other aspects are. We found limited distinctiveness in lack of access to weak ties and none for restricted geographic range, but all of the indicators of restricted range that we drew from social resources theory differentiated residents of poor urban areas from residents of middle-class areas. This suggests that future studies of network capital should broaden, conceptually and operationally, the aspects of restricted range on which they focus.

The second implication of this stage of our test of the distinctiveness proposition comes from the fact that we found greater distinctiveness on the resource element of network capital than on the structure element: five of our six indicators of the resource element differentiated residents of poor urban areas from residents of middle-class areas, with residents of poor urban areas reporting lower levels of these instrumental resources in every case. This pattern highlights the importance of separating the two elements of network capital, conceptually and empirically, in future social isolation studies or future studies of the urban poor. It suggests further that policy makers should consider these two elements of network capital separately when seeking ways to improve conditions of the urban poor. For example, they may consider how to craft programs to augment or alter the two elements of network capital—particularly the resource element.

Our exploration of the effect of the network structure on the network resources dimension of network capital goes to the heart of our focal question regarding why the urban poor suffer disadvantage. Our findings suggest that the answer to the question, "Is low network capital really the problem?" is "Yes." They also suggest that the relationship between the structure and resource elements of network capital is complex, with different aspects of restricted range constraining access to different instrumental resources.

One of the expanded measures of restricted range suggested by social resources theory, restricted voluntary organization integration, constrained access to all three types of instrumental resources that we considered. But we found mixed effects of the diversity dimension of network range. Although religious homophily decreased access to employment resources and mainstream individuals, age homophily increased access to employment resources. This pattern suggests two possibilities that future research should explore. First, the aspects of diversity that we considered salient in this context may be less consequential than other aspects of restricted diversity. Second, the diversity aspect of range may simply be less consequential among the urban poor than it is in the general population. In future research, it would be interesting to explore whether the aspects of network diversity that Lin (2002) emphasizes—aspects that focus more heavily on status or position—yield similar results.

Turning to the aspects of restricted range that Wilson (1987) and Granovetter (1982) emphasized, we did not find the urban poor sample to be distinct in restricted geographic range, but we did find that restricted geographic range decreased access of the urban poor to mainstream individuals and to communication and transportation resources. Evidence for the effect of restricted access to weak ties (density) was less compelling. Although he could not test it empirically, Granovetter's (1982) argument attributed the utility of weak ties to their association with network range. The question arises, then, whether individuals living in poor urban areas differ from residents of other areas in the degree to which weak ties lend range to their networks (as Sanders et al. 2002 suggest).

To begin exploring that possibility, we examined differences in the average characteristics of alters named in response to our friends-of-friends/acquaintances name generator between residents of poor and middle-class areas. These analyses show that, compared to friends-of-friends/acquaintances of individuals in the middle class, friends-of-friends/acquaintances of respondents in poor areas are significantly less likely to be of a different race than the respondent, are significantly more likely to be kin, are significantly less educated than the respondent, and are significantly less likely to be of a different religion than the respondent. These differences suggest that the effects of the prevalence of weak ties may be indirect, through other aspects of the structure element of network capital. We will explore that possibility in later work. In addition, we will investigate whether the definition of a "friend-of-a-friend or an acquaintance" may differ across samples.

The concept of social isolation will continue to play a major role in theoretical controversies, empirical studies, and policy debates about the causes and consequences of living in areas of concentrated poverty. Our analyses contribute to these discussions by demonstrating how residents of areas of concentrated poverty are distinct on the structure and resource elements of network capital. But our exploration of the relationship between the two dimensions of social isolation goes beyond that to show that restricted network range not only distinguishes residents of poor areas from residents of more affluent areas but also plays an important role in explaining the lack of resources in their networks. Recent research (McPherson et al. 2006) suggests that in the general population of the United States, low density, rather than low range, may affect access to another form of network capital. Their work shows that Americans' stocks of close personal ties are dwindling, which could decrease their access to social support. Thus, whereas this chapter shows that members of the urban poor population in the United States lack instrumental resources because of the restricted range of their social networks, more mainstream Americans may be experiencing declining levels of social support because of the decline in dense network sectors containing close personal ties. Future research should explore whether the structure and resources elements of network capital in the general population are, in fact, related in the way that the work of McPherson et al. suggests. For the urban poor population, our approach to asking and answering the question, "Is low network capital really the problem?" provides an important step forward in understanding why the urban poor are "truly disadvantaged" (Wilson 1987).

NOTES

This work was supported by Grant #SBR–9512005 from the National Science Foundation. We thank Edward S. Shihadeh, Sally Robicheaux, two anonymous reviewers, and the editor for helpful comments. Please direct all correspondence to Jeanne S. Hurlbert, Department of Sociology, 126 Stubbs Hall, Louisiana State University, Baton Rouge, LA 70803 (E-mail: sohurl@lsu.edu).

1. Consistent with the distinction in social resources theory between instrumental and expressive action, we do not treat instrumental forms of social support as instrumental resources. Like Wilson, we examine employment resources, access to mainstream individuals, and communication/transportation resources.
2. We classify isolation from mainstream institutions in the network structure dimension and isolation from mainstream individuals under the network resources dimension because lack of integration into mainstream institutions limits access to mainstream individuals who possess resources.
3. Tie strength represents a dyadic property, whereas range describes a network or network sector. At the network level the proportion of weak or strong ties represents a key aspect of restricted range (the density dimension; Campbell et al. 1986).
4. Wilson's (1987) and Granovetter's (1982) arguments assume that the patterns social resources researchers identify in the general population hold among the urban poor.
5. We note that this research tends to rely on name generators rather than using Lin's (2002) approach to studying social capital, which relies on position generators.
6. Although kin ties are not uniformly strong, they are disproportionately strong; reliance on kin has been cited as a key aspect of poor individuals' dependence upon strong ties and lack of access to weak ties (Stack 1974).
7. Homophily taps the average similarity in a network between a focal individual (ego) and alters. We note that religious homophily demonstrates construct validity as a diversity measure (see the following).
8. Our data include a measure of whether currently employed respondents used informal methods to find their jobs. Using this measure would necessitate excluding from the analysis individuals who are not employed and are most likely to be socially isolated. For analysis of job finding among employed individuals, see Hurlbert, Beggs, and Haines (2001).
9. Considerable evidence (see, for example, McPherson and Smith-Lovin 1982, 1986; Fischer and Oliker 1983; Marsden 1987; Beggs and Hurlbert 1997) suggests that women's networks exhibit less range and offer fewer instrumental resources than men's networks.
10. Because little within-area variation by race exists (e.g., the middle-class areas are predominantly white and the urban poor areas are predominantly black), race may not exert a significant effect.
11. In 1989, the "poverty line" for a family of four was $12,674.
12. The local Emergency Medical Service office provided a list of telephone exchanges for the area. We included a screener question to verify that respondents lived within the study area.

13. All field contacts were African American residents of the focal urban poor area. We used both African American and white interviewers for the main telephone sample; we did not attempt to match race of interviewer to race of respondent in that sample.
14. For example, for the focal urban poor area 89 percent of respondents were black (compared to 94 percent in the census), 24 percent were married (28 percent in the census), 4 percent reported incomes above $50,000 (which mirrors the census figure), and 80 percent reported incomes below $25,000 (78 percent in the census).
15. This name generator elicited a total of 471 alters. Of those, 84 percent (396) were unique to this name generator. These 396 alters were on average less close to the respondent than the alters named in response to the other two name generators (.56 for these alters, .81 for those elicited from the other two name generators), less likely to be kin (8 percent vs. 29 percent), less likely to be neighbors (23 percent vs. 36 percent), and the respondent–alter ties were less likely to involve multiple relationships (7 percent vs. 35 percent). Thus, this name generator decreases the strong tie bias of earlier studies. However, because it is new we do not know what, if any, additional biases it may introduce.
16. It is possible that urban poor respondents thought in terms of the time required to reach alters by walking or via public transportation, whereas most middle-class respondents thought in terms of "driving time." Even if this is true, we do not think it compromises the measure: the key element is the time taken to reach an alter, by whatever means of transportation the respondent typically used.
17. This measure does not consider whether those ties were also named in response to the other two name generators.
18. We measure race dichotomously because the population of this area contains extremely low percentages of non black non whites. Our sample includes only 26 non-Black non-Whites.
19. We asked respondents to place their income in one of seven categories. We recoded the first six categories to their midpoints and the seventh to $85,000. We developed a prediction equation to estimate family income for the 59 respondents who failed to report it. Details are available, on request, from the first author.
20. We report Model 1 only for interpreting differences in R^2 between the model that includes network structure and the model that includes only individual characteristics.
21. We calculated these figures as follows: (R^2, Model 2—R^2, Model 1) / R^2, Model 2.

REFERENCES

Bailey, S., and P. V. Marsden. 1999. "Interpretation and Interview Context: Examining the General Social Survey Name Generator Using Cognitive Methods." *Social Networks*, 21: 287–309.

Bane, M. J., and P. A. Jargowsky. 1988. "The Links Between Government Policy and Family Structure: What Matters and What Doesn't." in *The Changing American Family and Public Policy*, ed. A. J. Cherlin, 219–55. Washington, DC: Urban Institute.

Beggs, J. J., V. A. Haines, and J. S. Hurlbert. 1996. "Situational Contingencies Surrounding the Receipt of Informal Support." *Social Forces*, 75: 201–22.

Beggs, J. J., and J. S. Hurlbert. 1997. "The Social Context of Men's and Women's Job Search Ties." *Sociological Perspectives*, 40:601–22.
Bourdieu, P. 1986. "The Forms of Social Capital." In *Handbook of Theory and Research for the Sociology of Education*, ed. J. G. Richardson, 241–258. New York: Greenwood.
Bridges, W. P., and W. J. Villemez. 1986. "Informal Hiring and Income in the Labor Market." *American Sociological Review*, 51: 574–82.
Browne, I., and L. M. Tigges. 1999. "The Intersection of Gender and Race in Atlanta's Labor Market." In *The Atlanta Paradox: Race, Opportunity, and Disadvantage in a New Southern City*, ed. D. L. Sjoquist, 158–184. New York: Russell Sage Foundation.
Burt, R. S. 1985. "Network Items and the General Social Survey." *Social Networks*, 6: 293–339.
———. 2005. *Brokerage and Closure*. Oxford, NY: Oxford University Press.
Campbell, K. E., P. V. Marsden, and J. S. Hurlbert. 1986. "Social Resources and Socioeconomic Status." *Social Networks*, 8: 97–117.
Coleman, J. S. 1990. *Foundations of Social Theory*. Cambridge, MA: Harvard University Press.
Elliott, D. S., W. J. Wilson, D. Huizinga, et al. 1996. "The Effects of Neighborhood Disadvantage on Adolescent Development." *Journal of Research in Crime and Delinquency*, 33: 389–426.
Feagin, J. R., and K. D. McKinney 2003. *The Many Costs of Racism*. Lanham, MD: Rowman & Littlefield.
Fernandez, R. M., and Harris, D. 1992. "Social Isolation and the Underclass." In *Drugs, Crime, and Social Isolation*, eds. A. Harrell and G. Peterson, 257–293. Washington, DC: Urban Institute.
Fischer, C. S. 1982. *To Dwell Among Friends: Personal Networks in Town and City*. Chicago: University of Chicago Press.
———. and S. J. Oliker. 1983. "A Research Note on Friendship, Gender, and the Life Cycle." *Social Forces*, 62: 124–33.
Gramlich, E., D. Laren, and N. Sealand. 1992. "Moving Into and Out of Poor Urban Areas." *Journal of Policy Analysis and Management*, 11: 273–87.
Granovetter, M. S. 1973. "The Strength of Weak Ties." *American Journal of Sociology*, 78: 1360–80.
———. 1974. *Getting a Job: A Study of Contacts and Careers*. Cambridge, MA: Harvard University Press.
———. 1982. "The Strength of Weak Ties: A Network Theory Revisited." In *Social Structure and Network Analysis*, eds. P. V. Marsden and N. Lin, 105–30. Beverly Hills, CA: Sage.
Green, G. P., L. M. Tigges, and I. Browne. 1995. "Social Resources, Job Search, and Poverty in Atlanta." *Research in Community Sociology*, 5: 161–82.
Green, G. P., L. M. Tigges, and D. Diaz. 1999. "Racial and Ethnic Differences in Job Search Strategies in Atlanta, Boston and Los Angeles." *Social Science Quarterly*, 80: 263–78.
Green, G. P., R. B. Hammer, and L. M. Tigges. 1999. "'Someone to Count On': Informal Support in Atlanta." In *The Atlanta Paradox: Race, Opportunity, and Disadvantage in a New Southern City*, ed. D. L. Sjoquist 244–263. New York: Russell Sage.
Greenbaum, S. D. 1982. "Bridging Ties at the Neighborhood Level." *Social Networks*, 4: 367–84.
Haines, V. A., J. S. Hurlbert, and J. J. Beggs. 1996. "Exploring the Determinants of Support Provision: Provider Characteristics, Personal Networks, Community Contexts, and Support Following Life Events." *Journal of Health and Social Behavior*, 37: 252–64.

Hogan, D. P., L.-X. Hao, and W. L. Parish. 1990. "Race, Kin Networks, and Assistance to Mother-Headed Families." *Social Forces*, 68: 797–812.

Holzer, H. 1987. "Informal Job Search and Black Youth Unemployment." *The American Economic Review*, 77:446–52.

———, K. R. Ihlanfeldt, and D. L. Sjoquist. 1994. "Work, Search, and Travel Among White and Black Youth." *Journal of Urban Economics*, 35:320–45.

Hurlbert, J. S., V. A. Haines, and J. J. Beggs. 2000. "Core Networks and Tie Activation: What Kinds of Routine Networks Allocate Resources in Nonroutine Situations?" *American Sociological Review*, 65:598–618.

———. 2001. "Social Networks and Social Capital in Extreme Environments," In *Social Capital: theory and research*, eds. N. Lin, K. Cook, and R. S. Burt, 209–31. Chicago: Aldine De Gruyter.

Katz, M. B. 1993. "The Urban 'Underclass' as a Metaphor of Social Transformation," In *The 'Underclass' Debate: Views From History*, ed. M.B. Katz, Princeton, NJ: Princeton University Press.

Lin, N. 2002. *Social Capital: A Theory of Structure and Action*. Cambridge, MA: Cambridge University Press.

———. and W. Ensel. 1989. "Life Stress and Health: Stressors and Resources." *American Sociological Review*, 54:382–99.

Lomnitz, L. 1977. *Networks and Marginality*. New York: Academic Press.

McPherson, J. M. and L. Smith-Lovin. 1982. "Women and Weak Ties: Differences by Sex in the Size of Voluntary Organizations." *American Journal of Sociology*, 87: 883–904.

———. 1986. "Sex Segregation in Voluntary Associations." *American Sociological Review*, 51: 61–79.

———, L. Smith-Lovin, and M. E. Brashears. 2006. "Social Isolation in America: Changes in Core Networks Over Two Decades." *American Sociological Review*, 71:353–75.

Marsden, P. V. 1987. "Core Discussion Networks of Americans." *American Sociological Review*, 52: 122–31.

Mouw, T. 2002. "Racial Differences in the Effects of Job Contacts: Conflicting Evidence From Cross-Sectional and Longitudinal Data." *Social Science Research*, 31: 511–38.

Munch, A., J. M. McPherson, and L. Smith-Lovin. 1997. "Gender, Children, and Social Contact: The Effects of Childrearing for Men and Women." *American Sociological Review*, 62: 509–20.

Murray, S.O., J. H. Rankin, and D. W. Magill. 1981. "Strong Ties and Job Information." *Sociology of Work and Occupations*, 8: 119–36.

Portes, A. 1998. "Social Capital: Its Origins and Applications in Modern Sociology." *Annual Review of Sociology*, 24: 1–24.

Quane, J. M., and B. H. Rankin. 1998. "Neighborhood Poverty, Family Characteristics, and Commitment to Mainstream Goals: The Case of African American Adolescents in the Inner City." *Journal of Family Issues*, 19: 769–94.

Rankin, B. H., and J. M. Quane. 2000. "Neighborhood Poverty and the Social Isolation of Inner-City African American Families." *Social Forces*, 79: 139–64.

Reingold, D. 1999. "Social Networks and the Employment Problem of the Urban Poor." *Urban Studies*, 36: 1907–33.

Sanders, J., V. Nee, and S. Serneau. 2002. "Asian Immigrants' Reliance on Social Ties in a Multiethnic Labor Market." *Social Forces*, 81:281–314.

Smith, S. S. 2000. "Mobilizing Social Resources: Race, Ethnic, and Gender Differences in Social Capital and Persisting Wage Inequalities." *The Sociological Quarterly*, 41: 509–37.

Stack, C. B. 1974. *All Our Kin: Strategies for Survival in a Black Community*. New York: Harper and Row.

Taylor, R. J., and L. M. Chatters. 1986. "Church-Based Informal Support Among Elderly Blacks." *The Gerontologist*, 26: 637–42.

Tienda, M. 1991. "Poor People and Poor Places: Deciphering Neighborhood Effects on Poverty Outcomes." In *Micro-Macro Linkages in Sociology*, ed. J. Huber, 244–62. Newbury Park, CA: Sage.

Tigges, L. M., I. Browne, and G. P. Green. 1998. "Social Isolation of the Urban Poor: Race, Class, and Neighborhood Effects on Social Resources." *The Sociological Quarterly*, 39: 53–77.

U.S. Bureau of the Census. 1992. *Census of Population and Housing, 1990: Summary Tape File 3 on CD-Rom*. Washington, DC: U.S. Bureau of the Census.

Wilson, W. J. 1987. *The Truly Disadvantaged: The Inner City, the Underclass, and Public Policy*. Chicago: University of Chicago Press.

———. 1991a. "Public Policy Research and the Truly Disadvantaged." In *The Urban Underclass*, eds. C. Jencks and P. E. Peterson, 460–82. Washington, DC: Brookings Institution.

———. 1991b. "Studying Inner-City Social Dislocations." *American Sociological Review*, 56: 1–14.

———. 1993. *The Ghetto Underclass*. Beverly Hills, CA: Sage.

———. and T. F. J. Tolson. 1990. "Familial Support in the Black Community." *Journal of Clinical Child Psychology*, 19: 347–55.

Part IV

Families and Social Capital

12 Parental Closure Effects on Learning

Coleman's Theory of Social Capital on Learning Revisited

Ly-Yun Chang

By focusing on a special form of social capital, network closure among a child's parents and the parents of the child's good friends in school (hereafter "parental closure around school"), the 1999 debates on the effect of social capital on learning centered around three related issues: (a) Does the concept of social capital refer to a school attribute or an individual attribute? (b) Will parental closure around school increase or decrease students' learning? and (b) Because the second issue refers to the possible underlying mechanism for parental closure effects on learning growth, norm enforcement (Coleman and Hoffer 1987) or horizontal expansion (Morgan and Sørensen 1999a) were respectively suggested to explain positive or negative effect on learning growth. Rather than revisiting the debate on the effect of intergenerational social closure on students' learning, this chapter engages in the debate from a different angle. I argue that although I agree with Morgan and Sørensen (1999a) that the concept of social capital in a form of parental closure around school refers to a school attribute, we need to understand individual parental behavior and its relationship to learning because the reproduction and sustenance of the school level of social capital depends on the behavior of the students' parents, voluntarily or in response to school programs and the child's situation. I engage the debate by gaining an understanding of the role of individual parents' behavior.

PARENTAL CLOSURE AROUND SCHOOL AND STUDENT LEARNING

Despite the disparity in their theoretical interests, both Bourdieu (1986) and Coleman (1988) argued that social capital can be translated into human capital and generate desirable social outcomes for individuals. Although based on limited empirical analysis, the social capital advantage on learning has been widely quoted in explaining home, school, and community advantages in boosting children's learning outcomes (see Dika and Singh's extensive review in 2002). The major empirical debate on the effect of social capital on educational outcome was first set by Coleman and Hoffer (1987). Coleman and Hoffer attributed Catholic schools' learning advantage to the large endowment of social capital formed by the students' parents. Although Carbonaro (1998) found a positive association between parental closure around school and mathematics achievement, he later agreed with Morgan and Sørensen (1999a) that school-level parental closure does not behave in a manner consistent with Coleman's prediction. Contrary to Coleman's prediction of a positive effect of parental closure on educational outcomes, social capital as defined by a summary of network closure for students' parents is found to be detrimental to students' learning growth in mathematics performance (Morgan and Sørensen 1999a).

The 1999 debates on the effect of social capital on learning (Morgan and Sørensen 1999a, 1999b; Carbonaro 1999; Hallinan and Kubitschek 1999) centered around the issues of proper representation of the concept of social capital, which characterizes effective schools. Schools with which parents maintain constant contact are hypothesized to be effective in fostering student learning. Parental closure around school represents a school characteristic. Coleman and Hoffer (1987) attributed a positive return of network closure to its capacity to transmit values as well as enforce norms and discipline. Being a member of a close-knit community entails pressure to conform to the obligations associated with roles and status. Parents are the major mediating agents in transmitting community norms to the children. Parental closure indicates tight control over children's behavior via effective exchange of information among parents of the students. In contrast, Morgan and Sørensen (1999a) contended that an open network, that is, lack of parental closure, is embedded with more capacity for information exchange than a closed network. Horizon expansion due to nonclosure networks provides students with an opportunity to experience exposure. Students in norm-enforcing schools actually possess less social capital because less information is brought in, due to the closed network built among the parents of students.

A paradox arises when parental closure around school, as a measure of the concept of social capital, is derived from the aggregate parenting behavior of the students and is considered a school attribute. Specifically, when schools with an abundance of social capital do increase students' learning growth, the first thing parents do is to explore every possible way to help the child get into the school that endows students with social capital advantages. According to Morgan and Sørensen's (1999a) interpretation of Coleman's (1988) social capital theory of learning, schools with ample social capital benefit not only students whose parents engage in networking around school, but also those whose parents take no part. The issue of the free rider emerges. The paradox refers to the reproductive process of school climate. Parents can stop investing but still enjoy advantages due to other parents' investment. School climate with ample social capital will not be maintained if the parents of the admitted students make no effort to connect with the parents of classmates after admission. The level of social capital via parental closure hinges on the behavior of individual parents. There are at least five conditions that affect the reproduction of school climate regarding the degree of parental closure around school: (a) the school's ability to recruit students whose parents are more likely to attend to the child's peers and form connections with the parents of those peers; (b) the degree of pressure that the school can place on parents to participate in school activities; (c) evidence of social capital advantage, so that parents realize their devotion enables their children's admittance into desirable schools; (d) the capacity of parents to engage in networking; and (e) parents' need to intervene and monitor child's behavior.

Notwithstanding that the first two refer to school practice, parent's behavior and perception occupy a pivotal position in the reproduction of social capital in school. I therefore argue that when parental closure around school is used to map the intensity of social capital in school, we must return to the parenting behavior that is at the center of social capital measurement in the 1999 debate. With such an understanding, we may be able to put Coleman's (1988) social capital theory on learning under proper empirical examination. For this reason, this chapter departs from what Morgan and Sørensen (1999b) advocated. Instead, I focus on individual parental closure as the first step in the empirical examination of Coleman's social capital theory on learning. Considering the possibility that parental behavior can be adjusted according to the affordability of the parents and the child's situation, I propose that the relation between parental closure around school and learning outcomes may not be linear in either direction. Rather, the relation between parental closure around school and learning outcomes can be curvilinear as the theses of the strength of the weak ties would suggest (*weak tie hypothesis;* Granovetter 1973).

Moreover, school practice mentioned in the first two conditions implies the role of the institutional forces of the schooling system. One may expect the parent to act differently in response to different schooling systems, such as student recruitment methods. In this study, I test this idea to see whether any observed patterns of parental closure on learning are institutionally invariant or not (*institutional dependence hypothesis*). This chapter takes advantage of newly released data sets in Taiwan, the Taiwan Education Panel Survey (TEPS), by employing two cohorts of middle school students in comparing similarities and differences in parental closure patterns on learning. The two cohorts are not only different in terms of age/grade, but are also located in different institutional settings in the Taiwanese schooling system (see next section for a detailed description). Cohort comparison can shed light on the possible impact of institutional setting on parental behavior as a response to educational environments.

DATA AND METHODS

Data used in the study were collected through the TEPS of 2001. In Taiwan, community-based compulsory education is nine years, including six years of elementary schooling and three years of junior high schooling. Academic merit–based sorting begins when students enter higher secondary and higher education levels through standardized entrance examinations.[1] Junior high graduates are sorted into different tracks including academic, comprehensive,[2] vocational high school, or vocational junior colleges,[3] and sectors such as public or private. Students are admitted to the best possible school according to their scores on the entrance examination. Specifically, schools select the most qualified students according to the standardized scores set by the schools. Students with high test scores are more likely to choose academic track and public schools over vocational and comprehensive tracks and private schools. This transitional point is crucial for educational mobility because students admitted to prestigious colleges or universities usually graduate from elite academic higher secondary schools.

In 2001, 99.45 percent of the school-age population was in school. According to the 2001 statistics provided by the Ministry of Education, there are 708 junior high schools, 495 senior high schools, and 148 five-year junior colleges in Taiwan. Because many senior high schools offer multiple programs, such as academic, vocational, and comprehensive, the sampling unit is thus programs but not schools. For the TEPS project, 333 junior high schools (47 percent) and a total of 287 programs of higher secondary were sampled, including 154 academic tracks (53.6 percent), 45 comprehensive tracks (15.7 percent), 62 vocational high schools (21.6 percent), and 26 vocational five-year junior colleges (9.1 percent).

A total of 20,004 students in junior high schools and 19,333 students in the higher secondary schools were surveyed in September 2001 to constitute representative samples of seventh-grade and eleventh-grade students in Taiwan, respectively. For this study, 70 percent of the data were used for analysis. That is, the sample size used in this analysis was 11,945 and 11,708 for junior high and higher secondary, respectively. Because TEPS is a multistage cluster sample, weights were used to calculate the population parameters. Further, the estimates of standard errors were smaller than they should otherwise be, so proper standard errors were adjusted.

Note that Wave 1 data employed for analysis in this chapter were collected at the beginning of the seventh grade for the junior high cohorts and the eleventh grade for the higher secondary cohorts, i.e., the second year in senior high or junior college. Consequently, the Wave 1 cognitive ability measure for the higher secondary cohorts to some extent entails school effect on learning. Given the sorting mechanism, students can come from very different geographical districts. Parents of the students would have to make a great deal of effort to get acquainted with the parents of their child's good friends in a one-year time period. Wave 2 data were collected in the last semester of the ninth grade and twelfth grade, respectively.

The Dependent Variable

The students took a 75–item test that covered general analytical ability, reading (Chinese and English), mathematics, and science. The estimated right scores based on the Item Response Theory for all five subjects were used as the measure for cognitive ability (IRT score). The IRT scores for all five subjects together ranged between –3.1 and 3.1, with a mean of –0.01 and a standard deviation of 0.94. The psychometric properties of the tests used in TEPS are found in Yang and Tam (2004).

The Independent Variable: Parental Network Closure Around School

Central to the focus of this chapter is the nature of social networks formed between students' parents and their friends' parents. Parental closure is found when a child's parents and the parents of their friends maintain ties to each other. For the measures of parental closure around school, the questions about the student's social circle in TEPS2001 are parallel to those of NELS88 (National Education Longitudinal Study of 1988). That is, the parents were first asked, "How many of your children's friends do you know?" The answer could be "Don't know or claim that the child has no friends at all" (*ignorant parents*), "Don't know the name of the child's friend" (*not naming any*), "Know few of them by name," and "Know all of them by name." They were then asked a set of three questions: first, could they give the name of one of their child's friends? If the parents offered a name, they were next asked, "Is he or she a classmate of your child?" and "How well do you know the parents of your child's friend?" The answer categories for the latter question were "Chat or meet a lot" (*strong parental closure*), "Have talked to each other a few times" (*weak parental closure*), or "Know them through child's information" (*no parental closure*). Again, those who could not provide even one name of their child's friends were labeled "not naming any," even if they claimed to know their child's friends.

The variable "individual parental closure around school" is derived from the parent questionnaire. It is measured as the strongest contacts that the parents of the respondent student maintained with the parents of the school friends of the child. The statistics shown in Table 12.1 indicate that 27 percent of the junior high parents either did not know whether their child had a friend or claimed that the child had no friends (i.e., ignorant parents); for higher secondary the number is 29 percent. Twelve percent of the junior high parents claimed to know the names of every good friend of their child, and 8 percent of the higher secondary. In response to the request to provide the names of friends, more than 22 percent of the parents of the junior high cohorts could

Table 12.1 Descriptive Statistics of the Variables Under Study

	Junior High School	*High School*
Major independent variables		
The child's friends—parents' knowledge		
Don't know or no friend	27.10	29.09
Don't know their names	15.97	17.27
Names of few friends	44.93	45.48
Names of every friend	12.00	8.16
Number of friends named by parents		
0	46.99	57.37
1	14.45	17.71
2	15.97	12.22
3	22.60	12.69
Mean	1.13	0.82
Parental closure around school		
Not knowing friend	47.02	57.40
Not naming any	10.65	12.25
No parental closure	6.61	9.23
Weak parental closure	21.43	15.74
Strong parental closure	14.29	5.38
Visiting relatives and friends of parents		
Never	5.26	4.58
Seldom	34.59	44.87
Sometimes	38.63	35.41
Often	21.51	15.15
Visitor at home		
Never	2.91	1.70
Seldom	40.94	42.35
Sometimes	36.34	35.93
Often	19.81	20.02
Total	11,945	11,708

	Junior High School	*High School*
Family backgrounds		
Parents' education		
Junior high and below	29.19	31.44
Senior high school	43.45	41.86
Junior college	15.97	15.73
University	8.72	8.42
Graduate school	2.68	2.55
Family income		
Less than NT$20,000	11.78	9.34
NT$20,000–49,999	42.67	43.79
NT$50,000–99,999	33.69	35.32
School characteristics		
Urbanity		
Rural	17.80	6.89
Township	37.93	44.95
Urban	44.28	48.16
Sector		
Public	85.98	46.12
Private	14.02	53.88
Programs		
Academic	—	32.14
Comprehensive	—	10.77
Vocational	—	31.09
Junior college	—	26.00
Peer characteristics		
Types of friends		
High academic achiever	74.27	76.70
High talent	67.81	65.82
Sharing	67.63	83.67
Deviant	10.36	20.70
Issuing warning	18.47	39.23
Mean of good friend numbers		
	4.53	4.67
Total	11,945	11,708

provide the names of three school friends of their child. In contrast, 12.7 percent of the parents of the higher secondary cohorts could do so.

As a result, for the junior high cohorts more than 14 percent of the parents of the junior high students fell into the strong parental closure group, but only 5.38 percent were in the higher secondary cohort. Note that the categories of "ignorant parents," "not naming any," and "no parental closure" indicate no network closure among the parents of children in school. They differ in terms of their knowledge of the friends of their child. To repeat, "ignorant parents" refers to no knowledge of the child's peers on the parents' side. The category "not naming any" indicates that the parents know that the child has good friends in school, but claim not to know any of them. The category "no parental closure" indicates that (a) the parents know that the child has good friends in school, and (b) the parents provide the name of the child's good friend in school, but (c) the parents maintain no contact with the parents of the child's friends. The descriptive statistics are presented in Table 12.1.

Explaining Variables

Measures of *family background* are self–explanatory. For instance, parental education is the highest education level either parent has achieved. Because the average number of years of schooling is 12 years for the cohort born around 1970, students whose parents received a senior high education are used as the reference group. Family income is monthly and divided into six categories. Students coming from family with monthly income between NT$50,000[4] and NT$99,999 are used as the reference category. Family structure indicates coresidence with both father and mother, father only, mother only, or with no parents.

School characteristics refer to sector and program. School sectors refer to public or private; school programs include academic track, comprehensive track, vocational high school, and vocational junior college. Among the 11,945 students in junior high under study, 86 percent are in public schools, and 14 percent are in private ones. Forty-four percent of students are from schools located in urbanized areas, 17.8 percent in rural areas, and 37.9 percent are in areas in between. Among all 11,708 higher secondary cohorts, 32.14 percent are on the academic track, 10.77 percent on the comprehensive track, 31.09 percent on the vocational track, and 26 percent are in vocational junior college. About 53.9 percent are from private schools, and 46.1 percent are from public ones. Forty-eight percent of students are from schools located in urbanized areas, 6.9 percent in rural areas, and 45 percent in between.

Intergenerational transmission of social networks from parents to child indicates parents' efforts to deliberately form networks around the child. Two variables are constructed to indicate intergenerational transmission of social networks in this study. The variable "social" is derived from the question, "How often do your parents take you to visit relatives or their friends?" The variable "visit" is derived from the question, "How often do your parents have visitors at home?" Both variables signify a deliberate action initiated by the parents to engage their children in their own social ties. The engagement of the children in the parents' social network may lead to more exposure, as compared to those who have no such engagement. It is found in Table 12.1 that the majority reported experiencing the intergenerational transmission of social resources to varying degrees. Among the two cohorts, a small proportion reported visiting their parents' relatives and friends and having visitors at home frequently; only a few have never had this kind of experience. Note that the high-income families are more likely than the low-income families to bring their children to visit relatives and friends.

The students in TEPS2001 were asked various questions about their peers, such as, "How many friends do you hang out with often?" "Among the friends with whom you are hanging out, are there any who are high achievers academically?" The same type of question was repeated four more times, asking whether the student has a friend "who is highly talented," "who you can share personal affairs with," "who smokes, drinks, or chews betel nuts," or "who receives warnings from school." On average, junior cohorts have 4.53 friends, and more than 45 percent indicate having more than six good friends. The higher secondary cohorts on average have 4.67 friends and about 46 percent have more than six good friends. The descriptive statistics are presented in Table 12.1.

The Analytical Plan

The IRT ability score is the dependent variable for the analysis reported in this chapter. To assess the observed pattern of parental mediated network closure on learning, the models expressed in Equations 1a, 1b, and 1c are designed to assess the extent to which parental closure around school affects learning. The dependent variables are cognitive ability measured in Wave 1 and Wave 2, respectively. The model in Equation 1c includes the Wave 1 ability score to illustrate the possible effect of individual–parental closure on learning growth. As is shown in the following section, individual–parental closure measured in Wave 1 exerts a similar effect on both Wave 1 and Wave 2 cognitive ability scores, but little effect on learning growth. To simplify, the model in Equation 1b is used as the base model for comparison with the estimations of other model specifications. We also assess whether the observed pattern of individual–parental closure on cognitive ability can be attributable to the difference in family backgrounds (Equation 2), school characteristics (Equation 3), intergenerational transmission of social resources (Equation 4), and peer structure (Equation 5). The same sets of analyses are run separately for the junior high and higher secondary cohorts. The model is expressed as follows:

$$W1\_IRT^{*}_{i} = [\text{Parental Closure}_{I}] + e_{i} \quad [1a]$$

$$W2\_IRT^{*}_{i} = [\text{Parental Closure}_{I}] + e_{i} \quad [1b]$$

$$W2\_IRT^{*}_{i} = [\text{Parental Closure}_{I}] + [W1\_IRT^{*}_{i}] + e_{i} \quad [1c]$$

$$W2\_IRT^{*}_{i} = [\text{Parental Closure}_{I}] + [\text{Family Backgrounds}]_{i} \quad [2]$$

$$W2\_IRT^{*}_{i} = [\text{Parental Closure}_{I}] + [\text{Program, Sector, Urbanity}] \quad [3]$$

$$W2\_IRT^{*}_{i} = [\text{Parental Closure}_{I}] + [\text{Social, Visit}_{i}] \quad [4]$$

$$W2\_IRT^{*}_{i} = [\text{Parental Closure}_{I}] + [\text{Peers}_{i}] \quad [5]$$

DESCRIPTIVE STATISTICS ABOUT TAIWANESE SECONDARY SCHOOLING

In Taiwan, junior high schools are all community based, and the higher secondary schools are merit based. Descriptive analyses shown in Table 12.2 offer two sets of information that correspond to previous descriptions of the Taiwanese middle school system. First, parental education, family income, and family structure are associated with school characteristics. Private junior schools are the minority in Taiwan and attract students from high socioeconomic classes (Panel 1, Table 12.2). Social origin concentration by program and sector is evident during higher secondary schooling. For instance, students from higher-educated families are less likely to attend the vocational track, including both senior high vocational and junior college (Panel 2). They are also less likely to attend private school (Panel 3). Students from families whose monthly income is less than NT$50k are more likely to attend vocational schools. Students from families with different incomes do not differ in terms of attending public or private schools. Students from single-parent families or who are not residing with a parent are less likely to attend academic track, although they are no different in terms of attending private or public schools.

Second, parental education, family income, family structure, and school characteristics are associated with ability score (Panels 4 and 5). Cognitive ability is regressed by school attributes and family backgrounds for the junior high and higher secondary cohorts, respectively. Using parents with senior high schooling as the reference category, students with parents who have at least a college education have high cognitive ability scores, and students with parents who have a junior high school education or less have lower ability scores. Using students coming from families with monthly income between NT$50,000 and NT$99,999

Table 12.2 Descriptive Analyses of the Schooling Systems by Program, Sector, and Family Background

	Junior High School	*Higher Secondary*		*Junior High School*	*High School*
	Private	*Program*	*Private*	*W1 IRT*	*W2 IRT*
Dependent Variable	(1)	(2)	(3)	(4)	(5)
Parents' education (senior high school = reference category)					
Junior high and below	–0.856**	–0.046	0.021	–0.258**	–0.047+
	(0.195)	(0.074)	(0.102)	(0.025)	(0.024)
Junior college	0.374**	–0.232**	0.020	0.315**	0.112**
	(0.104)	(0.083)	(0.076)	(0.026)	(0.023)
University	0.447**	–1.223**	–0.560**	0.506**	0.161**
	(0.162)	(0.142)	(0.138)	(0.038)	(0.035)
Graduate school	**0.082**	**–1.211****	**–0.658****	**0.625****	**0.340****
	(0.227)	**(0.209)**	**(0.182)**	**(0.061)**	**(0.055)**
Family income (NT$50,000-NT$99,999 = reference category)					
Less than NT$20,000	–1.859**	0.192	0.038	–0.281**	–0.126**
	(0.315)	(0.121)	(0.175)	(0.035)	(0.037)
NT$20,000-NT$49,999	–0.731**	0.221**	0.010	–0.119**	–0.042**
	(0.084)	(0.078)	(0.082)	(0.021)	(0.016)
NT$100,000-NT$149,999	0.550**	–0.160	–0.075	0.107**	0.081**
	(0.105)	(0.098)	(0.077)	(0.036)	(0.027)
NT$150,000-NT$199,999	0.841**	–0.547**	0.191	0.103+	0.150**
	(0.177)	(0.190)	(0.159)	(0.061)	(0.049)
NT$200,000 or more	**1.213****	**0.044**	**0.094**	**0.121**	**0.113+**
	(0.177)	**(0.183)**	**(0.175)**	**(0.074)**	**(0.068)**
Presence of parents (both parents = reference category)					
No parent	-0.442	0.381**	0.257	–0.224**	–0.152**
	(0.305)	(0.121)	(0.184)	(0.052)	(0.056)
No father	-0.190	0.158*	0.215+	–0.032	0.126**
	(0.188)	(0.070)	(0.125)	(0.058)	(0.042)
No mother	–0.061	0.242*	0.096	–0.159**	–0.080
	(0.261)	(0.113)	**(0.179)**	**(0.060)**	**(0.076)**

(continued)

Table 12.2 Descriptive Analyses of the Schooling Systems by Program, Sector, and Family Background (continued)

	Junior High School	*Higher Secondary*		*Junior High School*	*High School*
	Private	*Program*	*Private*	*W1 IRT*	*W2 IRT*
Dependent Variable	(1)	(2)	(3)	(4)	(5)
Sector (private = reference category)					
Public				0.382**	-0.541**
				(0.059)	(0.061)
Urbanity (rural = reference category)					
Township				0.204**	0.297**
				(0.064)	(0.097)
Urban				0.286**	0.505**
				(0.061)	(0.099)
Programs (comprehensive = reference category)					
Academic					0.709**
					(0.073)
Vocational					-0.469**
					(0.087)
Junior college					0.175*
					(0.070)
Constant				–0.147*	–0.394**
				(0.059)	(0.110)
R^2-squared				0.20	0.50

Note. Junior high: $N = 11{,}945$. Higher secondary: $N = 11{,}708$.
Robust standard errors are in parentheses. $+p < 0.1$. $*p < 0.05$. $**p < 0.01$.

as the reference category, students in higher socioeconomic status families perform better than those from low socioeconomic status families. Students with higher ability scores tend to be from families where parents have higher education and family income, although students in the highest bracket of family income do not have the highest cognitive ability. The highest scores are found among students in single-mother families, followed by tacit families, single-father families, and no-parent families. Among them, students from tacit families do not differ from those in single-father families. Students in schools in urban areas have the highest ability score, followed by those in township and rural areas.

Such patterns hold for both junior and higher secondary cohorts, except for sector and program. For junior high cohorts, students of private schools, on average, have higher scores than those in public schools. In contrast, students in public higher secondary schools, on average, have lower ability scores than those in private schools. Moreover, results shown in Table 12.2 also clearly indicate a strong program differential on students' ability scores (Panel 5). Good students disproportionately cluster in academic track and public schools. Highest ability scores are found among students on the academic track, followed by those on the junior college and senior vocational track.

FINDINGS

Does Parental Closure Affect Cognitive Ability?

Parents' knowledge about the peer group of the child matters. First, the cutoff point lies at whether the parents come to know their child's friends. As long as parents know whether the child has a friend or not, this knowledge provides an advantage in learning. It does not matter whether the parents know the name of the child's friends or the parents are acquainted with the parents of the child's friends. Using "not naming any" as the reference category, "ignorant parents" present significant ability liability. Junior high cohorts suffer greater liability than the higher secondary cohorts.

Second, consistent with Carbonaro (1998), parental closure around school is found to have a significant positive effect on ability scores. However, the positive effect on learning is observed for weak parental closure around school. The relationship between parental closure and learning is not linear. Curvilinear patterns of parental closure effects on learning are found for both the junior high and higher secondary cohorts. Weak parental closure advantage is much higher among the higher secondary cohorts than the junior high cohorts. Specifically, we observed an advantage of weak parental closure on ability scores. The highest ability scores are found among those students whose parents are reported to have chatted or met with the parents of their friends only one or two times (weak parental closure). The point estimate of the coefficient for weak parental closure is significantly higher than that of the "not naming any" category. Third, whether at the junior high or higher secondary stage, students do not benefit from strong parental closure. The point estimate of the coefficient for the "chat and meet frequently" group (strong parental closure) does not differ statistically from that of the "not naming any" group. In other words, it does not appear to be necessary to have strong parental closure around school for students to gain social capital benefits on ability scores. Students can benefit from having parents who are acquainted with their friends. Weak parental closure brings the greatest advantage on ability score.

Fourth, such patterns of parental closure effects on learning remain similar no matter whether Wave 1 or Wave 2 cognitive ability is employed as the dependent variable. It appears that the effect of parental closure on learning is stable across different schooling periods. Wave 1 parental closure affects not only Wave 1 learning but also Wave 2 learning with similar patterns, although in slightly different degrees. A positive weak parental closure effect is found for both junior high and higher secondary cohorts. Finally, parental closure does not affect learning growth. The pattern holds for both cohorts. Parental closure presents no effect on learning growth for the two cohorts under study.

In sum, the findings shown in Table 12.3 suggest that students whose parents know their friends and maintain limited ties with the parents of those friends gain advantages on ability scores. Students receive a stronger advantage when the parents are able to establish loose contacts with the

Table 12.3 Regression Analyses of Parental Closure Effects on Wave 1 and Wave 2 Ability Scores, Respectively

	Junior High			*Higher Secondary*		
	Wave 1 (1)	Wave 2 (2)	Wave 2 (3)	Wave 1 (4)	Wave 2 (5)	Wave 2 (6)
Parental closure around school (not naming any = reference category)						
Parents' ignorance	–0.155**	–0.156**	–0.036	–0.100*	–0.116**	–0.036
	(0.030)	(0.035)	(0.023)	(0.043)	(0.042)	(0.022)
No parental closure	0.010	-0.037	–0.050	0.011	0.013	0.003
	(0.050)	(0.052)	(0.035)	(0.046)	(0.045)	(0.029)
Weak parental closure	0.094*	0.078+	–0.004	0.202**	0.199**	0.028
	(0.039)	(0.041)	(0.023)	(0.046)	(0.048)	(0.024)
Strong parental closure	0.013	–0.021	–0.038	–0.039	0.012	0.030
	(0.042)	(0.049)	(0.032)	(0.072)	(0.070)	(0.039)
Wave 1 IRT			0.790**			0.848**
			(0.009)			(0.011)
Wave 1 IRT squared			0.078**			0.065**
			(0.008)			(0.007)
Constant	–0.067*	–0.086**	–0.095**	–0.248**	–0.272**	–0.122**
	(0.029)	(0.030)	(0.021)	(0.067)	(0.060)	(0.018)
R^2	0.01	0.01	0.60	0.01	0.01	0.65

Note. Junior high N = 11,945, Higher secondary N = 11,708.
Robust standard errors are in parentheses. $+p < 0.1$. $*p < 0.05$. $**p < 0.01$.

parents of the child's friends. The benefit of parental closure diminishes as parental closure becomes "too much." Findings in Table 12.3 lend partial support to the findings of Carbonaro (1998). Nonetheless, a ceiling effect of parental closure on learning is found.

Sources of the Observed Pattern of Parental Closure Effects on the Attainment of Cognitive Ability

Considering the schooling systems faced by both cohorts and the fact that social networking is known to be a social economic status-bound phenomenon, we first assess the extent to which parental closure effect on learning can be attributable to family background variables and school characteristics. Results shown in Table 12.4 are derived from the regression analyses of Wave 2 cognitive ability on individual parental closure when taking into account family background variables and school characteristics, respectively. The same models are applied to the junior and higher secondary cohorts separately. Two major findings are observed. First, the curvilinear pattern remains as family backgrounds and school characteristics are included in the models. The ignorant parent liability and weak parental closure advantage remain significant, although the point estimates of the respective coefficients change to a varying degree. Second, sources of parental closure effects are different for the two cohorts. For instance, the observed liability due to "parents' ignorance" is due, to a larger extent, to the effects of family backgrounds for the junior high cohorts, although such liability can be due to both the effects of family backgrounds and school characteristics for the higher secondary cohorts. During the junior high stage, advantage due to weak parental closure cannot be attributable to the effect of family background. Moreover, weak parental closure advantage becomes even larger when school sector and urbanity are considered. In contrast, during the stage of the higher secondary, advantage due to weak parental closure can be accounted for by both the effects of family background and school characteristics. Weak parental closure advantage is due more to the effect of school characteristics on learning than the effect of family background variables. The coefficient for weak parental closure drops by about 53 percent when school characteristics are taken into account. It drops by only 20 percent when family background variables are included in the model.

Parental closure is a deliberate action by parents, as is learning enhancement. Parents spend more time on school-related networking when there is a need to do so. The formation of parental closure can be initiated by parents. That is, children become friends because parents are acquainted with each other. Taking a child to visit friends and relatives and/or having friends and relatives visit at home provides a child with more opportunities to get acquainted with the children of friends and relatives. Such visits are one way to expand the child's social horizon. Intergenerational transmission of social resources from parents to a child indicates the effort made by

Table 12.4 Regression Analyses of Parental Closure Effects on Wave 2 Cognitive Ability Score, Net of Family Background and School Characteristics

	Junior High			*Higher Secondary*		
	(1)	(2)	(3)	(4)	(5)	(6)
Parental closure around school (not naming any = reference category)						
Parents' ignorance	–0.156**	–0.060*	–0.135**	–0.116**	–0.059	–0.042+
	(0.035)	(0.028)	(0.033)	(0.042)	(0.037)	(0.024)
No parental closure	–0.037	–0.053	–0.030	0.013	0.004	–0.020
	(0.052)	(0.053)	(0.056)	(0.045)	(0.040)	(0.036)
Weak parental closure	0.078+	0.066+	0.103*	0.199**	0.159**	0.091**
	(0.041)	(0.037)	(0.041)	(0.048)	(0.042)	(0.032)
Strong parental closure	–0.021	–0.002	0.057	0.012	0.027	0.007
	(0.049)	(0.046)	(0.048)	(0.070)	(0.061)	(0.046)
Parents' education (senior high school = reference category)						
Junior high and below		–0.226**			–0.143**	
		(0.026)			(0.038)	
Junior college		0.347**			0.211**	
		(0.034)			(0.033)	
University		0.625**			0.511**	
		(0.034)			(0.064)	
Graduate school		0.825**			0.745**	
		(0.066)			(0.073)	
Family income (NT$50,000–NT$99,999 = reference category)						
Less than NT$20,000		–0.383**			–0.336**	
		(0.039)			(0.060)	
NT$20,000–NT$49,999		–0.210**			–0.167**	
		(0.024)			(0.039)	
NT$100,000–NT$149,999		0.146**			0.168**	
		(0.039)			(0.039)	
NT$150,000–NT$199,999		0.134*			0.290**	
		(0.064)			(0.066)	
NT$200,000 or more		0.208*			0.142+	
		(0.090)			(0.085)	
Presence of parents (both parents = reference category)						
No parent		–0.171**			–0.233**	
		(0.048)			(0.068)	
No father		–0.082			0.092*	

(continued)

Table 12.4 Regression Analyses of Parental Closure Effects on Wave 2 Cognitive Ability Score, Net of Family Background and School Characteristics (continued)

	Junior High			*Higher Secondary*		
	(1)	(2)	(3)	(4)	(5)	(6)
		(0.053)			(0.045)	
No mother		–0.181*			–0.057	
		(0.076)			(0.087)	
Sector (private = reference category)						
Public			0.632**			–0.520**
			(0.075)			(0.055)
Urbanity (rural = reference category)						
Township			0.277**			0.284**
			(0.089)			(0.072)
Urban			0.453**			0.513**
			(0.082)			(0.068)
Programs (junior high = reference category)						
Academic						0.773**
						(0.081)
Comprehensive						0.000
						(0.000)
Vocational						–0.426**
						(0.085)
Junior college						0.084
						(0.083)
Constant	–0.086**	0.024	–0.445**	–0.272**	–0.207**	–0.452**
	(0.030)	(0.036)	(0.087)	(0.060)	(0.056)	(0.096)
R^2	0.01	0.18	0.08	0.01	0.11	0.43

Note. Junior high $N = 11{,}945$, Higher secondary $N = 11{,}708$.
Robust standard errors are in parentheses. $+p < 0.1$. $*p < 0.05$. $**p < 0.01$.

parents to deliberately form networks around the child, as discussed in the previous section.

Both indicators of social resources, *visiting relatives and friends of the parents* and *visitors at home,* are introduced to the base model to estimate the extent to which the observed parental closure effect on learning can be accounted for by the effects of social resources. Table 12.5 presents the results of regression analyses. Intergenerational transmission of social resources is found to have advantages for the child, as shown in Table 12.5.

Table 12.5 The Effects of Parental Closure, Intergenerational Transmission of Social Resources, and Peer Structure on Wave 2 Cognitive Ability Score

	Junior High			*Higher Secondary*		
	(1)	(2)	(3)	(4)	(5)	(6)
Parental closure around school (not naming any = reference category)						
Parents' ignorance	–0.156**	–0.141**	–0.106**	–0.116**	–0.106*	–0.087*
	(0.035)	(0.034)	(0.034)	(0.042)	(0.042)	(0.037)
No parental closure	–0.037	–0.031	–0.041	0.013	0.016	–0.005
	(0.052)	(0.051)	(0.050)	(0.045)	(0.045)	(0.044)
Weak parental closure	0.078+	0.078+	0.076+	0.199**	0.205**	0.190**
	(0.041)	(0.040)	(0.039)	(0.048)	(0.048)	(0.046)
Strong parental closure	–0.021	–0.019	–0.021	0.012	0.031	0.024
	(0.049)	(0.046)	(0.045)	(0.070)	(0.068)	(0.067)
Visiting relative and friends of parents (never = reference category)						
Seldom		0.343**			0.222**	
		(0.057)			(0.059)	
Sometimes		0.411**			0.241**	
		(0.055)			(0.058)	
Often		0.546**			0.353**	
		(0.066)			(0.073)	
Visitor at home (never = reference category)						
Seldom		0.344**			0.134	
		(0.056)			(0.086)	
Sometimes		0.304**			0.032	
		(0.063)			(0.091)	
Often		0.259**			0.023	
		(0.059)			(0.099)	
Types of friends						
High academic achiever			0.273**			0.266**
			(0.036)			(0.038)
High talent			0.138**			0.126**
			(0.030)			(0.028)
Sharing			0.157**			0.074+
			(0.032)			(0.040)
Deviant			–0.328**			–0.293**
			(0.042)			(0.058)
Issuing warning			–0.106*			–0.018
			(0.043)			(0.039)
Constant	–0.086**	–0.786**	–0.376**	–0.272**	–0.581**	–0.556**
	(0.030)	(0.070)	(0.043)	(0.060)	(0.109)	(0.097)
R^2	0.01	0.03	0.07	0.01	0.02	0.05

Note. Junior high N = 11,945, Higher secondary N = 11,708.
Robust standard errors are in parentheses. $+p < 0.1$. $*p < 0.05$. $**p < 0.01$.

Taking a child to visit relatives and friends is found to be associated with incremental positive return on learning for both junior high and higher secondary cohorts (Models 2 and 5, Table 12.5). The incremental positive return of visiting is stronger for the junior high than for the higher secondary cohorts. Having visitors at home is also associated with a positive return on learning. The positive return is only observed for the junior high cohorts, but not for the higher secondary cohorts. Moreover, the positive return on learning in the case of junior high cohorts is in a decreasing form as the frequency of visitors increase. Nonetheless, the estimates of the coefficients for liability of ignorant parent and advantage of weak parental closure do not change much as both indicators of social resources are included in the model. This pattern holds for both junior and higher secondary cohorts. The observed patterns of parental closure on learning have little to do with the effects of social resources on learning.

The formation of parental closure may also start from the child side. The significant return to learning from peers when parental closure around school starts from the child side has been documented elsewhere (Brown 1990; Berndt 1992; Hartup 1996). The Chinese proverb, "Became red when close to red, but became black when close to black," perfectly illustrates the peer effect beyond sheer number of peers. Peer groups affect academic outcomes through the mediation of types of friends when friends are considered an important agent of socialization for adolescents (Ennett and Bauman 1994; Urberg, Deggrimencioglu, and Pilgrim 1997; Nichols and White 2001). The formation of parental closure is related to peer structure of the child because of the propensity of selectivity from the child's side. A child may selectively introduce friends to his/her parents; the parents' opportunities to meet the parents of the child's friends are, thus, not random. From the child's point of view, reluctance to introduce friends to parents may be due to the friends not belonging to a socially acceptable group—those exhibiting high academic performance, talent, presence of "good" behavior, absence of "deviant" behavior, and so forth. Parents are less likely to meet the parents of a child's friends who are socially unacceptable than those who are regarded as socially acceptable. In other words, network closure around school between parents and the parents of a child's friends involves an issue of selectivity when the parental link is initiated from the child side. The reported peer structure may to some extent entail an aspect of norm enforcement.

Students' peer network has a positive effect on the ability score. However, the effect is observed on types of friends, but not the number of friends. "Good" friends generate advantages on ability scores; "bad" friends create deficits on ability scores (Models 3 and 6, Table 12.5). The students who have friends with high academic performance or with many talents tend to achieve higher ability scores. The students who have friends who smoke, drink, or chew betel nuts tend to have lower scores. A significant advantage of "good" friends on learning and the peer deficit due to "bad" friends is found for both cohorts. The exception is observed for the higher secondary cohorts: having friends who can share personal matters makes no difference on ability scores.

The curvilinear pattern of parental closure effect on learning remains when students' peer structure is taken into account. More important, the observed patterns of parental closure on learning have to do with the effects of peer structure on learning depending on level of parental closure. On the one hand, the liability due to "ignorance of parents" seems to be due to some extent to the effect of peer structure on learning for both cohorts. On the other hand, learning advantage due to weak parental closure cannot be attributable to the effect of peer structure on learning. In sum, the observed patterns of parental closure effects on learning have little to do with the effects of intergenerational transmission of social resources or of peer structure on learning. Even the type of friends cannot explain the observed liability and advantage of parental closure on learning.

CONCLUDING REMARKS

Although family and school are recognized as structuring norm transmission and opportunity for exposure that enable a child to learn, family and school may also jointly create something irreducible to either family background or school characteristics that affects learning outcomes. Social capital is the general term used to capture the "social fact" embedded jointly in families with different educational levels and financial resources and schools with different characteristics. This chapter empirically examines the effects of parent–mediated networks around school on the child's learning.

My findings reveal that parenting behavior, unsurprisingly, is constrained by personal socioeconomic resources. Parenting behavior also tends to adjust according to the institutional schooling system. Their behavior strategically takes into account institutional opportunities and constraints. To be specific, parental closure around school is found to have a positive effect on the student's ability score. Parental closure around school does yield advantage on learning growth. However, a positive effect on learning is observed only among those with weak parental closure. Students gain the highest advantage when parents maintain loose contacts with the parents of their friends. The optimal parental closure effect on cognitive ability is found in weak parental closure. Learning liability is found among students whose parents are ignorant about the friends of the child. Such patterns are found for different time points of schooling and schools in different institutional settings. The strength of the weak tie thesis (Granovetter 1973) finds support here.

More important, the extent to which learning liability due to parents' ignorance of a child's peers and learning advantage due to weak parental closure can be attributable to the fact that effects of family background and school characteristics depend on stages of schooling. Family background, but not school characteristics, account for learning liability due to parents' ignorance of a child's peers in the junior high cohorts. In contrast, family background and school characteristics are the major source of observed learning liability for the higher secondary cohorts.

Moreover, for the junior high cohorts, weak parental closure advantage is found to be independent of the effects of school characteristics on learning. Only a small proportion of weak parental closure advantage can be reducible to family background. In contrast, school characteristics are far more important than family background variables in understanding the learning advantage due to weak parental closure for the higher secondary level. A large proportion of the learning advantage due to weak parental closure can be attributable to the effect of school characteristics on learning. School characteristics are the common source directly affecting both parental closure and ability score for the higher secondary cohorts, or through family background. This is not the case for the junior high cohorts.

Contrary to our expectation, the effect of parenting behavior is not related to either the effect of intergenerational transmission of social resources or that of child's peer structure on learning. Although social resources and peer structure affect students' ability scores, none can substantially explain the observed curvilinear pattern of the parental closure effect on learning.

At this juncture, note again that, in Taiwan, junior high schools are part of compulsory education. The majority of junior high schools are public and community based. Private schools are in the minority. At this stage of schooling, compulsory education has led 99.15 percent of primary school graduates to continue on to junior high degrees. Parental behavior appears to be an extra force in the child's learning. Family background underlies both learning liability due to parents' ignorance of their children's situation and what Carbonaro labeled as a little help from the parents of friends (1998). School characteristics do not have a similar influence.

When students enter the higher secondary school level, they are sorted into schools by their academic performance on a standardized entrance examination. Family socioeconomic status is associated with both school characteristics and cognitive ability. Schools in the higher secondary system are stratified by social origin concentration, as revealed in tracking, sectors, and geographic locations. School characteristics at the higher secondary school level become a dominant force, which explains away the effect of parental behavior on learning. School characteristics not only explain away the liability of parent's ignorance but also to a significant extent the advantage of weak parental closure for the higher secondary cohorts.

For practical reasons, parents' investment in education at the higher secondary level appears to be strategically individually oriented. Senior high students face university entrance examinations in three years and most junior college students continue their education following graduation; to ensure success, parents concentrate on areas that could help their children achieve high scores on these examinations. Once the students get into good schools and onto the right track, the school takes on the task of structuring learning opportunities. At this point, parents can no longer affect the learning of the child; their position in affecting children's learning has become secondary.

Finally, study findings shed light on empirical examinations of Coleman's (1988) social capital on learning theory. Because social capital is measured by parental closure around school as a school attribute, and school-level social capital is derived from the reports of individual parents/students, social capital as parental closure appears to be reproduced through examination of the institutional design of the school system. As long as parental closure appears to respond in different degrees to the institutional settings of the school system, the level of social capital that takes the form of parental closure around school will remain constant. In this chapter, I reveal that the institutional design of the school system cannot be overlooked in such studies.

NOTES

This research was supported by Academia Sinica through the Learning 2000 Project and National Science Council (NSC 94–2412–H–001–028). Direct correspondence to Ly–yun Chang, Academia Sinica, Institute of Sociology, Nankang, Taipei, 11529, Taiwan (E-mail: gacloud@gate.sinica.edu.tw). TEPS is an ongoing data collection project jointly funded by the Ministry of Education, the National Science Council, and Academia Sinica. The views expressed here do not reflect the opinions of the funding agencies.

1. Starting in 2003, graduates of junior high schools no longer have to take entrance examinations to be admitted into high schools of different tracks or junior college. Instead, graduates of junior high schools take a key competency test, which is similar to the SAT in the United States, and apply to schools by submitting their key competency scores.
2. The comprehensive track is a program that emphasizes both academic and vocational learning.
3. The first three years of the five-year junior college are considered part of higher secondary schooling in Taiwan.
4. The exchange rate of NT dollars to U.S. dollars is roughly 33:1.

REFERENCES

Berndt, T. J. 1992. "Friendships and friends' influence in adolescence." *Educational Psychology,* 34: 15–29.

Bourdieu, P. 1986. "The forms of capital." In *Handbook of Theory and Research for the Sociology of Education,* ed. John B. Richarson, 241–258. Westport, CT: Greenwood Press.

Brown, B. B. 1990. "Peer Groups and Peer Cultures." In *At the Threshold: the developing adolescent,* eds. S. S. Feldman and G. R. Elliot, 171–196. Cambridge, MA: Harvard University Press.

Carbonaro, W. J. 1998. "A Little Help From my Friend's Parents: Intergenerational Closure and Educational Outcomes." *Sociology of Education*, 71: 295–313.

———. 1999. "Opening the Debate on Closure and Schooling Outcomes: Comment on Morgan and Sørensen." *American Sociological Review*, 64: 682–6.

Coleman, J. S. 1988. "Social Capital in the Creation of Human Capital." *American Journal of Sociology*, 94: S95–120.

———, and T. Hoffer. 1987. *Public and Private Schools: The Impact of Communities*. New York: Basic Books.

Dika, S. L., and K. Singh. 2002. "Applications of Social Capital in Educational Literature: A Critical Synthesis." *Review of Educational Research*, 72(1): 31–60.

Ennett, S. T., and K. E. Bauman. 1994. "The Contribution of Influence and Selection to Adolescent Peer Group Homogeneity: The Case of Adolescent Cigarette Smoking." *Journal of Personality and Social Psychology*, 67: 653–63.

Granovetter, M. 1973. "The Strength of Weak Ties." *American Journal of Sociology*, 78: 1360–80.

Hallinan, M. T., and W. N. Kubitschek. 1999. "Conceptualizing and Measuring School Social Networks: Comment on Morgan and Sørensen." *American Sociological Review*, 64: 687–93.

Hartup, W. W. 1996. "The Company They Keep: Friendships and Their Developmental Significance." *Child Development*, 67: 1–13.

Morgan, S. L., and A. B. Sørensen. 1999a. "Parental Networks, Social Closure, and Mathematics Learning: A Test of Coleman's Social Capital Explanation of School Effects." *American Sociological Review*, 64: 661–81.

———. 1999b. "Theory, Measurement, and Specification Issues in Models of Network Effects on Learning: Reply to Carbonaro and to Hallinan and Kubitschek." *American Sociological Review*, 64:694–700.

Nichols, J. D., and J. White. 2001. "Impact of Peer Networks on Achievement of High School Algebra Students." *Journal of Educational Research*, 94: 267–74.

Urberg, K. A., S. M. Deggrimencioglu, and C. Pilgrim. 1997. "Close Friend and Group Influence on Adolescent Cigarette Smoking and Alcohol Use." *Developmental Psychology*, 33: 934–44.

Yang, M. L., and T. Tam. 2004. "Mental Health Inequality in the Adolescent Society: Family Background and the Paradox of Academic Success in Taiwan."Taipei, Taiwan: Academia Sinica.

13 Childcare Networks and Embedded Experiences

Joseph Galaskiewicz, Beth M. Duckles, and Olga Mayorova

Social capital theory has been very successful in explaining a wide variety of behaviors and outcomes. Even before Putnam's (1993, 2000) landmark works, and certainly since, study after study has shown that those who had social ties realized benefits and advantages that those without ties did not. Research at the individual level has shown the benefits for health and happiness, educational attainment and social welfare, and career advancement and material gain. Research at the organizational, community, and state levels has shown how social capital results in improved performance, power, and political stability (see Portes 1998).

One of the earliest applications of social capital theory was that by James Coleman (1988), who argued for the value of network closure for parents raising small children. We extend this work by arguing that a strong childcare network enables parents to send their children to venues or providers where the child is in the presence of adults that the parent knows well, or in the presence of other children whose parents are known by them. In contrast, parents who lack a childcare network must send their children to venues or providers where the child is supervised by or in the presence of adults who they do not know well, or with children whose parents are unknown to them. *Our proposition is that having an extensive childcare network enables parents to provide their children with experiences that are more deeply embedded in their own social networks and are thus more trustworthy and secure.*

Although this seems like a straightforward proposition, it can be complicated by the venue or provider chosen. When the venue or provider is another household, we expect to find support for our proposition. However, having a childcare network may also enable parents to send their children to organizational settings and realize the same advantages. The childcare network not only ensures that children will be taken care of in households and be in the company of children that the parent is familiar with, but also that the child will have embedded experiences in organizational settings. In other words, a household like experience can be replicated in nonhousehold environments through a dense network of informal childcare providers.

After briefly reviewing social capital theory, we formulate hypotheses to test our propositions. We test if having family and friends in the Phoenix metropolitan area who are available for childcare increases the chances of parents taking their children on Saturdays to households where there is a relative or friend on-site, or they know the adult present for a longer period of time. We then turn to a broader array of providers and test if having a strong family and friend childcare network results in children going to households *and organizational venues* (e.g., restaurants, theatres, schools, parks, and so on) where the parent knows the parents of the other children. We use data collected from a 2003–2004 random sample survey of families with children between 5 and 12 years of age in the Phoenix metropolitan area. We focus exclusively on children's activities outside of the home on Saturdays during the school year.

NETWORKS AND CHILDREN'S WELFARE

Coleman's (1988) seminal article triggered a debate in the child development literature that has been very fruitful. In essence, Coleman argued that intergenerational network closure produces information and control benefits for parents who are raising children. By "closure," Coleman was referring to the condition where the parents of those children that their children were going to school or playing with were well known. Coleman argued that when parents of children knew one another, they could exchange information on their children and come to a consensus about standards and sanctions. The example is a familiar one: your child, Kate, states that her friend Mary's parents say that it's OK for her to stay out until 10 o'clock, so why can't she? The child gains leverage in this encounter because Kate makes an explicit threat that she will lose her friendship with Mary if Kate's parents are not more reasonable (like Mary's parents), and an implicit threat that Kate will "hate" her parents if they don't relent (which is unpleasant for the parent). If Kate's parents knew Mary's parents, the former could confirm Kate's claim and, if true, perhaps negotiate a time that both parents could be comfortable with. In other words, the parents' ability to control their own child is increased if their child has friends who are, themselves, embedded in the parents' network.

Coleman (1988) then presented evidence that the likelihood of children dropping out of school was lowered by the fewer times a family moved, if children attended Catholic schools, and by the children attending religious services more frequently (see also Hagan, MacMillan, and Wheaton 1996). These variables were supposedly correlates of intergenerational closure in the parents' networks. Looking at individual level performances, Carbonaro (1998) found that closure had a modest positive effect on twelfth-grade math achievement. McLanahan and Sandefur (1994) showed the consequences of single parenthood for school achievement and attrition, teenage pregnancy, and other adolescent outcomes (see Portes 1998). Although Morgan and Sørensen (1999) found that the density of parental networks increased mathematics learning in Catholic school settings, it decreased learning in public schools. The results that Coleman assumed were due to network closure may have as much to do with the culture of Catholic and public schools. Wilson's (1996) analysis of children's poor school performance in areas of concentrated disadvantage added a twist to Coleman. He argued that in areas with high levels of criminal activity, parental closure may backfire and encourage antisocial behavior among children. Portes and Rumbaut (1996) argued that the closed social network in immigrant enclaves that focuses on the continuity of enclaves may subvert students' learning. It is also consistent with the observation that parental and/or organizational norms matter in explaining structural effects.

Our chapter is inspired by Coleman's (1988) research, but we go in a slightly different direction. Instead of assessing the effects of intergenerational closure on children's performance or dropout rates, we focus on its effects on children's leisure time experiences outside the home. We focus on two types of experiences: one where the provider herself is a friend or relative of the parent or the parent has known the provider for a long time, the other where the child is with children whose parents are known by the parent. Coleman's work highlights the importance of parents having information and control by virtue of being closely connected to caregivers and/or to the parents of children who are also receiving the same services. By having these ties to those responsible for their child's care or to the parents of other children, parents can get quick feedback on their children and their experiences, especially if the parent is not present at the venue. In contrast, if children are being watched over or served by adults whom the parent does not know well, or if children are with children whose parents are unknown to the parent, the parent's control over the situation is diminished. We label the former "embedded" experiences and the latter "anomic" experiences.

CHILDCARE SUPPORT NETWORKS: A LITTLE HELP FROM ONE'S FRIENDS AND FAMILY

How is it that parents can ensure embedded and avoid anomic experiences for their children? Although parents could make an effort to get to know the parents of their children's friends, they will always be playing "catch up," which certainly gives their children an advantage. A more proactive strategy is to arrange the child's life so that she does things with the children of one's friends and relatives or in the presence of a close or strong tie. But to accomplish this, parents need a large social support network that is available for childcare where the members of the network have strong ties to them.

Research on social support constitutes an important subfield within the social capital literature (for an overview see Lin, Dean, and Ensel 1986;

Walker, Wasserman, and Wellman 1994). Researchers such as Wellman (1979) and Wellman and Wortley (1990) focused on who provides assistance in everyday life and who provides support; Fischer (1982) focused on who has social support in communities and who does not (see also McLanahan and Sandefur 1994). Researchers have done extensive work on the effects of social support on family life and children (see Portes 1998, as well as Stanton-Salazar and Dornbush 1995 and Valenzuela and Dornbusch 1994), and the literature on the effects on health is vast (e.g., House, Umberson, and Landis 1988; Kawachi 1999; Kunitz 2004). There is, however, little work on informal childcare support networks and the benefits they provide to parents and child (Hayes, Palmer, and Zaslow 1990; for an exception see Parcel and Menaghan 1990, 1994).

Who is more likely to have a childcare support network of strong ties? First, families that have lived in a community longer are able to make friends that can help with childcare (Sampson, Morenoff, and Earls 1999). Newcomers may quickly socialize with their new neighbors (Fischer 1982), but we believe that the strong ties needed for a trustworthy childcare network take time to build. If the parents were raised in the community, they are also likely to have parents, siblings, cousins, etc. available for child care. Second, families with both parents present are more likely to have larger childcare networks of strong ties (McLanahan and Sandefur 1994). The mere fact that two adults are present in the household instead of one opens up worlds to the family that are not available with only one parent. There are two sets of families and two friendship networks to draw support from instead of one. Also single parents have less time to socialize and create networks. Third, families that participate in the associational life of their communities are more likely to have support networks (Fischer 1982). Church attendance, for example, is a way of meeting others who are similar to oneself, building friendships, and finding strong ties to stock a childcare network. This leads to our first hypotheses.

H1a: Families that have lived longer in the community are more likely to have friends and/or family members who are available for childcare.

H1b: Families that have both parents present are more likely to have friends and/or family members who are available for childcare.

H1c: Families that attend church regularly are more likely to have friends and/or family members who are available for childcare.

How can a childcare support network of strong ties help parents provide embedded experiences for children? Having many people available for childcare provides parents with a large stock of "warm bodies" to care for their children after school or on a weekend. Thus, if the goal is to have friends or family look after your child at their home, those who have more friends and family in the metropolitan area that are available for this duty are likely to take advantage of these network ties and provide more embedded experiences for their children. In fact, having a stock of caregivers and not using them would seem odd. This explanation is rational and consistent with social capital theory that focuses on how people will use their ties to realize benefits for themselves (Lin 2001). In this case, parents use their childcare network to ensure their child has embedded experiences in other's homes.

> H2: Children of families that have friends and/or family members living in the metropolitan community who are available for childcare are more likely to spend Saturday at a household of a family friend or family member than that of a neighbor, coworker, or other.

> H3: Children of families that have friends living in the metropolitan community who are available for childcare are more likely to spend Saturday at a household of someone their parents have known longer.

> H4: Children of families that have friends and/or family living in the metropolitan community who are available for childcare are more likely to spend Saturday at a household where the parent knows the parents of other children present.

DOES IT WORK OUTSIDE THE HOUSEHOLD SECTOR?

Households are not the only venues where children spend Saturdays. Many children spend time in organizational settings or in unorganized or unstructured venues. The former include restaurants, stores, gyms, sports leagues, churches, and dance classes; the latter include malls, streets, parks, and the desert. Organized settings are closed environments where there is adult supervision. Sometimes it is intense, such as a dance class, and sometimes it is lax, such as a restaurant. However, in both cases there is a clear boundary between the organization and the outside world; once that boundary is crossed there are rules and limits on behavior that the organization's agents enforce. Unorganized or unstructured venues are open environments. There is no supervision, no rules, and no barriers to cross when entering or leaving the venue.

In the organizational setting, children are more likely to interact with other children whose parents are unknown to their parents and to be taken care of by people who are strangers to the parents. This is because in these organized settings, the organization's agents control who has access to the venue, not the parent. Thus, sending a child to these venues entails a certain amount of risk for the parent, although organized venues may have greater capacity and the resources to provide children with a high-quality experience. Thus we hypothesize,

H5: All else equal, the parents of children who have Saturday experiences in formally organized settings are less likely to know the parents of the other children present.

Parents may be able to overcome the anomie of organizational venues if they can use their childcare network to provide embedded experiences for their children in these settings. Granovetter (1985) argued that people's economic actions are often embedded in social relations. Social structure affects the choices that people make and the meaning of their actions, and people use their social relations to achieve certain economic ends. We want to extend Granovetter's agenda into the realm of childcare in a way not dissimilar to DiMaggio and Louch's (1998) efforts to analyze household purchases. The attractive feature of Granovetter's approach is that it does not polarize the world into rationalist (market-centered) versus sentimentalist (culture-centered) views (Zelizer 2005). Rather, it recognizes that as people make consumer choices, they are influenced by their social relations, but they also use their relations to further their own ends. As Zelizer observes, economic sociologists have made great strides in developing this framework to study production, it is time to use it to study consumption.

Recent research shows that a person's day-to-day activity, which includes both organizational activity and informal interaction, is an "an expression of kinship and other relationships" (Miller 1998, 35). Focusing on commercial establishments, Miller (2001) noted that the hairdresser's salon and hardware store, and, to a lesser extent, the betting shop, cafe, and pub, in the community he studied were places that provided an opportunity for social interaction with those already known. People chatted with storeowners and clerks as well as with other customers on a regular basis. As quoted in Zelizer (2005), "In a direct challenge to individualistic accounts of consumption, Miller provides evidence that sociability and purchasing of goods support each other, while isolation promotes withdrawal from consumption (Miller 1998, 34; 1995, 24)" (p. 334). The outcome is that one does things with friends, family, acquaintances, ex-spouses, and children, i.e., experiences in these organizational environments are embedded, not anomic. As the activities of the network shift from the household to some public venue such as a park or a restaurant, the same people are there.

Lyn Lofland (1973/1985) described how, in urban environments, primary groups will transform public space into private space as they go about their business. Some public places, such as a local park or store, become home territories where groups of residents will carry on their private conversations and agendas, indifferent to the owners or caretakers and suspicious of outsiders. She also described how urban dwellers will "travel in packs"; when they leave their neighborhoods the group will appropriate public space as their own as they move from place to place, creating mobile homes for themselves (Lofland 1973/1985, p. 137). One often observes teenagers "capturing" and then releasing malls, public spaces, and eateries as they go about their daily life, but extended families, bachelor/wedding parties, softball teams, conventioneers, and office and factory workers will often exhibit similar behavior as they take road trips to bars, hotels, convention sites, casinos, stadiums, and airports. They will talk loudly, yell at each other across a crowded room, laugh loudly at private jokes, and use obscene language. There is value in being with those "special someones" and maintaining group solidarity—even if it means taking over public venues or invading others' private spaces.

In our example, parents could purposely use their childcare network of strong ties to embed their children's experiences when in organizational settings. They could intentionally "travel in packs" to buffer their children from strangers. If parents have an extensive social network of caregivers, it is likely that these people are also available for these purposes. Alternatively, it could happen that embedded experiences are simply the product of the household's day-to-day routines, and there is no intentionality. How one behaves is the product of people playing out roles in the context of relationships with others, e.g., friend, sister, parent, coworker, student, or lover. If their friends, relatives, and acquaintances are doing an activity, e.g., eating, going to a movie, or playing sports, we suspect that parents and their children will be doing it with them. Thus, people who are deeply embedded in social relations will engage more frequently in embedded activities without thinking twice. In contrast, if one has few close friends or relatives available for childcare, it is likely that the parent's social life will be less rich and thus the children's organizational experiences less embedded. We thus hypothesize:

> H6: Children of families that have friends or family members living in the metropolitan community who are available for childcare are more likely to spend Saturday in both household and organizational venues where the parent knows the parents of other children present.

LITERATURE REVIEW ON CHILDREN'S ACTIVITIES

There has been a considerable amount of research on what children do outside the home after school and on weekends. Those doing time budget studies of children have found that boys are more involved in group sports (Timmer, Eccles, and O'Brien 1985), and girls are more likely to take dance or cooking classes (Medrich et al. 1982). They also found that younger children spend more time going to church than older children (Timmer et al. 1985; Hofferth and Sandberg 2001), and whites spend more time in sports than minorities (Medrich et al. 1982; Hofferth and Sandberg 2001). Looking at time diary data for 2002, Bianchi, Robinson, and Milkie (2006) found that children between 5 and 11 years of age have, on average, 38.3 hours of "free time." Most is spent on watching television (13.9

hours), playing (10.5 hours), visiting (2.3 hours), and sports (2.2 hours). The effects of social class are more subtle. Lareau (2002, 2003) found that middle-class families scheduled many more organized events for their children, and poorer children spent their free time around the house. Medrich et al. (1982) found that families with higher incomes tend to use a mix of private and public facilities or only private providers; poorer families tend to use a mix of private and public facilities or only public providers. Family structure also seems to affect what children do in their leisure time, but not to a large extent. For example, children from female homemaker families tend to spend less time in church than children from two-parent families (Hofferth and Sandberg 2001). Bianchi et al. (2006) found that children between 5 and 18 from single-mother households tend to spend less time on home computer activities, religion, sports, art, and reading, and more time watching television than children from two-parent homes, but the differences were not that great.

We agree with Medrich et al. (1982), who state that out-of-school/out-of-home activities are more than simply leisure. Although this time may not be as important as time spent at home or in school in explaining future gains or losses, we suspect that this "free time" exacerbates whatever advantages or disadvantages a child realizes from home and school. There is some evidence that after-school activities can increase academic achievement (Valentine et al. 2002; Marsh and Kleitman 2002; Cooper et al. 1999); reinforce parental ideologies (Dunn, Kinney, and Hofferth 2003); contribute to less delinquency in low minority schools (Hoffman and Xu 2002); and, for inner-city youth, lessen the likelihood that they will be substance abusers (Zimmer et al. 2001). Extracurricular activities have been shown to help with adolescent social integration, which is a strong predictor of adult social integration (Spady 1970; Otto 1976). Some studies also suggest that involvement in extracurricular activity increases future civic involvement (Hanks and Eckland 1978; Verba, Schlozman, and Brady 1995; McFarland and Thomas 2006). There is evidence that the relationships formed with the staff of after-school programs can promote positive youth development (Kahne and Bailey 1999). For an excellent overview of the literature on the effect of childcare on children's development, see Hayes et al. (1990).

METHODOLOGY

We studied both children's activities and who served these children. We collected information on 1,036 children, between the ages of 5 and 12, in the Phoenix–Mesa metropolitan area. The Survey Research Laboratory (SRL) at Arizona State University began collecting data in September 2003 and finished in February 2004. The SRL suspended interviews during the Thanksgiving, Christmas, and New Year's holidays so that we would not include reports on holiday activities.

We selected study participants using random digit dialing methods (see Bianchi and Robinson 1997, and Harvey 1999). Our response rate for families with children between the ages of 5 and 12 was 55 percent. Upon calling, we obtained a list of all children in our age range living at the residence. The interviewer randomly selected one child and asked to speak to the adult who had the best knowledge about the child's activities on the previous Saturday.[1] Parents composed 93.4 percent of the respondents; the rest included legal guardians, grandparents, aunts/uncles, older brothers/sisters, and other; one person refused to identify themselves. We then asked for a diary of the child's activities outside the home for that day from midnight on Friday to midnight on Saturday (Robinson, 1999). We collected information on what the child did, whom they did it with, when they did it, where they did it, and who provided the service. If the activity benefited either the child or an adult and the child, we asked if the service provider was a household, a business or other organization, or if the child was at another location.

Following the phone survey, we selected 55 households from a pool of respondents who agreed to a follow-up interview and conducted in-depth face-to-face interviews with the parent or guardian. As much as possible, we selected respondents representative of different income and race/ethnicity categories, as well as new residents and those who lived longer in the Phoenix area. We interviewed 22 Hispanic families; 28 non-Hispanic white families; and 5 families with other racial/ethnic backgrounds. Fifteen families were low income, 29 were middle income, and 11 were upper income. The purpose of these interviews was to gather more qualitative data on how parents and guardians and their children decided on weekend activities. We wanted to know what they gained from the activities their child participated in and how they evaluated the child's experience (if they did). We asked about the role of religion, race/ethnicity, language, and culture in the selection of activities. We also asked about their fears and how they determined that a provider was trustworthy. We integrate these data into the discussion at the end of this chapter to add context and understanding to the quantitative results.

DESCRIPTIVE STATISTICS

We begin with some descriptive statistics. We draw a distinction between household respondents, activities, and providers. As noted, we had 1,036 household respondents with data on one child per household. One hundred and ninety-six households reported no activities for the child outside the home on the previous Saturday. Ninety-six households reported children participating in activities outside the home, but these did not benefit the child (e.g., running an errand with an adult). One refused to tell us if it benefited the child or not. In total, 743 children participated in 1,256 activities outside the home that benefited them in some way.

Table 13.1 cross-tabulates activity by type of service provider. As noted, 71.7 percent of the families reported activities outside the home that benefited the child, and the total number of these activities was 1,256. Of these, 167 were eating (13.3 percent); 179 (14.3 percent) were other personal care activities (shopping, doctor's visits, haircuts); 305 (24.3 percent) were sports related (individual, dual, and team sports); 165 (13.1 percent) were simply play; 212 (16.9 percent) were social activities (visiting, partying, sleepovers); 88 (7.0 percent) were entertainment (going to a movie, attending a festival or sporting event); 71 (5.7 percent) were developmental (education, arts, religion, scouting); 66 (5.3 percent) were miscellaneous activities (animal care, looking for a house, travel out of town, helping parent at work, running errands with adult); and 3 (.2 percent) were missing data. For the 1,256 activities, 279 (22.2 percent) were provided by households other than the respondent's; 650 (51.8 percent) were provided by organizations or businesses; and 327 (26.0 percent) were reported as "other." The latter included passive venues where no one, *per se,* provided a service, e.g., parks, shopping centers, church lots, schoolyards, streets and highways, the desert, or "our neighborhood." In our analysis, we excluded activities in "other locations." This left us with 929 activities to analyze.

Table 13.1 Cross Tabulation of Providers and Activities

	Activity type				
Provider:	*Eating*	*Other Personal Care*	*Sports*	*Play*	*Social*
Household	8	4	10	80	160
Organization/ business	145	154	174	11	29
Other	14	21	121	74	23
Total	167	179	305	165	212

	Activity type				
Provider:	*Entertainment*	*Developmental*	*Miscellaneous*	*Missing*	*Total*
Household	2	4	11	0	279
Organization/ business	69	53	12	3	650
Other	17	14	43	0	327
Total	88	71	66	3	1,256

MEASUREMENT OF VARIABLES

Dependent Variables

Different hypotheses have different dependent variables because we were trying to look at different examples of embedded experiences. Our measures of embedded experiences were: the activity was in the household of a friend or relative, the parent knew the people in the household for a long period of time, and the parent knew the parents of all the other children present at the venue (household or organization/business) where the child went on Saturdays. Of the 279 respondents who said that they used another household for the child's activities, we asked: "Was (the child's name) at the home of a friend, neighbor, coworker, relative, or someone else?"[2] One hundred seventeen said a friend, 46 said a neighbor, 2 said a coworker, 110 said a relative, and 4 said other. We dichotomized responses as: 0 = *neighbor, coworker, or someone else* (18.6 percent), and 1 = *relative or friend* (81.4 percent). We wanted to distinguish between weak and strong ties, and we dichotomized on this basis. Of the 177 who mentioned nonkin, we asked: "How long have you known this person?" The average number of years was 5.11, the range was less than 6 months (coded 0) to 30 years, and the standard deviation was 6.37. We experimented with many cut-off values, and finally dichotomized the variable: 0 = *less than three years* (83), and 1 = *3 years or more* (94).[3]

For the 279 activities that were provided by households and the 650 activities that were provided by organizations or businesses, we first asked, "Were there other children present?" Seven hundred fifty-five said yes (81.3 percent); 171 said no (18.4 percent); and 3 either did not know or refused to answer (.3 percent). Of the 755 who said that children were present, we then asked, "Do you know the parents of the children who were present?" Five hundred eighty-six said yes (77.6 percent); 96 said yes, but only some of them (12.7 percent); and 73 said no (9.67 percent). We created a dichotomous variable where: 0 = *knew none or only some of them*, and 1 = *knew all the parents of the children present.*

Independent Variables

Two items were used to construct our measure of childcare support. We asked these items of all 1,036 respondents. First, "Do you have any family members in the Valley area that you call on for help with childcare?" Five hundred said yes (48.3 percent); 533 said no (51.4 per cent); and 3 said they did not know or refused to answer (.3 percent). Second, "Do you have any friends, acquaintances or former spouses in the Valley area that you call on for help with childcare?" Five hundred thirty-four said yes (51.5 percent); 499 said no (48.2 percent); and 3 said that they did not know or refused to answer (.3 percent). Independently, neither variable had much of an effect on our dependent variables.[4] Thus we opted for an additive index. Three hundred forty-one respondents were coded as having relatives *and* friends/acquaintances/ex-spouses that could help with child care (32.9 percent); 352 were coded as having one or the other (34.0 percent); and 339 were coded as having neither (32.7 percent). Cronbach's alpha for the index was a modest .484 due to the low correlation between these variables, $r = .319$. This does not present a problem for us, given that our research goal is to assess the effect of a family's volume of childcare support on children having embedded experiences. The variables measuring the family's potential to build childcare networks of strong ties included years of residence in the Phoenix metro area (asked of respondent; $M = 15.7$ years), whether the respondent was married or not (19.3 percent widowed/separated/divorced/never married), and whether the family attended church regularly (70.5 percent answered that they did).

Control Variables

There were three types of control variables: activities (as discussed previously), the child's demographic characteristics, and parental resources. Data on all the control variables were gathered from respondents over the phone as well. The variables for the child included gender (46.4 percent girls); the child's age ($M = 8.5$ years); and whether the child was Hispanic (39.2 percent), white non-Hispanic (51.3 percent), or non-white non-Hispanic (9.5 percent), which included African-Americans, Asians, Pacific Islanders, and Native Americans.[5] Parental resources included household income ($M = \$64,840$); education of the respondent (mean = 13.4 years); and whether the respondent worked last Saturday (16.5 percent worked either part time or full time). Using regression techniques, we imputed values for cases with missing data using all the control variables measured on the individual/child and family and the additive index for family and friends providing child support in the metro areas. We imputed values for four variables: family/friends in the metro area to provide child support, household income, family length of residence in the metro area, and education of the respondent.[6]

ANALYSIS

To test the first hypothesis, we estimated an ordinary least squares model where our additive index for whether the family had friends or family members available for childcare was the dependent variable. Our N is the number of families in our sample, 1,036, but with missing data we analyzed 983 cases. The results are in Table 13.2. We see that only one of the family social capital variables, length of residence in the community, had a statistically significant effect on our dependent variable. Thus,

Hypothesis 1a but not Hypotheses 1b or 1c was confirmed. We also learn that the parents of Hispanic children, less-educated caregivers, and the parents of older children were less likely to have friends and/or relatives in the area available for childcare; however, the latter two effects were only significant at the .10-level.

In our subsequent analyses, the units of analysis are the activities that the children engaged in, not the family or household. Approximately 28 percent of our respondents reported that either the child had no activities outside the home or participated in no activities that benefited the child. Also, in testing Hypotheses 2 and 3, we only looked at cases where the activity was at another household. In testing Hypotheses 4, 5, and 6, we only considered cases where the activity was at another household or provided by an organization. The exclusion of so many sampling units from

Table 13.2 OLS Regression Model with Family and Friends Providing Childcare as Dependent Variable

Dependent variable: Family and friends provide childcare (0=none; 1=family or friends; 2=family and friends)	*Coefficient (SE)*
Independent variables:	
Child female (ref. category=male)	.050 (.050)
Child's age	-.021 (.011)#
Child Hispanic (ref. category=non-Hispanic, white)	-.203 (.062)**
Child non-Hispanic, nonwhite (ref. category= non-Hispanic, white)	-.062 (.090)
Family income	.001 (.001)
Caregiver's years of education	.018 (.010)#
Caregiver worked Saturday (ref. category=did not work)	-.052 (.067)
Family years lived in Phoenix metro area	.011 (.002)***
Family typically attends church (ref. category=does not attend)	.014 (.056)
Caregiver not married (ref. category=married)	.081 (.066)
Constant	.780 (.177)***
N	983
F (10, 972)	8.38
Prob>F	.000
R-squared	.079

the analyses suggests that there may be sample selection bias. To address this issue, we tested our hypotheses using probit models with sample selection (Van de Ven and Van Praag 1981). These models estimated a sample selection model and a substantive probit model and assessed the correlation between their respective error terms using the statistic ρ. If the correlation is near zero, then the potential for sample selection bias is low, and the results of estimating models with and without taking sample selection into account will not differ greatly (Berk 1983). If the correlation is high, then it is important to focus on coefficients from the probit analysis with sample selection.[7]

Another methodological concern is that our units of analysis are activities, and not households. The reader should recall that we sampled 1,036 households and they reported on 1,256 activities. Because 28.3 percent of the households did not have activities for children that benefited them, this means that those children who had such activities performed 1.69 activities on average. Thus, we utilized the cluster option in Stata to correct for the nonindependence in observations and estimated robust standard errors.[8]

The results from our second analysis are in Table 13.3. Here the dependent variable is the characteristics of the household where the respondent sent his/her child last Saturday. The total *N* is 1,549 activities/households, but of these, 1,270 are censored observations (no activities outside the home [196]; no activities that benefited the child [96]; we do not know if they benefited the child or not [1]; and activities that took place somewhere other than a household [977]). This left 279 uncensored activities/households. When Stata estimated the probit model with sample selection, it took the number of cases for which we had (or should have) observations, 279, plus the number of censored observations, 1,270. Thus the total *N* is 1,549. However, because of missing data on various items, the *N* in Table 13.3 was 1,492, and we had 271 uncensored cases.

Table 13.3 presents two sets of results. Column 1 shows the results from a simple probit analysis where we ignored the sample selection issue. Our *N* was 271, which included only activities that took place in households. We see that respondents who had more family and friends available for childcare were more likely to send their child to households where the adults were relatives or friends. This supports Hypothesis 2. Also, boys or older children were more likely to go to households where the adults were relatives or friends of the family. Social activities typically took place in households where the adults were relatives or friends of the parent, but the effect was only significant at the .10-level.

Column two presents the results taking into account possible sample selection bias.[9] In the sample selection model, we included the three family resource variables: family income, caregiver's years of education, and whether or not the caregiver worked on Saturday (a measure of time available for caregiving). We also have three social capital variables: caregiver not married, years living in the Phoenix metro area, and church attendance. We should first note that ρ was moderately strong (–.428), suggesting that

Table 13.3 Probit Models with Home of Relative/ Friend (vs. Other) as Dependent Variable

Dependent variable: Relation to head of household (0=neighbor, co-worker, other; 1=friend, relative)	*Column 1 Coefficient (Robust SE)*	*Column 2 Coefficient (Robust SE)*
Independent variables:		
Family and/or friends provide childcare	.267 (.114)*	.256 (.125)*
Child female (ref. category=male)	-.436 (.196)*	-.403 (.211)#
Child's age	.091 (.042)*	.085 (.047)#
Child Hispanic (ref. category=non-Hispanic, white)	.371 (.249)	.328 (.228)
Child non-Hispanic, nonwhite (ref. category=non-Hispanic, white)	.494 (.388)	.445 (.405)
Family income	.001 (.002)	.001 (.002)
Caregiver's years of education	- .043 (.040)	-.039 (.039)
Caregiver worked Saturday (ref. category=did not work)	.478 (.317)	.439 (.332)
Family years lived in Phoenix metro area	-.006 (.008)	-.009 (.009)
Family typically attends church (ref. category=does not attend)	-.119 (.224)	
Caregiver not married (ref. category=married)	-.013 (.255)	-.068 (.291)
Social	.525 (.313)#	.493 (.301)
Play	-.375 (.324)	-.341 (.337)
Constant	.419 (.711)	1.000 (1.311)
N	271	1492
Censored N		1221
Uncensored N		271
Wald statistic	43.66***	24.75*
Degrees of freedom	13	12
Log likelihood	-113.247	-813.112
Pseudo R^2	.136	
Selection model		
Dependent variable: Relation to head of household (0= did not answer question; 1=answered question)		
Independent variables:		
Family income		.001 (.001)
Caregiver's years of education		.000 (.013)
Caregiver worked Saturday (ref. category=did not work)		.026 (.096)
Family years lived in Phoenix metro area		.009 (.003)**
Family typically attends church (ref. category=does not attend)		-.095 (.083)
Caregiver not married (ref. category=married)		.203 (.095)*
Constant		-1.080 (.174)***
ρ		-.428 (.783)

sample selection was somewhat a problem, and two variables in the sample selection model were significant. Caregivers who were not married or families that had lived in the Phoenix metro area were more likely to use households on Saturday than other options. The results for the probit model with sample selection (column 2) were essentially the same as in column 1. The results in the substantive model showed that respondents that had family and/or friends to take care of their children were more likely to send their children to households of friends or family members than to households of coworkers, neighbors, or someone else. Again, we found support for Hypothesis 2. Also, males or older children were more likely to be at homes of relatives or friends, but the results were significant only at the .10-level. Finally, if the activity was social in nature, the activity was more likely to be at the home of relatives or friends, but the effect was significant only at the .11-level.

The dependent variable for Hypothesis 3 was the number of years that the respondent knew nonkin household members where the child was spending time on Saturday. For this analysis we only focused on nonkin households, because respondents would know relatives all their lives. The variable was dichotomized: 0 = *knew less than three years;* 1 = *knew three years or more.* In Table 13.4 there were only 177 cases where children were at nonkin households on Saturday. Thus the total *N* was 1,549; the number of censored cases was 1,372; and the number of uncensored cases was 177. However, our number of censored and uncensored cases was somewhat less because of missing data. Because we were only considering nonkin households, we substituted the dummy variable "Do you have friends in the valley to help with childcare?" (0 = no; 1 = yes) for our additive index that measured the availability of family and friends.[10]

Looking at the probit model in Table 13.4, we see that having friends in the valley had very little effect on knowing the adults in the household for three years or more.[11] Looking at the control variables, higher-income respondents were likely to know household members longer. If the child was older or the activity was social in nature, caregivers were more likely to know household members three years or more, but these effects were only significant at the .10-level.

In the probit model with sample selection (column 2), we see that ρ was larger than in Table 13.3 (.717). In the selection model, we see that higher income families were more likely to use households on Saturday where nonkin were present. Turning to the substantive model, we see that none of the substantive effects were statistically significant. We concluded that Hypothesis 3 was not supported.

The final three hypotheses tested whether the respondent knew the parents of all the children who were with their child. The *N* in Table 13.5 included the 620 censored observations, as well as the 929 activities that took place in households or at businesses/organizations (but not in other venues such as the street, desert, or shopping mall). However, the data set had a nuance. Of

Table 13.4 Probit Model with Knowing Nonkin Household Members Three Years or More as Dependent Variable

Dependent variable: Know non-kin household members (0=less than three years; 1=three years or more)	*Column 1 Coefficient (Robust SE)*	*Column 2 Coefficient (Robust SE)*
Independent variables:		
Friends provide childcare (0=no; 1=yes)	.208 (.220)	.154 (.314)
Child female (ref. category=male)	-.172 (.208)	-.128 (.288)
Child's age	.085 (.049)#	.064 (.103)
Child Hispanic (ref. category=non-Hispanic, white)	.430 (.267)	.329 (.507)
Child non-Hispanic, nonwhite (ref. category=non-Hispanic, white)	-.161 (.342)	-.117 (.335)
Family income	.006 (.002)*	.006 (.005)
Caregiver's years of education	-.062 (.044)	-.044 (.087)
Caregiver worked Saturday (ref. category=did not work)	-.375 (.311)	-.280 (.490)
Family years lived in Phoenix metro area	.000 (.009)	.002 (.006)
Family typically attends church (ref. category=does not attend)	.086 (.227)	
Caregiver not married (ref. category=married)	.124 (.276)	.155 (.211)
Social	.575 (.330)#	.438 (.579)
Play	.580 (.355)	.442 (.582)
Constant	-.901 (.831)	-1.998 (1.789)
N	171	1494
Censored N		1323
Uncensored N		171
Wald statistic	16.13	4.35
Degrees of freedom	13	12
Log likelihood	-108.630	-636.455
Pseudo R^2	.082	
Selection model		
Dependent variable: Know nonkin household members (0=did not answer question; 1=answered question)		
Independent variables:		
Family income		.002 (.001)*
Caregiver's years of education		.004 (.014)
Caregiver worked Saturday (ref. category=did not work)		.009 (.114)
Family years lived in Phoenix metro area		.003 (.003)
Family typically attends church (ref. category=does not attend)		-.090 (.090)
Caregiver not married (ref. category=married)		.104 (.117)
Constant		-1.395 (.194)
ρ		.717 (1.319)

Table 13.5 Probit Model with Know Parents of All Children (vs. Not) as Dependent Variable

Dependent variable: Know parents of all children present (0=no; 1=yes)	*Column 1 Coefficient (Robust SE)*	*Column 2 Coefficient (Robust SE)*
Independent variables:		
Family and/or friends provide childcare	.696 (.168)***	.591 (.149)***
Child female (ref. category=male)	.087 (.126)	.057 (.106)
Child's age	.052 (.028)#	.040 (.024)#
Child Hispanic (ref. category= non-Hispanic, white)	-.066 (.147)	-.051 (.116)
Child non-Hispanic, nonwhite (ref. category=non-Hispanic, white)	-.047 (.204)	-.042 (.165)
Family income	.001 (.001)	
Caregiver's years of education	-.033 (.025)	-.051 (.020)*
Caregiver worked Saturday (ref category=did not work)	.018 (.161)	.016 (.129)
Family years lived in Phoenix metro area	-.005 (.005)	-.008 (.004)#
Family typically attends church (ref. category=does not attend)	.242 (.136)#	.186 (.127)
Caregiver not married (ref. category=married)	-.156 (.177)	-.109 (.149)
Social	-.095 (.239)	-.077 (.183)
Play	.376 (.296)	.291 (.238)
Eating	1.047 (.197)***	.847 (.164)***
Other personal care	1.089 (.213)***	.870 (.185)***
Entertainment	.774 (.226)**	.626 (.195)**
Developmental	.119 (.236)	.108 (.181)
Miscellaneous	.541 (.401)	.442 (.324)
Business/organization provider (ref. category=household)	-.519 (.268)#	-.410 (.213)#
Family and friends provide childcare X business/organization provider	-.607 (.186)**	-.526 (.158)**
Constant	.454 (.535)	1.478 (.488)**
N	721	1484
Censored N		763
Uncensored N		721
Wald statistic	100.37***	78.99***
Degrees of freedom	20	19
Log likelihood	-315.730	-1307.562
Pseudo R^2	.159	

(continued)

Table 13.5 Probit Model with Know Parents of All Children (vs. Not) as Dependent Variable (*continued*)

Dependent variable: *Know parents of all children present (0=no; 1=yes)*	*Column 1 Coefficient (Robust SE)*	*Column 2 Coefficient (Robust SE)*
Selection model		
Dependent variable: Know parents of all children present (0=did not answer question; 1=answered question)		
Independent variables:		
Family income		.003 (.001)***
Caregiver's years of education		.051 (.012)***
Caregiver worked Saturday (ref. category=did not work)		-.015 (.092)
Family years lived in Phoenix metro area		.008 (.003)**
Family typically attends church (ref. category=does not attend)		-.003 (.072)
Caregiver not married (ref. category=married)		.003 (.082)
Constant		-1.058 (.158)***
ρ		-.838 (.212)

these 929 activities, only 755 had other children present; thus we could only measure our dependent variable on these 755 activities. Because of missing data, our *N* was 1,484 and we had 721 uncensored cases.

We tested Hypotheses 4, 5, and 6 in a single model (see Table 13.5). We argued that the effects of childcare networks on knowing the parents of other children would be positive regardless of the venue. This network effect should hold up if the child was at another household (Hypothesis 4) or the provider was an organization (e.g., business, government agency, nonprofit organization, or church; Hypothesis 6). Columns one and two show that Hypothesis 4 was supported, but Hypothesis 6 was not. In these models, we included a product or interaction term where we multiplied our additive index for family and friends support by the dummy variable for organizational provider. The results showed that when the child was at another household the effect of having family and friends providing child support was quite strong, but when the provider was at an organization, the effect of the childcare network variable on the likelihood of knowing the parents of all the children present was much weaker. These effects were smaller in the probit model with sample selection (see column two), but still statistically significant at the .01-level. We found support for Hypothesis 5 in both our probit model and probit model with selection. Respondents who sent their child to

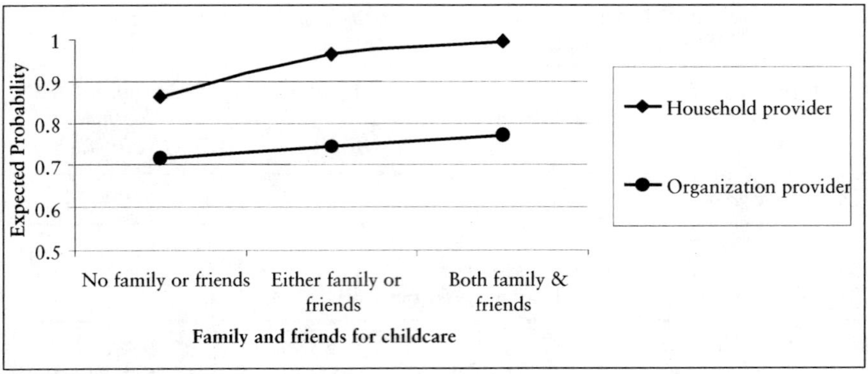

Figure 13.1 Probability of knowing parents of other children.

organizational venues on Saturday were less likely to say that they knew the parents of all the children present at their child's activities than those who sent their children to households, whether or not the family had a child care network.

To illustrate these effects, we graphed the results from the probit model in Figure 13.1.[12] First, we see that using a household rather than a business or organization increased the expected probability that parents/guardians knew the parents of all children present regardless of the size of their childcare network (Hypothesis 5). Second, we see that having friends and family available for childcare increased the probability of knowing the parents of other children when using household providers (Hypothesis 4), but having a network of childcare providers only slightly increased the likelihood of embedded experiences for children when using organizational providers (Hypothesis 6). The effect of family-and-friend networks on knowing the parent when the provider was an organization was not significant at even the liberal .10-level (b = .089), and the expected probability increased only from .715 to .773 as we moved from having no family or friends for childcare to having both family and friends. A network of childcare providers was, therefore, not useful in insulating children from strangers in these organizational settings.

Finally, parents were more likely to know the parents of the other children present if the activities were eating, entertainment, or other personal care (including shopping) than if the child was playing sports (the reference category). In sports, children were often playing an opponent that neither the child nor parent selected, so this was understandable. Also, it was apparent that when parents were in public places like restaurants, stores, and theatres, where there were many other children present, they did not perceive those children as being with their child.

Discussion

This chapter distinguishes between Saturday experiences for children that were embedded in social relations and those that were atomistic. We have not argued that one type of experience is better than another, and one can make arguments in favor of each type (see Morgan and Sørensen 1999). On the one hand, having your children at sites where the homeowner is a friend or relative or one knows the parents of all the other children there can make the parent or guardian more secure. The parent or guardian has a close personal tie to the one providing the service and/or the parents of the other children. These are childcare experiences that take place in a closed, dense network, and all the benefits of network closure—trust, security, and monitoring—are available to parents and guardians. On the other hand, embedded experiences can be stifling. In all likelihood, embedded settings are homogeneous. Children are not exposed to new people or new ideas. The parent or guardian may be reluctant to change providers or venues because it would mean breaking out of their networks. Yet a new venue or provider with new people may provide a higher quality experience for the child.

The main findings were that living longer in the metropolitan area resulted in having family and friends/acquaintances/ex-spouses to help with childcare. This led to more embedded experiences for children, but only if providers were other households. We argued that people are influenced by their primary group ties when making decisions about their everyday lives. Parents who have many relatives and friends/acquaintances/ex-spouses around them to provide childcare tend to provide a very sheltered or embedded Saturday experience for their child but, again, only if the provider was another household not if the provider was an organization.

In our in-depth interviews with parents and guardians, respondents who lived in the area longer provided several examples of how family and friendship ties helped to provide embedded experiences for their children. A middle-income Hispanic mother who lived in the Phoenix area for over 30 years remarked in the face-to-face interview, "With family, pretty much they spend a lot of time with my sisters, and with my sisters they go everywhere; I mean they'll go to the movies, to the mall, to the grocery store, wherever, and I feel comfortable with them taking my children places." She allows her 12-year-old son to go to a coach's house or a friend's house: "I'm OK with that once I've gotten to know the person more one-on-one and feel comfortable with them." These ties become an almost unnoticed part of the fabric of their daily lives that serves to bring families even further into the community. Another middle-income mother who lived in Phoenix for 15 years put it this way:

> Well, we're not dealing with strangers when we go to these things, We always know most of the people that are involved because they're

> all kinds of friends that get involved and I know the parents and then there might be a few other kids from other schools that might come in and then you meet them. You see the same people . . . go almost to the same sports, they go from one sport to the next, so you're kind of dealing, we're kind of dealing with the same people . . . so it's a good thing because you can trust these people. . . . You're not joining an organization of strangers every single time.

Although these accounts suggest that childcare networks insulate children in household *and* organizational venues, the quantitative results did not show that informal childcare networks ensured embedded experiences in organizational settings for the typical child.

What about the parents and children who just moved to the area and did not have relatives or friends/acquaintances/ex-spouses to help with childcare? Nearly one-third of our households had none of these network resources to draw on. These families had distinct experiences. A low-income white family that had lived in Phoenix for a year and had no family members in the area expressed some difficulty even finding activities: "Again, if I can count the school, it really seems to be the only one that I've really had contact with. . . . So, I don't really have that much information or knowledge." A low-income Hispanic family who had just moved to the area suggested that the information was not available to them and that they largely relied on religious education classes to keep their child occupied. There were also challenges to letting the child do activities because it was difficult for the mother to take time off from work to take the child to the activity. Without friends or relatives to provide information or take care of their child, these families relied on organizational actors and had no choice but to accept the anonymity that came with them.

The isolation of these families had greater consequences with regard to using other households. One middle-income white mother who had just moved to the area with no family nearby said, "I've dropped them off at birthday parties. . . . I dropped him off there, but it took me a while to do that because I don't know anybody here and there's so many weirdoes. . . . No, I haven't dropped him off too many times with just anybody." With the need to be cautious and to figure out whom to trust, this family tended to be more atomistic in their Saturday activities, going to movies or spending time together as a family rather than risking misfortune by sending the children to households they were unfamiliar with. Many parents without ties mentioned having to "go with your instincts," "be careful," "be cautious," and "pick and choose" when allowing their children to be in social situations with other children or families. One parent who had been in the Phoenix area five years related a story where she did not trust the parents of her child's friend. In this case, she insisted that the friend stay over at her house rather than allowing her child to go to the other household. As she put it, "I sound like I was getting [the child] maybe out of a bad situation by inviting her to come over to our house for the weekend, but there was no way it was going to happen the other way around." It was clear that newcomers who were more isolated were paying a price for the household's lack of a childcare network.

CONCLUSION

In conclusion, the most conservative interpretation of our quantitative findings is that they verified that when respondents said that they could call on family and friends/acquaintance/ex-spouses for childcare, this meant that family and friends took care of their children at their homes. The people who said they had extensive childcare networks sent their children to their friends' or relatives' homes for all or part of Saturday. This is why the adult present in the household was a friend or family member and why the parent knew the parents of the other children present. However, calling on family and friends for childcare did not mean family and friends took one's kids, along with their own, to organizational or commercial venues. Sometimes this happened, but often it did not. Thus, our empirical analysis perhaps did nothing more than verify what people meant by "providing childcare." The only substantively important empirical finding was that families that were newer to the metropolitan were less likely to have anyone who they could call on for help with childcare.

We had thought that childcare networks would provide embedded experiences for children outside the household. Our qualitative interviews unearthed evidence that parents often knew the parents of other children in organizational venues beforehand, but our quantitative analysis showed that children often obtained services in anomic organizational settings even though the parents had a childcare network to draw on. Apparently the function of a childcare network was not to ensure more embedded experiences in organizational settings. Although childcare networks provided embedded experiences in the household sector, they did not perform the same function in the formal economy.

Because we argued that these networks should be functional in organizational venues, we now need to explain why they were not. There are two possible reasons. First, organizational providers may be more trustworthy than households, and thus it is not necessary to have intergenerational closure. Parents are comfortable using households, but only if they know the adults present or the parents of the children very well. Organizations are corporate actors that have reputations that they want to protect. They often have fairly firm boundaries that organizational personnel watch over, and there is someone who has a material stake in providing a safe and satisfying experience for the children who patronize the establishment. This is true for government, nonprofit, and for-profit providers. Thus, entrusting a child to an organizational entity is not as risky as entrusting a child to a household. There is not a strong incentive to avoid strangers. All else being equal, corporate actors are more accountable than natural persons (Hannan and Freeman 1989).

A second reason why parents sent children to anomic organizational settings, even though they had a childcare network that could have provided embedded organizational experiences, is that "hanging out" with friends and families all the time may restrict the array of experiences that parents want for their children. Parents could coordinate their children's organized activities with friends and family in their childcare network, e.g., send children to venues frequented by one's network, but often they do not. Limiting their children's experiences to those that could be embedded in their networks would radically reduce the options for their children. As our qualitative data suggests, some families and children travel in packs, but this is apparently not always the case. Because one rarely meets someone new or learns something different in these dense and redundant caravans, parents may prefer, on occasion, to break away from the crowd and expose their children to richer, although more anomic, experiences.

NOTES

We acknowledge Steve Corral, Matt Greene, Joy Inouye, Paola Molina, Mike Jacobs, Sarah Lauro, and Ali Fogarty, who worked so diligently on this project. We also thank Shap Wolf and Bill Edwards for their expert help in collecting the data. The editors' suggestions were very useful, and we thank them for their input. Funding for this research was provided by the National Science Foundation, SES 0531650. We also acknowledge the support of the Social and Behavioral Science Research Institute and the Udall Center at the University of Arizona.

1. We weighed interviewing children and asking about Sunday as well. Although many studies do interview children, e.g., Timmer et al. (1985); Bianchi and Robinson (1997); Hofferth and Sandberg (2001), we decided against interviewing children because the pretests with adult respondents were averaging 20 minutes, and interviewing children would add considerably more time. We also wanted to get parents/guardians' evaluations of providers. Our pretests also taught us that there was more activity outside the home on Saturday than on Sunday, and so we restricted our questions to Saturday's activities.
2. We suspected that there might be some overlap in these categories, e.g., relative could be a friend as well, or a coworker a friend, so we read all five options to them and had respondent select the one they felt best described the relationship.
3. In our analysis, we found that the results did not change if we used different coding schemes. There was no effect of our childcare network variable on this item.
4. We first used these variables as separate items in our equations. We found that only the interaction term was statistically significant. We thus decided to use the index instead of the items separately.
5. Our clustering may seem odd, but it reflects the reality of the Phoenix metropolitan area. We asked two questions to derive our categories. First, we asked about the child's race: 56.4 percent said white, 3.7 percent said black, 1.5

percent said Native American, 1.4 percent said Asian or Pacific Islander, 13 percent said other, and 24.0 percent refused to answer. We then asked about "other" and all but one person gave us a codable response. We then asked whether the child was of Spanish or Hispanic origin. All but 16 respondents (1.5 percent) answered this item. Combining the items on race and ethnicity, we derived our measure of ethnic/racial identity. The U.S. Census reported that in 2000 the population in the Phoenix metropolitan area was 25.1 percent Hispanic and 3.5 percent non-Hispanic black (www.censusscope.org/us/m6200/chart_race.html). The reader needs to remember that our sample included households with children between 5 and 12 years of age.

6. We redid all our analyses excluding cases with missing data. The coefficients changed slightly but the *p*-values and the substantive results did not.
7. If we simply ignore the sample selection issue, we make the assumption that the cases missing from our substantive model are irrelevant to the estimation of our model coefficients and the model we estimate may be misspecified, i.e., estimates the wrong functional form (Berk 1983). Furthermore, the error terms are likely to be correlated with regressors producing biased and inconsistent estimates of the parameters. The approach developed by Van de Ven and Van Praag (1981) not only assesses the correlation among the errors terms of the selection and substantive model, but also includes a correction term that produces consistent, efficient estimates of the parameters in the substantive model.
8. Before beginning our analysis, we checked for multicollinearity. We used the 1,256 activities/households as our cases. The listwise correlations (N = 1,202) among the control variables and our independent variables were quite low, never greater than .419 (education of respondent and income of household) or less than –.354 (play activities and organizational venue). The correlation matrix is available upon request.
9. The selection model should have at least one variable that is not in the probit equation (StataCorp, 2005). In testing Hypotheses 2 and 3, we dropped a control variable—whether the family attended church regularly—that had very little effect on the dependent variables in the probit models. The choice of the variable was influenced by its weak effect, whether or not the model converged, and how quickly it converged when the variable was eliminated. In testing Hypotheses 4, 5, and 6, we dropped family income from the probit model with sample selection, because church attendance was related to knowing the parents of all children present but family income was not.
10. We also estimated the model with the additive index but found no effect on the number of years that the caregiver knew the nonkin household adults.
11. We tried dichotomizing at different values of the dependent variable, but found "support from friends" had no effect on this dependent variable. The model we settled on was the best-fitting model that we tried.
12. It is important to remember that the coefficients in a probit analysis are measuring the change in a z-score (the inverse of the normal cumulative distribution function) for a unit change in the independent variable (Liao 1994). To graph probabilities, we converted the z-scores into expected probabilities before plotting our results.

REFERENCES

Berk, R. A. 1983. "An Introduction to Sample Selection Bias in Sociological Data." *American Sociological Review*, 48: 386–98.

Bianchi, S. M., and J. Robinson. 1997. "What Did You Do Today? Children Use of Time, Family Composition, and the Acquisition of Social Capital." *Journal of Marriage and Family,* 59: 332–44.

Bianchi, S. M., J. P. Robinson, and M. A. Milkie. 2006. *Changing Rhythms of American Family Life.* New York: Russell Sage Foundation.

Bourdieu, P. 1984. *Distinction.* London: Routledge & Kegan Paul.

Carbonaro, W. 1998. "A Little Help From my Friends' Parents: Intergenerational Closure and Educational Outcomes." *Sociology of Education,* 71: 295–313.

Coleman, J. S. 1988. "Social Capital in the Creation of Human Capital." *American Journal of Sociology,* 94(Supplement): S95–S120.

Cooper, H., J. C. Valentine, B. Nye, and J. J. Lindsay. 1999. "Relationships Between Five After-School Activities and Academic Achievement." *Journal of Educational Psychology,* 91:369–78.

DiMaggio, P., and H. Louch. 1998. "Socially Embedded Consumer Transactions: For What Kinds of Purchases do People Most Often Use Networks?" *American Sociological Review,* 63:619–37.

Dunn, J. S., D. A. Kinney, and S. L. Hofferth. 2003. "Parental Ideologies and Children's After School Activities." *American Behavioral Scientist,* 46: 1359.

Fischer, C. S. 1982. *To Dwell Among Friends: Personal Networks in Town and City.* Chicago, IL: University of Chicago Press.

Galaskiewicz, J., O. Mayorova, P. Molina, J. Inouye, and S. Lauro. 2005. "Spatial Effects in the Market for Youth Services." Paper presented at the Annual Meetings of the American Sociological Association, Philadelphia, PA, August 2005.

Granovetter, M. 1985. "Economic Action and Social Structure: The Problem of Embeddedness." *American Journal of Sociology,* 91: 481–510.

Hagan, J., R. MacMillan, and B. Wheaton. 1996. "New Kid in Town: Social Capital and the Life Course Effects of Family Migration in Children." *American Sociological Review,* 61: 368–85.

Hanks, M., and B. K. Eckland. 1978. "Adult Voluntary Associations and Adolescent Socialization." *Sociological Quarterly,* 19: 481–90.

Hannan, M. T., and J. Freeman. 1989. *Organizational Ecology.* Cambridge, MA: Harvard University Press.

Harvey, A. S. 1999. "Guidelines for Time Use Data Collection and Analysis." In *Time Use Research in the Social Sciences,* eds. W. E. Pentland, A. S. Harvey, M. P. Lawton, and M. A. McColl, pp.19–45. New York: Kluwer.

Hayes, C.D., P. L. Palmer, and M. J. Zaslow, eds. 1990. *Who Cares for America's Children? Child Care Policy for the 1990s.* Washington DC: National Academy Press.

Hofferth, S. L., and J. F. Sandberg. 2001. "How American Children Spend Their Time." *Journal of Marriage and Family,* 63: 295–308.

Hoffmann, J. P., and J. Xu. 2002. "School Activities, Community Service, and Delinquency." *Crime & Delinquency,* 48: 568.

House, J. C., D. Umberson, and K. R. Landis. 1988. "Structures and Processes of Social Support." *Annual Review of Sociology,* 14: 293–318.

Kahne, J., and K. Bailey. 1999. "The Role of Social Capital and Youth Development: The Case of 'I Have a Dream' Programs." *Educational Evaluation and Policy Analysis,* 21: 321–343.

Kawachi, I. 1999. "Social Capital and Community Effects on Population and Individual Health." *Annals of the New York Academy of Sciences,* 896: 120–30.

Kunitz, S. J. 2004. "Social Capital and Health." *British Medical Bulletin,* 69: 61–73.

Lareau, A. 2002. "Invisible Inequality: Social Class and Childrearing in Black Families and White Families." *American Sociological Review,* October, 67: 747–76.

———. 2003. *Unequal Childhoods: Class, Race and Family*. Berkeley: University of California Press.
Liao, T. F. 1994. *Interpreting Probability Models: Logit, Probit, and Other Generalized Linear Models*. Thousand Oaks, CA: Sage Publications.
Lin, N. 2001. *Social Capital: A Theory of Social Structure and Action*. Cambridge, UK: Cambridge University Press.
———, A. Dean, and W. Ensel, eds. 1986. *Social Support, Life Events, and Depression*. Beverly Hills, CA: Sage.
Lofland, L. H. 1973. *A World of Strangers: Order and Action in Urban Public Space*. Prospect Heights, IL: Waveland Press, 1985.
Marsh, H. W., and S. Kleitman. 2002. "Extracurricular School Activities: The Good, the Bad, and the Nonlinear." *Harvard Educational Review*, 72: 464.
McFarland, D. A., and R. J. Thomas. 2006. "Bowling Young: How Youth Voluntary Associations Influence Adult Political Participation." *American Sociological Review*, 71: 401–25.
McLanahan, S., and G. D. Sandefur. 1994. *Growing Up With a Single Parent: What Hurts, What Helps*. Cambridge, MA: Harvard University Press.
Medrich, E. A., J. Roizen, V. Rubin, and S. Buckley. 1982. *The Serious Business of Growing Up: A Study of Children's Lives Outside School*. Berkeley: University of California Press.
Miller, D. 1995. *Acknowledging Consumption*. London: Routledge.
———. 1998. *A Theory of Shopping*. Ithaca, NY: Cornell University Press.
———. 2001. *The Dialectics of Shopping*. Chicago, IL: University of Chicago Press.
Morgan, S. L., and A. B. Sørensen. 1999. "Parental Networks, Social Closure, and Mathematics Learning: A Test of Coleman's Social Capital Explanation of School Effects." *American Sociological Review*, 64: 661–81.
Otto, L. B. 1976. "Social Integration and the Status-Attainment Process." *American Journal of Sociology*, 81: 1360–83.
Parcel, T. L., and E. G. Menaghan. 1990. "Maternal Working Conditions and Children's Verbal Facility: Studying the Intergenerational Transmission of Inequality From Mothers to Young Children." *Social Psychology Quarterly*, 53: 132–47
Parcel, T. L., and E. G. Menaghan. 1994. "Early Parental Work, Family Social Capital and Early Childhood Outcomes." *American Journal of Sociology*, 99:972–1009.
Portes, A. 1998. "Social Capital: It's Origins and Applications in Modern Sociology." *Annual Review of Sociology*, 24: 1–24
———, and R. G. Rumbaut. 1996. *Immigrant America: A Portrait*. Berkeley, CA: University of California Press.
Putnam, R. 1993. *Making Democracy Work: Civic Traditions in Modern Italy*. Princeton, NJ: Princeton University Press.
———. 2000. *Bowling Alone: The Collapse and Revival of American Community*. New York: Simon & Schuster.
Robinson, J. R. 1999. "Time Diary Method: Structure and Uses." In *Time Use Research in the Social Sciences*, eds. W. E. Pentland, A. S. Harvey, M. P. Lawton, and M. A. McColl, pp. 47–89. New York: Kluwer.
Sampson, R. J., J. D. Morenoff, and F. Earls. 1999. "Beyond Social Capital: Spatial Dynamics of Collective Efficacy for Children." *American Sociological Review*, 64: 633–60.
Spady, W. G. 1970. "Lament for the Letterman: Effects of Peer Status and Extracurricular Activities on Goals and Achievement." *American Journal of Sociology*, 75: 680–702.
Stanton-Salazar, R. D., and S. M. Dornbusch. 1995. "Social Capital and the Reproduction of Inequality: Information Networks Among Mexican-Origin High School Students." *Sociological Education*, 68: 116–35.

StataCorp. 2005. *Stata Statistical Software: Release 9*. College Station, TX: StataCorp LP.

Timmer, S. G., J. Eccles, and K. O'Brien. 1985. "How Children Use Time." In *Time, Goods, and Well-Being*, eds. F. T. Juster and F. P. Stafford, pp. 353–382. Ann Arbor, MI: Survey Research Center, Institute for Social Research, University of Michigan.

Valentine, J. C., H. Cooper, A. B. Bettencourt, and D. L. DuBois. 2002. "Out-of-School Activities and Academic Achievement: The Mediating Role of Self-Beliefs." *Educational Psychologist*, 37: 245.

Valenzuela, A., and S. M. Dornbusch. 1994. "Familism and Social Capital in the Academic Achievement of Mexican Origin and Anglo Adolescents." *Social Science Quarterly*, 75: 18–36.

Van de Ven, W. P. M. M., and B. M. S. Van Praag. 1981. "The Demand for Deductibles in Private Health Insurance: A Probit Model With Sample Selection." *Journal of Econometrics*, 17: 229–52.

Verba, S., K. L. Schlozman, and H. E. Brady. 1995. *Voice and Equality: Civic Volunteerism in American Politics*. Cambridge, MA: Harvard University Press.

Walker, M. E., S. Wasserman, and B. Wellman. 1994. "Statistical Models for Social Support Networks." In *Advances in Social Network Analysis: Research in the Social and Behavioral Sciences*, eds, S. Wasserman and J. Galaskiewicz, pp. 53–78. Thousand Oaks, CA: Sage.

Wellman, B. 1979. "The Community Question." *American Journal of Sociology*, 84: 1201–31.

———. and S. Wortley. 1990. "Different Strokes From Different Folks: Community Ties and Social Support." *American Journal of Sociology*, 96: 558–88.

Wilson, W. J. 1996. *When Work Disappears: The World of the New Urban Poor*. New York: Alfred A. Knopf.

Zelizer, V. 2005. "Culture and Consumption." In *The Handbook of Economic Sociology* (2nd ed.), N. J. Smelser and R. Swedberg (eds), pp. 331–354. New York and Princeton, NJ: Russell Sage Foundation and Princeton University Press.

Zimmer, M. H., A. Duggan, G. Howard, and R. Sturner. 2001. "Participation in After-School Activities and Psychological Well-Being During Adolescence." *Journal of Developmental & Behavioral Pediatrics*, 22:345.

14 The Immediate Returns on Time Investment in Daily Contacts

Exploring the Network—Overlapping Effects from Contact Diaries

Yang-Chih Fu

INTRODUCTION

Like any form of capital, social capital involves essential components such as investment and returns. Unlike other capital, however, social capital may be so intangible that its values vary significantly depending on how actors establish and maintain social ties, and on how such ties overlap between different personal networks. Strong and positive interpersonal ties lead actors directly to social support and potential resources. The extent of network overlapping further contributes to how indirect support and resources are available or accessible to the actors (Coleman 1988, 1990; Lin 2001b). Although ties or relationships are core to the social network perspective of social capital, network analysis has benefited by focusing more on the extent to which personal networks intersect.

This chapter explores the role of network overlapping in daily contacts in terms of the investment–return mechanism. According to the "network closure" argument, closed or overlapped networks tend to contain richer social capital than open or nonoverlapped networks. In nonoverlapped networks, actors are tied to each other only directly, without being connected through other, mutual acquaintances. When this occurs, what people gain depends exclusively on what they invest in that direct tie. In overlapped networks, by contrast, not only are actors directly connected, but they also become further intertwined by mutual acquaintances. Because the intersecting ties in such networks provide additional social support and valued resources, one need not invest as much to gain desirable returns from any specific tie. In other words, the marginal utility of investment in social interactions declines as actors' personal networks intersect, even though the total returns in interactions may be higher in overlapped networks. It seems that, overall, actors need to invest more in overlapped networks, but they make less effort to obtain support and resources from other actors within the networks.

This chapter analyzes how immediate returns on time investment in daily contacts vary across three kinds of networks: nonoverlapped, partially overlapped, and overlapped. One starting argument is that immediate returns tend to diminish in overlapped networks. Data were drawn from contact diaries that fifty-two informants in Taiwan kept for three months in spring 2004. After screening out ineligible contacts, I used 45,457 contacts in multilevel analyses. Using time, or the duration of each interpersonal contact, as the measure of investment, the chapter examines its effects on two forms of immediate returns that the informants evaluated after each contact: how significant the contact was to them, and the extent to which they regarded the contact as pleasant.

The goals of the study are, thus, twofold. First, it aims to demonstrate a practical way to construct and analyze how investment yields immediate returns in dyadic contacts. Second, it verifies whether such returns on time investment are, indeed, less significant in overlapped networks, within which social capital may already be well embedded. The first goal responds directly to the problem in "the weakest aspect in social capital theorizing . . . the analogy to investment in 'real capital'" (Kadushin 2004, 87). The second goal aims to clarify the utility of a core element in the social network perspective—the degree of network overlapping (Coleman 1988, 1990; Burt 2001; Lin 2001a, 2001b).

THE CONCEPTUALIZATION OF SOCIAL CAPITAL: THE NEED FOR INVESTMENT AND RETURNS

Social capital has gained prominence in the social sciences and has added substantially to the understanding of personal networks, as well as social structure, phenomena, and actions (Astone et al. 1999; Schuller, Baron, and Field 2000; Lin, Cook, and Burt 2001). Due to its very simplicity and flexibility, however, social capital seems to suffer from being used in obscure and ambiguous ways, and its misuse is likely to threaten its theoretical meaning and implications (Wall, Ferrazzi, and Schryer 1998). Like preceding popular sociological concepts, social capital faces severe challenges to its original meaning and academic value. Without rigorous refinements in conceptualization and measurement, the concept is likely to become inappropriate for serious scientific inquiry (Portes and Landolt 1996; Portes 1998; Flora 1998).

Researchers have conceptualized, defined, and measured social capital in empirical studies in diverse ways, sometimes risking the loss of the term's value. For example, a common usage of social capital refers to sociability, social networks and social support, trust, reciprocity, community, and civil engagement. More broadly, social capital has been referred to as a "mother's expectation" for her child to go to college (Johnson 2001) or as "how parents interact with their children." (Morrow 1999, 749) Some historical studies refer to social capital as "social practices, customs, groups and institutions that strengthen civil society." (Grew 1999, 407) Such a broad and loose usage could even expand to include cultural capital (Schuller et al. 2000). These examples show that various researchers conceptualize and define social capital in an ad hoc fashion (see Snijders 1999). Some even treat it as a metaphor and borrow concepts from other disciplines.

It may be useful to apply a metaphor to social capital, but it can also mislead empirical studies, making it more difficult to make systematic comparisons across studies and accumulate knowledge (Baron and Hannan 1994; Burt 1997; Sandefur and Laumann 1998; Clemens 1999; Lin 2001a, 2001b). To avoid such difficulty, it is crucial to clearly conceptualize social capital and develop valid measures (Lin, Fu, and Hsung 2001). To prevent empirical studies from deviating from the original meaning, researchers need to examine the measurement and instruments that are useful for verifying propositions about how social capital operates. As the key term "capital" implies, it is particularly critical to stipulate how actors invest in social interactions and how they gain returns on the investment.

A serious challenge to the study of social capital thus lies in how to conceptualize and measure investment. Because the term "capital" derives from economics, critics argue that social capital needs to be conceptualized as the way that economic capital (including material capital and financial capital) operates. The essential elements of capital usually include the *invention of resources, investments,* and *opportunity costs.* Once accumulated, these resources can be readily utilized when necessary (Baron and Hannan 1994; Boisjoly, Duncan, and Hofferth 1995). Any social resources that meet such criteria may become social capital. Some of the common conceptualizations and definitions of social capital do not meet these requirements, however. For example, children may benefit from their parents' human capital and other advantageous family backgrounds, or get ahead by means of their parents' networks, but they do not invent these advantages or resources, nor do they incur opportunity costs by taking these advantages.

Some studies overemphasize the effects or outputs of social capital. Social capital differs from other forms of capital. Although in some studies social capital is treated as an "input," it also can be an "output" of a preexisting production—a feature foreign to other inputs, such as land or labor. That is, precedent social actions create or accumulate social capital, which in turn becomes an input to subsequent social actions. Once relationships between actors change, the outputs from precedent social actions also change (Coleman 1990; Astone et al. 1999). Therefore, the values embedded in social capital often fluctuate over time. To maximize returns, actors may wait for social capital to appreciate before cashing it in (Lin 2001b).

According to the core argument of social exchange theory, social activities and interactions create surplus value in addition to accomplishing specific purposes. These surpluses are, themselves, products of social actions, which become potential resources that drive further social processes. As a result, a sequence of surpluses helps accumulate social capital (Astone et al. 1999; Portes 1998). Because investments and returns are part of this accumulating process of surpluses, it helps to identify and clarify their specific roles.

It appears more practical to identify and measure returns, which usually manifest in desirable social outcomes such as better jobs, higher income, more favorable treatment, and more rewarding affection. Investment in social capital, however, seems so difficult to conceptualize and measure that few empirical studies examine it explicitly. For some, the actions that actors take to protect existing valued resources or to gain additional ones qualify as investment. For others, actors may gain such "networked resource advantages" simply because they occupy strategic structural positions, not necessarily because they deliberately "cultivate" friendships (Lin 2001b; Kadushin 2004). That is, actors may not "invest" in social relationships with intent, although all actions that serve to build or maintain relationships incur some kind of resource depletion as well as opportunity costs.

Among the resources that actors typically use, time and money are probably the most widespread and universal. Nearly all social actions and human behaviors are mediated by time and space (Alheit 1994; Bond and Feather 1988). Not only does time condition everyday life, but it also affects individuals' quality of life and interpersonal relationships. For example, studies show that the amount of time that parents spend with their young children may affect the children's future well-being (Szalai 1972; Davies 1990; Campbell and Lee 1992). The amount of leisure time also affects family relationships and correlates highly with divorce rates. For women in particular, time use can be a key to how they organize daily life and how extensively they are able to build neighborhood networks. Time is thus an indispensable element in creating social capital, one that deserves scrutiny.

Time Investment and Overlapping Networks in Daily Contacts

Time serves as a good index of investment in social capital. When actors invest in social capital, time constitutes an essential part of the process. Not only is time essential in social actions, it is also universal and readily measurable under different circumstances and across various segments of the population. More important, the allocation of time, a limited and fixed resource, is a zero-sum game, because we recognize, count, and arrange it. Allocating time thus always incurs an opportunity cost. Whenever actors spend time doing something, whether interacting with a person or participating in activities, they simultaneously lose an equal amount of time that they could have used to do something else. Based on the most critical account of the requirements for "capital," (Baron and Hannan 1994; Castle 2002) the nature of investment and opportunity cost qualifies time as a meaningful concept for gauging inputs in social capital.

In the few studies that explicitly examine investment in social capital, time and money are treated as resources that actors use in their social actions. For example, how much an employee's referral network is worth can be measured by an exact amount of real money. That amount of money spells out what a firm actually gains by investing (real money) in using the employees' preexisting networks as the basis for recruiting new staff, a strategy that saves relevant costs (Fernandez and Castilla 2001).

Another study examines both the time and money that actors devote to helping relatives or friends in emergencies, a function that helps explain the extent to which they expect a return of similar help that they may need in the future. Such "time investment" and "money investment" correspond well to "time stock" and "money stock," respectively (Hofferth, Boisjoly, and Duncan 1999). By linking investment to returns, researchers can test specific propositions, which in turn help determine causal relations between inputs and outputs in social capital.

These studies, however, draw from preexisting survey data, which leads to severe limitations. Due to the retrospective nature of questionnaire surveys in particular, respondents needed to estimate both inputs and outputs. Rather than asking about the actual amount of time spent, for example, the survey used in Hofferth et al. asked whether respondents or anyone living with them had ever spent "a lot of time" (1999, 89) helping others. Likewise, instead of measuring the amount of time actually received in emergency help, that study estimated the "time stock" based on whether respondents believed that someone would take time to help them during an emergency. Although moving in the right direction, such a research design does not make the best use of the universal measurement of time. Although the input was a dichotomous measure taken from previous experiences, the output was a mere perceived, anticipated return. Thus, to evaluate time investment and its effects, researchers need a more systematic research design and measurement.

It may be difficult to conceptualize and measure time investment at the group, community, or higher level, but time constitutes a natural component (or more precisely, an artificial component; see Zerubavel 1985) in actions and interactions at the individual level. In terms of the network approach, it would require composite and complex measures to study time investment in such large entities as structures and networks. At the tie or contact level, however, it should be more straightforward to measure time investment. Interpersonal contacts are particularly suitable for such an inquiry.

In addition to being straightforward to measure, daily contacts provide an ideal vehicle for studying time investment for other compelling reasons. Structurally speaking, a network is composed of various ties among actors. In their dynamic dimension, ties and networks are formulated by interactions and actions. As the core of all interactions and actions, therefore, contacts should be the primordial unit of analysis for social ties and networks. Although many empirical studies focus on structures and ties, the literature gives less attention to actions and contacts. To fill the gap, this study examines time investment in daily contact, a rudimentary element of social actions. Because all activities on which social capital is built involve interactions among actors, contacts bear detailed information about the contexts of such social actions. Using contact as the unit of analysis thus enables us to explore basic principles of how actors invest in each transaction.

This study analyzes how time investment contributes to the immediate returns in daily contacts. Furthermore, and more fundamental to the network approach, the analyses follow the distinction between varying degrees of network overlapping. According to Coleman (1988, 1990), one of the most effective network structures for constructing social capital lies in network closure or network overlapping (i.e., an enclosed network in which many network members know one another). Network closure or network overlapping has been applied to topics ranging from academic achievements to career development (Flora 1998; Sampson, Morenoff, and Earls 1999). Using this structural dimension as a key dimension of social capital, one can explore ties and interactions beyond first-tier relationships and focus on the valued resources embedded in secondary social ties.

Various types of networks often contain different kinds of social capital. In overlapped networks, homophilous and multiple ties facilitate better social support and other expressive needs. In contrast, heterophilous ties and ties that bridge structural holes in open networks help achieve instrumental actions and gains (Lin 2001a, 2001b; Coleman 1988, 1990; Burt 1992, 2001; Granovetter 1973). In terms of expressive ends, then, it follows that the immediate returns on time investment should be less obvious in overlapped networks than in nonoverlapped networks. Although it takes a significant amount of time investment in each contact to gain expressive returns in nonoverlapped networks, such a time investment seems less necessary and less critical in overlapped networks, where intersecting social ties are already sufficient for providing social support.

Using data from contact diaries, this study examines how people achieve immediate returns on the time they spend on daily contacts. I propose that for each contact, immediate returns will be higher if the actor spends more time on the contact. Furthermore, such an investment–return process is closely mediated by the degree of network overlapping. Because valued resources are rich in overlapped networks, contact within such networks need not be long for the actors to gain meaningful returns. I, therefore, propose that the immediate returns on time investment are less distinguishable in overlapped networks. In nonoverlapped networks, the immediate returns clearly rely on the amount of time spent in social interactions. Such an investment–return relationship seems less straightforward in overlapped networks. Because valued resources are already rich and readily available in overlapped networks, the members' needs are easier to satisfy. Although the embedded social capital abounds, a slight increase in time investment in each contact creates little gain in support and resources. Only when actors make substantial extra effort or prolonged contact can they experience significant returns. This study examines such an investment–return relation and the network-overlapping effects through an analysis of detailed information from contact diaries.

DATA AND MEASURES

The study drew on data from contact diaries that fifty-two informants kept for three consecutive months during the period March through June 2004 (see Freeman and Thompson 1989; Lonkila 1999; and Fu 2005, 2007 for details about using contact diaries as a means of collecting data on personal networks). More than one-third of the informants were selected from a random sample of respondents from a previous survey conducted near the end of 2002. Others were volunteers recruited by several survey field supervisors of that particular survey. Female, young, and highly-educated people were slightly overrepresented in the informants (Appendix Table A14.1). Unskilled workers, who turned out to be the most difficult to recruit and instruct in the rigid task of diary keeping, were underrepresented (see Fu 2007 for a detailed description of the study).

These fifty-two diaries yielded a total of 95,325 contacts (with an average of 1,833 contacts in three months, Table 14.1). Among these daily contacts, the contacts with strangers (17.8 percent among all contacts) do not suit the purpose of this study because 99.2 percent of the strangers' networks do not overlap at all with the diary keepers' networks, nor do the contacts with the diary keepers' family or kin members. Because family or kin ties are often the strongest ties of all, the personal networks of family members tend to intersect with one another fairly extensively (because 94.3 percent of these members' networks overlap with the informants' networks). In addition, social norms stipulate that family or kin members are obliged to offer mutual support. Under such unique circumstances, it would be difficult to explain whether and how time investment in daily contact with family or kin members is directly linked to social support or immediate returns. Such a linkage, however, is quite apparent within nonkin or friend networks (Hofferth et al. 1999).

Due to the lack of variation in network overlapping, I excluded the contacts with strangers (no overlapped networks) and the contacts with family and relatives (nearly all overlapped networks). Moreover, because routine contacts (those inevitable contacts with family members living together, roommates, and coworkers who share the same office)

Table 14.1 Number of Contacts in Fifty-Two Diaries

Types of Contacts	N	%
Total contacts	95,325	100.00
Contacts in 3 months per informer		
Minimum	691	
Maximum	3,968	
Average	1,833	
Contacts excluded from analyses		
Contacts with strangers	16,969	17.8
Contacts with kin members	19,744	20.7
Routine contacts with nonkin acquaintances	13,155	13.8
Valid contacts after exclusions		
Nonroutine contacts with nonkin acquaintances	45,457	47.7

are typically so long that they lack variation in contact duration, I also excluded them from this study. As a result, 45,457 contacts were used for multilevel analyses (Table 14.1). All of these contacts refer to one-on-one contacts. Multiple contacts with the same individual that occurred in the same day were recorded only once for each means of contact (in person, by phone, by mail, or by e-mail). In all models, the level-1 unit is contact (n = 45,457), and the level-2 unit is the individual (n = 52). The analyses resemble those of Wellman and Frank (2001) that used multilevel network data, except that the level-1 unit in this study is not a tie, but a contact.

Dependent Variables

The immediate returns were measured by two indices. First, the informant evaluated how significant each contact was to him or her after the contact. The responses ranged from 1 (*not significant at all*) to 4 (*very significant*). Second, the informant evaluated how pleasant he or she regarded each contact immediately afterward. The responses were recoded as dichotomous: 0 (*not pleasant;* 62.9 percent) and 1 (*very pleasant;* 37.1 percent; Appendix Table A14.2). The first dependent variable (significant) required an ordinal analysis. Because the reference category is the lowest value (not significant at all), higher coefficients in the models indicate better returns. The second dependent variable (pleasant) was analyzed with Bernoulli logit modeling (Raudenbush et al. 2001). The higher the coefficient, the more pleasant the informant regarded the contact after it occurred.

Explanatory Variable—Duration of Contact

Each informant recorded the approximate amount of time spent in each specific contact, using one of the following five ordinal categories: (a) less than 1 minute, (b) 1–5 minutes, (c) 6–29 minutes, (d) between 30 minutes and 2 hours, and (e) more than 2 hours. Although the scale does not take full advantage of the precise measurement of exact time, the ordinal scale enabled the informants to record each contact more easily—an important incentive for keeping the diary.

Control Variables

Control variables include the characteristics of both ties and contacts. The tie characteristics measure age homophily (or similarity) and the overall strength of the tie. Of all the eligible contacts, about 37.3 percent occurred between informants and those who were members of the same age cohorts (Appendix Table A14.2). The strength of tie is a factor score that combines the length of acquaintanceship, the frequency of face-to-face contacts, the frequency of phone contacts, closeness, importance, and affection. All factor loadings and scoring coefficients are listed in Appendix Table A14.3. The very high alpha coefficient (0.8842) indicates that the items are coherent and the composite score is valid.

The contact characteristics cover two kinds of situations. "Expectation" measures the extent to which an informant anticipated or expected the contact beforehand. "Contact initiative" distinguishes whether the contact was initiated by the informant (ego), by the contacted person (alter, the comparison group), by both, or by chance. These contextual factors of daily contacts serve to mediate or differentiate the effects of time investment on immediate returns. The expectation and initiative of contacts are particularly relevant. According to arguments of the rational choice and purposive action perspectives, anticipated and ego-initiated contacts are expected to generate higher returns. Taking such an "expectation" variable into account should alleviate possible spurious effects on the outcome. Based on the principle of reciprocity in the network perspective, furthermore, the contacts that are initiated by both parties should be more rewarding.

These possible effects are particularly important for setting the causal direction between how long a contact lasted and how the informants perceived it. It could be true that "significant and pleasant" contacts last longer because the actors value them more, but the duration of many interpersonal contacts is beyond one's control, especially when the ego did not initiate such contacts. Moreover, because the informants were instructed to evaluate each contact according to what they judged or felt afterward (in the diary log such evaluation items were also deliberately printed after all other contact characteristics), it is more plausible to treat the subjective evaluations, rather than the duration of contacts, as the returns.

RESULTS AND DISCUSSION

The level-1 analyses in Table 14.2 clearly confirm that the longer a contact lasted, the higher returns the informants received from the contact. As the ordinal model shows, all of the contacts that lasted longer than one minute were more significant to the informants than the shortest contacts (higher coefficients in the model indicate better returns). The significance of contacts also varies by other contact situations, tie characteristics, and the informants' age groups. For example, the informants perceived contacts as more significant when the contacts were expected beforehand, initiated by the informants, or occurred with someone whose ties to the informants were stronger. When all of these characteristics are held constant, however, the duration effects remain highly significant (Table 14.2, Model 1).

The immediate returns as measured by whether the feeling was very pleasant also varied significantly by the duration of contact. Because the dependent variable was transformed to become dichotomous (1 = *very pleasant,* 0 = *not pleasant*), the effects were examined with a Bernoulli logit model. The higher coefficients indicate a more pleasant feeling. As shown in Model 2, the feeling about a contact becomes increasingly pleasant when that contact lasts longer. Although the same positive feelings are also apparent with the contacts that are initiated by someone other than the alter, in the same age cohort, and with strong ties, the positive effects of the duration remain very strong—the longer a contact lasted, the more pleasant the informants regarded it afterward.

At level 2, age groups turn out to be a crucial factor in distinguishing whether the informants regard their contacts as significant. Older informants regarded every nonroutine contact with nonkin acquaintances more positively, regardless of how long the contact lasted, whether it was expected, who initiated it, who the contacted person was, and how strongly that person was tied to them (Table 14.2, Model 1). In contrast, this individual characteristic shows little variation in explaining how pleasant the contact was (Model 2).

The overall initial effects at level 1 are robust. But do these effects remain equally strong with different kinds of contacts and within various kinds of networks? Do the immediate returns on time investment differ by the degree of network overlapping? To answer these questions, I divided the contacts into three types of networks. The criterion for division is "how well the ego or the alter knows each other's family" for every contact he or she has made or encountered. The first type, nonoverlapped networks, contains the contacts in which neither ego nor the alter knows each other's family members (that is, both ego and alter are "total strangers" to each other's family, 48.5 percent, Table 14.3). The third type, overlapped networks, is composed of the contacts in which either the ego knows the alter's family well, the alter knows the ego's family well, or

Table 14.2 Multilevel Effects on the Subjective Evaluation of Contacts

Independent Variables	*Dependent Variables = Significance (1–4, Reference = 1)*	*Dependent Variables = Pleasant Feeling (0,1)*
	Model 1 (Ordinal Model)	Model 2 (Unit-Specific Bernoulli Logit Model)
Level 1 (contacts)		
Contact situations		
Duration [< 1 minutes]		
1–5 minutes	.769 (.117)***	.200 (.095)*
6–29 minutes	1.127 (.129)***	.492 (.099)***
30 minutes–2 hours	1.204 (.206)***	.546 (.186)**
Over 2 hours	1.608 (.260)***	.963 (.214)***
Expected contact	.174 (.048)**	.075 (.044)
Initiated by [alter]		
By ego	.210 (.090)*	.194 (.072)**
Mutual	−0.277 (.148)	.349 (.129)**
By chance	−0.732 (.167)***	.314 (.142)*
Character ego/alter ties		
Same age groups	.062 (.045)	.176 (.062)**
Tie strength	.326 (.073)***	.550 (.096)***
Threshold2	3.019 (.242)***	—
Threshold3	5.603 (.301)***	—
Level 2 (individuals)		
Intercept	−5.752 (.676)***	−2.690 (.619)***
Age groups	.609 (.221)**	.311 (.255)
Level 1 d.f.	44899	44902
Level 2 d.f.	50	50

Note. Both models are based on HLM6. The ordinal model lists the final estimation of fixed effects (with robust S.E.). The Bernoulli logit model is unit specific. Numbers in parentheses are standard errors. After each independent variable, the category in brackets indicates the comparison group among the dummy variables.

$^{*}p < .05$. $^{**}p < .01$. $^{***}p < .001$.

both know each other's family well (about 13.4 percent of all contacts). All other kinds of second-tier ties (either the ego or the alter knows each other's family, but not well, about 38.1 percent) belong to the second type, partially overlapped networks. Thus the degree of network overlapping increases from the first to the third type.

This operative definition represents one example of "knowing a tie's ties," the core concept that depicts network overlapping or intersection. As

Table 14.3 Construct of Family Network Closure (Unit: Contact)

How Well Ego/Alter Know Each Other's Family		*Ego's gender*		
		Male	*Female*	*Total*
Total strangers	N	9,620	12,431	22,051
[Nonoverlapped networks]	%	48.1	48.8	48.5
Acquaintances	N	7,842	9,494	17,336
[Partially overlapped]	%	39.3	37.3	38.1
Know very well	N	2,520	3,550	6,070
[Overlapped network]	%	12.6	13.9	13.4
Total	N	19,982	25,475	45,457
	%	100.0	100.0	100.0

stated earlier, family members have primordial ties that are so strong that they are easily known or tied to other close ties. When people get to know each other well, they have a greater chance to talk about or meet each other's family. In other words, within a personal network family members are often located near the core that tends to intersect with other subsets of close circles. Thus the measure may also reflect the "depth of a tie" with the contacted persons—knowing a friend's family may indicate the existence of a "deeper" tie that penetrates into each other's core network. The degree of network overlapping may also be measured by other indices, such as how well the actors know each other's friends. However, for the informants in this study, "family" proved to be a clear boundary, and how well the actors knew each other's family was an easy question to answer and record in the diaries.

When the contacts are divided into these three types of networks, the age effect at level 2 remains positive and significant when the networks are not heavily overlapped. In both nonoverlapped and partially overlapped networks, older informants clearly see each contact as more significant than younger people do. However, such an age effect becomes nonsignificant in overlapped networks (Table 14.4).

At level 1, likewise, the significance of contacts continues to vary substantially and consistently on contact duration in both nonoverlapped networks and partially overlapped networks. Other contact situations and tie characteristics being equal, the informants tend to evaluate the contacts that last longer as more significant (Table 14.4, Models 1 and 2). However, such effects remain significant in overlapped networks only if a contact lasts longer than two hours; the magnitude of effects also decreases. In other words, unlike the contacts in other types of networks, all contacts

Table 14.4 Multilevel Effects on the Significance of Contacts by the Degree of Network Closure (Ordinal Models)

Independent Variables	*Nonoverlapped*	*Partially Overlapped*	*Overlapped*
	Model 1	Model 2	Model 3
Level 1 (contacts)			
Contact situations			
Duration [< 1 minutes]			
1–5 minutes	1.005 (.136)***	.674 (.100)***	.296 (.295)
6–29 minutes	1.393 (.164)***	1.013 (.127)***	.686 (.360)
30 minutes–2 hours	1.242 (.253)***	1.297 (.225)***	.850 (.453)
Over 2 hours	1.704 (.258)***	1.619 (.304)***	1.367 (.489)**
Expected contact	.165 (.039)***	.236 (.073)**	.092 (.132)
Initiated by [alter]			
By ego	.459 (.118)***	–.058 (.099)	.073 (.148)
Mutual	–0.168 (.135)	–0.548 (.212)*	–0.201 (.295)
By chance	–0.489 (.259)	–0.996 (.158)***	–0.872 (.153)***
Char. ego/alter ties			
Same age groups	.084 (.066)	–0.040 (.078)	.249 (.126)*
Tie strength	.280 (.107)*	.541 (.104)***	1.104 (.210)***
Threshold2	3.046 (.260)***	3.227 (.318)***	3.069 (.269)***
Threshold3	5.564 (.330)***	5.896 (.392)***	6.304 (.516)***
Level 2 (individuals)			
Intercept	–6.143 (.739)***	–5.952 (.735)***	–5.901 (1.22)***
Age groups	.750 (.241)**	.632 (.230)**	.634 (.363)
Level 1 d.f.	21570	17262	6039
Level 2 d.f.	50	50	45

Note. Dependent variables = significance of contact (1–4, reference = 1 "not significant at all"). Numbers in parentheses are standard errors. After each independent variable, the category in brackets indicates the comparison group among the dummy variables.

$^{*}p < .05$. $^{**}p < .01$. $^{***}p < .001$.

in overlapped networks that last shorter than two hours are no longer distinguishable (Table 14.4, Model 3). The immediate returns on time investment thus diminish remarkably in overlapped networks. Only the longest contacts are significant to the informants.

Such a unique pattern with the overlapped networks becomes more evident with regard to whether the informants have a pleasant feeling about the contacts. Table 14.5 shows the effects on this "pleasure" item across these three types of networks. For all network types, informants obviously perceive the contacts as more pleasant if they make these contacts with people who are strongly tied to them. Otherwise, the feelings vary inconsistently on the tie and contact characteristics across different types of networks.

Table 14.5 Multilevel Effects on the Perception of Contacts by the Degree of Network Closure (Unit-Specific Bernoulli Logit Models)

Independent Variables	*Nonoverlapped*	*Partially Overlapped*	*Overlapped*
	Model 1	Model 2	Model 3
Level 1 (contacts)			
Contact situations			
Duration [< 1 minutes]			
1–5 minutes	.341 (.111)**	.106 (.106)	–0.058 (.188)
6–29 minutes	.587 (.126)***	.379 (.107)**	.219 (.201)
30 minutes–2 hours	.429 (.258)	.624 (.198)**	.351 (.340)
Over 2 hours	1.076 (.233)***	.808 (.335)*	.683 (.368)
Expected contact	.107 (.041)*	.080 (.059)	.098 (.085)
Initiated by [alter]			
By ego	.072 (.085)	.171 (.107)	.346 (.098)**
Mutual	.163 (.135)	.413 (.181)*	.644 (.272)*
By chance	.397 (.151)**	.190 (.170)	.307 (.231)
Char. ego/alter ties			
Same age groups	.251 (.085)**	.201 (.083)*	–0.137 (.158)
Tie strength	.405 (.168)*	.460 (.146)**	.873 (.269)**
Level 2 (Individuals)			
Intercept	–3.131 (.724)***	–2.271 (.704)**	–1.688 (.864)
Age groups	.428 (.299)	.194 (.299)	.227 (.229)
Level 1 d.f.	21573	17264	6041
Level 2 d.f.	50	50	45

Note. Dependent variable = feeling about contact (1 = *very pleasant,* 0 = *less pleasant*). Numbers in parentheses are standard errors. After each independent variable, the category in brackets indicates the comparison group among the dummy variables.

$^{*}p < .05$. $^{**}p < .01$. $^{***}p < .001$.

When these tie and contact characteristics are taken into account, the duration of contacts plays various roles in different networks. For example, with the exception of the contacts that last between thirty minutes and two hours, the informants rated the longer contacts within the nonoverlapped networks as more pleasant (Table 14.5, Model 1). Such duration effects remain significant within the partially overlapped networks (Model 2), although not as strong as that in Model 1. Thus the previous findings (see Table 14.2) about how pleasant feelings vary based on the duration of daily contacts are unchanged within the nonoverlapped and partially overlapped networks.

Within the overlapped networks, however, the informants did not differentiate markedly in how pleasant they regarded the contacts by how long they lasted. Although they seemed to regard the longer contacts as more pleasant, none of the differences between the duration categories are statistically meaningful (Table 14.5, Model 3). In short, the duration effects weaken as the degree of network overlapping increases. In nonoverlapped networks in which the actors do not know each other's family or kin members, how long a contact lasts plays a decisive role in differentiating how pleasant the actors regarded the contact. In contrast, when at least one of the actors knows the other's family or relatives well, the contact's duration no longer plays a critical role. Having a pleasant feeling about a contact varies on other tie or contact situations, particularly on whether the ego initiated the contact or how well the ego was connected with the contacted person, but how long that contact lasted reduces almost to a nonfactor.

As a key measure of time investment, then, the duration of contacts generates differential effects on immediate returns by the degree of network overlapping. These differential effects reveal an important role that network overlapping might play in mediating how time investment brings about various returns in daily contacts. Such key findings shed light on the network approach to the study of social capital.

CONCLUSION

The existing literature on social capital lacks studies on the effect of the investment of social interactions on immediate returns and how these effects vary across different networks. Based on data from fifty-two diaries in which each informant recorded all one-on-one contacts for three months, this study used actual, although approximate, amounts of time to differentiate how actors perceive the significance and pleasure of daily contacts. It then compared the variation of these effects between three types of network overlapping.

It appears straightforward to verify whether the ego receives more significant immediate returns on time investment. The findings in this study further confirm the extent to which time investment helps explain returns differently by the degree of network overlapping. Network overlapping represents a core concept of the network approach for exploring social capital. Most of all, it underlines a unique structure in which influence, information, support, and affection flow through the intersecting connections among actors. As these valued resources flow, social capital accumulates and flourishes more easily. Such a network structure evidently differs from others in how the ego gains immediate returns from investing in social interactions.

This study has found that, in nonoverlapped networks and partially overlapped networks in which the majority of nonroutine contacts with nonkin acquaintances takes place, the immediate returns vary positively and consistently by how much time one invests in a contact. Other circumstances being equal, the longer a contact lasts, the more significant and more pleasant that contact tends to be. The returns on time investment thus seem pretty clear-cut.

In overlapped networks in which the ego knows the alter's family well or vice versa, the returns on time investment are far less significant. Network overlapping appears to alleviate what actors are required to invest to obtain certain immediate returns. Becasue the marginal utility of time investment declines when personal networks intersect, it may be less necessary to spend a substantial amount of time on contacts or interactions to achieve substantial returns. In other words, when the valued resources are more firmly embedded in intertwined social connections, actors tend to be more assured that they will receive positive and meaningful returns with a minimum of instant inputs in their social interactions.

In terms of the total amount of time spent in all normative interactions, people may actually invest more time in overlapped networks. However, they are able to gain immediate returns on time investment by making less effort in each individual contact. But when they invest a very substantial amount of time on a specific contact, the immediate outcome still tends to be positive, regardless of the degree of network overlapping.

Although the general inquiry has targeted social capital at the individual level, this study has focused on the effects at the contact level by means of contact diaries and multilevel analyses. Because the sample size of the informants in this study was small ($n = 52$) and the sampling procedure could not follow a probability procedure, the findings at the individual level may be preliminary and unsubstantial. With a sample that underrepresents unskilled workers, furthermore, the findings cannot be applied to the general population.

Despite the limitations, however, the study adds to the literature on social capital by exploring such intricate components as investment and returns at the contact level, while controlling for individual-level characteristics. The contact-level data reveal dynamic social situations in detail, which have been scarce in previous analyses based on individuals and interpersonal ties. In addition to differentiating the effects among various degrees of network overlapping, focusing on the variation at the contact level with the help of contact diaries is another contribution of the current study. Future studies should further untangle how investment and returns work by combining contacts, ties, individuals, and other network properties. As large-scale probability surveys on social networks become more available, studies on the returns of contact investment at the individual level should also be more feasible.

The findings of this study demonstrate how investment and returns function in daily contacts across various types of social networks. Although the data are limited to the approximate amount of time in ordinal categories and subjective evaluations that took place immediately after one-on-one contacts in daily life, these measures show valid indices. Meanwhile, the multilevel analyses give insight into how social capital operates differently when personal networks intertwine to various degrees. In the future, such intricate interactions between investment, returns, and network overlapping could also be examined by different measures, such as investment in subjective terms, long-term returns, and overlapped friendship networks. Analyses with various measures like these should further exemplify the fruitful conceptualization of social capital and elaborate theoretical interpretations.

APPENDIX

Table A14.1 Sociodemographic Characteristics of Informers (Level-2 Data, Unit: Individual)

Characteristics	*N*	%
A. Sources of informers		
Random sample follow-up	19	36.5
Recruited by interviewers	33	63.5
B. Sex		
Male	23	44.2
Female	29	55.8
C. Age		
20s	11	21.2
30s	21	40.4
40s	15	28.8
50s	3	5.8
60s	2	3.8
D. Marital status		
Single	14	26.9
Married	38	73.1

(continued)

Table A14.1 Sociodemographic Characteristics of Informers (Level-2 Data, Unit: Individual) (continued)

Characteristics	N	%
E. Education		
Elementary	1	1.9
Middle school	4	7.7
High school	14	26.9
Junior college	14	26.9
University	14	26.9
Graduate school	5	9.7
F. Work status/class		
No full-time job	18	34.6
Unskilled workers	1	1.9
Skilled workers	15	28.9
Assistant professionals	10	19.2
Professionals	2	3.9
Managers/supervisors	6	11.5
G. Urbanization of residence		
Rural	4	7.7
Towns/small cities	38	73.1
Large cities	10	19.2
Total	52	100.0

Table A14.2 Characteristics of Contacts (Level-1 Data, Unit: Contact)

Response Categories	N	%
A. Significance of contact (first dependent variable)		
1. Not significant at all	4,644	10.2
2. Somewhat nonsignificant	13,529	29.8
3. Somewhat significant	20,636	45.4
4. Very significant	6,647	14.6
Total	45,456	100.0
B. Feeling about contact (second dependent variable)		
0. Less pleasant (not pleasant)	28,602	62.9
1. Very pleasant	16,855	37.1
Total	45,457	100.0
C. Duration of contact (major explanatory variable)		
1. Less than 1 minute	3,914	8.6
2. 1–5 minutes	13,923	30.6
3. 6–29 minutes	14,082	31.0
4. 30 minutes–2 hours	7,290	16.1

(continued)

Table A14.2 Characteristics of Contacts (Level-1 Data, Unit: Contact) (continued)

5. More than 2 hours	6,248		13.7	
Total	45,457		100.0	
Measures	*Mean*	*SD*	*Min.*	*Max.*
D. Ego/alter ties				
Same age group	.373	.484	0	1
Strength of tie (Factor score, see Appendix Table A14.3)	.152	.609	−1.58	1.53
Length of acquaintanceship	2.121	.889	1	4
Frequency of face-to-face contacts	3.236	.795	1	4
Frequency of phone contacts	2.244	.991	1	4
Closeness	3.118	.872	1	4
Importance	2.522	.835	1	4
Affection	3.178	.585	1	4
Indices of Situations	*Mean*	*SD*	*Min.*	*Max.*
E. Contact situations				
Anticipated/expected	3.177	.932	1	4
Initiated:				
By ego	.357	.479	0	1
By alter	.316	.464	0	1
By both	.268	.442	0	1
By chance	.056	.231	0	1

Table A14.3 Factor Analysis of the Ego/Alter Tie Strength

Tie Characteristics	*Factor Loadings*	*Scoring Coefficients*
Length of acquaintanceship	.78024	.21511
Frequency of face-to-face contacts	.74036	.20412
Frequency of phone contacts	.73281	.20204
Closeness	.89588	.24699
Importance	.84007	.23161
Affection	.65182	.17971
Eigen value	3.62713	
% variance explained	60.5	
Alpha coefficient	.8842	

Note. Principal component factor analysis.

REFERENCES

Alheit, P. 1994. "Everyday Time and Life Time: On the Problems of Healing Contradictory Experiences of Time." *Time and Society*, 3: 305–19.

Astone, N. M., A. Constance, R. S. Nathanson, and J. K. Young. 1999. "Family Demography, Social Theory, and Investment in Social Capital." *Population and Development Review*, 25: 1–31.

Baron, J. N., and M. T. Hannan. 1994. "The Impact of Economics on Contemporary Sociology." *Journal of Economic Literature*, 32: 1111–46.

Boisjoly, J., G. J. Duncan, and S. Hofferth. 1995. "Access to Social Capital." *Journal of Family Issues*, 16: 609–31.

Bond, M. J., and N. T. Feather. 1988. "Some Correlates of Structure and Purpose in the Use of Time." *Journal of Personality and Social Psychology*, 55: 321–29.

Burt, R. S. 1992. *Structural Holes: The Social Structure of Competition*. Cambridge, MA: Harvard University Press.

———. 1997. "The Contingent Value of Social Capital." *Administrative Science Quarterly*, 42:339–65.

———. 2001. "Structural Holes Versus Network Closure as Social Capital." In *Social Capital: Theory and Research*, eds. N. Lin, K. Cook, and R.S. Burt, 31–56. New York: Aldine de Gruyter.

Campbell, K. E., and B. A. Lee. 1992. "Sources of Personal Neighbor Networks: Social Integration, Need, or Time?" *Social Forces*, 70: 1077–1100.

Castle, E. N. 2002. "Social Capital: An Interdisciplinary Concept." *Rural Sociology*, 67: 331–49.

Clemens, E. S. 1999. "Securing Political Returns to Social Capital: Women's Associations in the United States, 1880s–1920s." *Journal of Interdisciplinary History*, 29: 613–38.

Coleman, J. S. 1988. "Social Capital in the Creation of Human Capital." *American Journal of Sociolog,y* 94: S95–S120.

———. 1990. *Foundations of Social Theory*. Cambridge, MA: Belknap Press of Harvard University Press.

Davies, K. 1990. *Women, Time and the Weaving of the Strands of Everyday Life*. Aldershot, UK: Avebury.

Fernandez, R. M., and E. J. Castilla. 2001. "How Much Is That Network Worth? Social Capital in Employee Referral Networks." In *Social Capital: Theory and Research*, eds. N. Lin, K. Cook, and R. S. Burt, 85–104. New York: Aldine de Gruyter.

Flora, J. L. 1998. "Social Capital and Communities of Place." *Rural Sociology*, 63: 481–506.

Freeman, L. C., and C. R. Thompson. 1989. "Estimating Acquaintanceship Volume." In *The Small World*, M. Kochen, 147–58. Norwood, NJ: Ablex.

Fu, Y. 2005. "Measuring Personal Networks With Daily Contacts: A Single-item Survey Question and the Contact Diary." *Social Networks*, 27:169–86.

———. 2007. "Contact Diaries: Building Archives of Actual and Comprehensive Personal Networks." *Field Methods*, 19:194–217.

Granovetter, M. S. 1973. "The Strength of Weak Ties." *American Journal of Sociology*, 78: 1360–80.

Grew, R. 1999. "Finding Social Capital: The French Revolution in Italy." *Journal of Interdisciplinary History*, 29:407–33.

Hofferth, S. L., J. Boisjoly, and G. J. Duncan. 1999. "The Development of Social Capital." *Rationality and Society*, 11:79–110.

Johnson, D. 2001. "Society: Investing in Human Relations." *The Futurist*, 35: 9–11.

Kadushin, C. 2004. "Too Much Investment in Social Capital?" *Social Networks*, 26:75–90.

Lin, N. 2001a. "Building a Network Theory of Social Capital." In *Social Capital: Theory and Research*, eds. N. Lin, K. Cook, and R. S. Burt, 3–29. New York: Aldine de Gruyter.

———. 2001b. *Social Capital: A Theory of Social Structure and Action*. Cambridge: Cambridge University Press.

———, K. Cook, and R. S. Burt. 2001. "Preface." In *Social Capital: Theory and Research*, eds, N. Lin, K. Cook, and R. S. Burt, vii–xii. New York: Aldine de Gruyter.

———, Y. Fu, and R. Hsung. 2001. "The Position Generator: Measurement Techniques for Investigations of Social Capital." In *Social Capital: Theory and Research*, eds. N. Lin, K. Cook, and R. S. Burt, 57–81. New York: Aldine de Gruyter.

Lonkila, M. 1999. *Social Networks in Post-Soviet Russia: Continuity and Change in the Everyday Life of St. Petersburg Teachers*, Helsinki: Aleksanteri Instituutti. http://ethesis.helsinki.fi/julkaisut/val/sosio/vk/lonkila/, accessed June 2007

Morrow, V. 1999. "Conceptualising Social Capital in Relation to the Well-Being of Children and Young People: A Critical Review." *Sociological Review*, 47: 744–65.

Portes, A. 1998. "Social Capital: Its Origins and Applications in Modern Sociology." *Annual Review of Sociology*, 24: 1–24.

———, and P. Landolt. 1996. "The Downside of Social Capital." *The American Prospect*, 26: 18–21, 94.

Raudenbush, S. W., A. S. Bryk, Y. F. Cheong, and R. T. Congdon, Jr. 2001. *Hierarchical Linear and Nonlinear Modeling*. Lincolnwood, IL: Scientific Software International.

Sampson, R. J., J. D. Morenoff, and F. Earls. 1999. "Beyond Social Capital: Spatial Dynamics of Collective Efficacy for Children." *American Sociological Review*, 64: 633–60.

Sandefur, R. L., and E. O. Laumann. 1998. "A Paradigm for Social Capital." *Rationality and Society*, 10: 481–501.

Schuller, T., S. Baron, and J. Field. 2000. "Social Capital: A Review and Critique." In *Social Capital: Critical Perspectives*, eds. S. Baron, J. Field and T. Schuller, 1–38. New York: Oxford University Press.

Snijders, T. A. B. 1999. "Prologue to the Measurement of Social Capital." *Tocqueville-Review/Revue-Tocqueville*, 20:27–44.

Szalai, A. 1972. *The Use of Time: Daily Activities of Urban and Suburban Populations in Twelve Countries*. The Hague/Paris: Mouton.

Wall, E., G. Ferrazzi, and F. Schryer. 1998. "Getting the Goods on Social Capital." *Rural Sociology*, 63: 300–22.

Wellman, B., and K. Frank. 2001. "Network Capital in a Multilevel World: Getting Support from Personal Communities." In *Social Capital: Theory and Research*, eds. N. Lin, K. Cook, and R. S. Burt, 57–81. New York: Aldine de Gruyter.

Zerubavel, E. 1985. *Hidden Rhythms: Schedules and Calendars in Social Life*. Berkeley: University of California Press.

Contributors

Dan Ao is an assistant professor of sociology at the Chinese University of Hong Kong, b116619@mailserv.cuhk.edu.hk

John J. Beggs is an associate professor of sociology at Louisiana State University jbeggs@lsu.edu

Ronald L. Breiger is a professor at the Department of Sociology, University of Arizona, Breiger@Arizona.edu

Ly-Yun Chang is a research fellow at Institute of Sociology, Academia Sinica, Taiwan, gacloud@gate.sinica.edu.tw

Chieh-Hsuan Chen is a professor at the Department of Sociology, Tunghai University, Taiwan, chench@thu.edu.tw

Chih-Jou Jay Chen is an associate research fellow at Institute of Sociology, Academia, Sinica, Taiwan, jaychen@sinica.edu.tw

Rochelle R. Côté is a doctoral student at NetLab, the Department of Sociology, University of Toronto, rcote@chass.utoronto.ca

Beth M. Duckles is a doctoral student at the Department of Sociology, University of Arizona, bduckles@u.arizona.edu

Bonnie H. Erickson is a professor of sociology at the Department of Sociology, University of Toronto, ericson@chass.utoronto.ca

Henk Flap is a professor of sociology at the ICS/Department of Sociology, Utrecht University, The Netherlands, h.flap@fss.uu.nl

Yang-Chih Fu is a research fellow and director at the Institute of Sociology, Academia Sinica, Taiwan, fuyc@sinica.edu.tw

Joseph Galaskiewicz is a professor at the Department of Sociology, University of Arizona, galaskie@email.arizona.edu

Valerie A. Haines, is an assistant professor at the Department of Sociology, University of Calgary, Canada, haines@ucalgary.ca

Ray-May Hsung is a Professor of Sociology, at the Department of Sociology, National Chengchi University, Taiwan, hsung@nccu.edu.tw

Jeanne S. Hurlbert is a professor at the Department of Sociology, Louisiana State University, sohurl@lsu.edu

Ken'ichi Ikeda is a professor at the Department of Social Psychology, Graduate School of Humanities and Sociology, The University of Tokyo, Japan, ikeken@l.u-tokyo.ac.jp

Tetsuro Kobayashi is a junior research fellow at National Institute of Informatics, Japan, k-tetsu@nii.ac.jp

Gerald Mollenhorst is a doctoral student at the ICS/Department of Sociology, Utrecht University, The Netherlands, g.w.mollenhorst@uu.nl

Nan Lin is the Oscar L. Tang Professor of Sociology, at the Department of Sociology, Duke University, nanlin@duke.edu

Jar-Der Luo is a professor of sociology at Tsinghua University in Beijing, China, jdluo@mail.tsinghua.edu.cn.

Olga Mayorova is a doctoral student at Department of Sociology, University of Arizona, ovm@u.arizona.edu

Gabriele Plickert is a doctoral student at NetLab, Department of Sociology, University of Toronto, gabriel.plickert@utoronto.ca

Lijun Song is an doctoral student at Department of Sociology, Duke University, Lijun.song@duke.edu

Róbert Tardos is senior researcher of the Research Group for Communication Studies of the Hungarian Academy of Sciences at Eötvös Loránd University, tardos.robert@ppk.elte.hu

Beate Völker is a professor at the ICS/Department of Sociology, Utrecht University, The Netherlands., B.G.M.Volker@fss.uu.nl

Yung-Chu Yeh is a PhD candidate at Department of Business Administration, Yuan-Ze University, Taiwan.

Barry Wellman is a professor at NetLab, Department of Sociology, University of Toronto, wellman@chass.utoronto.ca

Index